WESTMINSTER COMMENTARIES

EDITED BY WALTER LOCK D.D.
FORMERLY LADY MARGARET PROFESSOR
OF DIVINITY IN THE UNIVERSITY OF
OXFORD

AND D. C. SIMPSON D.D.
ORIEL PROFESSOR OF THE INTERPRETA-
TION OF HOLY SCRIPTURE, CANON OF
ROCHESTER

THE EPISTLE TO THE

COLOSSIANS

AND THE EPISTLE TO

PHILEMON

THE EPISTLE TO THE
COLOSSIANS
AND THE EPISTLE TO
PHILEMON

WITH INTRODUCTION
AND NOTES
BY

LEWIS B. RADFORD, M.A., D.D.
BISHOP OF GOULBURN, AUSTRALIA

METHUEN & CO. LTD.
36 ESSEX STREET W.C.
LONDON

First Published in 1931

PRINTED IN GREAT BRITAIN

is to be exegetical,
...ook of the Bible in the light
...ern knowledge to English readers. The Editors will not
deal, except subordinately, with questions of textual criticism or
philology; but, taking the English text in the Revised Version as
their basis, they will aim at combining a hearty acceptance of
critical principles with loyalty to the Catholic Faith.

The series will be less elementary than the Cambridge Bible
for Schools, less critical than the International Critical Commentary, less didactic than the Expositor's Bible; and it is hoped
that it may be of use both to theological students and to the
clergy, as well as to the growing number of educated laymen
and laywomen who wish to read the Bible intelligently and
reverently.

Each commentary will therefore have

(i) An Introduction stating the bearing of modern criticism
and research upon the historical character of the book, and
drawing out the contribution which the book, as a whole, makes
to the body of religious truth.

(ii) A careful paraphrase of the text with notes on the more
difficult passages and, if need be, excursuses on any points of
special importance either for doctrine, or ecclesiastical organization, or spiritual life.

But the books of the Bible are so varied in character that
considerable latitude is needed as to the proportion which the
various parts should hold to each other. The General Editors will
therefore only endeavour to secure a general uniformity in scope
and character; but the exact method adopted in each case and
the final responsibility for the statements made will rest with the
individual contributors.

By permission of the Delegates of the Oxford University
Press and of the Syndics of the Cambridge University Press the
Text used in this Series of Commentaries is the Revised Version
of the Holy Scriptures.

WALTER LOCK
D. C. SIMPSON

PREFACE

THE preparation of this Commentary, undertaken in 1920, has been hindered by long delays and frequent interruptions. The care of an Australian country diocese slightly larger than Ireland involves constant travelling; and with only fifty priests and less than fifty parishes, containing, however, more than three hundred centres and congregations, it brings all the responsibilities of a closer personal knowledge of clergy and laity and a more intimate pastorate of places and people than is possible for an English bishop. Moreover, the Anglican Church of Australia has no 'general staff', and it is a hard fight for a few of the Australian bishops to carry a share of the national problems and enterprises of the Church in addition to their own diocesan work. Finally, the building stage of Canberra, the new Federal Capital City, which lies within the diocese of Goulburn, has brought exacting problems of its own—the founding of Church secondary schools, the planning of a cathedral, the consideration of the future ecclesiastical position of the city. The author can only trust that this multiplicity of interests and engagements may have saved his intermittent studies from the danger of an unduly academic outlook.

The Commentary has been a labour of love in fragments of leisure and overtime—the revival of former associations of sacred study, the refreshment of an often tired mind. It is the fulfilment of an old desire to make some contribution to the knowledge of the New Testament for the benefit of reading and thinking layfolk and of the many priests who are students rather than scholars, and at the same time to repay a fraction of a life-long debt to St. Paul by an attempt to illustrate the funda-mentality, and therefore the permanent value, of his teaching. The necessity of selection enforced by the limits of space has involved the omission of some important subjects, e.g. the sources and influences to which St. Paul owed his Christian theology, the relation of Christianity to the mystery-religions of the Hellenistic world, the strategy and statesmanship of the greatest of Christian missionaries. The attention given to the comparative study of the various uses and contexts of words and ideas may seem disproportionate; but a bishop may perhaps be forgiven for yielding to the desire to encourage and guide the kind of study that supplies the wants of those who are called to teach the New Testament as well as to preach the Christian faith.

With all the faults and defects which the author recognizes or which critics may discover, the work is now offered to the world in the hope that it may give to English readers the best of what Greek scholars derive from the original text, and may interpret to some extent the language and teaching of an epistle which is at once perhaps the most difficult and the most fruitful of St. Paul's bequests to modern Christian thought.

In its final form the book owes much to the careful observation and helpful advice of the two general editors, whose suggestions on particular points of the text and on larger questions of the plan of the book have been a happy blending of generous encouragement and wise criticism. And in the case of the senior general editor, Dr. Lock, gratitude is deepened by the knowledge that his latest contributions to the revision of the book have been given, with unstinted labour and unfailing interest, out of the precious hours of convalescence after a grievous breakdown, which has quickened into prayerful sympathy the reverent affection felt by so many scholars and students for the veteran *doctor doctorum* and *ductor discentium*.

LEWIS B. RADFORD
BISHOP OF GOULBURN, N.S.W.

St. Barnabas's Day, 1930

Postscript

It is difficult for students overseas to get into touch with the latest investigations. I have only just discovered the *Monumenta Asiae Minoris Antiqua* (American Society for Archaeological Research in Asia Minor), vol. i (ed. W. M. Calder), which throws a flood of light on the pagan and Christian life of the Phrygo-Lycaonian border; e.g. the inscriptions indicate clearly that the earliest Biblical names to pass into common use (in the third century A.D.) were Luke, Mark, and Paul; John and Peter came into use in the next century.

L. B. R.

CONTENTS

EPISTLE TO THE COLOSSIANS

INTRODUCTION:

EPISTLE TO PHILEMON

INTRODUCTION:

INTRODUCTION

I

THE AUTHENTICITY AND INTEGRITY OF THE EPISTLE

THE prefatory note by the General Editors of this series of commentaries requires that each commentary shall have an introduction dealing with the historical character and the religious value of the book. There is an intimate connexion between these two questions. A view of Christ and the Christian religion from the pen of an unknown early Christian writer might have a real interest and value of its own, such as attaches, for example, to the anonymous *Epistle to Diognetus*. It might give an illuminating glimpse of the life and thought of the Church of the first age. It might make a distinct contribution to religious truth, to be judged of course by its conformity to indisputably apostolic teaching and verified by its correspondence with catholic Christian experience. But the *Epistle to the Colossians* is not an anonymous writing nor a general treatise. It purports expressly to be a letter written by a particular apostle to a particular Church with reference to a particular phase of local religious thought. The value of its teaching therefore depends on the vindication of its supposed authorship and the verification of its supposed occasion— on the question whether we have here an authentic record of St. Paul's own theology in its latest stage and of his answer to an early heresy, or only the work of a Pauline disciple in the sub-apostolic age, even if that work were a genuine communication to the Colossian Church written in St. Paul's name after his death, in the sincere belief that it represented the mind of the great Apostle and might therefore honestly claim his authority.

(i) *The evidence of tradition*

The tradition of the Pauline authorship of *Colossians* rests on indisputable evidence from the second century, evidence which points back to a still earlier date. In the West, Irenaeus (III. xiv. 1, *c.* A.D. 180–90) quotes the salutation of 'Luke the beloved physician' as from St. Paul's Epistle to the Colossians. In the East, Clement of Alexandria (*Strom.* vi. 8, *c.* A.D. 190–210) quotes Col. ii. 8 as a warning addressed by St. Paul ' to Greek converts at Colossae'. These are not the earliest references to an epistle to the Colossians. Marcion, the anti-Judaic Gnostic, who taught at Rome about A.D. 140, included an epistle to the Colossians in his *Apostolicon*, his own revised canon

B

or list of Pauline epistles which he regarded as representing the true Gospel; and this private canon implies the existence of a still earlier catholic canon, a traditional list of epistles generally accepted in various parts of Christendom. The Latin fragment known as the Muratorian Canon (not later than A.D. 170) mentions an epistle to the Colossians as one of the epistles written by St. Paul to the seven Churches (Corinth, Ephesus, Philippi, Colossae, Galatia, Thessalonica, Rome) which are compared to the letters to the seven Churches in the Apocalypse, the idea being that in both cases the number seven stands for the complete unity of the Catholic Church.[1]

Tertullian and Origen, early in the third century, frequently quote and occasionally name the epistle; and it is included in the Old Latin version of the New Testament which dates from the second century. There are a few almost certain quotations from the epistle in the early half of the second century, e.g. in the epistles of Ignatius, Polycarp, 'Barnabas', and in the writings of Justin Martyr, though without any mention of the name or author of the epistle. These quotations are far less frequent than quotations from *Ephesians*—a fact due not to 'the superior size and value' of that epistle (Moffatt, *ILNT*., p. 154) but to the more general character and therefore wider interest of its teaching. But, few as they are, they prove that *Colossians* was known over a large area of the Church. Quotations are also found in the fragments of various heretical writings of the second century preserved in Hippolytus, *Refutation of all heresies* (c. A.D. 200–35). Two things emerge from these evidences taken together, viz. (1) the existence of this epistle (without any mention of its author or its destination) as a doctrinal authority or a formative influence not much more than fifty years after its traditional date; (2) the identity of this epistle with the epistle to the Colossians quoted expressly as Pauline. 'The external testimony to its genuineness is the best possible: ever since a collection of Pauline letters existed at all, *Colossians* seems to have been invariably included' (Jülicher, in *Encycl. Bibl.* i. 865). Such evidence would be held more than sufficient to establish the authenticity of any classical literature.

(ii) *The challenge of criticism*

The traditional acceptance of *Colossians* in its present form as an authentic Pauline epistle was first challenged by historical criticism a century ago. The criticism of the epistle in the nineteenth century

---

[1] Victorinus, a Danubian bishop of the third century, who wrote a valuable commentary on the Apocalypse, goes so far as to suggest that this idea of the completeness of the sacred number seven was the reason why St. Paul addressed his later letters not to churches but to individuals.

took two successive forms, (1) the denial of its Pauline authorship, (2) the denial of its literary integrity.

1. *The denial of Pauline authorship.*

The age of criticism began with F. C. Baur and the other German critics known as the Tübingen school. In pursuance of their theory that the first age of the Church was marked by a sharp conflict between the Judaistic and the Pauline views of the Christian religion —a conflict only reconciled in the Catholic Church of the second century—they regarded the New Testament in its present form as the result and monument of this reconciliation, and post-dated to a later age those books which appeared to them to bear signs of the process and indeed of the conscious purpose of reconciliation. Baur recognized as Pauline only four epistles, viz. *Galatians, 1* and *2 Corinthians,* and *Romans* i–xiv. Later critics of the school recognized also as Pauline *Romans* xv, xvi, *1 Thessalonians, Philippians,* and *Philemon.* A more judicious exercise of the very principle of historical criticism introduced by the Tübingen school has driven its theory from the field. But *Colossians* and *Ephesians* and the Pastoral Epistles are still challenged by some few critics of balanced judgement who doubt the Pauline authorship of one or other or all of these documents.

The denial of the Pauline authorship of *Colossians* rests upon three grounds, (*a*) its lexical and literary peculiarities, (*b*) its apparent anticipation of later Gnosticism, (*c*) its advance upon or its departure from the theology of the earlier and accepted epistles.

(*a*) *Lexical and literary evidence.*

Questions of Greek vocabulary cannot be discussed in detail in a commentary for English readers; but two or three points stand out clearly. (1) The argument from lexical peculiarities breaks down by proving too much. It is true that *Colossians* 'contains 33 words that are not found elsewhere in the N.T. and 32 phrases and 28 words which occur in other N.T. documents but not in St. Paul's writings, but a study of any one of the letters universally acknowledged to be Pauline reveals a precisely similar situation' (M. Jones, p. 7). (2) The absence of familiar Pauline words and phrases is no valid argument against Pauline authorship. The word 'cross' is not found in *Romans,* nor the word 'law' in *2 Corinthians,* nor the word 'righteousness' in *1 Thessalonians,* nor the word 'salvation' in *1 Corinthians.* Yet these omissions are not cited as evidence of non-Pauline authorship. (3) Variation in diction between writings of the same writer may result from special circumstances. Prof. Mahaffy compares St. Paul in this

B 2

respect to Xenophon; both were great travellers, and their vocabulary borrows from the various linguistic and literary environments in which they moved and wrote. (4) The occurrence or emphasis or repetition of special words or words used in a special sense, e.g. 'knowledge', 'wisdom', 'perfect', 'pleroma', 'mystery', 'elements', may be due to their prominence in the language of the Colossian heretical teachers; other peculiarities may be due to the necessity of a new vocabulary to meet a new religious problem.

The style of the epistle, however, as distinct from the vocabulary, is a more serious difficulty. There is a marked contrast in the argumentative portion of the epistle between the slow and laboured movement of its language and the rapid flow and clearer sequence of the language of the earlier epistles. Participles are left in suspense; relative sentences follow each other in sometimes ambiguous connexions; phrases are flung out abruptly in almost unintelligible constructions which have suggested the possibility of a corruption in the text, e.g. ii. 23. Various explanations have been offered, e.g. the weakening of mental grasp by age or ill-health, the difficulty of correspondence between quick transitions of thought and the slow pace of an amanuensis, the unfamiliarity or indefiniteness of the religious situation that the apostle was facing in contrast to the clearly defined and familiar situation faced in *Galatians* and *Corinthians*. Whatever the right explanation may be, the differences and difficulties of style are not too great to be explained by the special circumstances of the epistle, and are not in any way conclusive against its Pauline authorship. Genius cannot be restricted to one type of verbal expression in all cases.

(b) *The theological evidence.*

(a) *Signs of antignosticism.* The historical objection to Pauline authorship was based upon the idea of the Tübingen school that the controversial portion of the epistle appeared to be directed against a form or stage of Gnosticism which was not in existence before the second century. Some critics saw in this Colossian heresy a Jewish type of Gnosticism, viz. Ebionitism; but others saw the more elaborate Greek Gnosticism of the school of Valentinus. But this assumption, in whatever form, that the epistle points to a late type of Gnosticism, has been discredited by more recent investigation into the Graeco-Oriental origins of Gnosticism and the developments of Judaism. That investigation has brought to light all sorts of stages and phases of gnostic and syncretistic tendencies in cult and creed, Judaistic, Hellenistic, and Oriental, all earlier than Christianity, which might well have produced, in fusion with Christianity, the kind of teaching confronted in this epistle. 'At any time after A.D. 40 early Christianity was upon the edge of such speculative tendencies' (Moffatt, *ILNT*., p. 154). On the other hand, a more careful study of the epistle reveals two facts which are fatal to the Tübingen hypothesis. Those terms in the epistle which appeared to the critics to be drawn from the language of second-century Gnosticism, e.g. *fullness* (*pleroma*), *perfect* (*teleios*), *knowledge* (*gnosis*), are not used in the epistle in the technical sense in which later Gnosticism used them. And some of the most distinctive and prominent features of later Gnosticism, both in language and in doctrine, do not occur in the epistle at all. There is, therefore, nothing in the references to the Colossian heresy which requires a later date for the epistle.

(β) *Signs of Gnosticism.* The main objection of Baur himself was that the theology of the epistle showed signs of a departure in the direction of Gnosticism. Regarding the Colossian heresy as mainly a development or variant of Judaistic Christianity, he regarded the epistle as an answer from the pen of a sub-apostolic writer whose faith was tinged with an early gnosticism which could still pass muster as an innocent venture of Christian thought. For example, in the idea of reconciliation in *Colossians* and *Ephesians* Baur saw traces of the root-idea of Gnosticism that the soul of man is a part of the divine nature which descends to earth and ultimately reascends to its divine origin. In the idea of the Church as the bride of Christ he saw the later Gnostic pairs of aeons or emanations, male and female, from the divine nature. In the *pleroma* of these epistles he saw the Gnostic idea of *pleroma* as denoting not the essence but the expression of divinity, not the Absolute but its external self-realization, and in the Christ of these epistles he saw the supreme aeon, the highest and fullest of these self-realizations of the divine nature. But it is sufficient to reply that the root-idea of Gnosticism proper is a descending chain of emanations of inferior spiritual existences, an idea which might be compatible with the Colossian heresy, but which is neither implied in the teaching of *Colossians* nor capable of development by inference from that teaching; that the idea of a return of these emanations to the original unity of the divine nature not merely fails to do justice to the idea of reconciliation to God, but lies in a different region from that idea, which is not metaphysical but moral, not a speculative conception but a practical experience of the spiritual life; that in the union of Christ and the Church the idea of marriage is subordinated to the idea of headship; that the *pleroma* of the epistle is not the total sum of a series of emanations, of which Christ is the culminating term, but the complete and unique revelation of the divine in Christ. The writer of the epistle is not fighting one gnosticism with the weapons of another. He is unfolding the implications of the Christian faith as the full and final answer to all gnosticism.

(γ) *A new Christology.* The Christology of the epistle does at first sight seem to present a serious difficulty. New expressions are used, new conceptions unfolded, which undoubtedly go beyond the language and teaching of the earlier epistles of St. Paul. But these advances beyond his earlier expositions of doctrine are not necessarily departures from the principles of his earlier doctrine. Even where the differences are greatest, even when they are stated in the fullest contrast, they do not involve any contradiction of his former teaching. They are right in the line of such evolution as a master mind may well experience, either as the result of continued thinking over the contents of his original belief, or as the reaction to the challenge of a new crisis or the stimulus of a new environment. There is nothing in this doctrinal advance which justifies the suspicion that we may be in the presence of another mind or in the atmosphere of another age. This judgement may be illustrated by a brief notice of the chief points of advance. (1) There is the great Christological passage in Col. i. 15 ff. This involves the eternal pre-existence of Christ. But so does the great Christological passage in Phil. ii. 5 ff. *Philippians* is now secure once more in its recognition as an authentic epistle of St. Paul. The authenticity of *Colossians* cannot be logically denied on the ground of a doctrinal advance when that advance is evident in an epistle accepted as authentic. The real advance in Col. i. 15 ff. is in the conception of Christ in relation to the universe. Three points emerge here. Christ is the original mediator or agent in the creation of the universe, the present principle of its coherence, and the final goal of its progress. The first idea is stated expressly in 1 Cor. viii. 6, 'through whom all things'. The second is a logical corollary of this statement. The third does seem to contradict 1 Cor. xv. 28 and Rom. xi. 36, where the final goal of creation is God the Father. But there is a similar apparent contradiction between 1 Cor. viii. 6 and Rom. xi. 36. The contradiction in either case is only apparent, not real. The immediate supremacy of Christ is quite compatible with the ultimate supremacy of God the Father.

(2) Another advance is in the doctrine of reconciliation. In Col. i. 20 the Cross is the reconciliation not only of mankind but of the universe, angels and all. But there is a pointer in this direction already in 2 Cor. v. 19, 'God was in Christ, reconciling the world unto

himself'. (3) In Col. ii. 14, 15, the Cross is the dethronement not only of the Law but of the powers of the spirit-world. But there is a glimpse of the latter conception in Gal. iii. 19, where the super-session of the Law by the Incarnation is connected with the idea of angelic mediation in the origin of the Law (cp. Gal. iv. 9), and in 1 Cor. ii. 6–8, where the doom of the 'rulers of this world', already in process, is connected in some mysterious way with the crime and blunder of their crucifixion of 'the Lord of glory'. (4) The relation of Christ to the Church in Col. i. 18, 24 (cp. ii. 9, 10) has been cited as a new conception. But already in 1 Cor. xii. 27, Rom. xii. 5, the Church is the Body of Christ, though the dominant idea there is the mutual relation of Christians as members of the Body; and in 1 Cor. xi. 3 Christ is 'the head of every man', i.e. of humanity. The headship of Christ in and over the Church in *Colossians* is not a new conception but the combination of earlier conceptions. It is evident, therefore, that though here and elsewhere in *Colossians* there is 'a very sub-stantial extension of St. Paul's realm of ideas and a marked develop-ment of concepts', yet 'the germs are clearly discernible in his earlier writings' (M. Jones, p. 4). Baur admits these 'hints of similar views' in acknowledged Pauline writings, but regards them as ob-scure and inconclusive, whereas in *Colossians* and *Ephesians* they are dominant and pervasive. But such prominence and emphasis is intelligible enough as the response to the challenge of a new peril. The history of St. Paul's theology finds a parallel in the history of the Catholic creeds. Each truth of the Christian faith came into prominence in turn in the creed in response to a heresy which raised that particular question. The most remarkable example of this process of development is the later extension of the Nicene Creed to give full expression to the implicit belief in the person and operation of the Holy Spirit.

This development of St. Paul's theology may have been quickened or even occasioned by the demands of the Colossian crisis. But more probably it was at work already under the circumstances of his enforced retreat at Rome, with its narrowed range of labour and its widened range of outlook upon the empire, the Church, and the uni-verse. What the Colossian crisis brought was the necessity of concen-trating his thoughts upon particular truths in his world-view and the opportunity of expressing those truths in the light of his recent thinking. Here again the difficulties urged by critics fall far short of any justification for challenging the authenticity of the epistle.

2. *The denial of literary integrity*

Recent criticism, with a few eccentric exceptions, in particular a group of Dutch scholars (e.g. the articles of Van Manen in the *Encyclopaedia Biblica*), has abandoned the attack upon the authenticity of the epistle, and turned to attack its integrity. It has adopted a theory of interpolation to solve a twofold problem, viz. (1) the literary relation between *Colossians* and *Ephesians*, (2) the mixture of Pauline elements with apparently non-Pauline or sub-Pauline. The problem of the relation of *Colossians* to *Ephesians* is indeed complicated. The resemblances between the two epistles are large and obvious. There are parallel passages, similar constructions, identical words and phrases, and a correspondence in general outline and in particular details which is only to be appreciated in its continuity and in its exceptions by printing the two epistles side by side with every word common to the two underlined. The resemblances 'point unmistakably to one of two conclusions: they must either be the work of one and the same author, or the writer of the one must have borrowed on a large scale from the work of the other' (M. Jones, p. 9). The latter conclusion is highly improbable in view of the fact that the supposed writer of the later epistle, whichever it was, has not merely borrowed and adapted paragraphs and sentences, but has borrowed phrases and words from one context to use them in another context. 'The terminology of the one epistle is frequently transferred to the other, but the terminology and the thought of the one are seldom found in combination in the other' (M. Jones, p. 10). Each epistle has a literary unity and a literary individuality of its own. The only satisfactory reconciliation of this fact with the fact of their mutual resemblances is to accept both as the work of one and the same author. But there still remains the problem of priority. Sometimes the one seems clearly prior, sometimes the other. In some cases a passage in *Ephesians* seems clearly to be an amplification or an abbreviation of a passage in *Colossians*; sometimes the process seems to have been the reverse. The question of relation between the two epistles is discussed at length in Ch. III of this Introduction. It is sufficient here to say the priority of *Colossians* is the only conclusion that does justice to the whole of the evidence.

To return to the other half of the problem, viz. the mixture of Pauline and non-Pauline elements in *Colossians*, Ewald in 1856 met the difficulty by supposing that the epistle was written by Timothy (others suggest Tychicus), acting not as amanuensis at St. Paul's dictation but as the editor of material provided by St. Paul. This supposition seems to be excluded by the personal intimations in i. 23, ii. 1, 5. In any case it is almost incredible that so intimate a friend and so loyal a disciple would diverge in his own views from his master's teaching, still less introduce into an epistle to go forth in his master's name any language or thought that was not essentially in accord with his teaching. Moreover, the epistle was almost certainly written in close touch with St. Paul for immediate dispatch (iv. 4, 7–9), and would surely be submitted to the apostle for endorsement or revision. Its conclusion bears the apostolic autograph. Its contents must be taken as carrying the apostle's approval.

Holtzmann, in 1872, propounded an ingenious theory of successive interpolations. In his opinion there was an original *Colossians*, an authentic Pauline epistle dealing with a legalistic and ascetic movement at Colossae. This was expanded into our *Ephesians* 'as a protest against a Jewish-Christian theosophy' by an unknown writer who subsequently expanded the original *Colossians* by interpolations from *Ephesians* and other sources to give it an antignostic turn. This elaborate hypothesis served to account for the fact that sometimes *Ephesians* seems to borrow from *Colossians* and sometimes *Colossians* from *Ephesians*. It ignored the possibility that St. Paul may not have copied from the one in writing or dictating the other, but may have repeated passages from memory, or simply given similar though not identical expression to the same conceptions in two contemporary letters without any deliberate repetition or even conscious recollection. Holtzmann's hypothesis fails to account for the fact, already noted, that many of the phrases in *Ephesians* supposed to be borrowed from *Colossians* do not occur in the same context as in *Colossians*, and seem to fit quite naturally into the contexts in which they do occur in *Ephesians*. The hypothesis, moreover, creates more difficulties than it removes. Why did this ingenious redactor borrow from *Colossians* alone in writing his *Ephesians*, and not from other Pauline epistles also? What authority is there for dividing the Colossian heresy into two sections or stages? How did the redactor manage to get his own later expansion of *Colossians* into circulation in the presence of the original Pauline letter? How did the original vanish while the substitute survived? Soltau elaborated a still more complicated theory in which the original Pauline *Colossians* was expanded by an editor who drew from an epistle to Laodicea, which was used also in the composition of *Ephesians*, which in turn was used as the source of later interpolations in *Colossians*. Both Holtzmann and Soltau are far too subjective and arbitrary in the criteria by which they decide that this or that passage is an interpolation. The theory is condemned by its results: Holtzmann's restoration of the supposed original of *Colossians* is a bare and bald substitute indeed for the warmth and wealth of the *Colossians* that we know. Detailed discussion of these reconstructive hypotheses is superfluous. Later criticism has passed sentence upon them; see for example Sanday's criticism of Holtzmann in Smith's *Dictionary of the Bible* (2nd ed.). It is interesting to note that one scholar, Von Soden, who subjected Holtzmann's theory to drastic criticism, himself first rejected only a few passages as interpolations (viz. i. 15–20, ii. 10, 15, 18 *b*); then came to accept the epistle almost as it stands; then again decided to reject i. 15–20 once more, and finally rejected only i. 16 *b*, 17.

The integrity of the epistle as a whole is now practically beyond dispute. But there is some ground for doubting here and there the integrity of the text. There are a few passages in which the evidence of the MSS. points to the later introduction of phrases from parallel passages in *Ephesians* or to the insertion of marginal glosses into the text. Interpolations have been suspected in a few places by scholars unbiassed by any prejudice against the epistle as a whole, e.g. in i. 15–20, i. 23, ii. 1. The present text of ii. 18 and 23 is so difficult to understand that various scholars have taken refuge in 'attempts at emendation and hypotheses of interpolation' (Moffatt, *ILNT*, p. 165). Dr. Hort (*WH*. ii. 127) remarks that 'the epistle, and more particularly the second chapter, appears to have been ill-preserved in ancient times', and suggests that perhaps 'some of its harshnesses are really due to primitive corruption'. But Moffatt (*ILNT*., p. 156) is right in insisting that 'such interpolations and glosses as may be reasonably conjectured do not point to any far-reaching process of editing, least of all upon the part of the author (or under the influence) of *Ephesians*'.

II

THE HISTORICAL SETTING OF THE EPISTLE

(i) *The place of writing*

The date of the epistle depends upon the place, upon the question whether the imprisonment during which it was written was at Rome or at Caesarea or at Ephesus. Until thirty years ago the traditional answer, Rome, held the field almost undisputed. Since that date Caesarea and Ephesus have been advocated on grounds that deserve serious consideration. To-day Ephesus is the only formidable rival to Rome.

1. *Caesarea.*

The two chief advocates of the Caesarean hypothesis are Dr. Eric Haupt (*Die Gefangenschaftsbriefe* in Meyer's Commentary) and Dr. Hicks, Bishop of Lincoln (*Interpreter*, April 1910); an earlier discussion will be found in Hort's *Romans and Ephesians*, pp. 103–10. The case for Caesarea was based on two main arguments. (*a*) *Philippians* seemed to differ so markedly from the *Colossians-Ephesians-Philemon* group that the only conclusion appeared to be to leave *Philippians* in its traditional Roman setting and to assign the three other epistles to an earlier date. The attempt to determine the dates of St. Paul's letters by a comparison of their contents and style is somewhat discredited by modern scholarship. But if the attempt is to be made, there is a marked resemblance between *Philippians* and the earlier group of epistles, *Romans* and *Corinthians*. And it is scarcely credible that St. Paul would pass from that group to the Colossian group, so different in character from the earlier group, and then revert to that earlier type of epistle. (*b*) In *Colossians* and *Philemon* St. Paul seems to feel the burden of imprisonment keenly and heavily, and to miss sorely his lost freedom of missionary activity, while in *Philippians* he writes cheerfully and hopefully. This difference seemed to point to different conditions of imprisonment, closer confinement at Caesarea and greater freedom at Rome. A comparison of the two experiences as recorded in *Acts* does leave the impression that there was a difference in the two confinements. At Caesarea he was a prisoner under trial; at Rome he was a defendant awaiting the result of his own appeal to a higher tribunal. But even at Caesarea (Acts xxiv. 23) his friends were given a liberty of access almost equal to the liberty of intercourse allowed at Rome (Acts xxviii. 30). In any case the difference between the two cases was not so great as to justify the assignment of *Philippians* to Rome and of *Colossians* to Caesarea. There is, moreover, an obvious explanation of the difference in the tone of St. Paul's references to his confinement in the two epistles. In *Colossians* he is protesting against a public peril to the Christian faith; in *Philemon* he is making a private appeal to the Christian love of a convert and a friend. The burden of confinement was a powerful plea in support of both protest and appeal. Despite the incidental warnings in *Philippians*, there was apparently no need at Philippi for any such protest, and therefore no need for the pathetic plea of his 'bonds'.

There are other considerations which tell solidly for Rome as against Caesarea. (1) The desire and prayer for a door of missionary opportunity (iv. 3) seems quite inappropriate in a letter from Caesarea if it means opportunities within reach there as distinct from the distant opportunities of the mission fields from which his imprisonment had separated him. Caesarea lay within the recognized sphere of the apostles at Jerusalem (Gal. ii. 9), and St. Paul was scrupulously loyal to this division of labour (cp. 2 Cor. x. 13–16). That desire and prayer would be entirely appropriate at Rome; there he had reached the long-distant goal of his early hopes and plans (Rom. i. 13, xv. 22–4, Acts xix. 21, xxiii. 11), the starting-point perhaps of a new extension of his own peculiar mission. (2) Philip the evangelist was living at Caesarea with his four daughters, the 'virgins which did prophesy' (Acts xxi. 8–15). In all probability Philip was among the friends permitted to visit St. Paul there in prison (Acts xxiv. 23). Could St. Paul, writing from Caesarea at the latest within two years from this hospitable welcome, leave Philip unmentioned among the friends around him, or, worse still, leave him open to the suspicion that, as he was not mentioned among the 'fellow-workers for the kingdom of God who had been a comfort to him' (Col. iv. 11), he was perhaps to be reckoned among those other Jewish Christians who were apparently rivals or opponents of the Apostle's mission, or at least indifferent and unsympathetic? (3) In *Philemon*, a companion epistle to *Colossians* in date, St. Paul asks Philemon to arrange hospitality for him in view of the hope of an early visit to Colossae. At Caesarea he was waiting to be sent to Rome for trial as the result of his appeal to the imperial tribunal, and no such hope could have been entertained. But such a hope was intelligible at Rome, with his trial apparently imminent and the prospect of freedom in sight not far beyond.

2. *Ephesus.*

Ephesus was suggested by Deissmann in 1897, and strongly advocated by a German scholar, Lisco, in his *Vincula Sanctorum*, in 1900. A stronger case can be made out for Ephesus than for Caesarea.[1] Some scholars assign only *Ephesians*, *Colossians*, and *Philemon* to an imprisonment at Ephesus; others assign *Philippians* also to Ephesus; others so assign *Philippians* alone. Only those arguments which

---

[1] Kirsopp Lake, *Critical Problems of the Ep. to the Philippians* in *Exp.* viii. 42, June 1914. Bacon, *Again the Ephesian imprisonment of Paul*, *Exp.* viii. 51, March 1915. Winstanley, *Pauline Letters from an Ephesian prison*, *Exp.* viii. 54, June 1915. For a balanced statement concluding in favour of Rome, see M. Jones, *The Epistles of the Captivity, where were they written? Exp.* viii. 58, October 1915. The case for Ephesus has been stated afresh by Dr. Michaelis, *The Trial of St. Paul at Ephesus, Journ. Theol. Studies*, xxix. 116, July 1928, and by Dr. Geo. Duncan, *The Ephesian Ministry*, 1930. For a full bibliography of the question see Deissmann, *St. Paul*, p. 17, 2nd ed., 1926.

relate to the three connected epistles will be considered here. It should be noted in this connexion that *Ephesians* was probably not addressed to the Ephesian Church alone, but to some, if not all, of the churches of the province of Asia.

(*a*) There is evidence of a tradition that St. Paul was for a time in prison at Ephesus. (1) A ruined tower in the walls of the ancient city still bears the name of 'St. Paul's Prison'. (2) The *Acts of Paul and Thekla*, a second-century document, mentions an imprisonment at Ephesus during which two women of social eminence in the city visited him at night.   (3) There are short introductions prefixed in some versions of the Vulgate to the epistles of St. Paul. These introductions, called the 'Monarchian Prologues', are based upon Marcion's work, and go back therefore to the earlier part of the second century. The preface to *Colossians* states: 'ergo apostolus jam ligatus scribit eis ab Epheso'. These evidences are not conclusive. The ruined tower is, in the judgement of scholarly travellers, an unsuitable building for the custody of prisoners. The preface to *Colossians* may mean merely that its writer believed that St. Paul wrote at Ephesus as a prisoner on his way from Caesarea to Rome.

An imprisonment at Ephesus is quite probable. Only one confinement is recorded in *Acts* before the date of *2 Corinthians*, viz. at Philippi; but in 2 Cor. xi. 23 St. Paul says that he has been 'in prisons more abundantly'. There are only four imprisonments mentioned in *Acts*; but Clement of Rome says that St. Paul was 'seven times in bonds'. St. Paul's own references to many adversaries, hourly peril, daily dying, and 'fighting with beasts at Ephesus' (1 Cor. xv. 30–2, xvi. 9) seem in combination to indicate opposition, persecution, imprisonment, condemnation to death in the arena, from which he escaped by reprieve or rescue. The language of 2 Cor. i. 8–9, iv. 8–10, vi. 9, points apparently to the present or recent prospect of death; in fact the eschatology of that epistle in contrast to *1 Corinthians* seems to suggest that St. Paul had abandoned the hope of meeting his Lord again on earth. In the last chapter of *Romans*, perhaps not an original part of the epistle but a letter or part of a letter to Ephesus, Andronicus and Junias are described as 'my fellow-prisoners', and Aquila and Priscilla as having 'laid down their necks for my life' (Rom. xvi. 3–4, 7); and Ephesus seems the only place where these friends could respectively have shared the apostle's imprisonment and risked their lives for his.

On the other hand, this presentation of the evidence of the N.T. is open to criticism in detail. The term 'fellow-prisoner', even if it refers to actual imprisonment (see notes on Col. iv. 10 and Phm. 23), does not prove that the imprisonment was shared with St. Paul in actual companionship; it may mean 'who like me have been imprisoned for the Gospel'. The reference to the self-sacrifice of Aquila and Priscilla does not read like a reference to imprisonment; it may refer to a courageous intervention against popular fury. The distress and almost despair of soul revealed in *2 Corinthians* finds sufficient explanation in the lingering trouble within the Church at Corinth and in recent personal peril at Ephesus, without any supposition of actual imprisonment. His language about fighting with beasts at Ephesus is probably metaphorical, like the delivery from the mouth of the lion in 2 Tim. iv. 17 and the use of the very word 'fighting with beasts' by Ignatius to describe his treatment by the 'leopards' of his soldier escort (Ign. *Rom.* v). As a Roman citizen St. Paul was exempt from execution in the arena. The cumulative weight of the evidence alleged is seriously weakened by these criticisms of the various links in the chain.

(*b*) The Ephesian hypothesis is supported by arguments drawn from *Philemon*. Onesimus, it is argued, would have found his way to Ephesus more naturally and easily than to the far-distant capital of the Empire. But Ephesus, if nearer, was unsafer for a runaway slave. St. Paul's supposed confinement at Ephesus may have been eased by facilities of intercourse with friends, as at Rome; and these facilities would give Onesimus a chance of meeting the apostle. But Onesimus would probably avoid Ephesus in view of the 'constant risk of recognition and detection' in a city in such close touch with other Asian towns. Rome, on the other hand, was notorious as a customary refuge and a safe hiding-place for runaways.

It is argued that St. Paul's hope of an early visit to Colossae (Phm. 22) can scarcely be reconciled with his dream of a mission to Spain (Rom. xv. 28), which probably occupied his thoughts at Rome. At Ephesus such a hope was natural; Colossae was within easy reach in the event of his liberation. But St. Paul's plans may have been entirely changed by recent experiences. The hardships of persecution and imprisonment may have told heavily upon his strength. The idea of breaking new ground in the western provinces of the empire seems to have faded from his mind. There were doctrinal and disciplinary problems in some of the churches of Greece and Asia; and in the event of liberation St. Paul might well feel that he must turn to 'the consolidation of churches already in existence rather than the founding of new communities' (M. Jones, *Exp.* viii. 58, p. 306).

(*c*) There are various considerations which cast grave doubt upon the Ephesian hypothesis. (*a*) The first is the general tone of *Ephesians*.

The absence of personal greetings is of course intelligible and indeed inevitable in an encyclical letter. But *Ephesians*, whether addressed to a single church or to a group of churches, was clearly intended for a church or churches within reach of Ephesus. In that case it is strange indeed that its language should read so 'distant and impersonal', and in particular should be so indirect and tentative in its references to the faith of his readers (e.g. Eph. i. 15, iii. 2, iv. 21), as though he had no first-hand knowledge of their religious history. Such language points rather to the letter having been written at a later date and a distant place, from which he views the whole group of churches without any vivid remembrance of personal interest.

(β) There is the question of time. The duration of St. Paul's stay in Ephesus was roughly three years. There is scarcely room within such a space of time for the establishment of a strong church in Ephesus itself, for the evangelization of Colossae and Laodicea and Hierapolis, and for the rise and growth of a syncretism of Jewish, Hellenic, and Oriental elements to a stage and an extent which imperilled the faith and life of Christianity in SW. Phrygia.

(γ) In *Colossians* St. Mark and St. Luke are seen in close companionship with St. Paul. The date of any possible Ephesian imprisonment is probably too early for St. Mark's restoration to the confidence which he had forfeited by his defection. And the evidence of the 'we' sections of *Acts* seems to prove clearly that St. Luke was not with St. Paul at Ephesus, but remained at Philippi between the apostle's first visit there and his second visit after his hastened departure from Ephesus.

(δ) The most conclusive argument against the Ephesian hypothesis is the absence of any reference in the N.T. to any imprisonment of St. Paul at Ephesus. It is quite possible that there was such an imprisonment. But the imprisonment in which *Colossians* and its companion epistles were written was an experience which left a deep mark upon St. Paul's life and outlook. It is almost incredible that an imprisonment long enough to give room for the writing of these epistles, and serious enough to make a landmark in the apostle's ministry, should not be mentioned in the detailed story of his Ephesian mission (Acts xix), in which St. Luke is apparently drawing upon ample information from trustworthy sources, nor again in St. Paul's own retrospect of that mission in his farewell address to the presbyters of Ephesus at Miletus (Acts xx. 17–25).

3. *Rome.*

The arguments in favour of Ephesus are attractive but inconclusive. The early tradition of the Roman origin of the epistle still holds the field. The imprisonment at Rome is a known fact. The references in *Philippians* to the Praetorium (whether that means the imperial palace or the imperial guards) and to Caesar's household obviously suggest the idea of Rome. There is indeed evidence for the existence of slaves or freedmen of the imperial household on imperial service at Ephesus and also for the presence of 'praetorian' troops on duty in that city and for the existence of a 'government house'. But such evidence is only corroborative; it proves that *Philippians* might have been written from Ephesus, as far as its local colouring is concerned. Rome still remains the natural interpretation of such local touches. But the most substantial argument in support of the Roman origin of these epistles lies in the background of *Ephesians*. 'The imagery of that epistle manifests a very real influence of imperial ideas on the mind of St. Paul. The majesty and unity of the Empire, its widely spread dominion, the unique position of the Caesar as supreme ruler of the world and the object of actual worship, these and cognate ideas are clearly discernible behind the glorious vision of the Empire of Christ, the Church Universal, which is the central theme of the epistle' (M. Jones, *Col.*, p. 15). Glimpses of these imperial ideas, touches of these imperial influences, were possible, perhaps inevitable, in any great provincial city. But only at Rome could their splendour be seen and their pressure felt at its full height. There the Roman citizen in St. Paul must have thrilled with pride to live even as a prisoner in the imperial city whose franchise he shared and whose central seat of judgement he had claimed as his one hope of justice. But the Christian apostle in him must have thrilled with a deeper thrill of pride in the service of the Cross and the Kingdom of Christ. The submission of the peoples of the world to Caesar, the attribution of divinity to the universal benefactor, the heaping of titles of supremacy upon his name—these would all suggest a comparison which would blaze into contrast as he penned the tribute of faith to the Jesus 'in whose Name every knee should bow' (Phil. ii. 10):

> For all wreaths of empire
> Meet upon His brow.

The very franchise which had given him his right of appeal to Caesar would point a comparison and a contrast with the freedom of the adoption of the sons of God of every race into the kingdom of Christ. The *Pax Romana* would fade into impotence before the *Pax Christi* which all humanity was finding and to find in the Gospel of the Church, which is the dominant conception of the epistle to the Ephesians. And *Ephesians* is inseparable from *Colossians*. If the ency-clical epistle unfolds the vision of the Catholic Church as the Empire of Christ, the local epistle unfolds no less vividly the vision of the cosmic sovereignty of the Christ, in which even the Catholic Church is but one kingdom, though it be the kingdom which is to win all other kingdoms in earth and heaven for God.

(ii) *The date of writing*

The traditional view of Rome as the place of origin of the epistle is free from the objections incurred by the Ephesian hypothesis, and fits far more naturally into the known framework of St. Paul's life and ministry. Upon the determination of the place depends the date. The apostle's work in Ephesus is placed by recent scholar-ship with fair certainty in A.D. 52–5 (or 53–6); his imprisonment at Caesarea 56–8 (or 57–9); his first imprisonment at Rome 59–61 (or 61–3 according to Lightfoot). Any preciser dating within the period 59–61 (or 61–3) depends upon the question whether *Colossians* was written before or after *Philippians*, a question to be discussed in the next section of this introduction. An attempt has been made to fix the date by the earthquake which devastated Laodicea in A.D. 60 (Tacitus, *Ann.* xiv. 27). Eusebius places this disaster just after the burning of Rome in A.D. 64, and states that Colossae and Hierapolis shared the disaster. In that case it was obviously subsequent to the writing of the epistles of the captivity. If Tacitus is right in dating it A.D. 60, or if there were two earthquakes, one in 60 and one in 64, then *Colossians* must be placed at the close of the two years 59–61, or still later, where Lightfoot places it; for it is unlikely that no reference would be made in a letter written immediately after a catastrophe which wrecked Laodicea and can scarcely have left Colossae uninjured. On the other hand this very argument may point to a date before the earthquake, viz. 59 or early in 60.

The exact date of the epistle is comparatively unimportant. No question of interpretation is affected by the precise year of its writing. It is the approximate date which is significant, and its significance lies in the fact that the Crucifixion was only thirty years distant. Twenty years after the Crucifixion the first epistle to the Thessa-lonians, probably the earliest Christian document, reveals the Church as a community founded on belief in Jesus the Christ as Son of God and Lord and Saviour of mankind. Ten years later, while the earliest gospel was yet unwritten, this letter to Colossae reveals a far richer development of that simple faith, resting partly on the meditation of the apostle on his own spiritual experience, and partly on the

c

experience of the faith in the life of the Church. The doctrine of the
sovereignty of Christ in the realm of nature as well as in the realm of
grace—the doctrine of the Cross as not only an atonement but also
a triumph—the doctrine of the Christian life as a mystical union
with a living Christ—these are not late developments of a post-
apostolic Christianity influenced by Hellenistic or Oriental religious
ideas; they are early developments of an apostolic theology thought
out on the basis of personal experience—the individual experience
of a 'Hebrew of Hebrews' for whom the whole world was altered by
the entry of Christ into his soul,—the corporate experience of communities of men and women, Jewish, Syrian, Phrygian, Greek, Latin,
to whom Christ was not a pathetic memory of their own or their
teachers' recollection, but an immediate presence and an abiding
power.

III. THE RELATION OF COLOSSIANS TO CONTEMPORARY EPISTLES

Philemon is more than a contemporary; it is a pendant to *Colossians*.
Its contents and bearings are the subject of a separate study in its own
Introduction. The present section deals only with the two epistles
whose relations to *Colossians* affect the interpretation of that epistle
as a whole, viz. *Philippians* and *Ephesians*, and with the identity of
the 'epistle from Laodicea' to which reference is made in Col. iv. 16.

(i) *Colossians and Philippians*

Philippians is almost certainly a product of the same imprisonment which produced *Colossians* and *Ephesians*. Two questions call
for consideration, (1) the comparison and contrast of the contents of
the two epistles, (2) the priority of the one or the other in order of
time.

(1) The resemblances between *Philippians* and *Colossians* are few
and slight. (*a*) In their vocabulary Von Soden notes seventeen cases
of identical or almost identical expressions. Several of these are not
peculiar to the epistles of the imprisonment: e.g. the figurative use
of 'circumcision' (Phil. iii. 3, Col. ii. 11) is found in Rom. ii. 28–9:
'perfect' (Col. i. 28, Phil. iii. 15) in 1 Cor. ii. 6, xiv. 20; 'conflict'
(*agon*, Phil. i. 30, Col. ii. 1) in 1 Thess. ii. 2; 'prize' (Phil. iii. 14,
Col. ii. 18) in 1 Cor. ix. 24. The only noteworthy resemblances in
language peculiar to the two epistles are the 'upward' calling of
Phil. iii. 14 and the upward look and thought of Col. iii. 1; the 'heart
of compassion' in Col. iii. 12, Phil. ii. 1; the 'energy' of God in Phil.

iii. 21, Col. i. 29, ii. 12 (cp. Eph. iii. 7); 'humility' in Phil. ii. 3, Col. ii. 23, iii. 12 (cp. Eph. iv. 2); and the references to the apostle's 'bonds' in Phil. i. 7, 13, 14, 17 and Col. iv. 18. (b) In ideas there are a few noteworthy resemblances, e.g. the peace of God (Christ) in the heart, Phil. iv. 7, Col. iii. 15; the prayer for knowledge, Phil. i. 9, Col. i. 9; the apostle's fellowship with the Lord's passion, Phil. iii. 10, Col. i. 24; the supplying of what is lacking in service or suffering, though in very different connexions, Phil. ii. 30, Col. i. 24. These two groups of resemblances confirm the belief that the two epistles belong to the same short period of the apostle's experience. But they also bring into stronger relief the difference in the general contents of the two epistles.

Philippians was written to a church of St. Paul's own founding, knit closely to him in personal intimacy; *Colossians* to a church with which he is claiming fellowship in spite of the absence of any personal connexion. The Philippian church had its dangers; the unity of its life was imperilled by pride and partisanship, and the purity of its faith apparently by Judaistic and by libertinist error, unless the third chapter of the epistle is an interpolation of part of another letter, written perhaps to another church. The Colossian church was in danger from an entirely different quarter; its peril lay in the attractions of a false asceticism and a fanciful mysticism. To both churches the apostle speaks in thankful recognition of their spiritual progress. To both he tempers protest with sympathy; but in *Philippians* it is the sympathy of a spiritual father, a personal friend, grateful for proofs of their generosity; in *Colossians* it is the sympathy of an apostle anxious to safeguard the faith of a church founded by his disciples and friends. To the Philippians he can reveal the secrets of his own soul; to the Colossians he can only unfold the spiritual significance of his apostolic mission. It is noteworthy that it is only in *Colossians* and *Ephesians* that he applies the teaching of the new life in detail to all social and domestic relationships. The Philippian church seems to have been stronger in applied Christianity. At first sight it seems strange that this exposition of Christian ethics should have been included in the epistle to Ephesus, a church upon which he had spent nearly three years' pastoral labour; but it must be remembered that *Ephesians* was probably an encyclical letter addressed to a group of churches in south-western Asia, some of which had not had the benefit of St. Paul's own personal teaching and training.

(2) The question of priority between *Philippians* and *Colossians* still remains undecided. In favour of a later date for *Philippians* it

convey any idea of the way in which, or the extent to which, phrases and even clauses in *Colossians* appear here and there in *Ephesians* in a different context or with a different turn of thought, or the whole section in *Ephesians* varies from the parallel in *Colossians* in the order of ideas and the connexion of thought. Here the analysis gives first the two general ideas common to this section in both epistles, without any attempt at detailed comparison or contrast, and then the particular points peculiar to the one or the other:

<table>
<tr><td align="center">COLOSSIANS</td><td align="center">EPHESIANS</td></tr>
</table>

i. 1, 2.   Opening salutation.   i. 1, 2.

Thanksgiving.

COLOSSIANS	EPHESIANS
	i. 3–14. for the mystery of God's purpose: election, adoption, redemption, revelation, consummation, in an inheritance including Jew and Gentile.
i. 3–5. for their faith, love and hope.	i. 15. for their faith and love.
i. 6. for the growth and fruit of the Gospel in all the world.	
i. 7–8. for the work of Epaphras at Colossae.	

i. 9–11.   Prayer for their advance in knowledge and power.   i. 16–19.

COLOSSIANS	EPHESIANS
i. 12–20. Thanksgiving for their redemption into the kingdom of the Son who is	
1. the revelation of the love of God.	i. 20–23. The power of God seen at work in Christ:
2. the agent, centre and goal of all creation.	1. His resurrection and ascension.
3. the head of the Church, the Body of Christ, who is	2. His supremacy over all powers.
(a) the embodiment of the *pleroma* of the Godhead;	3. His headship over the Church, which is
(b) the reconciliation of the universe.	(a) the Body of Christ; (b) the *pleroma* of Christ.
i. 21–23. They have been reconciled from the alienation of sin to the hope of holiness through fidelity to the Gospel.	ii. 1–22. They have been reconciled
	1–10. from the death and doom of sin to the life of grace.
	11–22. from the alienation of a hopeless heathenism to fellowship with the saints in the household and temple of God.

i. 24–ii. 7.   *The mission and ministry of the Apostle.*   iii. 1–20.

i. 24. A ministry of joyful suffering in fulfilment of the afflictions of Christ for the sake of His Body the Church.

i. 25–29. His mission a dispensation of God

    (*a*) to proclaim the mystery of God.

    (*b*) to preach 'Christ the hope of glory' among the Gentiles.

    (*c*) to perfect every Christian.

ii. 1–7. Anxious prayer for their preservation and progress in the Christian faith and life.

ii. 8–iii. 4. *The peril to their faith :*

ii. 8. A philosophy of life offering what can all be found in Christ and in Christ alone.

ii. 9–10. The supremacy and sufficiency of Christ.

ii. 11–13. The true redemption and consecration of life.

ii. 14–15. The liberating victory of the Cross.

ii. 16–18. The fallacy and futility of this asceticism and angelolatry.

ii. 19. The necessity of holding fast the Head, the source of life and growth for the Body.

ii. 20–23. The folly of reverting from the freedom of redemption to the bondage of an asceticism plausible but powerless to save.

iii. 1–4. The secret of holiness: the *sursum corda* of a risen life hidden in Christ.

cp. Col. iii. 14, 15.

iii. 1–21. His mission

    (*a*) to 'bring to light the dispensation of the mystery', the fellowship of the Gentiles in the Gospel.

    (*b*) to preach the riches of Christ.

iii. 13. His afflictions are their glory.

iii. 14–19. Prayer to the Father for their strengthening by the Spirit and for the indwelling of Christ.

iii. 20, 21. Doxology.

iv. 1–16. *The call of unity.*

1–3. Exhortation to fulfil their calling in love and peace.

4–6. The unity of the fellowship of the faith: one Spirit, one Lord, one Father.

7–11. The unity of the ministry of grace: all ministries are gifts of the ascended Christ

   (*a*) to train the saints for ministry and so build the Body.

cp. Col. ii. 19.

   (*b*) to preserve them from false teaching and lead them to the Head, the source of growth for the whole Body.

iii. 5–17.   *The old life and the new.*   iv. 17–v. 21.

(*a*) the dying of the old life of passion and sin.

(*b*) the development of the new life of grace and holiness.

iii. 11. The transcending of all human distinctions: Christ all in all.

iv. 17–21. Christian renunciation of pagan vices.

iv. 25. Truthfulness a mutual duty between members of the Body.

iv. 29. Foul language to give place to healthy and helpful talk (cp. v. 4).

iv. 30. Warning against grieving the Holy Spirit, the seal of redemption.

v. 5. Sins that exclude from the kingdom of God and of Christ.

v. 7–13. The contrast and conflict between darkness and light.

v. 14. A hymn of awakening to the Light.

iii. 14, 15. The ruling influence of the peace of Christ.

Col. iv. 5.

v. 15, 16. The wisdom of redeeming the time.

v. 18. The wine of intoxication and the wine of inspiration.

iii. 16.   The mutua helpfulness of sacred song.   v. 19.

iii. 17.   The habit of constant thanksgiving.   v. 20.

> v. 21. Mutual submission in the fear of Christ.

iii. 18–iv. 1.   *The transformation of human relationships.*   v. 22–vi. 9.

1. The submission of the wife.

> v. 23, 24. The headship of the husband in the home like the headship of Christ in the Church.

2. The love of the husband.

> v. 25–32. Its mystical exemplar: the devotion of Christ to the Church.
>
> v. 31. Its divine law: the unity of marriage (Gen. ii. 24).

3. The obedience of the children.

> vi. 2, 3. 'The first commandment with promise' (Ex. xx. 12, Dt. v. 16).

4. The patience of the father.

> vi. 4. The duty of religious training.

5. The mutual obligations of slave and master.

iv. 2–6.   *Practical counsels.*   vi. 10–20.

iv. 2. Perseverance in prayer and thanksgiving.

iv. 3, 4. Request for their prayers for his own freedom to preach and for faithfulness in preaching the mystery of Christ.

iv. 5. Wisdom of redeeming the time.

Eph. v. 15.

iv. 6. Need of 'grace' and 'salt' in conversation.

cp. Eph. iv. 29.

vi. 10–17. The spiritual conflict: the Christian soldier and the whole armour of God.

vi. 18. Perseverance in prayer and thanksgiving.

vi. 19, 20. Request for their prayer for his own freedom to preach and for faithfulness in preaching the mystery of the Gospel.

Various features in the character and relation of the two epistles emerge from this comparative analysis.

1. The thanksgiving in *Ephesians* begins with the successive stages and the universal range of the divine plan of human salvation. In *Colossians* it centres at once upon the Christian life of the Church addressed, and with an incidental glance at the missionary progress of the Church at large passes into a thankful retrospect of the mission that founded the Church at Colossae. This section of the analysis is almost conclusive in itself for the earlier date of *Colossians*. It is scarcely credible that the thanksgiving in *Ephesians* for the whole 'mystery' of divine purpose could have been omitted from any immediately subsequent letter.

2. In the Christological section which develops out of the thanksgiving *Colossians* begins with the supremacy and centrality of Christ in the *cosmos*, the universe, and lays upon this an emphasis appropriate in view of the exaltation of powers and angels in the Colossian heresy. The theme of *Colossians*, viz. Christ in relation to God, creation and the Church, is also the theme of *Ephesians*, but there creation is less prominent than the Church; the consummation of all things in Christ is included as a stage in the divine purpose (i. 10), but Christ is viewed rather as 'the immanent Principle in the unity and spiritual growth of the Church'; and the whole theme is viewed not in contrast to any false teaching, but as an exposition of the eternal purpose of God for humanity.

3. The idea of reconciliation is worked out differently in the two epistles. In both it includes the change in the spiritual character

and moral life of the hearers. But in *Colossians* it has a cosmic range; it includes the celestial powers, in obvious antithesis to the tendency of the Colossian heresy to regard the angels as mediators. In *Ephesians* the reconciliation has no cosmic significance. The consummation of the world in Eph. i. 10 is not associated with the Cross. Emphasis is laid instead on the reconciliation of the Gentiles—not merely their personal reconciliation to God, as in *Colossians*, but also their collective reconciliation together with Jews in the one Body.

In *Colossians* the thought of their reconciliation passes into a warning against drifting away from the Gospel. In *Ephesians* there is no hint of any such danger; the idea of reconciliation is worked out in its bearing on the unity of the Church, which is the key-note of *Ephesians* as clearly as the purity of the faith is the key-note of *Colossians*.

4. The place of the Gentiles in the Church is more prominent in *Ephesians*. In Col. i. 27 the 'mystery' is the indwelling of Christ in the Christian, which Gentiles share with other Christians. In Col. iii. 11 the union of Jew and Gentile is implied in the vanishing of racial and other human distinctions, apparently in contrast to the exclusivism of the false teachers. But in *Ephesians* the union of Jew and Gentile is a main idea; the 'mystery' itself is the inclusion of the Gentiles in the Body of Christ.

5. The two prayers at the close of the passage dealing with the apostle's mission repay careful comparison. The prayer in *Colossians* is tinged with anxiety and apprehension amid all its most thankful and hopeful touches. The prayer in *Ephesians* has a higher background and a wider outlook, and culminates appropriately in a doxology.

6. The difference in the purpose of the two epistles comes out most vividly in the contrast between the two next sections. There is indeed a brief but striking appeal for peace and unity in Col. iii. 14, 15. And in Eph. iv. 14 there is an incidental but grave warning against vacillations and vagaries of belief. But the titles here given to the two sections, 'the peril to the faith' and 'the call of unity', might almost serve as descriptions of the two epistles in their entirety. *Colossians* has in view a crisis in a particular church, *Ephesians* the character of the Church Catholic.

7. The terse precepts of *Colossians* for the Christian family are given in *Ephesians* a sacramental bearing and a scriptural basis. Christian marriage is set in analogy to the union of Christ and the Church, and also in continuity with the primitive ideal. The rights and duties of Christian parenthood are placed in the line of traditional Hebrew piety. The absence of these explanations and references

in *Colossians* can scarcely be attributed to abbreviation. Their presence in *Ephesians* is intelligible, if it was written in a more quietly reflective hour in which Colossae and its crisis had passed out of the foreground of the apostle's mind.

8. The description of the warfare of the Christian life in *Ephesians* is an appropriate epilogue. It blends in one picture the spiritual world of unseen foes and the Roman soldier at the apostle's side. In *Colossians* he had given the theological and practical antidote to the local peril of a mystical asceticism based upon the belief in the intervention or mediation of angelic powers, perhaps beneficent, at least neutral rather than hostile. In *Ephesians* he calls attention to a constant and universal danger from that unseen world, the influence of personal forces of evil not remotely celestial but immediately insidious, and meets the danger with a parable or allegory of personal spiritual discipline and preparation.

This comparative analysis of the two epistles in general outline and in particular contents points clearly towards the conclusion that *Ephesians* is the later document. The Colossians were intended to have the benefit of this fuller teaching, if 'the epistle from Laodicea' (Col. iv. 16) was our *Ephesians*, as in all probability it was. There is no evidence to indicate whether the writing of *Ephesians* was prompted by any special circumstances or conditions of Church life in Ephesus or other cities in Asia and Phrygia. The evidence of the messages to the seven churches in the Apocalypse belongs to a later though perhaps not distant date. We are left to conjecture. (*a*) It is possible that St. Paul, after writing his letter of corrective or precautionary instruction to Colossae, may have felt conscious that the Colossians needed something of a wider vision and richer interpretation of the Christian faith and the Catholic Church, and not the Colossians only but all the churches in their neighbourhood, and that this consciousness bore fruit in the letter which we know as *Ephesians*. (*b*) The journey of Tychicus to Colossae would take him through a succession of cities where there was already a Christian church, and afforded the opportunity and suggested the wisdom of a circular pastoral letter that would give them all the benefit of a message from the apostle who was the founder of one at least of these churches and the spiritual father of the founders of others. (*c*) It may have been a relief and a joy to turn from controversial to constructive teaching, from polemic to something like prophecy, and to give written expression, as he surveyed the world from the centre and heart of the Roman empire, to the vision of a wider realm, a higher sovereignty, a profounder peace for humanity.

(iii) *The Epistle from Laodicea*

The Church at Colossae is to see that *Colossians* is read in the 'congregation of the Laodiceans' and in its turn to read 'the letter from Laodicea' (Col. iv. 16). The identification of this 'letter from Laodicea' is still under discussion. The history of the question as it is traced by Lightfoot (*Colossians*, pp. 272–98) is an illuminative epitome of the history of biblical criticism. Here only the barest outline of the question can be given. (*a*) The first theory is that the epistle in question was a letter written by the Laodiceans, either to St. Paul or to Epaphras or to the Colossian Church. These alternatives are all open to the same obvious objections. The two epistles in view in Col. iv. 16 are clearly in the same category; 'ye also' implies a parallel as well as an exchange. A letter from the Laodiceans to St. Paul would not be a counterpart to a letter from him to the Colossians. A letter from Laodicea to Colossae is unthinkable; why should the Colossians be urged to read a letter written to themselves? A letter from Laodicea to St. Paul implies a copy retained at Laodicea, a possibility on which St. Paul could scarcely count with certainty. Why could he not get one of his companions at Rome to make and send to Colossae a copy of the original letter from Laodicea?

(*b*) The second theory is that the letter was written from Laodicea by St. Paul himself; and it has been identified in turn with *1 Timothy*, with either *1* or *2 Thessalonians*, and with *Galatians*, on the ground of doubtful indications in, or inferences from, notes appended to these epistles in some manuscripts or versions. But these epistles are all years distant from *Colossians*, and can be assigned on solid grounds to other places of writing; and the very idea of a recent letter sent by St. Paul from Laodicea is untenable in view of the fact that for some considerable time before writing *Colossians* he had been in confinement at Rome.

(*c*) The only remaining solution of the problem, and the most obvious, is that it was a letter written to the Laodiceans by St. Paul himself, which the Laodiceans are to send on to Colossae, as the Colossians are to send on to Laodicea the letter received by them. The alternative form of this theory, viz. that it was a letter to the Laodiceans from Epaphras or Luke, is improbable; it would have been natural and almost inevitable in that case that St. Paul would mention its author. On the assumption that it was a letter from St. Paul, it has still to be identified. It has been supposed to be one of the letters which have not survived. But in view of the fact that there are three known epistles from St. Paul to the province of Asia at this time, it is superfluous to suggest a fourth in the absence of any evidence requiring this addition. On the strength of a tradition mentioned by a fourth-century writer, some modern scholars have identified the epistle with *Hebrews*; but even apart from the weight of argument against the Pauline authorship of *Hebrews*, the general contents and character and purpose of that epistle are so entirely different from *Colossians* that it is almost incredible that two such letters could have come from the pen of St. Paul so near together and gone to the same little group of neighbouring churches. Others have suggested *Philemon*; but even if Philemon's home was Laodicea and not Colossae, it is unthinkable that a private letter on a delicate question of personal Christian duty should have been read by express instruction of St. Paul himself to two congregations.

(*d*) A startlingly novel theory was propounded in 1910 by Harnack (*Sitzungsberichte d. k. p. Akademie d. Wissenschaften*, xxxvii, 1910). He argued that 'the letter from Laodicea' was our *Ephesians*, and that it was not a Laodicean copy of an encyclical to the churches of Asia, but a special letter to the Church of Laodicea. Marcion's copy of *Ephesians*, about A.D. 140, bore the title of 'the epistle to the Laodiceans'. Harnack believes that this was the original title and address. The disappearance of this address in orthodox circles from the beginning of the second century was the result of the condemnation pronounced upon the Church of Laodicea in the Revelation of St. John. In ancient times, when individuals and communities disgraced their earlier reputation, their names were erased from the tablets or documents which recorded their former distinctions. The name of Laodicea was thus erased from the current copies of the epistles. The epistle itself was treasured still as a pastoral of catholic value, and the name of Ephesus as a leading church in Asia was used to fill the blank. Laodicea recovered its spiritual life before the end of the second century, but its title to the epistle remained only among the Marcionite heretics. Harnack's theory is a brilliant conjecture. It links together historical facts hitherto unconnected. It gives a new significance to Rev. iii. 16 in the light of Rev. iii. 5, 12. But it remains only a brilliant conjecture. It is strange indeed that action so drastic has left no trace in the history or literature of the Church in Asia during the second century. It is strange that Laodicea failed to regain its title to the epistle when it recovered its good name as a church half a century later. Nor does Harnack offer a convincing explanation either of the absence of those personal references in the epistle which might have been expected in a letter to Laodicea alone, or of the interpolation of 'Ephesus' in place of the erased 'Laodicea', or of the general character of the teaching of a letter addressed to a particular church.

(e) The theory now commonly adopted is that the 'letter from Laodicea' was our *Ephesians*, and that the uncertainty of its address is to be explained in one of two ways. (a) It may have been a circular letter to the churches of Asia, with a space left blank for the insertion of the name of each church in the copy intended for it. The absence of any copy for Colossae itself has been explained by the supposition that, as the Colossians were receiving a letter of their own, they might be left to content themselves with receiving the Laodicean copy of the encyclical letter. Their own letter contained so much that was identical or similar that St. Paul may have thought it unnecessary to send them also a copy of the encyclical; but at the last moment he may have thought that perhaps they ought to see it, and might make a copy of it for themselves if they wished to keep it for the sake of its fuller teaching on some points. The question arises here, whether the mention of the letter from Laodicea in Col. iv. 16 does not prove that *Ephesians* was already written. Internal evidence, however, is almost conclusive for the priority of *Colossians*. And Col. iv. 16 may have been a later addition after *Ephesians* too was ready for dispatch. It still seems the more natural thing that St. Paul should have sent a copy of the circular-letter to Colossae as well as to the other churches. But it is possible that the true explanation, after all, is that there was only one copy of the circular-letter, viz. the original manuscript; that this was left to each church to copy if it so desired; and that the 'letter from Laodicea' was this original manuscript on its way to the last church perhaps on the list, viz. Colossae. In that case Colossae was treated in just the same way as all the other churches. On the other hand, as in the Apocalypse, so it may have been here; Laodicea, with its civil and social prominence as the local metropolis, may have been selected as the centre of circulation for the eastern district, as Ephesus was for the western.

(β) The difficulty of the address may be explained otherwise. The letter may have been written originally to a single church, and would probably in that case include personal greetings and references. The original address and the salutations may have been omitted later, when the letter came to be adopted, and therefore needed to be adapted, for wider circulation, since its teaching seemed to be of general value for all churches. This explanation is quite compatible with the belief that the letter in question was our *Ephesians*. Our manuscripts may have descended from a copy in which Ephesus had been inserted because it was a copy preserved at Ephesus, and the absence of a place-name in the opening address was felt to be awkward.

(γ) It is quite possible, however, that the church to which the letter was originally written on this hypothesis was Laodicea. In that case it was either our *Ephesians* or some other letter. The latter possibility is not disproved by the fact that there is no trace of any such letter. Other letters of St. Paul have certainly perished. The former supposition is open to the objection that the theme and contents of *Ephesians* are too wide and too deep for a letter written to Laodicea alone, a church with no history before its sad appearance in the Apocalypse a generation later. We seem almost driven by the majestic sweep of *Ephesians* to postulate a larger object for the letter than the instruction of any single church. After all, the theory of an encyclical letter to the churches of Asia remains the most probable and the most satisfying.

(iv) *The Epistle to the Laodiceans*

No survey of the problem would be complete without a glance at a document which once commanded an acceptance which it did not deserve, viz. the apocryphal 'Epistle to the Laodiceans'. Here is an English version:

'Paul an apostle not from men nor through man but through Jesus Christ, to the brethren which are at Laodicea. Grace to you and peace from God the Father and the Lord Jesus Christ. I thank Christ in every prayer of mine that ye are abiding in Him and persevering in His works, awaiting His promise unto the day of judgment. Let not the vain talk of false teachers beguile you, that they should turn you away from the truth of the gospel which is preached by me. And now God will make those things which belong to me [at this point the text is corrupt] . . . to the progress of the truth of the gospel . . . serving and doing good works which belong to the salvation of life eternal. And now my bonds which I suffer in Christ are seen of all men ; in which I am glad and rejoice. And this is for my lasting salvation, which is wrought by your prayers and by the ministration of the Holy Spirit, whether by life or by death. For to me to live is to live in Christ, and to die is joy. And this very thing His mercy will work in you, to have the same love and to be of one mind. Therefore, beloved, as ye heard in my presence, so hold fast and do in the fear of God, and ye shall have life for ever. For it is God that worketh upon you. And whatsoever ye do, do without wavering. Finally, beloved, rejoice in Christ ; and beware of them that are base in pursuit of gain. Let all your petitions be open in the sight of God ; and be ye stedfast in the mind of Christ. And what things are honest and true and modest and just and lovely, these do. Hold fast in your heart what ye heard and received ; and ye shall have peace. The saints salute you. The grace of the Lord Jesus be with your spirit. And see that this is read to the Colossians and the Colossians' letter is read to you.'

The letter is a transparent forgery, 'a cento of Pauline phrases', most of them from *Philippians*, a few from *Galatians*, 'strung together without any definite connexion or any clear object' (Ltft.). It was evidently written to satisfy Col. iv. 16. Its Grecisms and its variations from the Old Latin and Vulgate versions point to a Greek original, but it had a far wider circulation in the West than in the East. Jerome and Theodore of Mopsuestia, in the fourth century, rejected it as spurious, but the second council of Nicaea (A.D. 787) found it still necessary to warn people against 'a forged epistle to the Laodiceans' which 'was given a place in some copies of the Apostle'. Still it retained its place in many manuscripts of the Pauline epistles from the sixth to the fifteenth century, though some medieval scholars, while not doubting its Pauline authorship, doubted or denied its canonicity. 'Thus for more than nine centuries this forged epistle hovered about the doors of the sacred Canon, without either finding admission or being peremptorily excluded.' The revival of learning sealed its doom, and papist and protestant scholarship were at one in its condemnation. 'The dawn of the Reformation had effectually scared away this ghost of a Pauline epistle, which (we may confidently hope) has been laid for ever, and will not again be suffered to haunt the mind of the Church' (Ltft., *Col.*, pp. 297, 298).

IV

CHRISTIANITY IN PHRYGIA

(i) *Cities of the Lycus Valley*

The central portion of what is known now as Asia Minor, or more correctly as Anatolia, was occupied for centuries before the Christian era by invaders from Thrace called Phrygians. The Roman provincial system ignored racial and historical facts for reasons of administrative convenience, and attached eastern Phrygia to the province of Galatia (hence the double name in Acts xvi. 6 and xviii. 23) and western Phrygia to the province of Asia, extending the name Phrygia at the same time to include the Lycus valley and the district north of Lycia. The Roman province of Asia, originally the kingdom of Attalus of Pergamum, included all the coastal regions from the Hellespont to the Mediterranean, Mysia, Lydia, and Caria. Mysia is mentioned in Acts xvi. 7, 8. Lydia and Caria survived only as racial

D

descriptions. Five churches in Lydia, viz. Ephesus, Smyrna, Thyatira, Philadelphia, Sardis, are grouped in the Apocalypse along with Pergamum in Mysia and Laodicea in Phrygia as 'the seven churches which are in Asia'. The cities of the Lycus valley may therefore be described with equal accuracy as Phrygian or as Asian, the former racially or geographically, the latter politically.

Less than a hundred miles south-east of Ephesus the valley of the Meander narrows to a pass, the open gate through which Greek civilization and Roman imperialism travelled eastwards and the trade of Phrygia flowed westwards to the Aegean seaboard. Fifteen miles farther east the great eastern trade route from Ephesus to the Euphrates leaves the Meander at its sharp bend from its southward course, and strikes south-east along its tributary the Lycus. Ten miles farther east, less than ten miles to the north of the highway, lies the city of Hierapolis, and on the highway itself lies Laodicea, to the south of the river. Both cities were situated on the terraces of the hills that form the north and south walls of the once more widening valley. Twelve miles east of Laodicea, in a little glen which forms the higher shelf of the Lycus valley, lies the site of Colossae, with the Lycus running through its midst in a deep ravine.

The Lycus valley has a character of its own. Its towns have been devastated again and again in ancient and modern times by violent earthquakes. There are no signs of recent volcanic action; but hot springs and mephitic vapours still prove the presence of subterranean fires. Calcareous deposits from the tributaries of the Lycus have buried here and there ruins and fields alike, and 'gleam like glaciers on the hillside' (Ltft., p. 3). Yet the district was fertile enough to breed large flocks of sheep with wool of rare excellence; its mineral streams provided materials for the dyers; and both Hierapolis and Laodicea had a guild of dyers, and probably Colossae also, which gave its name to a rich purple dye known as *colossinus*.

Three races met in this valley—Phrygians, Lydians, and Carians. Colossae was Phrygian until it became more or less superficially Greek. Laodicea was regarded as both Phrygian and Carian. Hierapolis was described by different authors as Carian and as Lydian. Yet while Laodicea began life afresh as a Greek colony, Hierapolis became 'the focus of Phrygian national feeling and religious ideas' (Woodhouse, *Enc. Bibl.* ii. 2064). The Carians and Phrygians were victorious invaders of European stock; the Lydians were apparently a mixed race, earlier immigrants of Thracian origin who had absorbed Asiatic elements. All three merged into an Anatolian type. 'The warrior element was gradually eliminated from their character, as the native strain overpowered the blood of the immigrant stock' (Ramsay, *CBP.* i. 9). In later times 'Phrygian' even became a synonym of 'slave'. Yet the original differences survived in their religion. In the Phrygian and Carian cults the male element still predominated, in the Lydian the female; in the former Zeus and the native Father-gods with whom he was identified, in the latter the Mother-goddess and her son. 'From the dawn of history to the present day the development of Asia Minor turns on the conflict between the European and the Oriental spirit' (Ramsay, *CBP.* i. 8).

1. *Colossae.*

Colossae[1] owes its place in history to St. Paul. It was 'a great city of Phrygia', Herodotus tells us, when Xerxes halted his huge army there in 480 B.C. on its way to the invasion of Greece. It was 'a populous city, prosperous and great' when Xenophon spent a week there in 401 B.C. in the service of Cyrus on his ill-fated expedition against Artaxerxes. But it declined steadily before the political and commercial supremacy of Laodicea and the social attractions of Hierapolis. About fifty years before St. Paul wrote the epistle which planted Colossae on the map of Christendom, the historian-geographer Strabo notes that it was a small town in the district of which Laodicea was the capital. Its site was not identified until the nineteenth century; and its ruins since discovered are few and meagre, a fragment of a mediocre theatre, and of an unimposing acropolis, and little more worth noting. Its Christian history will be sketched later in this chapter.

2. *Hierapolis.*

Hierapolis was famous on both social and sacred grounds. In addition to its prosperous wool-trade it had a source of wealth in the medicinal waters and the natural baths provided by the ample streams in its environs. Its name points to a sacred origin. The city grew round a *hieron* or shrine of the old Phrygian religion. Its original name was Hieropolis, 'the city of the sanctuary', but with the dominance of Greek civilization it gave place to the form Hierapolis, 'the sacred city', as the Phrygian shrine yielded in importance to the Hellenic city. Yet native religion held its ground. The patron deity of the city was Apollo Archegetes, i.e. the Founder, an appro-

---

[1] The name Colossae may have been derived from a lake named Koloe. Its present form was perhaps a Greek development from a fancied connexion with *colossos*, though there is no evidence of any statue to support this idea. Some Greek MSS. of *Colossians* have the form *Colassae*. The adjective varies similarly between *Colossenos* and *Colassaeus*, the latter, like *Colassae*, probably representing the native pronunciation, the former the Greek.

Laodicea owed its rapid later advance to Roman administration. It
stood at the junction of four highways in the imperial road-system,
and became the metropolis of the local district of some twenty-five
towns known as the Cibyratic *conventus* or *dioecesis* from its original
head-quarters at Cibyra. At Laodicea Cicero, on his periodic visits as
proconsul of Cilicia, held his assizes, cashed his bills on the Roman
treasury, and wrote some of the letters which he afterwards published.
The city numbered among its citizens orators, sophists, and philosophers, famous in their day—one local magnate who 'became a king
and a father of kings', Polemo, whose services to the Roman government were rewarded by Mark Antony with the governorship of part
of Cilicia, and then with the kingdom of Pontus, and whose son
Polemo resigned Pontus on its formation into a Roman province in
A.D. 62, the very year perhaps in which St. Paul wrote his letter to
Laodicea—and at least one benefactor, Hiero, who spent his fortune
on public buildings. The wealth of the city, and its pride, were proved
by the fact, which Tacitus (*Ann.* xiv. 27) notes with surprise and
admiration, that after a disastrous earthquake in A.D. 60 the city
rebuilt itself without appealing for the imperial grant usually made
in aid of such reconstructions. Further evidence of that wealth also
remains in the magnificence of the ruins which still survive, despite
the quarrying thence of the materials for the building of the modern
Turkish town of Denizli. Of the religious life of Laodicea there is
little distinctive evidence. Between the city and the 'gate of Phrygia'
to the west there was a famous temple of Men Carou, the Carian form
of the old Phrygian deity, variously identified or associated with
Zeus and Apollo and Asklepios by the Hellenic immigrants. Round
this cult grew a famous school of medicine, which had its seat in
Laodicea itself. Its chief physicians in the time of Augustus are
mentioned on Laodicean coins bearing the snake-wreathed staff of
Asklepios or the figure of Zeus. From this school an ear-ointment and
an eye-powder passed into general use far and wide. The bearing of
this medical school, as of the dyed-wool trade and the wealth of the
city in general, on the message to Laodicea in the Apocalypse will be
noted in that connexion. In that connexion too it is significant that
Laodicea failed as signally as Philadelphia succeeded in fulfilling the
missionary duty expected of them as centres of Hellenic civilization.
Its material wealth had proved a moral weakness; it had all western
Phrygia at its feet, but apparently lived a self-centred life without
any educative influence upon its less favoured neighbours. It was
seemingly as lukewarm in the cause of civilization as it was afterwards in the cause of Christianity.

(ii) *Foundation and development of churches*

1. *Their foundation not the work of St. Paul.*

Colossians itself is the earliest evidence of Christian churches in the three cities of the Lycus valley; and the language in which St. Paul refers to their origin and growth and to his own relation to them seems to prove clearly that they were not churches of his own foundation. He writes as though he owed his knowledge of their conversion as well as their progress to information derived from others (i. 4, 9). There is no hint of any personal contact with his readers, and no reference to any incident of any visit to Colossae. He refers often to his own preaching of the Gospel, and to their first hearing or their later knowledge of the Gospel, and these two references occur near to each other; but they are never connected as two sides of one and the same event or process; in fact the day when they heard the Gospel is distinguished clearly from the day when he heard the news of their conversion (cp. i. 6 and i. 9). And the wording of his avowal of anxiety on their behalf implies, in its most natural interpretation, that Colossians and Laodiceans alike were among the many Christians who had never seen his face (ii. 1).

The literary evidence of the epistle is borne out by the historical evidence of *Acts.* There is no hint there of any visit to the Lycus valley, nor is there room for such a visit. 'Phrygia' was a general and ambiguous term, requiring definition either by further specification or by the indications of the context. It is true that St. Paul is twice described as passing through territory called Phrygia (Acts xvi. 6, xviii. 23). But in both cases the district is also called Galatian or is coupled with Galatian territory. The most natural interpretation of the double designation is that it refers to that part of the original Phrygia which was included in the Roman province of Galatia. (*a*) The first case is the second missionary journey. St. Paul had completed his visitation of churches founded on the first journey, and came, apparently from Antioch in Pisidia, to the frontier of the province of Asia, evidently intending to break new ground by entering that province, but was 'forbidden by the Holy Ghost to preach the word in Asia' (Acts xvi. 6). We are left to conjecture as to whether this prohibition was internal or external—the direct prohibition of a divine inspiration or the indirect prohibition of circumstances interpreted as the guidance of the Spirit. In obedience to this conviction, St. Paul turned northwards along the Asian frontier in a journey that was guided ultimately into a mission to Macedonia. Now the Asia of *Acts* is the Roman province, which included the Phrygia of the Lycus valley, lying south-west of Pisidian Antioch. If this was the point at which he had intended to enter Asia, travelling along the great east-to-west highway, the Lycus valley was obviously the actual field from which he was warned off by the divine prohibition. In any case, even if he was thinking of entering Asia by the minor road north of the Lycus valley, SW. Phrygia as part of the province was closed against him by that prohibition. (*b*) The second reference to this region is in the account of the third missionary journey. It is described this time in inverse order as Galatian-Phrygian, in view of the direction of the Apostle's route. Starting from his original base, Antioch in Syria, St. Paul traversed for a third time the region of his first mission, 'strengthening all the disciples' (xviii. 23). Then he came to Ephesus, 'having passed through the upper country' (xix. 1). The impression left by the turn and tone of the language in both contexts is that they refer to two different and successive stages of the journey, viz. (1) a confirmatory visitation of churches already established, (2) a journey westwards from this group of churches, starting probably from Pisidian Antioch as his last place of call. Now there were two westward roads from Antioch in Pisidia, the most western of the churches of that first mission, viz. (1) the great highway running south-west through the Lycus valley and then bending northward to Ephesus, (2) a minor road running more directly westward to the north of the Lycus valley. The latter road seems clearly indicated by the phrase 'the upper country'. The southern route would have taken St. Paul through Colossae and Laodicea and near to Hierapolis. But the evangelization of those cities would have postponed for some time his visit to Ephesus; and Ephesus, as the metropolis of the whole province, was apparently the immediate goal of the Apostle's mission, as it was indeed the strategic centre of any provincial movement. The result of thus striking at the heart of the province justified this policy; from Ephesus, within the three years of his mission there, 'all the inhabitants of Asia heard the word of the Lord Jesus' (xix. 10).

2. *The fruit of St. Paul's Ephesian ministry.*

The record of *Acts* seems to leave no room for a visit of St. Paul to the Lycus valley. And this negative evidence is confirmed by the positive evidence of the epistle, which points conclusively to Epaphras, himself a Colossian (iv. 12, 'one of you'), as the evangelist of SW. Phrygia (Col. i. 6–8). There is no indication of his religious status; he is described only as 'a faithful minister of Christ' (i. 7), 'a bond-man of Christ' (iv. 12), and 'a dear fellow-bondman' (i. 7) of St. Paul and his companions. The terms are general. But whether presbyter, deacon, or layman, he was not only the evangelist of Colossae (perhaps also of Laodicea and Hierapolis), but also its pastor in a true sense, interceding for them during his absence in Rome with the apostle (iv. 12, 13), with an urgency peculiarly intelligible on behalf of Christians who owed to his preaching the faith which was now imperilled by a false 'philosophy'.

Yet in a very real sense the Colossians owed their faith to St. Paul. Epaphras had been his delegate and representative (i. 7, 'who is a faithful minister of Christ on our behalf'), faithful in devotion to his Lord and faithful in discharge of a mission which he may have undertaken at the suggestion of St. Paul or with his approval, but which in any case was a mission which he undertook as the substitute and perhaps, he may have hoped, the forerunner of the Apostle. The conversion of the Colossians was the indirect result, as the conversion of Epaphras himself was probably the direct result, of St. Paul's great mission at Ephesus. That mission seems to have been confined immediately to Ephesus itself. St. Paul reminds the Ephesian elders how he 'was with them all the time', and 'for three years night and day ceased not warning every one with tears' (Acts xx. 18, 31). There is scarcely room left for anything beyond flying visits to other Asian cities, especially if we have to allow for a brief visit to Corinth (2 Cor. xii. 14, xiii. 1); and there is no hint in *Acts* of any absence from Ephesus during this period. Yet the Gospel travelled somehow to Asian cities near and far. Demetrius the silversmith may have been exaggerating when he declared that 'almost throughout all Asia this Paul had persuaded and turned away much people' (Acts xix. 26); but the author of *Acts* himself says that 'all they which dwelt in Asia heard the word of the Lord, both Jews and Greeks' (xix. 10). Such language indicates that the Apostle's teaching and influence had extended far beyond Ephesus and its vicinity; and 'St. Luke, it should be observed, ascribes this dissemination of the Gospel, not to journeys undertaken by the Apostle, but to his preaching at Ephesus itself' (Ltft., *Col.*, p. 31). The work went far beyond evangelization; it bore fruit in the foundation of Christian communities. Writing from Ephesus to Corinth, St. Paul sends greetings not from congregations at Ephesus alone but from 'the churches of Asia' (1 Cor. xvi. 19). The explanation of this extension of his Ephesian ministry is to be found in the activities of his fellow-workers, whether companions like Timothy or converts like Epaphras and Philemon and his family. Traders and travellers from towns and villages near and far carried back from the metropolis 'each to his own neighbourhood, the

spiritual treasure which they had so unexpectedly found' (Ltft.,
p. 31); and much of the fruits of the Ephesian mission must have
come from seed sown by these returning converts in their own native
soil. The Christianity of the Lycus valley was such a secondary harvest. Its cities were in close touch with Ephesus; there are extant
medals struck in commemoration of the 'Concord of the Laodiceans
and Ephesians' and the 'Concord of the Hierapolitans and the
Ephesians'; and Colossae cannot have been remote from this commercial or religious fellowship. It was probably on visits to Ephesus that
Epaphras and Philemon and Archippus of Colossae, and perhaps
Nymphas of Laodicea, heard the Gospel from the lips of the Apostle,
and found in him not only a teacher but a friend, whose teaching they
repaid by passing it on to their friends and neighbours at home. But
though Philemon and Nymphas served the Church in Phrygia by pro-
viding a home for the worship of Christian congregations (Col. iv. 15,
Phm. 2), yet it was to Epaphras that the churches of the Lycus valley
owed their birth and early growth. The coupling of Laodicea and
Hierapolis with Colossae in his affections and intercessions (iv. 12, 13)
points not merely to a Christian interest and sympathy in the progress of their faith, but to a sense of spiritual responsibility peculiarly
appropriate if he was the father of that faith.

(iii) *Occasion and purpose of the three epistles*

1. *The Colossian peril.*

There is no record of any communication between the Apostle and
the infant churches of SW. Phrygia. Probably there was a series of
messages to and fro during the Ephesian mission, verbal messages
or brief letters, but nothing more. No importance should be attached
to the absence of representatives from the inland churches at St.
Paul's conference with the presbyters of the Ephesian Church at
Miletus (Acts xx. 16, 17). The conference was summoned by a hurried
message on landing at Miletus, and there was no time to collect
delegates from distant congregations. Yet it is true that Colossae
had no great importance of its own or direct claim upon apostolic
notice. It sprang into prominence suddenly as a centre of danger and
a source of anxiety. Five or six years after the foundation of its
church St. Paul heard grave news from Colossae which drew from
him the epistle known to us as the *Epistle to the Colossians*. The
language in which he refers to their conversion and progress (Col. i.
3–8) and lays claim to their hearts (Col. ii. 1, 2) reads as though this
epistle was his first message to the Colossian Church as a body. Thus
far there had been no call for apostolic intervention. The early

history of Christianity in the Lycus valley was apparently uneventful but encouraging. But a visit from Epaphras to the Apostle at Rome revealed the rise of a grave peril to the faith, the emergence and advance of a strange heresy, half Judaic, half Oriental, which was tempting the Colossians away from the simplicity of the Gospel.

The visit of Epaphras may have been prompted by a desire to prove his sympathy with the Apostle in his own personal crisis; but the Colossian peril was urgent enough in itself to suggest such a visit for the primary purpose of giving the Apostle full information and seeking his advice. Epaphras was both distressed and alarmed. The heresy was still apparently in a partly critical, partly conciliatory stage (cp. ii. 16, 18 with ii. 4, 8), inclined to condemn the simplicity of Christian liberty in matters of dietary habit and ceremonial observance, but anxious to commend its own claim to superiority as a more philosophical faith and a more complete explanation of the mysteries of life. The Colossians were not yet lost to the true Gospel. Their faith in Christ, their love for their Christian neighbours, and apparently their hold of the hope of the future life, were still a source of encouragement and a ground for thanksgiving (i. 2–8). They were only as yet in danger of drifting from the great truths of the Gospel under the influence of the attractions of the new teaching (i. 23, ii. 4, 8). But the mischief was spreading. It was gravest in Colossae—hence the destination of this epistle of protest—but the reference to Laodicea and Hierapolis in contexts which imply anxiety on the part of St. Paul (ii. 1) and of Epaphras (iv. 12, 13) suggests that the new teaching was extending its campaign to those churches also. Its character and contents are reserved for a separate study. It is sufficient here to note two things. (1) The new teaching involved two distinct dangers. Its angelolatry obscured the supremacy of Christ in the universe; its asceticism obscured His sufficiency for all spiritual life, personal and corporate. The epistle begins, therefore, with a constructive exposition of the true faith, a vindication of both the supremacy and the sufficiency of Christ. In fact the answer of the Apostle to the twofold error comes almost in the form of a digression from the main theme. The particular heresy is analysed and exposed, as it must be if its errors are to be recognized and rejected. But the analysis and the exposure rest on a background of positive truth. (2) This penetrating criticism of a heresy that menaced the purity of the Christian faith and the power of the Christian life is enforced by a twofold appeal to Christian affection. It is preceded by a fearless and affectionate insistence upon the Apostle's own devotion to the spiritual welfare of Christians known to him only

from the remoter and higher standpoint of the imperial metropolis
presents itself to the Apostle under two aspects, viz. its relation to
the Gospel and its relation to the Empire. The Church is the embodiment and the instrument of the Gospel, being as it is 'the fullness
(*pleroma*) of Christ', in modern language the extension of the Incarnation; as the Body of Christ it is at once the treasure-house of faith
and the training-ground of fellowship. At the same time the Church
is the initiation and the instalment of a world-wide community, a
Christian civilization, not so much the spiritual counterpart of the
Empire as the revelation of a divine world-unity transcending and
transforming all and every human society. Existing within every
part of the Empire, it yet includes the whole Empire. It is the Pauline
parallel to the Johannine 'city of God', just as the encyclical *Ephesians*
is the Pauline parallel to the Johannine encyclical known as the
Apocalypse. Both are written to the churches of Asia; both contemplate the Catholic Church, which is the true home of the glory
and honour of the nations.

(iv) *Subsequent history of the three churches*

1. *Their apostolic connexions.*

The history of the three churches during the remainder of the
period covered by the New Testament has points of contact with
each of the chief apostles, St. Paul, St. Peter, and St. John.

(a) *St. Paul.*

St. Paul's movements after the writing of *Colossians* are uncertain. The evidence of the Pastoral Epistles, here assumed to be
historically correct, is so fragmentary and scattered that any inferences must be largely conjectural. From 2 Tim. i. 18, iv. 13, 20, it
seems clear that St. Paul visited Asia during the interval between
his first and his second imprisonment at Rome. Ephesus alone is
mentioned as a place of sojourn (2 Tim. i. 18), but the reference to the
defection of 'all that are in Asia' points to visits to other churches
also. Lightfoot ventures upon a tentative reconstruction in detail
of the last few years of the Apostle's life, in which he finds room for
(a) a flying journey to the East, including visits to Philippi, Ephesus,
and the churches of SW. Phrygia, to fulfil hopes and promises (Phil. i.
26, Phm. 22) and to ascertain and confirm the results of his answer to
the Colossian heresy, (b) the realization of his old dream of a missionary
visit to Spain and the West (Rom. xv. 28), and (c) a return to the
churches of Asia, and thence again by way of Miletus, Troas, Philippi,
and Corinth (2 Tim. iv. 13, 20) to winter at Nicopolis (Tit. iii. 12), a

journey cut short perhaps before reaching Nicopolis by his arrest and final imprisonment (Ltft., *Biblical Essays*, pp. 430-7). It was on this visit perhaps that he met the grievous disappointment mentioned in 2 Tim. i. 15, 'all that are in Asia turned away from me'. This has been taken to mean that some Asian Christians visiting Rome, now back again 'in Asia', deserted or avoided the imprisoned Apostle, in striking contrast to the courageous affection of Onesiphorus (2 Tim. i. 16). But the more obvious explanation is that the desertion took place in Asia, probably at Ephesus, though it is still uncertain whether the reference is to a refusal of support on the part of individuals on some occasion of personal need or danger, or to a rejection of the Apostle's teaching and authority on the part of the churches of Asia. To this crisis probably belongs the opposition of Alexander the coppersmith (2 Tim. iv. 14), who may have been the Alexander excommunicated for his 'blasphemous' teaching (1 Tim. i. 20). The scathing references to 'seducing spirits and doctrines of devils' (1 Tim. iv. 1) certainly seem to point to the rise or recrudescence of a deadly heresy. The Apostle's prediction of trouble within the Church (Acts xx. 29, 30) had proved bitterly true. St. Paul reluctantly left Timothy in charge of the situation at Ephesus, and his first epistle to Timothy reveals the anxiety with which he still regarded that situation and contemplated a return to deal with it again in person. But there is no evidence to show whether this heresy was connected in any way with the apparently subtler and less flagrant heresy of Colossae, or whether St. Paul or Timothy visited the churches of the Lycus valley.

(b) St. Peter.

The first epistle of St. Peter, an encyclical conveyed by Silvanus from Rome, is addressed to the 'elect sojourners of the dispersion' (probably not Jewish-Christian communities but Christians, Jewish or Gentile, regarded as the true Israel) in Pontus, Galatia, Cappadocia, Asia, and Bithynia. The order of the names indicates the course of a journey beginning from a seaport on the Euxine coast and working round Anatolia, east, south, west, and north again. The epistle is written to churches of which some (Galatia and Asia) were directly or indirectly Pauline in origin, and some had received letters from St. Paul at Rome. It contains resemblances to *Ephesians* (and *Romans* too) which read like reminiscences. It contains no reference to St. Paul, but this silence may be due to the fact that three of the districts (Pontus, Cappadocia, and Bithynia) had lain outside the region of St. Paul's missionary labours. It is carried by Silvanus, a former companion of St. Paul, and it conveys a greeting from another of St. Paul's companions, Mark, now also in St. Peter's company. Its references to persecution indicate a nearer peril and a severer trial than had yet befallen these churches. It was probably, therefore, written after St. Paul's martyrdom, but not more than five or six years after *Colossians*. The course of its transmission lay almost certainly through the Lycus valley highway from Galatia to Asia. It was therefore probably read, and its message interpreted, to the churches of Colossae, Laodicea, and Hierapolis. The significance of the epistle, in view of these facts, lies in the twofold impression which it gives, (1) that St. Peter regarded himself as carrying now the burden of 'the care of all the churches' once carried by St. Paul, not as claiming a concurrent apostolic authority but as inheriting a residuary authority from his martyred brother-apostle; (2) that St. Peter is unconscious of any supposed discord between Pauline and Petrine Christianity, or at least is desirous of proving the unity and continuity of his mission with the mission of St. Paul (Ramsay, *CRE.*, pp. 279–88; Swete, *St. Mark*, pp. xvii–xviii; *Apocalypse*, p. lxvii; for a different view of some points see Bigg, *St. Peter and St. Jude* in *I.C.C.*, pp. 16–20, 67–74).

(c) *St. John.*

The next chapter of the history of these churches is Johannine, whether the John who taught the faith and fostered the growth of the Church in Asia was the apostle or less probably the shadowy personality known as John the Presbyter. It is uncertain whether his ministry at Ephesus preceded or followed his exile on Patmos. In the former case it is an interesting question whether it was this ministry which was the secret of the partial revival of the Church at Ephesus from the relapse apparent in the Pastoral Epistles. Colossae and Hierapolis are not mentioned again in the New Testament; but they are almost certainly included in the message to the Church of Laodicea in the Apocalypse (Rev. iii. 14–22). The seven churches there are not merely typical in character; they are representative in position. Each of them is the leading church of a group of neighbouring churches.

The significance of the message to Laodicea is not seriously affected by the question whether the Apocalypse dates from the end of the reign of Nero (A.D. 68) or from the last years of Domitian (A.D. 90–6). The later and more probable date gives more time and room for a spiritual decline which would certainly be amazing within some six years of the writing of St. Paul's epistles. It is amazing enough within thirty years of his one and only visit. The message reflects at once (1) the lingering presence of the Colossian heresy, (2) the unity of Pauline and Johannine theology, and (3) the local circumstances and conditions of Laodicea itself.

(1) Some of the titles given to our Lord in these messages to the churches are peculiarly appropriate to the needs and dangers of the church addressed. In the Laodicean message He is described as 'the faithful and true witness, the beginning of the creation of God' (Rev. iii. 14). 'Witness' certainly implies primarily the idea of fearless loyalty to truth as known by revelation and by experience, and this idea is predicated of Christ elsewhere, e.g. 1 Tim. vi. 13, John xviii. 37. But the combination of 'witness' with 'the beginning of the creation of God' recalls Col. i. 15, 'the image of the invisible God, the firstborn of all creation', and suggests that 'witness' may refer to the person of Christ as the perfect revelation of God to man (cp. the idea of the *pleroma* of God seen in Christ, Col. i. 19, ii. 9). In any case the second of the two titles, which is peculiar to this message, certainly seems to point to the failure of the Laodicean Church still to grasp or hold fast the supremacy of Christ over all angelic or spiritual powers.

Another phrase peculiar to this message, 'to sit with me in my throne' (Rev. iii. 21), recalls the appeal to 'seek the things above, where Christ sitteth on the right hand of God' (Col. iii. 1), and the reminder that 'God has made us sit together in heavenly places in Christ Jesus' (Eph. ii. 6). It is a parallel to St. Paul's answer to the Colossian heresy, viz. the centring of devotion upon Christ as the all-sufficient Saviour. The denunciation of lukewarmness as the special sin of the angel of the Church in Laodicea recalls the warning to Archippus to do full justice to his ministry (Col. iv. 17). The coincidence is even more vivid if the angel is the chief pastor of the Church, perhaps even Archippus himself, who may have been still living. Like priest, like people. But even if the angel is the personification of the Church, the coincidence is still suggestive. 'The "be zealous" of St. John (Rev. iii. 19) is the counterpart of the "take heed" of St. Paul' (Ltft., *Col.*, p. 43).

(2) In view of the insistence of some modern scholars upon a contrast between Pauline and Johannine teaching, such a parallel as Rev. iii. 14 and Col. i. 15 ff. is a valuable addition to the evidence for the close agreement between the two apostles on the great Christological questions, e.g. the pre-existence of Christ, His cosmic functions, His mystical union with the members of His Body. The verbal correspondence is so close as to suggest that St. John was acquainted

E

not only with the substance of St. Paul's teaching but with the contents of his epistles. St. John would be almost sure to find at Ephesus, even if he did not visit Laodicea or Colossae, copies of our *Colossians* and *Ephesians*.

(3) Several points in the scathing analysis of the spiritual condition of the Laodicean Church start into vivid prominence in the light of what is known of the place and the people. The boast 'I am rich and have need of nothing' recalls the pride of wealth which scorned to accept imperial assistance in the rebuilding of the shattered city (p. 38). Lightfoot reads between the lines a hint of 'the pride of intellectual wealth, the spirit of intellectual exclusiveness' (cp. Col. ii. 8, 18), which were fatal to the attainment of the true wealth of the Gospel and the true breadth of the Church, and which the seer contrasts with their real spiritual poverty and with the gold to be bought of Christ, gold tried in the fire of discipline and persecution: cp. the treasures of wisdom and knowledge hidden in Christ (Col. ii. 3). The eye-salve with which the eyes of their souls are to be anointed and their spiritual blindness cured recalls the famous specific of the Laodicean medical school; and there is a striking parallel in Eph. i. 18 in the connexion between the enlightenment of the eyes of the understanding and the riches of the glory of the Christian inheritance. The white raiment with which they need to be clothed recalls not merely the clothing with the 'new man' and the Christian virtues (Col. iii. 10, 12, cp. Eph. iv. 24), but also the rich garments of black wool which were the staple trade of Laodicea and its neighbours. Finally, the spewing out of the lukewarm soul, neither cold nor hot, recalls the fact that the water of the Hierapolitan medicinal hot springs, as it flowed down towards Laodicea, sank into a tepidity which produced nausea. Ramsay calls Laodicea 'the city of compromise' (*Letters to the Seven Churches*, ch. xxix, xxx). The besetting sin of its Christianity was in a true sense compromise with the world. The pursuit of prosperity was fatal to the purity and the power of the Christian faith and life. Laodicea stood rebuked by the contrast between its failure to bear witness and the Christ who was 'the true and faithful witness'. But compromise was only the expression of that besetting sin; the sin itself was indifference. Laodicea showed no more enthusiasm for Christian saintship than it had shown for Hellenic civilization (p. 38). It took a dilettante interest in religious thought, perhaps a fainter and shallower interest than the less sophisticated Colossians, who were captivated by the new theology of the prevalent syncretism. But religion has no subtler or deadlier enemy than the interest which will not rise to enthusiasm, or, worse

still, which itself represents the cooling and waning of an inevitably and righteously intolerant enthusiasm.

2. *Their later development and decline.*

'Christianity spread', writes Ramsay (*St. Paul the Traveller*, pp. vii f., ed. 1897), 'with marvellous rapidity at the end of the first and in the second century in the parts of Phrygia that lay along the road from Pisidian Antioch to Ephesus, and in the neighbourhood of Iconium, whereas it did not become powerful in those parts of Phrygia that adjoined northern Galatia till the fourth century.' Duchesne remarks that 'Phrygia was almost entirely Christian when Gaul possessed only a very small number of organized churches' (*Christian Worship*, p. 11). The importance of the three cities of the Lycus valley, however, was seriously diminished by the partial transference of the seat of government for the eastern half of the Empire from Rome to Nicomedia by Diocletian, and its final transference by Constantine to Byzantium in A.D. 330. The focus of the eastern road-system was shifted from the old to the new capital, and the cities of the Lycus valley, lying no longer on a great highway, sank into comparative obscurity. Laodicea and Hierapolis remained great for some time after Colossae had declined, but ultimately shared that decline. Seven centuries and a half later the valley was invaded by the Turks, and from 1071 to 1306 Turk, Byzantine, and Crusader passed to and fro in the oscillations of a series of conquests and reconquests which left the Turk in final possession.

The Christian history of south-west Phrygia bade fair at first to fulfil the promise of its early advance, but after the fourth century it is almost a blank. It is a history thenceforward of heresy and controversy, of conciliar activity and vacillating policy, and finally of decadence and decline.

(a) *Hierapolis.*

During the last generation of the first century and onwards, Hierapolis held pride of place in intellectual activity. Tradition relates that when St. John migrated after the fall of Jerusalem to Ephesus, some of the oldest survivors of the mother Church accompanied him into Asia, 'which henceforward became the head-quarters of apostolic authority' (Ltft., *Col.*, p. 45). Amongst their number were two apostles, St. Andrew and St. Philip, and two personal disciples of Christ, Aristion and 'John the Presbyter'. An alternative view of the evidence identifies the Philip in question with the Evangelist (Acts xxi. 8), but the earlier and stronger evidence points to the

E 2

Apostle. St. Philip found a new home at Hierapolis with his three daughters, two of whom survived long enough to pass on to Papias their reminiscences of the first preachers of the Gospel. Papias, the second bishop of Hierapolis,[1] whose name points to his being a native of Phrygia, was a disciple of St. John or perhaps of John the Presbyter, and a friend of Polycarp, the martyr bishop of Smyrna, and according to a doubtful tradition himself died a martyr's death at Pergamum in A.D. 164. His *Exposition of Oracles of the Lord* won for him the title of the first chronicler of the Church. His silence about St. Paul has been made an argument for a modern theory that Asian Christianity turned from the teaching of St. Paul to that of St. John. The silence is explicable on other grounds; and the theory postulates a conflict between Pauline and Johannine teaching which is disproved by an unbiassed comparison. In one respect Papias seems to have been a typical Phrygian. He taught an extreme form of literal millenarianism which perhaps reflects the sensuous element in the Phrygian religious temperament.

His successor Claudius Apollinaris was a learned theologian and a prolific author, whose large and varied output included treatises on truth and on piety, vindications of Christianity against paganism and Judaism, an apology addressed to the Stoic emperor M. Aurelius, and contributions to the Paschal controversy and to the refutation of the Phrygian heresy known as Montanism. This heresy he fought in its early stages with the weapons of scholarship and in its later developments with the machinery of ecclesiastical discipline; he summoned at Hierapolis, about A.D. 160 or later, a synod of twenty-six bishops, which condemned the heresy and excommunicated the heresiarch Montanus and his companion the prophetess Maximilla.

His successors are little more than names in history. Hierapolis itself henceforth was little more. It was represented at the great councils of the fourth and fifth centuries, but it left no mark upon the life of the Church. This stagnation of church life here and at Laodicea may have been due partly to the faults of Byzantine imperialism—'the over-centralization of government, the decay of municipal self-government, the indifference of the imperial administration to the duty of educating the people' (Ramsay, *CBP*. ii. 506). But it may have been due also to deeper causes, e.g. the secularization of church life by the reliance of theological controversialists upon dynastic or political support. Hierapolis, originally

---

[1] Tradition says that the first bishop was Heros, and that he was appointed by St. Philip. It is strange that tradition does not make St. Philip himself the first bishop.

a diocese in the ecclesiastical province of Laodicea, was made a metropolitan see by Justinian in the sixth century, perhaps on the ground of its old religious prestige, and had a number of cities in North Phrygia assigned to its jurisdiction; but its new ecclesiastical dignity brought no revival of religious activity.

(b) *Laodicea.*

Laodicea appears to have emerged at length from its earlier spiritual apathy. Nothing is known of its history during the traditional episcopates of Archippus and Nymphas, both perhaps later inferences from the mention of their names in *Colossians*. In the middle of the second century its bishop, Sagaris, died for the faith in 'one of those fitful persecutions which sullied the rule of the imperial Stoic', M. Aurelius (Ltft., p. 60). Somewhat later it became a centre of the Paschal controversy between the Asiatic or Quartodeciman custom of commemorating the Passion on the fourteenth day of the month regardless of the day of the week and the western custom of keeping the Friday and Sunday regardless of the day of the month. The controversy at Laodicea was probably caused by the influx of Christian traders and visitors accustomed elsewhere to the western use, whereas Laodicea followed the Asiatic use. The prominence of Laodicea in the controversy, which was finally decided by the Nicene Council in favour of the western use, is evidence of the continuing importance of the city. But its influence as a church waned a century later, despite its position as the metropolitan see of a province including Hierapolis and Colossae and other Phrygian dioceses. Its bishops attended the great councils of Nicaea, Ephesus, and Chalcedon, but between those dates more than one Laodicean bishop committed his church to the heresy of the day, Arian or Eutychian. Laodicea seems to have relapsed into the indifference which had merited the scathing judgement of the Apocalypse. 'The same vacillation and infirmity of purpose which had characterized her bishops in the earlier councils marks the proceedings of their later successors' (Ltft., p. 63).

There is one exception to the uneventful record of Laodicea after the second century, and that is the Council of Laodicea held about A.D. 365 (Hefele, *History of Church Councils*, ii. 295–325; Westcott, *N.T. Canon*, ed. 4, pp. 427–35). It was a local synod of bishops from Phrygia and Lydia which passed fifty-nine canons dealing with various questions of ecclesiastical discipline, from the functions of a subdeacon and rules for choirs to the regulation of the *agape* and of Lenten baptismal classes, and from the scandal of mixed bathing

comment may refer to the ethnological affiliation of the Colossae of St. Paul's day; it need not imply that Colossae was a thing of the past, which needed to have its geographical position stated. Theodoret, in the next century, refers to the survival of Philemon's house in his day. There was a bishopric of Colossae until late in the seventh century. In that century the population migrated to the shelter of a hill-fortress built at Chonae three miles to the south by the Byzantine government as a stronghold against Saracen raids, just as the Laodiceans migrated three centuries later to the hill-fortress of Denizli, though the new city retained for centuries the name Laodicea. The Colossian bishop at the second Nicene Council, in A.D. 787, signs as 'bishop of Chonae or of the Colossians'. At later councils Chonae is his sole title. The memory of Colossae disappeared so completely that the Colossians of the epistle were identified by some writers with the Rhodians, the possessors of the famous statue known as the Colossus. The great church of the archangel 'Michael the chief-captain' (*archistrategos*), which took the place of the oratory known to Theodoret, still remained in the suburbs of the old city as a centre of religious attraction on the score of its healing powers, until it was desecrated in A.D. 1070 by the stabling of the horses of the raiding Seljuk Turks within its walls, and burned down in a fiercer raid in A.D. 1189 (Ramsay, *CBP*. i. 213–16).

From the seventh century onwards the Saracens had made fitful raids into western Anatolia. But these were ineffective and tolerable in comparison with the chronic invasions of the Turks from the eleventh to the fourteenth century (Ramsay, *CBP*. i. 15–18). There is no trace of persecution under the Seljuk Turks; that trial was reserved for the Osmanli domination of a later age. Yet the Christian population of the Lycus valley steadily disappeared. Laodicea was a Christian city in A.D. 1210; in 1310 it was mainly Moslem. Ramsay attributes the change to voluntary conversion. 'The strong Oriental substratum in the Phrygian inhabitants of the Lycus valley asserted itself, and they were more ready to adopt an Oriental religion like Mohammedanism than the Christians in some other parts of the country were' (*CBP*. i. 28).

Elsewhere in another connexion (*CRE*., p. 465) Ramsay describes another relevant factor in the history of Anatolian Christianity, though without noting its bearing on the ruin of the Church. 'The national idiosyncrasies were too strongly marked, and these Oriental peoples would not accept the centralized and organized Church in its purity, but continued the old struggle of Asiatic against European feeling, which has always marked the course of history in Asia

Minor. The national temper, denied expression in open and legitimate form, worked itself out in another way, viz. in popular superstitions and local cults, which were added as an excrescence to the
forms of the Orthodox Church. A growing carelessness as to these
additions, provided that the orthodox forms were strictly complied
with, manifested itself in the Church.' This acquiescence brought its
own nemesis. The Church might have led these racial characteristics
'into captivity to the obedience of Christ', and so consecrated and
transformed each racial character into a distinctive type of Christian
devotion and service and of national development within the kingdom
of God—the true missionary function of the Church, indicated in the
very epistle which St. Paul wrote to the churches of Asia, viz.
Ephesians, and now at last realized and exemplified and justified in
the modern mission field. Instead, the Church surrendered to the
situation, and sacrificed the purity of Christian doctrine to the dic-
tates of ecclesiastical opportunism. The result was fatal. As the
faith of these peoples lost its purity, it lost its power to save either
the soul or the race. They had ceased to 'hold fast the Head', and
the Body went to pieces. First there came internal decay, and then
external disintegration under the pressure of an alien invasion strong
in the power of a strict creed and therefore of a fighting faith. Lightfoot sees in this decadence and destruction of Anatolian Christianity
a yet deeper significance in the light of the vision of the Apocalypse
written for the warning of the churches of Asia (*Col.*, pp. 69–70).
'When the day of visitation came, the Church was taken by surprise.
Occupied with ignoble quarrels and selfish interests, she had no ear
for the voice of Him who demanded admission. The door was barred
and the knock unheeded. The long-impending doom overtook her,
and the golden candlestick was removed from the Eternal Presence.'

V

THE COLOSSIAN HERESY

(i) *A Christian aberration or a non-Christian intrusion?*

The phrase 'the Colossian heresy' serves conveniently to denote
the movement or tendency to which we owe *Colossians*. But the
term 'heresy' connotes ideas which may or may not be true of this
movement. In a sense it begs the question. In the N.T. 'heresy'
(*haeresis*, choice) denotes a religious school or sect, e.g. the Sadducees
(Acts v. 17), the Pharisees (Acts xv. 5), the Nazarenes or Christians

(Acts **xxiv. 5**, 14, **xxviii.** 22), or a faction within the Church (1 Cor. xi. 19, Gal. v. 20, 2 Pet. ii. 1, cp. Tit. iii. 10); but in patristic literature and in conciliar records it denotes a doctrinal divergence from within the Church, a perversion or misrepresentation of the Christian faith. But that is just the question at issue in this case. Was the Colossian peril a Christian or a non-Christian movement ? Was it an aberration of Christian teaching, or an intrusion of alien teaching which sought either to seduce Christians from the Christian faith or to find a place for itself within the Christian Church ? In the stage at which St. Paul confronts the movement it may have been both; teachers within the Church may have been preaching a Christianity adulterated by admixture from foreign sources or depolarized by foreign attractions. The practical crisis before St. Paul was a heresy within the Church, whatever its origin was. But the use of the term 'heresy' for convenience must not be taken as implying in advance an answer to the primary question of the origin and character of the movement. That question is primary in the logical sense. Even if its origin, in the absence of direct evidence, has to be inferred from its character, the origin once determined or conjectured becomes itself a premiss from which other inferences may be drawn. This is not a case of arguing in a vicious circle. If the origin of a movement is clearly or probably traceable to Judaic or Hellenic or Oriental sources, we have in that fact or theory a basis for the interpretation of obscurer points in its character and contents. The question is primary in a practical sense. The movement must be analysed home to its origin if its bearing on later movements of similar character is to be traced or its significance for modern thought estimated. The answer to the question is not obvious. Colossianism, if the term may be coined, has been affiliated variously to Judaism and to Gnosticism, or to some movement of a composite or syncretistic character, whether a Judaic type of Gnosticism or a Gnostic type of Judaism. Later research into the background of Asian Christianity is now pointing rather to an indigenous source for the movement or indigenous elements in the movement. But these theories have perhaps all been influenced by the desire to identify the movement with some known contemporary movement. It may, on the other hand, have been distinct from other movements, though not independent of them. It may be a phenomenon of which there is no other example. In any case, the best procedure will be first to sketch the movement as it is presented in *Colossians*, and then to trace its relation to various elements in the religious conditions and environment of the place of its emergence.

(ii) *The evidence of the epistle*

The evidence of the nature of the movement is confined to the epistle itself. That evidence is twofold. It consists of (1) direct references to points or phases of the heresy—passages in which express statements are made with regard to its general character and its particular contents ; and (2) indirect references—passages in which there appears to be an implied antithesis to the heresy—in which a marked emphasis on some aspect or feature of Christian truth seems to suggest that the Apostle had in mind a particular fault or fallacy of the heresy in view.

1. *Direct references.*

(*a*) First comes a general description of the character of the heresy. It was clothed in a subtle and plausible rhetoric which misled its hearers (ii. 4). It posed as a philosophy or theory of life ; yet it was fallacious in argument and futile in result—it deluded with promises which it could not fulfil (ii. 8). It was 'not according to Christ', i.e. not centred in Christ as the divine source and the living substance of truth. If it did not reject the precepts of Christ (and there is no hint of any such rejection), it certainly did not recognize His person and position in the universe. Its source was human tradition, apparently the authority of dead or living teachers, the prestige of an ancient cult or the discipline of an established system—here we are left to conjecture. Its substance was a theory of cosmic control, a system of angelic or demonic powers intervening between God and man (ii. 8, 18).

(*b*) The Apostle refers incidentally to particular tenets or practices of the heresy in language intelligible enough for his original readers, who were familiar with the things to which he refers, but scarcely adequate for modern interpretation. If it was conciliatory in its desire to win acceptance for its teaching, it was critical or censorious in its attitude towards the ordinary Christian life. It made test questions of matters of ascetic or ceremonial observance, and judged ordinary Christians by these tests ; at least it insisted on the superiority of a religious life marked by these observances (ii. 16, 18). It inculcated rules of life, rules of abstinence from various foods and drinks, rules of observance of holy days, annual, monthly, and weekly. Between God and man it apparently placed the angels in a position of cosmic power and control over nature and humanity, and of mediation in things temporal and spiritual. It enthroned the angels as objects of worship, or exalted them as models of devotion. With the worship paid to them or the devotion shaped by them was connected somehow the idea of humility or humiliation (ii. 18). If the word means humility, what seems to be implied is a false idea of deity as something too remote for direct human adoration or appeal, which savoured therefore of a presumption from which angel-worship was supposed to be free in view of the closer resemblance or relation between the angels and mankind. If the word means humiliation, what seems to be implied is a false idea of religious discipline as something negative, lying in the prohibition of practices rather than in the pursuance of a spirit, in the condemnation of things rather than in the conversion of a life. At the same time this humility or humiliation was connected with a kind of mysticism, which sought satisfaction and took pride in visions. The language in which this ecstatic mysticism is described is obscure; but it seems to resemble some features of the 'mysteries' of popular Hellenistic-Oriental religion, though the resemblance is not clear enough to be pressed into identification or affiliation. This mysticism was evidently connected with the asceticism of the movement. Apparently the ascetic practices were advocated as purifying and preparing the soul for the mystic experiences. The mysticism in question appeared to St. Paul to have two grave faults. It fostered a pride quite inconsistent with any true humility or self-humiliation. It was intellectual rather than spiritual in character, and its intellectuality was of a materialistic type. The Apostle seems to mean that it was obsessed with the idea of the evil of matter and so failed to rise to the contemplation of spiritual truth. But the radical error of the heresy lay in its failure to do justice to the person and place of Christ in the universe. It had never attained or it had ceased to retain any real grasp of the nature and mission of Christ. Apparently it placed Him very little higher than the angels. Certainly it seems to have denied or minimized His supremacy in the world-order and His sufficiency for all human need as the fount of spiritual life and the food of spiritual growth (ii. 19).

2. *Indirect references.*

The indirect references can only be used tentatively and provisionally. It is possible that in some of these cases St. Paul is not laying any deliberate emphasis on a particular point of Christian truth, and still less deliberately countering any particular point in the heresy. Yet even here it is permissible to see an actual, even if not an intentional, answer to some heretical view of which we have evidence elsewhere in the epistle.

(*a*) St. Paul's insistence on knowledge (Gk. *gnosis* or *epignosis*, see notes on i. 9, 10) or wisdom or understanding as something moral and spiritual and practical (e.g. i. 9–11, 28, iii. 16), as a possession of which the secret lies in love rather than in learning (ii. 2, cp. 1 Cor. viii. 1), seems to imply that the vaunted knowledge of the heretics is intellectual and speculative, without any practical bearing on life.

(b) Progress in the spiritual life is made conditional upon faithful adherence to the purity of the Gospel (i. 23, ii. 7). The heretics seem to have advocated their teaching as an advance upon the simplicity of the Christian faith (ii. 8).

(c) Salvation is described in three ways, as deliverance (i. 13), as redemption (i. 14), as reconciliation (i. 21, 22, ii. 13). (a) Gnosticism set itself to conciliate or evade the neutral or hostile powers by which the world was dominated. St. Paul seems to have this attempt in mind when he insists that salvation lies in transference into another world; Christians have been lifted right out of the realm of darkness and bondage into a realm of love and light. (β) Redemption in various forms of Oriental-Hellenic mysteries was regarded mainly as liberation from matter or from fate; this is perhaps the point of St. Paul's insistence here that redemption is liberation from sin. (γ) His insistence on reconciliation as the work of God and the fruit of the Cross seems to imply a protest against the idea that it was to be won by human endeavour, whether by the worship of angelic mediators or by the works of a mystical asceticism. And the reference to the angels, clearly included in 'the things in the heavens' (i. 20), as themselves participating in the reconciliation of the world, is apparently intended to exclude any idea that they were in some way mediators or agents of that reconciliation.

(d) The references to the Christian faith as a mystery seem intended to lay stress on points in which it stood in sharp contrast to the Graeco-Oriental mysteries to which the Colossian heresy apparently had some relation or resemblance. (a) They were esoteric; their teaching was secret, at once expressed and disguised in dramatic and ritual representations of ideas of redemption and immortality. The Christian mystery was a revelation, an open secret; the ages of divine silence were now past, and the truth was now revealed to human minds. (β) The substance of the mystery-cults lay in myths depicting or symbolizing the life-story of unhistorical and imaginary beings, gods or heroes. The Christian mystery was a personal revelation, truth revealed in the life and mission of an historical person; it is to be seen in Christ, nay, it is Christ (i. 27, ii. 2, 3). (γ) The teaching of the Greek mysteries was given only to an inner circle of initiates. The Christian mystery was a universal revelation: it was for every man (i. 28).

(*e*) In references to the communication of divine power emphasis is laid upon the fact that the *pleroma*, the fullness of Godhead, was concentrated completely and permanently in Christ (i. 19, ii. 9). This emphasis seems to be an answer to the idea that the divine power was distributed among a hierarchy of celestial beings.

(*f*) Human nature is to be consecrated and sanctified by communion with Christ, by a mystical circumcision. Here is an implied contrast to the idea that it is to be consecrated and sanctified by ascetic discipline. The liberation of humanity has been won already by the victory of Christ upon the Cross over all unseen powers, angelic or demonic. There may be here an implied assertion that their intervention on human behalf is imaginary and superfluous. But the context points rather to the idea of the dethronement of a tyranny which cowed and crippled human endeavour.

(*g*) The new life of the Christian is pictured as a spiritual experience giving a new interpretation and a new power to ethical principles (iii. 5–17), apparently in antithesis to the idea of a progress to be achieved by the observance of ascetic practices. Its main principle is that morality lies in relation not to things but to persons (iii. 12–iv. 1). At the same time the moral is placed in its rightful relation to the spiritual. The new character is to find expression in a new conduct. Religion is not morality touched with emotion; it is a spiritual life, but it bears fruit in a higher morality and it may fairly be judged by its fruitfulness. The mysteries touched the springs of emotion, but it is doubtful whether they transformed lives. St. Paul does not suggest that the Colossian teaching ignored morality, still less that it encouraged or palliated immorality. But the space given in *Colossians* to Christian ethics does suggest that he was concerned to insist that mystical devotion should not merely indicate but also inspire moral duty. The Colossian teaching was apparently ego-centric; it was a system of self-culture, and that too a system of doubtful efficacy. Christian truth was altruistic; and it was centred in a Life which was at once an actual example and a real power.

(iii) *Environment and origin of the heresy*

Various attempts have been made to identify the Colossian heresy with more or less definite religious movements of the first century. The absence, however, of any clear evidence of any similar contemporary heresy in the apostolic mission field suggests or at least permits the idea that Colossianism was a local phenomenon, a reaction to a particular religious environment. It is necessary, therefore, to sketch first the general religious situation of the Graeco-Roman world and then the immediate environment of the Colossian Church.

1. *Paganism and religion.*

The dark picture of pagan life painted by St. Paul in Rom. i. 21–32 was painted from reality. But it is only one aspect of paganism; and there was another side to the picture. Professor Gilbert Murray in his *Five Stages of Greek Religion*, Dr. Glover in his *Conflict of Religions in the early Roman Empire*, and Dr. Dill in his *Roman Society from Nero to Marcus Aurelius* paint a pathetic picture of a world that was wistfully seeking redemption from the burdens of life; they depict a movement of thought that was feeling its way after a religion which could give peace and purity of life because it had the moral power of truth. Greek thought had undermined the old mythological faiths which had been the inspiration of art and literature. Macedonian and Roman imperialism had destroyed the fabric of national government and sapped the foundations of municipal activity. Peace and prosperity under Roman administration were only partial compensation for the loss of local patriotism and corporate enterprise. If men turned to philosophy, it was only to find scepticism instead of certainty on the ultimate principles of truth. The result of all these experiences was a state of mind which has been aptly described as 'a failure of nerve' and 'a softening of human pride' which was a real *praeparatio evangelica*. Meanwhile philosophy itself was turning from the problems of the cosmic and the divine to the more practical and pressing problem of human nature, from metaphysics to morality, from speculative research to spiritual reflection. It left the study for the street; the peripatetic moralist, whether the dignified Stoic or the Cynic who has been called 'the mendicant friar of imperial times', was a familiar figure in public places.

The religious environment to which the Gospel came in Anatolia was complex. There was the domestic religion of the worship of family gods, the *lares* or *genii*, tutelar or ancestral spirits. There was the great theocrasy of Hellenic times, the worship of the old local gods merged into or identified with the greater Greek deities, e.g. the mother-goddess Leto of SW. Phrygia and the Cybele of N. and E. Phrygia identified with the Greek Artemis; Attis the son or youthful consort of Cybele identified with Apollo; Sabazius the son of Leto identified with Apollo or elsewhere with Zeus. This worship was a municipal cult, historical rather than religious, ritual rather than doctrinal, like Shinto in Japan. Later came Caesar-worship, the deification of the emperor or the personification of the spirit of the empire, which was sometimes blended with the Greek cults, e.g. with the cult of Dionysus at Ephesus. Neither municipal nor imperial cults touched the souls of men. The religious instincts and desires found their satisfaction in the mystery-cults of Oriental origin which swept their way everywhere through the Hellenistic world. These cults offered glimpses of divine truth and human hope through impressive rites, and the offer was accepted eagerly by hungry souls of all races in all grades of society.

2. *Astrology and fatalism.*

'The denial or rather removal of the Olympian gods landed men in the worship of Fortune or of Fate', both of which beliefs cut the ground from under any moral motive or purpose of human endeavour. At first sight it seems as though 'the believers in Destiny were a more respectable congregation than the worshippers of Chance. It requires a certain amount of thoughtfulness to rise to the conception that nothing really happens without a cause' (Murray, p. 167). But the belief in Destiny was no mere philosophic fatalism. It was part of a religious outlook which centred round the stars of heaven and their relation to the life of man. Sun, moon, and planets were associated and then identified with gods or ruling spirits, the Elements (Gk. *stoicheia*, see note on Col. ii. 8) of the Kosmos. The month was redivided into the seven-day week derived from Babylon, the original home of astronomy and planet-worship; each day was named after its own ruling planet, Sun, Moon, Ares (Mars, Fr. *Mardi*), Hermes (Mercurius, Fr. *Mercredi*), Zeus (Fr. *Jeudi*), Aphrodite (Venus, Fr. *Vendredi*), Kronos (Saturn). In the Mithras-liturgy the seven vowels, the *stoicheia* of the alphabet, are the names of the 'seven deathless lords of the universe' (Gk. *kosmokratores*, cp. the use of this term in Eph. vi. 12). For the Stoic philosopher the belief in the omnipotence of the stars took shape in an 'astral mysticism'. The decrees of Fate became the law of a divine Providence, from which the human will could draw strength by its very self-surrender. The contemplation of the stars, the listening to 'the music of the spheres', lifted the mind above secular cares. The Stoic doctrine of 'the sympathy of the universe' seemed to find a vivid illustration in the connexion between the movements of the stars and the fortunes of men. But for the ordinary man the omnipotence of the stars was no comfort, but a terror. It meant the iron rule of powers 'either indifferent to his good or actively malignant'. Life was a dark bondage in an unfriendly universe.

3. *Gnosticism and mystery-cults.*

From this bondage of fear, fear of known perils here and unknown perils hereafter, men found no relief in official religion, or in academic philosophy. They looked for something to satisfy both mind and soul, to make the world intelligible and life tolerable. They sought light from every quarter. The syncretism of the last prechristian century was not, like modern theosophy, an intellectual effort to unify the various racial beliefs that were brought into contact by the wholesale migrations of Greek imperialism and the improved communications of Roman imperialism. It was rather an instinctive grasping after the possible help of truth from any and every source. Syrian ideas (themselves a syncretism in which Babylon and Persia played a large part), Egyptian ideas, Jewish ideas, popularized ideas of Greek philosophy, inherited ideas of ancient local faiths, were blended and fused in all sorts of combinations and permutations, which modern research is now slowly and patiently analysing. This syncretism took shape in two forms, a theosophical form known as gnosticism and a religious form known as the mysteries. (*a*) We are not concerned here with the Christian or semi-Christian gnosticism of the second and third centuries, but with the pre-Christian gnosticism which Reitzenstein has named 'Hellenistic theology'. It was a theology of dualism and pessimism. The universe and human nature were the scene of an inevitable conflict between spirit and matter, which were identified with good and evil. Endeavour was helpless and life was hopeless in view of the transitoriness of things, the obsession of human passion, the tyranny of unseen world-powers. In its more speculative forms this pagan gnosticism set itself to explain the universe. The chasm and the distance between God and man, the conflict between spirit and matter—these difficulties were overcome by a theory of creation which bridged the chasm and reduced the conflict by filling the *pleroma*, the upper world, with a series of emanations, more or less divine beings, dilutions of deity which were responsible for the material and evil element in creation. But this early gnosticism was mainly and mostly concerned with the history and destiny of the soul of man—its descent from the divine world and its reascension thither through the seven spheres, the realms of the seven planetary ruler-spirits, up to the eighth sphere, the Ogdoad, the home of God and the ultimate home of the soul of man. Later gnostic literature is full of spells or passwords with which the returning soul is to win its way past the planetary gods or demons at the gate of each sphere. To know a demon and to name his name

F

was to disarm his power to hurt. The story of the Christ from the Incarnation to the Ascension as presented in later semi-Christian gnosticism is 'a reduplication of the Hellenistic story of the soul' (Bevan, *Hellenism and Christianity*, p. 100). It reappears to-day in the 'mythical Christ' of theosophy (see p. 123).

Gnosticism was the philosophical and doctrinal phase of syncretism. The deeper needs of the soul were met by the popular and devotional phase of syncretism which found expression in the mystery-cults. Ancient Greece had its Orphic mysteries and later its Eleusinian mysteries. Later still came the mysteries of the Phrygian goddess Cybele, the Syrian god Attis, the Egyptian deities Isis and Serapis, the Persian god Mithras. They originated in nature-cults in which the recurring birth, death, and resurrection of nature were connected with the myth of a dying and reviving god and with the hope of human immortality. In the Hellenistic age they lent themselves readily to supply the craving for personal religion. They were mostly private and voluntary associations. They offered mystical ways of union with God through solemn initiations and sacramental rites; and they encouraged the belief in personal visions of divine beings. They required some measure of personal purity in one form or another of ascetic discipline. Some of them had sometimes an ugly side, in which the weird emotions of nature-cults ran riot in sexual orgies. The Phrygian mysteries had a reputation for the wildest perversions of natural instincts. But on the whole the mysteries did serve to foster, and in part to satisfy, religious instincts. Scholarship is still divided on the question whether the idea of a redeemer in later pagan gnosticism was developed independently or derived from Christianity. What is clear is that the redeemer of gnostic cults is an interpreter rather than a saviour, a guide to the way of the future life rather than himself 'the way, the truth and the life'. Knowledge (Gk. *gnosis*) is the supreme need of life. 'The possession of knowledge is enough to enable the soul to regain its heavenly home, whether by knowledge be understood intellectual enlightenment in the higher Platonic sense, or knowledge of magical formulas and mystic practices in the baser superstitious acceptance' (Bevan, p. 101).

4. *Anatolian Judaism.*

In the midst of this racial and religious fusion lay communities of 'Jews of the dispersion'. The policy of Macedonian imperialism had planted in Asia Minor large colonies of Jews from Babylonia and Palestine, subsequently enlarged by voluntary migration for the sake of trade. Jews from 'Asia and Phrygia' as well as other parts of Anatolia were among the colonial Jews present at the feast of Pentecost and probably among the first converts to the Christian faith (Acts ii. 8–11, 39–41). It was 'Jews from Asia' who raised the cry of desecration against the presence of St. Paul's companions from Ephesus in the courts of the Temple (Acts xxi. 27). Apart from their economic position, their faith and life remained distinct enough, and their missionary enthusiasm ardent enough, to exert a strong influence upon thoughtful pagans, due especially to 'their freedom from crude mythology, their sacred Book, their ethical standards, and their social rest-day' (Nock, p. 55, n. 1). Jewish influence is visible in the 'superstitious feeling attached to the Sabbath in pagan circles'. It told also upon pagan cults. The old Thraco-Phrygian god Sabazius was identified with the Lord God of Sabaoth, and the cult of Cybele seems also to have been influenced in a monotheistic direction by Jewish beliefs (Cumont, pp. 64–5). By a strange blending of Jewish and Phrygian traditions, Noah and the ark appear on coins of Apamea in the third century A.D. (Ramsay, *CBP*. ii. 672; Nock, p. 54, n.). On the other hand, Judaism yielded to influences from the side of paganism. Wealth weakened Jewish social exclusiveness. A rabbinist complains that 'the baths and wines of Phrygia have separated the Ten Tribes from Israel', though it is not certain whether his complaint is that they have been tempted into irreligious luxury or into acceptance of Christianity. The marriage of the Jewess Eunice (the Greek name is noteworthy) to a Greek at Lystra points to a relaxation of strict principle even in a devout Jewish family (Acts xvi. 1, 2 Tim. i. 5). The Jews of Asia Minor assimilated Graeco-Roman civilization, supported imperial policy, and in some cases apparently complied outwardly with the imperial religion; and they seem to have 'melted later into the general Christian population' (Ramsay, *CBP*. ii. 674–6). There is no evidence outside *Colossians* for any infusion of distinct pagan beliefs into Phrygian Judaism. But the evidence already quoted suggests that the Jews of Phrygia were exposed, and had perhaps to some extent yielded, to the danger of the infiltration of pagan ideas, just as their ancestral faith during or before the exilic period had yielded to the attractions of Chaldaean astrology with its magical associations. There is *prima facie* ground for the idea that Anatolian Judaism may have been responsible either for the main features of a Christian heresy with touches of Hellenistic gnosticism or for Judaic touches in a heresy mainly due to Hellenic gnosticism.

F 2

5. *Judaism and Gnosticism.*

Two leaders of Christian scholarship have sought the origin of Colossianism in the sphere of a more or less gnostic Judaism. Lightfoot leaned towards Essene Judaism. His case may be outlined briefly as follows. There are two elements in the heresy. The observance of sabbaths and new moons points conclusively, the distinction of meats and drinks and the implicit reference to circumcision point suggestively, to Judaism. The theosophic speculation, the mystic contemplation, the adoration of intermediate spiritual agencies, point to Gnosticism. There are not two distinct heresies, but a combination of two elements in one heresy. Already in pre-Christian days Gnosticism was allied with Judaism—not with Sadduceeism or Phariseeism, but with the Essenism which is 'the great enigma of Hebrew history'. To the strict observance of the Mosaic law the Essenes added a rigid asceticism which abstained from marriage, wine, flesh, and oil for anointing, on grounds not of Mosaic legalism but of a dualism which regarded matter as the principle or the abode of evil. On the other hand, the Essenes leaned towards sun-worship, denied the resurrection of the body, prohibited animal sacrifice, saw mystic importance in the names of the angels, speculated on God and creation, attached a value to apocryphal sacred books and occult science, and guarded their tenets with an exclusive spirit of reserve. Essenism was a sort of gnostic Judaism. In describing the Judaism of Colossae as Essene, Lightfoot is careful to explain that he does not assume 'a precise identity of origin but only an essential affinity of type' with the Essenism of Palestine. From the evidence of the exorcism and magical books of Ephesus (Acts xix) and of the Sibylline oracle of A.D. 80, Lightfoot concludes that 'this type of Jewish thought and practice had established itself in Asia Minor in the apostolic age'. He points out the traces of early Gnosticism in the Colossian heresy, and the continuance of the same type of heresy in the district to which the Apocalypse was addressed. Finally, he finds in the heresy attributed to Cerinthus (a Jew of Alexandria who lived and taught in the province of Asia at the close of the first century) a link between Judaism and Gnosticism and between the Colossian heresy and later Gnosticism. The Judaism of Cerinthus was seen in his teaching that Jesus was the son of Joseph and Mary, and in his insistence upon circumcision and the sabbath; his Gnosticism in his teaching that the Christ descended upon Jesus at his baptism, inspired his teaching and wrought his miracles, and left him before the Passion, and that the world was made by angels, to one of which, the God of the Jews, was due the law, which was not entirely good. Cerinthus also taught a stark and crude millenarianism.

Lightfoot's theory has been seriously shaken by criticism. Dr. Hort, who leaned once to this theory, later withdrew his support, having come to the conclusion that 'there is no tangible evidence for Essenism out of Palestine' (*Judaistic Christianity*, p. 128). Zahn (*Intr. N.T.* i. 376, 479) points out (*a*) that the evidence for Essene abstinence from flesh and wine breaks down; (*b*) that the most characteristic features of Essenism, e.g. the abstinence from marriage, the community of property, the abolition of slavery, the monastic order of their life, are absent from the Colossian heresy; (*c*) that there is no proof of angelolatry in Essenism ; (*d*) that pride in circumcision and strictness in observance of holy days were common to Judaism in general.

Dr. Hort himself thinks (*a*) that the 'philosophy' of Colossianism was not theosophical but ethical, and that the term 'philosophy' was adopted by the heretics 'to disarm Western prejudice against things Jewish by giving them a quasi-Hellenic varnish' (*JC.*, p. 120); (*b*) that 'the worship of angels was assuredly a widely spread Jewish habit of mind at this time', but did not involve any speculative doctrine of angelic power (*JC.*, p. 122); (*c*) that 'the pretensions to wisdom and philosophy' need not point to 'any outlying or outlandish sects of philosophy or religion', or to anything more than a possible but by no means certain 'accessory influence from some kind of popular Greek ethical philosophy' (*JC.*, p. 129). But Dr. Hort, while correct perhaps in his interpretation of the term 'philosophy' (see note on Col. ii. 8), seems to ignore the reference to mystic visions in Col. ii. 18, which appears to indicate some form of theosophical contemplation, and the references to the *pleroma* and sovereignty of Christ in Col. ii. 9, 10, which appear to imply an answer to some form of gnostic speculation about celestial powers. Hort's conclusion that 'we are dispensed from the need of trying to discover any peculiar or extraneous sources for the special form of Judaic Christianity gaining ground at Colossae', and that 'we are apparently on common Jewish ground', has had its weight gravely weakened by an elaborate study of the doctrine and worship of angels by Mr. Lukyn Williams (*Colossians*, pp. xxii–xxxvii, and *Journ. Theol. Stud.* x. 39, pp. 413–38), in which he reaches the conclusion (1) that 'although there has been among the Jews confessedly much speculation as to the nature and functions of angels, together with some belief in the intercession of angels for them, yet there is almost no evidence of the worship of them being recognized in early times by thoughtful Jews, save indeed in connexion with exorcism and magic' (p. xxxi), and (2) that the undeniable worship of angels by Colossian Christians of Jewish origin was no inheritance from Judaism, but the resultant of various general causes and local influences (see p. 75 of this introduction).

Lightfoot's attempt to affiliate or relate Colossianism to Essenism has not carried conviction. But an incidental remark of his, which reads almost like an unconscious admission of the weakness of his theory, points towards the probable explanation of the origin of the heresy. 'All along its frontier, wherever Judaism became enamoured of and was wedded to Oriental mysticism, the same union would produce substantially the same results. In a country where Phrygia, Persia, Syria, all in turn, had moulded religious thought, it would be strange indeed if Judaism had escaped these influences' (*Col.*, p. 93). Judaism was undoubtedly a contributing factor or element in Colossianism; but it is doubtful whether it was the main element or the original factor—in other words, whether the Colossian heresiarchs were syncretistic Jews (either Christian heretics of Jewish origin or non-Christian Gnostic-Jewish teachers attempting to seduce Christians from the Church's faith) or Graeco-Phrygian Gnostics who found room in their teaching for beliefs and practices either borrowed from Judaism or akin to Judaism.

Bishop Moorhouse, in his *Dangers of the Apostolic Age* (p. 137), took the Colossian teachers for Judaistic Christians. 'The spirit of Jewish exclusiveness . . . was neither dead nor disposed to confess itself finally defeated. If it could not attain its ends by asserting the claims of an exclusive law, it would endeavour to reach the same goal by claiming the possession of a superior wisdom. The Jew would be satisfied if only by some means he could set himself above the Gentile, if either by means of law or of gnosis he could vindicate his claim to superior privilege, and so break down the universality of the Gospel.' But the evidence is against this identification. (*a*) From Col. i. 21 (cp. Eph. ii. 12, 13, iv. 17, 18) and Col. i. 27 it seems clear that the Colossian congregation was predominantly Gentile; (*b*) there is no hint of rivalry between Jew and Gentile within the Church at Colossae; (*c*) the exclusiveness which St. Paul implicitly condemns by his recurrent 'every man' in *Colossians* is nowhere connected in any way with racial or religious ancestry, but seems clearly to lie in the alleged superiority of the mystic over the ordinary Christian, or of religious philosophy over simple faith, or of an elaborate cult over a plain creed. Curiously enough, Bishop Moorhouse, in his own preface

(p. x), consciously or unconsciously corrects his own mistake: 'The second danger by which the Apostolic Church was threatened had a mainly Gentile source; it arose not from a jealous and exclusive Judaism, but from what thought itself a liberal and enlightened philosophy.'

6. Heresies of the New Testament age.

The Colossian heresy must now be viewed in comparison with other heresies appearing in the N.T. In the earliest epistles, *1* and *2 Thessalonians*, Judaism is not the Judaizing of Christians, pro-legal and anti-Gentile, but the antagonism of unbelieving Jews to Christian apostles and converts. There is misapprehension or doubt of the Coming of Christ. But there is no sign of heresy in the sense of false teaching. 'The mystery of iniquity' is the power of moral evil, not merely anti-Christian but anti-religious. In *Galatians* the danger comes from Judaistic insistence on the permanence of the Law within the Gospel, a claim which reduced the Church to 'a somewhat liberalized form of the ancient Jewish communion' (Moorhouse, p. ix). In *Romans* the danger is twofold—the Judaistic insistence on the Law, and the reactionary antinomianism which perverted Christian liberty into moral licence. The questions faced in *1* and *2 Corinthians* are mainly moral and disciplinary, arising out of the social relations of Christian and pagan neighbours or the spiritual problems of Christian ministry and worship. The only sign of heresy is the denial of the resurrection, probably on the part of Greek converts who, without being in any formal sense Gnostics, regarded matter as evil and a future for the body as therefore an unspiritual prospect. In *Philippians* there are signs of a recrudescence of the old Judaistic antagonism to Christian liberty; but the 'enemies of the cross of Christ' (iii. 18–19) are not doctrinal but moral perils. There is no indication of heresy in the sense of a perversion of the Christian faith itself.

The peril of false teaching is faced as a grave problem in the later writings of the N.T. It is practically absent from the first epistle of St. Peter, which is concerned with the moral discipline of the spiritual life. But it is a large feature in the *Pastoral Epistles*, in *2 Peter* and *Jude*, *1* and *2 John*, and the Apocalypse. Dr. J. B. Mayor (*Jude and 2 Peter*, p. clxxiii) views the evidence of all these writings as 'a general picture' of 'the prevalence of antinomian heresy, resulting in corruption of morals and disbelief in God and Christ'— partly a picture and partly a prophecy of 'intellectual licence and moral laxity' (p. clxxx). In the main this is a true description. But the evidence is scarcely homogeneous enough to be satisfied by a single general description. Dr. Parry, in his introduction to the *Pastoral Epistles* (pp. lxxxi–lxxxix), distinguishes between warnings dealing with present conditions and warnings dealing with future developments. In the latter (1 Tim. iv. 1 ff.; 2 Tim. iii. 1 ff., iv. 3, 4) he sees the imminence of an apostasy of Christians due to influences at work from without the Church. The main features of this false teaching were that it claimed the authority of inspiration, and advocated a rigid asceticism, including abstinence from marriage and from certain kinds of food, on grounds not of Judaic distinctions between clean and unclean, but of the essentially evil nature of matter. Dr. Parry remarks that this asceticism was not peculiarly characteristic of Gnosticism, but generally characteristic of the pessimism of the age, and prevalent in various forms in the oriental cults and the current philosophies which met in the syncretisms of Asia Minor and other parts of the Graeco-Roman world. On the other hand, the false teaching confronted in the Pastoral Epistles generally is apparently not strictly heretical. The only specific heresy mentioned is the denial of any resurrection but the spiritual resurrection of the Christian soul in baptism (2 Tim. ii. 18). The error lay rather in the methods of teaching, in the concentration upon 'myths' and 'genealogies', which encouraged idle speculation, and conveyed a shallow kind of ethical instruction, fruitful only in controversy. Dr. Hort (*Jud. Chr.*, pp. 135–43) attributes this kind of teaching to the influence of later Judaism, in which the narratives of the Pentateuch were elaborated in the *Haggadah* into imaginary stories largely concerned with eschatological speculation and mythological theosophy, while the laws of the Pentateuch were elaborated in the *Halachah* into a detailed ethical code which gave rise to endless casuistry. There was a similar fashion in the Greek world, which did with Homer what the Jewish schools did with Moses. But it is almost certainly the Jewish development which is in view in the Pastoral Epistles.

The epistles to Timothy have a special interest for students of *Colossians* because they were written to Ephesus. The doctrinal and moral perils of which they give fragmentary and uncertain indications were a fulfilment of St. Paul's forecast of perils to the faith and the faithful from teaching both without and within the Church (Acts xx. 29, 30). The Johannine epistles and the Apocalypse are also pertinent evidence because they are the product of experience in Ephesus and the cities of the province of Asia. The heresy repudiated in *1 John* (ii. 22, 23; iv. 3; cp. *2 John*, 7) is clearly the docetism which, while recognizing the divinity of Christ, denied the reality of His human nature, and so destroyed the identity of Jesus with the Son of God. There is no trace of docetism in the heresy confronted by St. Paul in *Colossians*, unless we may read an anti-docetic emphasis in Col. i. 22, where he insists that the reconciliation effected by Christ was effected 'in the body of his flesh'. He is confronting rather a conception of Christ which recognized both His humanity and His divinity, but failed to recognize the cosmic sovereignty of Christ and the cosmic consequences of the Cross.

The message to the Church at Ephesus in the Apocalypse reveals two perils which may be, however, only two aspects of one peril. There are false teachers who claim an apostolate, a claim which the Ephesians had tested and found false (cp. the wolves of Acts xx. 29), and there are the Nicolaitans whose teaching is not stated but is described as finding expression in conduct which the Ephesians abominated. From Rev. ii. 14–15 it is clear that they advocated or tolerated sexual impurity and complicity in pagan worship. But there is no hint of doctrinal as distinct from moral peril. Nor is there any such hint in the message to the Church at Laodicea. It is doubtful, therefore, whether any light is thrown upon the Colossian heresy by the evidence of later epistles as to errors of teaching and practice at Ephesus. There may be some resemblance or connexion between the mythological and genealogical teaching condemned in the Pastoral Epistles and the 'traditions of men' in Col. ii. 8; but Col. ii. 22 seems to connect these traditions specially with the asceticism of the movement. The asceticism mentioned in 1 Tim. iv. 3 banned marriage, and was based on the dualistic view of matter as evil; the asceticism at Colossae was devotional in purpose rather than dualistic in principle. Nor are there any traces in *Colossians* (though there are perhaps in Eph. v. 6) of that philosophy of libertinism which regarded the indulgence of the flesh as a matter of indifference to the spirit. Nor, again, is there any evidence of angelolatry at Ephesus, unless it is latent in the 'myths and genealogies' of the Pastoral Epistles, which indeed some scholars have taken to refer to the angels of Judaism or the aeons of Gnosticism.

7. *Phrygian syncretism and the Colossian heresy.*

The evidence points towards the conclusion that Colossianism was a distinct local product. Much depends on the question, which of its contents was the starting-point of the heresy, the centre round which the floating elements of Phrygian religion crystallized? Or, if that metaphor suggests something too systematic, the original stream into which other tributaries flowed? Dibelius is probably right in thinking that angelolatry was the central factor in the movement (Excursus on *Die Irrlehrer von Kolossä*, p. 85 of his edition of the epistle in the *Handbuch z. N.T.*, 1912). The worship of the *stoicheia*, the cosmic angels, at Colossae was clearly due not to a speculative tendency without any practical bearing, but to an essential interest of the religious life of the Hellenistic age. The Colossian heresiarchs apparently taught that, while the Gospel had brought relief from the sense of sin, it had not relieved men from the obligation or necessity of serving and conciliating the Elements to which they were subject from birth to death. From Col. ii. 18 (see note there on 'dwelling') and from the antithesis implied perhaps in the emphasis on the 'mystery' of Christ (Col. i. 26 f.; ii. 2; iv. 3) it seems probable that this angel-cult took the form of a mystery-rite, like all cults of oriental origin. From the reference to the solid and orderly unity of the faithful at Colossae (ii. 5) it seems clear that the angel-cult had not yet found a distinct place within the Church (see the discussion of the later 'conventicles' on p. 101 of Ch. VII of this introduction); it was still an external temptation. But it may have already found a place in private or domestic observance. The term *threskeia* used in Col. ii. 18 denotes an act rather than an attitude of worship, and indicates that angel-worship had advanced from mere reverence to actual observance.

There is an intimate connexion between this angel-worship and the two other specific features of the movement, viz. the celebration of festival seasons and the observance of ascetic rules. This asceticism was probably prompted not merely by the need and duty of self-discipline as a condition of mystic vision, but also perhaps by the current idea that the organs and constituents of the human body, composed as they were of the elements, must be kept pure in honour of the spirits in charge of the elements of the universe. The celebration of days and seasons was connected with the belief that the cosmic spirits, especially the planetary angels, were 'the Lords of Time'. There may have been also a connexion between the ascetic rules and the sacred seasons; special purifications were customary before the mystery-festivals.

The history of the term *stoicheia*, used for the elements, is discussed in the notes on Col. ii. 8. The origin of the cult of the elemental spirits is to be traced to various converging influences, (*a*) the oriental religions, represented not merely by waves of influence from their home-bases along lines of inter-racial contact, but also by Syrian and Persian migrations into Asia Minor; (*b*) the religious philosophy of the Hellenistic age, which saw a correspondence and dependence between man and the cosmic elements, e.g. between the eye and the sun and stars, and between the human reason and the nature of the universe; (c) the angelology of Judaism, which in Phrygia in particular developed into angelolatry under various influences, e.g. Persian angel-worship, Hellenistic belief in demons (see p. 94), and the Anatolian animism which saw spirits behind the hot springs and earthquakes and the other abnormal phenomena of the Lycus valley. The Jews 'may not have been disinclined, the more educated from philosophical and the poorer from superstitious motives, to attribute power to the deities whom their neighbours worshipped, but regarding these not in any sense as independent powers, but rather as beings wholly under the direction of the one God and acting in some sort as His intermediaries' (Lukyn Williams, *Colossians*, pp. xxxv–vi). For the general syncretism of the Colossian heresy there were various materials present in its environment, (a) the cult of the old Phrygian moon-deity worshipped under the name of Men; (b) the oriental cults of Attis, Sabazius, and the Great Mother (Cybele), which spread far and wide through Anatolia; (c) the Egyptian theology seen in the pages of Philo the Hellenist-Jewish philosopher of Alexandria and developed later in the Hermetic writings; (d) perhaps also the Persian cult of Mithras the hero sun-god, though this cult had not yet reached farther west than Cilicia. In all these cults there appear in varying combinations the factors noted in the Colossian heresy. Last, but not least, (e) there was the Judaic contribution, e.g. circumcision, the bond of the law, the sabbath (Col. ii. 11, 14, 16).

In the light of this survey it seems probable that Judaism was not the main source but only a contributing factor of the Colossian movement. The movement was Phrygian rather than Jewish in origin and character. 'Asia' was not merely its birthplace but its parent. 'Cosmological speculation, mystic theosophy, religious fanaticism, all had their home here. Associated with Judaism or with Christianity the natural temperament and the intellectual bias of the people would take a new direction; but the old type would not be altogether obliterated. Phrygia reared the hybrid monstrosities of Ophitism. She was the mother of Montanist enthusiasm, and the foster-mother of Novatian rigorism. The syncretist, the mystic, the devotee, the puritan, would find a congenial climate in these regions of Asia Minor' (Lightfoot, *Col.*, pp. 95–6). One question remains unanswered, perhaps unanswerable—who were these Colossian heresiarchs and whence came they? Were they Jews attracted towards Christianity and yet unwilling to abandon beliefs and practices to which they were already attached ? Or were they Christians of Jewish origin who felt still the attraction of the religious syncretism of their past life ? Or were they Greeks or Graeco-Phrygians who had become prose-lytes of the local Judaism or had adopted some of its beliefs and practices, and now were attracted by the Christian Gospel and yet desired to find a place in the Christian faith and life for ideas and habits which they had inherited from pagan syncretism ? In any case the Colossian heresy represents an attempt to create a still larger and wider syncretism, in which all that seemed to them essential in Christianity was to be combined with the purest elements of the existing syncretism. The Colossian heresiarchs were proud of their improved Christianity, their new Christian theosophy. They and their Colossian disciples had now to learn that it was not merely less than Christian; it was in vital conflict with all that was most essential in Christianity. It is possible that their Christology was already defective, that they had not yet risen to more than the bare recognition of the divinity of Christ. St. Paul saw at once that their angelolatry was fatal to any true Christology, that Christ was reduced in their teaching to a place very little higher than the angels. The question has been raised whether St. Paul has done justice to the movement. It is true that his knowledge of the movement must have been derived almost entirely from Epaphras, unless indeed the movement began so early that some knowledge of its beginnings reached him during his long work at Ephesus. It is quite possible that it did begin early, if it came from men who were attracted by the first preaching of the Gospel at Colossae and who sought to combine what it offered with what they possessed already in the way of religion. In any case it has been urged that St. Paul's information was one-sided, and that he wrote with a polemical purpose and not with the impartiality of a student of the history of religion (Dibelius, p. 85). It is indeed unfortunate for the modern student that St. Paul's evidence is fragmentary, and his language allusive rather than descriptive. But his information came from those who felt the danger to the Christian faith and life, and it must have included therefore the salient features of the peril. 'Polemical', however, is scarcely the word to describe his purpose; it implies a suggestion of controversial injustice. It was no part of the duty of a Christian apostle to commend whatever may have seemed Christian or capable of Christianization in this new teaching. It was his duty to defend the Christian faith against teaching which menaced its purity and its power. Yet his defence is characteristic both of the Apostle and of the faith that he is defending. He is not attacking the false teachers; he is protecting Christian believers. So he begins, without a word of controversy, by unfolding the fullness of the truth of the person and place of Christ in the world; in the light of that truth he points out the essential falsehood and the inevitable failure of the new teaching; and then works out the bearing of the true life in Christ on all the relations of life. As far as it is controversial, the epistle is a model for all controversy on behalf of the Christian faith. He lays bare the central issues of the conflict with a trenchant criticism. The angelolatry of the new teaching dethroned Christ; its asceticism virtually destroyed Christianity. But his own teaching is positive and constructive. Over against the theory of cosmic powers he sets the sovereignty of the Son of God over all life, natural and spiritual. Over against the precepts of an asceticism which fought the flesh in detail with its own weapons he sets the principle of an ascension of the spirit in communion with the living Christ which would transform the whole life of the Christian.

VI

ANALYSIS OF THE EPISTLE

I. THE CHURCH AT COLOSSAE. i. 1–14.

(i) Personal introduction: Christian greetings to the Colossian Church from the Apostle and his companion Timothy. i. 1, 2.

(ii) Thanksgiving and intercession for their Christian life. i. 3–14.

1. Thanksgiving:
   (a) for their experience of faith, love, and hope. i. 4, 5.
   (b) for the fruit and growth of the Gospel at Colossae and in the world at large. i. 6.
   (c) for the work of Epaphras:
       (α) his ministry among the Colossians as the Apostle's representative. i. 7.
       (β) his message of information from Colossae for the Apostle's encouragement. i. 8.

2. Prayer for their spiritual progress:
   (a) in knowledge of the will of God, to be proved by a consistent walk of life. i. 9–10.
   (b) in active service, at once the fruit and the source of fuller knowledge of God. i. 10.
   (c) in a divine strength manifested in perseverance and patience. i. 11.

(*d*) in joyful thanksgiving to the Father
    (*α*) for their admission to 'the inheritance of the saints in light'. i. 12.
    (*β*) for their transference from the power of darkness into the realm of 'the Son of His love'. i. 13.
    (*γ*) for their redemption, the forgiveness of sins which they have found in Christ. i. 14.

II. CHRIST THE TRUE MYSTERY. i. 15–ii. 7.

(i) *The mystery of the Person of Christ.* i. 15–23.

1. In relation to God and the universe: i. 15–17.
    (*a*) He is the visible representation of the invisible God;
    (*b*) the firstborn Son, prior and superior to every created being or thing, terrestrial and celestial, visible and invisible;
    (*c*) the centre, the channel, the climax of all creation, and the secret of its coherence.

2. In relation to the Church, the new creation: i. 18.
    (*a*) He is the Head of the Body.
    (*b*) the beginning and the firstborn of the new life.

3. He is therefore supreme in the natural and in the spiritual realm.
    (*a*) The ground of His supremacy is His possession of the *pleroma*, the fullness of Godhead. i. 19.
    (*b*) Its purpose is the reconciliation of the universe to God (i. 20), a reconciliation which
        (*α*) consists in the peace made by the offering of His life upon the Cross;
        (*β*) includes in its scope the celestial as well as the terrestrial world, angels as well as men.
    (*c*) In this reconciliation the Colossians have a place: i. 21–2.
        (*α*) in the past they were alienated from God in thought and life.
        (*β*) in the present they are now reconciled to God by the life and death of the Son.
        (*γ*) in the future they are to be presented perfect before God.
    (*d*) The claims of the Gospel of reconciliation: i. 23.
        (*α*) its message is the standard of perseverance and the condition of progress.
        (*β*) its mission is world-wide.
        (*γ*) its ministry is now the life-work of the Apostle.

(ii) *The ministry of the Apostle of Christ.* 1. 24–ii. 7.

1. In relation to Christ: it is a ministry of suffering for the sake of the Body of Christ, the Church—a counterpart and a completion of 'the afflictions of Christ'. i. 24.
2. In relation to God: it is a ministry of service. i. 25–7.
   (a) its purpose is the proclamation of a divine mystery once hidden but now revealed to the saints.
   (b) its work is to bring this revelation home to the nations and to bring out the wealth of its meaning for their life.
3. In relation to the individual Christian: it is a ministry directed towards the perfecting of the saints. i. 28–9.
   (a) Its message, 'Christ in you the hope of glory', is for every man, not for a select few.
   (b) its methods are discipline and doctrine.
   (c) its aim is the presentation of every man perfect in Christ.
   (d) its discharge means a life of labour and conflict, in which the Apostle is sustained by the power of Christ, working in him.
4. In relation to particular churches: it is a ministry of fellowship in the faith. ii. 1–7.
   (a) His sense of responsibility is not confined to converts of his own mission; it extends to Colossian and Laodicean and all other Christians to whom he is personally unknown. ii. 1.
   (b) It finds expression in earnest prayer: ii. 2, 3.
     (a) for their spiritual life in general, for courage, love, understanding, conviction.
     (β) for their progress in knowledge of 'the mystery of God', viz. the Christ who is the treasury of all wisdom.
   (c) It prompts anxiety for the Colossians, now in danger of yielding to plausible error. ii. 4.
     (a) Such a surrender would be a serious blow to the unseen fellowship between them and him, and to the order and solidarity of their faith, which it is a joy to behold from afar. ii. 5.
     (β) It would be a grave departure from the path of union with Christ, a break in the life of steady and thankful progress in the faith. ii. 6, 7.

III. THE FALSE MYSTERY AND THE TRUE. ii. 8–iii. 4.

(i) Christ is the final and sufficient answer to the false and futile philosophy which is threatening to capture the Colossian Church.
1. It is not based upon Christ. ii. 8.
   (a) its religious discipline is based upon human tradition.

(b) its theological doctrine is based upon a theory of ruling cosmic powers.

2. But Christ is the source of all truth and the centre of all sovereignty. ii. 9–13.

(a) He is the fullness of Deity and the fulfilment of humanity. ii. 9, 10.

(b) He is the head of all spiritual powers and forces. ii. 10.

(c) He is the sole source of salvation: to their union with Him in their baptism they owe

(a) the destruction of their old life, the truth symbolized by the old rite of circumcision. ii. 11.

(β) the resurrection to a new life born of

1. the quickening power of God;

2. the forgiving love of God. ii. 12, 13.

3. Of this power and this love the Cross was the open vindication.

(a) It was the cancelling of the sentence of condemnation involved in the old law of righteousness. ii. 14.

(b) It was the disarming of the cosmic angelocracy or demonocracy that dominated the life of mankind. ii. 15.

(ii) The Cross has cut the ground from under any cult of angelolatry and asceticism. The old life is a thing of the past: its fear of spiritual powers has been conquered, its faith in ritual precepts condemned, by the Cross.

1. The question of religion is not

(a) obedience to a ritual system of food and festival: these are but the shadow of a reality which is to be found in Christ and in Christ alone. ii. 16, 17.

(b) nor the observance of angel-worship with its strange blending of

(a) the self-conscious humility of the devotee;

(β) the self-inflated pride of the visionary. ii. 18.

2. The test question is the place given to Christ: this heresy stands condemned by its failure to 'hold fast the Head', from whom is derived

(a) the sustenance of every member,

(b) the unity of all the members,

(c) the growth of the whole Body. ii. 19.

(iii) In the light of the Cross this plausible asceticism is both faithless and futile. ii. 20–3.

1. It is faithless: their 'dying with Christ' set them free from any real or imaginary domination of spiritual world-powers. Why

then yield obedience to rules of life based upon belief in that domination? ii. 20-1.

2. It is futile.
   (a) Such rules attach eternal significance to things of transient use and value. ii. 22.
   (b) They are human in origin and authority. ii. 22.
   (c) In spite of their apparent wisdom, their display of devotion, humility, and discipline, they fail to conquer the flesh. ii. 23.

(iv) In the light of the Resurrection the path of spiritual progress is plain: its one rule is *Sursum corda*. iii. 1-4.

1. The ascended Christ is now for them
   (a) the perspective of all effort: 'seek things above'. iii. 1.
   (b) the principle of all thought: 'think things above'. iii. 2.
2. Their whole life has been lifted to a higher plane:
   (a) it shares the secrecy of the present life of Christ in God. iii. 3.
   (b) it will share the future glory of His final revelation. iii. 4.

IV. THE OLD LIFE AND THE NEW. iii. 5-iv. 6.

(i) The dying of the old life of passion and sin. iii. 5-11.

1. There must be a resolute effort
   (a) to put to death the old habits of impurity and other self-seeking passions. iii. 5-7.
   (b) to put away the old sins of temper and speech—all that is fierce, foul or false. iii. 8, 9.
2. This effort is the necessary and practicable sequel of their new spiritual status.
   (a) They have a new nature instead of the old—a fresh beginning and a constant renewal in the knowledge of the truth and in the likeness of the Creator. iii. 10.
   (b) They have a new environment—an order of things in which all differences, racial, religious, cultural, social, cease to count, and Christ is everything to every man. iii. 11.

ii) The development of the new life of grace and holiness. iii. 12-17.

1. There are new habits to be formed in response to the call of God's love—sympathy, simplicity, patience, forgiveness and love, 'the bond of perfection'. iii. 12-14.
2. The peace of Christ, which is the purpose of the life of the Body, must be the ruling principle in the hearts of its members. iii. 15.
3. 'The word of Christ' with all its wealth of wisdom must find a home in their minds and an expression in their conversation and their worship, in speech and in song. iii. 16.

G

e.g. Ezekiel, Zechariah, Job, and Daniel, that angels proper in the sense of beings distinct from God appear as a prominent feature in Jewish belief. They are called by various names, e.g. sons of God, gods, heroes, keepers, watchers, holy ones, princes. They are the court, the army, the council, the choir of heaven. They intercede for men; they protect the righteous; they inspire and inform the prophet; they punish the wicked; they guard the nations. They are intermediaries between God and man in various phases of revelation and redemption. There are indications of various degrees of rank. Two chief angels are given names, viz. Michael and Gabriel. Moreover, there are also indications of a belief in demons, evil or unfriendly spirits—a belief due to a growing reluctance to attribute evil to God. In this connexion it is interesting to note the evolution of the idea of Satan. In the prologue of *Job* he is still one of the spirits in attendance upon Jehovah, but 'permanently sceptical of disinterested virtue'; God is responsible for evil, but overrules it for a good end. In Zech. iii. 1. ff., he is the accuser and adversary of the high-priest and the nation which he represents. In 1 Chron. xxi. 1, he is the tempter who 'moved David to number Israel'. But Satan in the O.T. has no relation to the evil spirits; 'the devil and his angels' is a N.T. development. There is little reference to angels in the philosophical books of the Apocrypha, *Ecclesiasticus* and *Wisdom*, or in a historical book like *1 Maccabees*; belief in angels seems to have faded or weakened under the influence of Greek rationalism. But in the apocalyptic literature which represents the popular religion of Judaism angelology is a prominent feature. The angels appear as protectors, vindicators, healers, revealers, but also as the spirits in charge of natural phenomena, and some are identified with the stars and planets. Their ranks are elaborated into a complicated hierarchy, headed by four 'angels of the throne', Michael, Gabriel, Uriel (or Phanuel), and Raphael. The demons appear as fallen spirits or as the spirits responsible for the particular sins of men.

Various explanations have been suggested to account for the origin and development of Jewish angelology. It has been suggested that the angels represent the gods of the nations, reduced by the growing monotheism of the Hebrews to a position of subordination to the true God—that they represent the spirits of early animism unified and moralized in the service of a divine purpose—and again, with greater truth, that they represent the result of a growing transcendentalism which removed God so far from contact with humanity and the universe that religious feeling was led to people the gap between God and the world with spirits which kept man in touch with

God. Yet these theories are after all only more or less probable explanations of a historical process. They are no argument against the reality of a religious experience or the truth of a religious belief. They may throw an instructive light upon the steps by which Hebrew faith found its way to belief in angels; they do not cast any real doubt upon the existence of angels. Even ancient myths and legends of theophanies may be corruptions of a true tradition, or crude anticipations of a true hope. It has been suggested again that Jewish angelology is the result of Babylonian and Persian influence. This may be true of some later elaborations of angelic grades and functions. There are indeed arresting resemblances, e.g. between the guardian angels of Hebraism and the *fravashis* of Iranian religion. But such resemblances are capable of three explanations. They may point to a process of borrowing. They may be due to a common origin. They may be the outcome of independent developments. The main ideas at least of Jewish angelology—the existence of angels, their activities as instruments and intermediaries of the revelatory and redemptive purposes of God—are not only prior to any probable influence from Persia, but an integral part of that faith of prophet and psalmist which was constantly protesting against the influence of alien faiths. Yet it is certain that between the Old Testament and the New Jewish angelology had become more elaborate, and it was this later development, and not the earlier simpler belief, which was in the background of the New Testament.

(ii) *Angels in the New Testament*

1. *The narrative of Gospels and Acts.*

In the Gospels the appearances of angels are nearly all in connexion with the Nativity and Resurrection of our Lord (to which must be added the Ascension in Acts i. 10), viz. in connexion with the manifestations of His Divinity. The appearances to Joseph, Zacharias, and the Blessed Virgin are in line with the angelic revelations to the seers and saints of the O.T. The 'multitude of the heavenly host' with the angel that appeared to the shepherds recalls the angel-choir of the heavenly temple of the majesty of God. It is significant that the only appearances in our Lord's own recorded experience are at the opposite pole; they are ministrations in His hours of human need, the temptation in the wilderness and the agony in Gethsemane. In *Acts* two angels bid the disciples return from the mount of Ascension to their work for Christ; an angel releases the apostles from prison and sends them back to preach in the Temple (v. 19), directs Philip's journey (viii. 26), prepares Cornelius for Peter's visit (x. 3, 30), delivers Peter from gaol (xii. 7, 9), smites Herod with deadly disease (xii. 23), and reassures Paul in the storm-tossed ship (xxvii. 23). Most of these appearances are essentially similar to those of divine messengers in the O.T. But in Herod's case the 'angel of the Lord' is, as often in the O.T., 'a Hebrew description of what we should call the action of divine providence' (Rackham, *Acts*, pp. 71–2). And in Philip's case 'the angel of the Lord', in the light of 'the Spirit' that bade him join the eunuch (viii. 29) and 'the Spirit of the Lord' that 'caught him away' (viii. 39), may imply 'an inward intuition rather than an external vision' (Rackham, p. 72), cp. the coupling of spirits and angels in Acts xxiii. 8, 9. It has been suggested that the expression 'angel of the Lord' in *Acts* and in Mt. i. 20, ii. 13, 19, Lk. i. 11, corresponds to the 'angel of Jehovah' in the O.T. which is really a manifestation of Jehovah Himself. But this view is ruled out (*a*) by the fact that in Lk. i. 11 the angel is identified with Gabriel, (*b*) by the apparently equivalent use of the expression 'angel of God' in Acts x. 3, (*c*) by the fact that 'the angel of Jehovah' occurs only in the oldest documents of the O.T., and seems to have given place later to the ordinary idea of an angel as a divine messenger distinct from God.

2. *The teaching of our Lord.*

Our Lord is represented as speaking of the nature and position of the angels. They need no reproduction, for they are immortal (Mk. xii. 25, Mt. xxii. 30, Lk. xx. 36); their knowledge is limited with regard to the future (Mt. xxiv. 36); some of them at least are in constant and immediate attendance upon the presence of God (Mt. xviii. 10). They are 'the angels of God' (Mt. xxii. 30, Lk. xv. 10, John i. 51), but they are also the angels of the Son of man (Mt. xvi. 27, xxiv. 31, cp. Rev. i. 1, xxii. 16).[1] They will be the retinue of the Son of Man in His final glory. They will gather the elect to meet Him (Mk. xiii. 27, Mt. xxiv. 31); they will reap the harvest of human life (Mt. xiii. 39), and separate the wicked from the just (Mt. xiii. 41, 49). They will be witnesses of the Son of Man's recognition or

---

[1] It is precarious, however, to lay stress on the exact wording of a saying of our Lord. In Mk. viii. 38 the Son of Man comes 'in the glory of His Father with the holy angels'; in the same saying in Mt. xvi. 27 'in the glory of His Father with His angels' (clearly in the light of the context 'the angels of the Son of Man'); in Lk. ix. 26 'in the glory of Himself and of the Father and of the holy angels'. The common element in all three versions of the saying is the attendance of the angels upon the Son of Man in the glory which is His as the Son of God.

rejection of men who have confessed or denied Him on earth (Mk. viii. 38, Mt. xvi. 27, Lk. ix. 26, xii. 8, 9). Meanwhile they share the joy of God over the sinner that repents (Lk. xv. 10). They carry the departing soul to its unseen home (Lk. xvi. 22). The angels of 'these little ones' (whether the children or the childlike disciples) have a place of their own in the presence of God (Mt. xviii. 10)—clearly guardian angels, though not necessarily one guardian angel for each soul. Angels ministered to the Son of Man in the wilderness of temptation (Mk. i. 13, Mt. iv. 11); this fact must have come to the disciples from our Lord's own lips. The legions of heaven are only waiting for the Father's bidding to come to the aid of the Son (Mt. xxvi. 53). The angels of God shall be seen 'ascending and descending upon the Son of Man' (John i. 51), a prophecy of the fulfilment of Jacob's dream—a reference not to angelic ministrations to our Lord in His earthly life, of which the disciples saw nothing except in Gethsemane, but to 'the continuing presence of Christ, in whom believers realize the established fellowship of the seen and the unseen' (Westcott). The prophecy is symbolic of the relation between God and the Church; yet it suggests irresistibly the idea of angels bearing the prayers and bringing the answers to the prayers of the Son of Man as representative of all humanity and so applies to each and every member of His Body.

Opinion is divided on the question whether our Lord's references to angels decide the question of their existence and activity. It is argued that His language is symbolical and pictorial. Thus Mt. x. 32, 'him will I confess before my Father which is in heaven', is used to prove that the phrase 'before the angels of God' in Lk. xii. 8 is a popular synonym for the presence of God. But this argument breaks down before the fact that in Mk. viii. 38, Mt. xvi. 27, Lk. ix. 26, the presence of God and the presence of the angels are both mentioned together in the same sentence. Moreover, our Lord refers to the angels not merely in the parables but also in His interpretation of the parables (Mt. xiii. 39, 41, 49). It has been urged again that our Lord quoted rather than confirmed popular belief—that He clothed spiritual truth in forms that would be intelligible and acceptable to His hearers, without necessarily implying that the imagery corresponded to fact—that He was concerned to teach higher truths and not to correct every element of untruth in current belief. On the other hand, belief in angels, though not in itself an essential or fundamental part of the Christian faith, plays an important part in shaping religious life and effort; and if it is unfounded in reality, He would surely have condemned it by corrective teaching, as He did in the case of wrong ideas of the Law and the Kingdom of God, or at least discouraged it by silence. 'If it were not so, I would have told you' (John xiv. 2).

Our Lord's references to angels, if the argument from silence may be pressed so far, seem by their silence to discourage the prevailing idea of angels as the intermediaries of revelation, an idea discouraged more positively by His teaching about the guidance of the Holy Spirit. Neither is there any hint of a hierarchy of angels. But His references cover most of the fundamental ideas of Jewish angelology. And it is almost certain that the Lord's Prayer implies the existence of angels. The obedience of earth is to correspond to the obedience of heaven, 'as in heaven, so on earth'. The reference can scarcely be to the harmony within the Godhead; such a reference would be premature and unintelligible, and obedience is not the right word for the relation of the Son and the Spirit to the Father. Nor can it be to the order of the heavenly bodies in obedience to the law of their creation; such obedience is impersonal. The only tenable interpretation is the obedience of the angels in the service of God.

3. *The Gospel according to St. John.*

Apart from the two angels at the tomb of the risen Lord (xx. 12) and the saying of our Lord to Nathanael (i. 51), there are no references to angels in the Fourth Gospel. The mention of an angel stirring the pool in v. 4 is a later interpolation; and the remark of the crowd in xii. 29 is a mere record of popular belief. No stress must be laid on the absence of any reference to angels in the Johannine epistles; their purpose and character gave no opening for any such reference. But the practical silence of the Gospel is significant. It seems to indicate that there was no room for the idea of angels as intermediaries of revelation alongside the doctrine of the abiding presence of Christ and the guidance of the Holy Spirit. Already in *Acts* the prompting of the Spirit appears in the case of Philip alongside the voice of the angel. In the Fourth Gospel the angel has virtually disappeared before the Spirit. In fact the absence of teaching on angelic ministry is so marked in the Gospel that it has been urged as an argument against its coming from the same pen as the Apocalypse in which that ministry is so prominent.

4. *Current Jewish belief.*

(*a*) Glimpses of popular belief in angels occur in *Acts* and in the Fourth Gospel. The periodic stirring which gave healing power to the pool of Bethesda was attributed to an angel (John v. 4). The voice from heaven which some of the crowd thought was thunder was taken by others for the voice of an angel (John xii. 29). The faithful praying for Peter in prison, when the maid reported his presence at the door, said 'It is his angel' (Acts xii. 15), perhaps meaning his ghost, but more probably the guardian angel who was supposed to resemble the person under his protection. The Sadducees, the priestly class, denied the existence of spirits and angels (Acts xxiii. 8), though it is not certain whether this means that their strict adherence to the O.T. as against later writings and oral tradition led them to reject the later elaborations of angelology, or that their rationalistic leanings under the influence of Greek thought led them to explain away even the angelophanies of the O.T. as mere personifications of natural forces. The Pharisees on the other hand believed in the existence and influence of angels (Acts xxiii. 8), and were prepared to believe that 'a spirit or an angel had spoken' to St. Paul (Acts xxiii. 9).

(b) In 2 Peter and Jude particular beliefs with regard to the angels emerge from the Jewish background. Jude quotes the apocalyptic Enoch's prophecy of the Lord coming in judgement with 'the holy myriads'. Both epistles refer to the doom of the fallen angels as an illustration of divine judgement. In 2 Pet. ii. 4 they are merely described as sinning, without any hint of either of the two traditional views of their sin, viz. the sexual indulgence of Gen. vi. 2 or the divulgence of divine secrets. In Jude 6 it is said that 'they kept not their own principality', i.e. the position of dignity and office assigned them by God, 'but left their proper habitation', i.e., apparently, descended from heaven to earth—perhaps a reminiscence of the mysterious story of Gen. vi. 2. Both contrast the irreverence of false teachers with the reverence of the angels. In 2 Peter ii. 11 the reference may be to the language of the Angel of the Lord in Zech. iii. 2, but probably it refers to the tradition mentioned in Jude 9 that the archangel Michael in defending the body of Moses against the devil contented himself with invoking the judgement of God.

(c) In the Apocalypse, even when allowance is made for the symbolism of visions, there remain traces of the popular Jewish angelology of the apocalyptic writings as well as the traditional belief of O.T. times. There is little trace, however, of the elaborate hierarchy so prominent in the apocalyptic books. The angels 'are seen engaged in the activities of their manifold ministries, now as worshipping before the Throne, now as bearing messages to the world, or as stationed in some place of trust, restraining elemental forces, or themselves under restraint until the moment for action has arrived, or as presiding over great departments of Nature. Sometimes their ministries are cosmic; they are entrusted with the execution of world-wide judgements, or they form the rank and file of the "armies of heaven", who fight God's battles with evil, whether diabolical or human; the Abyss is under their custody. Sometimes an angel is employed in the service of the Church, offering the prayers of the saints, or presiding over the destinies of a local brotherhood or ministering to an individual brother, e.g. to the Seer himself. No charge seems to be too great for an angel to undertake, and none too ordinary; throughout the book the angels are represented as ready to fill any place and do any work to which they are sent' (Swete, *Apocalypse*, p. clxv). There is a significant warning against any attitude of worship in their presence (xix. 10, xxii. 8, 9); it may have been meant as a protest against some such tendency in the Churches of Asia.

5. *The Epistle to the Hebrews.*

The angelology of *Hebrews* has a special value of its own. It deals chiefly with the contrast between Christ and the angels. The main theme of the epistle is the finality of Christianity which follows from the supremacy of Christ. Hebrew Christians were being tempted by disappointment into relapse. In Christ they have all and more than all that Judaism gave or promised. Christ is greater than the angels, than Moses, than Aaron. Revelation, leadership, priesthood—all that there was of these in the Israel of the past was partial and prophetic. In all three respects His superiority is complete and final. There is no clear reference to any danger of angelolatry among Hebrew Christians. The danger lies in the direction of a relapse into a Judaism which assigned to the angels an undue prominence and importance as intermediaries of divine revelation. It is the relation of the angels to the Word of God that is in question. The writer recognizes and apparently accepts the tradition, based on Dt. xxxiii. 2 and Ps. lxviii. 17, which interpreted the attendance of the angels at the revelation of Sinai as indicating their ministration in the giving of the Law (ii. 2). But he insists on the superiority of the Gospel as the message of the living Word, the Son of God. This insistence takes the form of a contrast between Christ and the angels in various respects. (1) By His Resurrection and Ascension He entered upon an inheritance of Sonship to which the angels have no claim (i. 4, 5, cp. Ps. ii. 7). (2) The Christ of the Resurrection, or perhaps the Christ of the future Advent, is entitled to receive the adoration of the angels (i. 6, cp. Dt. xxxii. 43 LXX, Ps. xcvii. 7). (3) 'Angels fulfil their work through physical forces and natural laws (Ps. civ. 4, "He

maketh his angels winds and his ministers a flame of fire "); the Son
exercises a moral and eternal sovereignty' (Westcott on i. 7, 8).
(4) The Son is enthroned in royal majesty, awaiting the triumph of
His kingdom; the angels are 'ministering[1] spirits sent forth to do
service for the sake of them that shall inherit salvation' (i. 13, 14).
(5) The angels are next contrasted both with Christ and with mankind (ii. 5–9). The writer takes as his text Ps. viii. 4–6, especially
'thou madest him (man) a little lower than the angels'. (a) He
argues virtually that what Scripture prophesies here is that the
supremacy over the world to come rests not with angels but with
man. Lower than the angels now, man will some day be higher
(cp. 1 Cor. vi. 3). The prophecy has been fulfilled in the Son, who
condescended to the position of man, and whose supremacy, not
indeed yet realized in actual triumph, has been vindicated by His
coronation with glory and honour as the reward of His Passion. He
stooped beneath the angels for man's sake. Now He stands above
them as the fulfilment of human destiny. (b) At the same time the
Incarnation bore testimony to the greatness of man. The A.V., 'He
took not on him the nature of angels' but human nature, suggests
that the Incarnation was a proof of man's superiority to the angels.
The R.V., 'Not of angels doth he take hold', i.e. to help them,
suggests the true idea of the context. It was man, not angels, that
needed divine assistance—man with his sin and his fear of death.
That was why the Son stooped beneath the angels to live the life of
flesh and blood. It was not angels but men that He came to save.
The writer pursues this idea no further; he has fulfilled his purpose,
which was to explain the temporary inferiority of the Son to the
angels. But we can scarcely avoid reflecting upon the paradox of
divine providence seen in the fact that man's sinful and sad experience has become the stepping-stone to an intimate communion with
the Son of God which is destined to exalt him above the angels. We
are led thence irresistibly to two ideas of St. Paul's. (a) In his protest
against Christians going to law with Christians he reminds the
Corinthians that the saints will judge the angels (1 Cor. vi. 3). Any
reference here to fallen or evil angels destroys the force of the argument which lies in the exalted nature of the angels. To awaken the
Church to 'a sense of its competence and dignity' (Godet) he reminds

---

[1] The word 'ministering' (like 'ministers' in i. 7) may refer to 'the general
office of the angels as spirits charged with a social ministry' (Gk. *leitourgia*) as
distinct from 'the particular services (Gk. *diaconia*) in which it is fulfilled'
(Westcott). But the former word in LXX and Gk. N.T. is nearly always used
of ministering to God; in that case the 'service' is probably service rendered to
man. Cp. the Collect for St. Michael and All Angels' Day.

them that the members of Christ are to share His sovereignty in judging, i.e. ruling, the world, angels included. (*b*) St. Paul tells the Colossians that the reconciliation of the universe which begins with the reconciliation of man to God is to end with the reconciliation of 'things in the heavens', in which the angels are in some sense included (see Additional Note on p. 188).

One passage in *Hebrews* remains to be noticed. The writer presses home the greater responsibility of his readers by reminding them that while their forefathers met at Sinai in a scene of law and fear, they themselves have come to a scene of grace and peace. In that heavenly world in which they are living now (xii. 22) 'myriads of angels in festal assembly' are present with 'the Church of the first-born enrolled in heaven', the Judge who is their God, the faithful departed, and the Saviour Himself, and the atoning blood that cries not for vengeance but for mercy. The scene thus pictured may be a picture of Christian worship in communion 'with angels and arch-angels and with all the company of heaven'. Dean Vaughan inter-prets the picture of the Christian life in general. 'In that heavenly city which is already your home, you have a host of sympathizing friends in those unfallen spirits who behold the face of your Father. They are there, not in selfish repose, but in perpetual ministry for sinful and suffering mankind. They have charge concerning you in your perilous pilgrimage, invisible helpers and guardians in your hours of loneliness and temptation.'

(iii) *St. Paul and the angels*

1. *Angels and demons.*

Of the reality of the existence of angels and demons St. Paul had no doubt. It was an article of Pharisaic belief, and he was 'a Pharisee, a son of a Pharisee' (Acts xxiii. 6). But the references in his epistles to the place of angels in divine providence and in human destiny show signs of not merely development but divergence. The problem can only be appreciated and solved by a historical survey of his teaching on the subject. At the outset some of his references to angels may be set aside as figures of speech, e.g. when he anathe-matizes any contradictory gospel even if preached by 'an angel from heaven' (Gal. i. 8)—when he recalls the enthusiasm with which the Galatians had welcomed him at first 'as an angel of God, as Christ Jesus' (Gal. iv. 14)—when he depreciates religious eloquence without love, even if it be 'the tongues[1] of men and of angels' (1 Cor. xiii. 1)—

---

[1] The Rabbis speculated upon the language of the angels, some maintaining that it was Hebrew. But 'men and angels' may be a synonym for 'heaven and

and when he warns the Corinthians against the subtlety of a Satan who can transform himself into 'an angel of light' (2 Cor. xi. 14).

In *Thessalonians*, his earliest epistles, the angels are included in his conception of the future Coming of Christ. In 1 Th. iii. 13 'with all his saints' may or may not include the angels (cp. 'the holy ones' in Zech. xiv. 5, evidently in St. Paul's mind here); and in 1 Th. iv. 16 'the voice of an archangel' may be a reference to Michael (see Milligan, l.c., and Cheyne in *Expositor*, VII. i. 289 ff.), or a pictorial touch like the trumpet of God with which it is coupled. But in 2 Th. i. 7 'the angels of his power' are clearly present as attendants and ministers of the Lord revealed in judgement. In the later epistles the thought of the future Advent recedes into the background. Its place is taken by questions of doctrine, discipline, and devotion which demand attention in the course of church development. References to angels are incidental but profoundly suggestive.

(a) *Their relation to the Christian faith and life.*

They are 'wondering spectators of the vicissitudes of the church militant here on earth'; God has exhibited the apostles as men doomed to death in the arena, 'a spectacle to the world, both angels and men' (1 Cor. iv. 9). They are present at the worship of the Christian congregation; women must not shock them by any disregard of reasonable convention of dress and behaviour (1 Cor. xi. 10). They are present witnesses of the heart of man and its motives; St. Paul makes his appeal to Timothy in the sight of God and Christ Jesus and 'the elect angels' (1 Tim. v. 21), i.e. probably the angels who had not fallen—not a title of superior rank among the angelic orders. They are deeply interested in the revelation of Christ as the Truth of God, the now visible mystery of divine purpose. The ascended Christ was not only preached among the nations and believed in the world, but had also been 'revealed to angels' (1 Tim. iii. 16— perhaps a quotation from an early creed-hymn), apparently as being intimately concerned with the fruits of the Incarnation of which they had been the heralds. As with the inception of the Gospel, so with its progress. The angels are to see the working out of the mystery of divine purpose in the new spiritual unity of mankind (Jew and Gentile) and to recognize therein the manifold character of the wisdom of God, like 'the intricate beauty of an embroidered pattern' (Arm. Rob. on Eph. iii. 10). The same idea is seen in

---

earth', i.e. all the eloquence in the world. Cp. perhaps 1 Cor. iv. 9, 'a spectacle to the world, both angels and men'.

St. Peter's picture of the angels peering wistfully into the fulfilment
of ancient prophecy in the passion and glory of Christ (1 Pet. i. 12).

(b) *Their cosmic and divine relations.*

The world of heaven is included in the reconciliation which begins
with the world of earth. 'All fatherhood' or 'every family' (not 'the
whole family' as in A.V.) in heaven as well as on earth derives its
name and character from the Father of our Lord Jesus Christ, who
is 'not only the universal Father but the archetypal Father' (Arm.
Rob. on Eph. iii. 15). Corporate life is a divine principle; the whole
world is one great family embracing all kinds of families—domestic,
social, national, religious—human and angelic. Angelic as well as
human life has a unity which flows from the universal Fatherhood of
God, and an ideal which comes from the archetypal Fatherhood and
its expression in the life of the Holy Trinity. In the apostolic philosophy of history all grades of being in heaven as well as on earth are
destined to find in Christ their consummation, each to find its own
perfection and all to find their common purpose (Eph. i. 10). This
consummation consists partly in their recognition of the lordship of
Christ over all life (Phil. ii. 10, Col. i. 16, 17, Eph. i. 21, cp. 1 Pet. iii.
22). But it is also described as a reconciliation (Col. i. 20), a term
which suggests not merely a synthesis of all life under the sovereignty
of Christ but also a restoration of all life in obedience to the will of
God, in a response to the love of God—an obedience formerly refused,
a response formerly imperfect either in its consciousness of divine
love or in its fulfilment of the claims of that love. And the emphasis
on heaven as well as earth indicates that even angelic life and service
needed this reconciliation, a more perfect harmony with the divine
purpose, a more complete devotion and obedience to the divine love
which is the law of all life. The language is too general to indicate
whether the reconciliation concerns only angels good but imperfect,
or includes also evil or unfriendly spirits.

(c) *Satan and the demons.*

Over against the 'angels' stand the 'demons'. Plato approves a
subsidiary worship of 'demons' as interpreters and intercessors
between God and man. Plutarch recognizes a threefold providence—
the supreme Godhead, the secondary gods, the demons. Philo insists
on the identity of the Hebrew angels and the Greek demons. 'Demon'
(Gk. *daimonion*) had originally a good or neutral meaning. For
St. Paul the demons are evil spirits. They are the dark reality behind
pagan idolatry; Christians m t choose between the table of the

Lord and the table of demons (1 Cor. x. 20, 21). They are 'the world-rulers' (Gk. *kosmokratores*) of this darkness, the spiritual hosts of wickedness in the heavenly places', against which the Christian has to wrestle and can only hope to stand when clad in the panoply of God (Eph. vi. 12, 13, cp. the war in heaven of Rev. xii. 7). At their head stands Satan, the antagonist of all good—the devil, the spirit of all falsehood in thought and life. He thwarts the Apostle's plans for the Gospel (1 Th. ii. 18); the stake in the flesh is 'an angel of Satan' (2 Cor. xii. 7); he disguises himself as an angel of light (2 Cor. xi. 14); he tempts the novice in the Christian ministry to fatal pride (1 Tim. iii. 6, 7), the Christian believer to deadly heresy (1 Tim. v. 15, 2 Tim. ii. 26) or to immorality (1 Cor. vii. 5). He is doomed to ultimate defeat and destruction (Rom. xvi. 20); meanwhile he finds an incarnation in Antichrist (2 Th. ii. 9). He exercises a real domination over the world, human life out of touch with God. He is 'the prince of the power of the air', 'the spirit that now worketh in the sons of disobedience' (Eph. ii. 2); he is 'the god of this age' who 'blinded the minds of the unbelieving' against the light of the Gospel (2 Cor. iv. 4). The expulsion of an offender from the Church is 'a delivery unto Satan' (1 Cor. v. 5, 1 Tim. i. 20), an exposure to the full force of his malignity; the restoration of the sinner who has learned penitence in the sufferings thus incurred is delivery from the designs of Satan (2 Cor. ii. 10, 11). The Christian must be armed against his subtle attacks (Eph. vi. 11), and must break definitely with pagan associations, for there can be no 'concord between Christ and Belial' (2 Cor. vi. 15).

(d) Dualism in St. Paul.

The demonology of St. Paul has been cited as a proof that he 'lived and moved in a world of dualisms, whereas the modern world is convinced of the ultimate unity of the universe' (Wilson, *St. Paul and Paganism*, p. 244). The dualism of St. Paul has been both misunderstood and exaggerated. The term needs defining. Antithesis is not dualism. Faith and unbelief, the first and the second Adam, the Church and the world, the present age and the age to come, flesh and spirit—these are not dualisms but antitheses. Dualism implies not merely antithesis but antagonism—not mere opposition but essential, inherent, permanent opposition. Ancient dualism, Greek or Persian, regarded the world as the scene of an original and irreconcilable conflict in the celestial sphere between a God and a Devil, in the terrestrial sphere between spirit and matter. Of this dualism St. Paul is innocent. 'He does teach an ethical dualism of flesh and spirit,' but only 'as the outcome of his own spiritual experience' (M. Jones, p. 32). Far from regarding matter as evil, and flesh and spirit as essentially antagonistic, he believes in the possibility of the consecration of the flesh by the spirit. He does recognize the existence of powers that influence the life of man, powers antagonistic to God and 'in some sense or degree independent of God'. He does regard evil as not merely human but cosmic. But the devil, though the enemy of God, is not the rival of God; the bold expression 'the god of this age' (2 Cor. iv. 4) is not theological but practical. 'The world is still for St. Paul fundamentally God's world' (M. Jones, p. 32). God is not in process of becoming God: St. Paul would have had some sympathy perhaps but certainly no approval for the pessimistic philosophy, largely the product of the Great War, which regards God as engaged in a hard and uncertain struggle to reduce chaos to order and to overcome evil with good. There is in St. Paul nothing of the pessimism which was the necessary result of pagan dualism, both philosophic and popular. The delay of redemption was not inevitable; it was providential. The victory of the Kingdom of Christ over every enemy is assured, and then 'God will be all in all' (1 Cor. xv. 28). The key-word of *Colossians* and *Ephesians* is reconciliation in heaven and on earth.

2. *The darker side of St. Paul's angelology.*

The real difficulty in St. Paul's angelology lies in his apparent conversion to an attitude of antagonism to the angels. This impression is not derived in any way from his condemnation of the practice of worshipping angels; that condemnation might have been pronounced in the interests of a true angelology. Nor does it depend upon the identification of the angels with 'the elements of the world' in Col. ii. 8, 20 and Gal. iv. 3, 9 (on which see notes on Col. ii. 8, 20). It is derived rather from a comparison of terminology and contexts in a group of passages in various epistles. (*a*) In Rom. viii. 38 he couples angels with 'principalities and powers' as belonging to the same category of existences, and as presenting possible obstacles to the Christian's realization of the love of God in Christ. (*b*) While in Col. i. 16 he merely insists on the supremacy of Christ over 'principalities and powers' in the natural order by virtue of His place as the agent of God in creation, and in Col. ii. 10 and Eph. i. 21 upon His supremacy over 'principalities and powers' in the spiritual order, on the other hand in Eph. vi. 12 he regards 'principalities and powers' as the enemies of the Christian life, and in Col. ii. 15 describes them as the enemies of Christ, disarmed and displayed in triumph on the

Cross. St. Paul seems in this group of passages to ignore the distinction between good and evil angels, or between angels and demons, whether these demons are to be identified with the fallen angels of Jewish tradition or with the hostile spirits of pagan belief. 'We are almost compelled to conclude that St. Paul regarded even angels as being ranged on the side of evil' (Jones, p. 36), and as being among the spiritual powers to which 'the present world', i.e. the pre-Christian age, was in bondage.

There are three other passages to be considered. (c) There is the almost contemptuous reference in 1 Cor. ii. 6, 8 to 'the rulers of this world' or 'age' who in their ignorance of the mystery of the wisdom of God had 'crucified the Lord of glory', and whose rule is now 'coming to nought'. These rulers of this world are regarded by some scholars as identical with the spiritual beings elsewhere designated 'principalities and powers', and therefore with the angels. In that case St. Paul would appear to have included angels among the forces that sent Christ to the Cross, and the Cross was not merely a crime but a blunder, for which they paid dearly by their own dethronement and degradation (Col. ii. 15). This conclusion is so startling that it would be a great relief to accept the possibility of another interpretation which identifies the rulers of this age with the rulers of the Jewish nation, Caiaphas, Herod, Pilate, to whose ignorance St. Peter refers as a palliation of their crime (Acts iii. 17). (d) There is the unsympathetic dismissal of 'the elements of the world' in Gal. iv. 3, 9 and Col. ii. 8, 20. Some scholars still maintain that these elements are the rudimentary stage of the world's religious education. But recent scholarship is mostly in favour of the view that the phrase refers to the elemental spirits supposed to inhabit the stars and to control all natural phenomena and the lives of men and nations (see note on Col. ii. 8 and p. 64). In that case, in the light also of Gal. iii. 19 and Col. ii. 14, 15, we can scarcely avoid the impression that St. Paul 'regarded the whole world before Christ, the Jewish world with its Law and presiding angels and the pagan world with its astral powers and fates, as a world in slavery, which attained its freedom only through the victory accomplished on the Cross' (M. Jones, p. 39). (e) Finally, there is the mysterious connexion which St. Paul sees between the angels and the Mosaic law. It was already an accepted Jewish tradition (based on Dt. xxxiii. 2, LXX) that angels were the givers, the guardians, and the agents of the Law. St. Stephen referred to this tradition to enhance the dignity of the Law and to accentuate the responsibility of disobedience (Acts vii. 53). St. Paul refers to it in Gal. iii. 19, 'It was ordained through

H

angels in the hand of a mediator,' in a context which suggests plainly
the inferiority of the Law compared with the Gospel, though it does
not necessarily involve 'a somewhat depreciatory view of angels'
(M. Jones, p. 37), for there is nothing depreciatory of angels as such
in contrasting their instrumentality with the absence of any such
instrumentality in the case of Christ and the Gospel. But in Col. ii.
14, 15 the abolition of the Law by the Cross is clearly connected with
the dethronement of the principalities and powers, with whom the
angels are to be identified or at least associated. St. Paul seems
clearly to regard the angels and the Law as bound up together in
such a way that 'freedom from the Law meant at the same time
freedom from the angels who in company with other principalities
and powers held the world in thraldom' (M. Jones, p. 38).

There would seem to be no necessary connexion between the two
ideas of the domination of the Law and the domination of the angels.
Liberation from the Law by the Cross would of course involve the
abandonment of the idea that its angelic associations gave it any
claim to permanence. The connexion of angels with the giving of
the Law was only an incidental circumstance of its Mosaic origin, and
even so only an inferential interpretation of the canonical scriptures.
But there is no proof that Hebrew tradition regarded the continued
administration of the Law by the angels as a tyranny to be compared
or associated with the tyranny of other celestial powers. Yet
St. Paul's language is emphatic and insistent. He certainly does
link the abolition of the bond of the Law with the breaking of the
power of a domination exercised by spiritual powers of a neutral or
inimical character. It is possible that the difficulty would be cleared
up if we knew to what extent and in what directions the Jews of
Asia Minor had mingled their belief in angels with the Graeco-
Oriental belief in 'demons'. St. Paul's alleged failure to distinguish
between angels and demons may be deliberate; he may have been
striking at a syncretism in which angels and demons were so inex-
tricably blended that in order to secure for human life and thought
the fresh start which it needed he had to cut the whole resultant
belief right away by the vindication of the Cross as the death-knell of
all usurpations, demonic or angelic.

Dr. M. Jones believes that the explanation of the whole difficulty
is to be found in the historical development of St. Paul's own thought
—a development partly due to the succession of environments and
experiences amid which he lived and worked, and partly to the growth
of his own spiritual life. Dr. Jones sees three stages in the development of the darker side of St. Paul's angelology. (1) Inheriting or

accepting the belief in the world-domination of various spiritual powers, a belief which darkened and saddened and crippled human life at every turn, as it does still in the unevangelized peoples of the modern world, St. Paul came to see in the Cross of Christ not merely redemption for the soul of man from sin and suffering but redemption for the world as a whole, the victory of the love of God over all the forces of evil. (2) St. Paul at first regarded the Law as a preparation for the Gospel; but the insistence of Judaizing Christians on the imperative necessity of the Law as a condition of admission to the Church of Christ led him to regard the Law as a system of spiritual bondage, the Jewish counterpart of the tyranny of pagan beliefs, 'an essential factor in the state of slavery and oppression from which the world was set free by the death of Christ' (M. Jones, p. 41), and the shadow of this darker view of the Law fell also upon the angels who were 'intimately associated with the Law as its promulgators and patrons'. (3) The last and decisive factor in St. Paul's attitude towards the angels was the Colossian heresy with its central tenet of angel-worship. The supremacy of Christ and the freedom of the Christian soul were both at stake; and his depreciation of angels passed into condemnation of the whole conception of the spirit-world which was threatening to invade and invert the Christian faith. 'The Law was in itself good and holy, but when it is set up as a rival to the Gospel it becomes for St. Paul a curse. So the angels may in themselves be the servants of God and the assessors of Christ at the last day, but when they are set against the Son and threaten His supremacy, even they are numbered among the principalities and powers who are triumphantly dethroned by the death of the Cross' (M. Jones, p. 44). 'He believed in angels, and the dominion that they were supposed to wield over the lives of men was a stern reality to him, but he set himself to show, with all the force at his command, that they possessed no shadow of right to the religious regard of men, and that whatever power they may have had in the age that had now gone by had been completely broken in the face of Christ. He set the Christian on the high road leading to religious freedom and joy in the fellowship of Jesus Christ' (M. Jones, p. 47).

This analysis seems in the main a correct account of St. Paul's experience. But it does not exhaust the possibilities of the case. (a) It ignores the possibility that St. Paul did not himself believe that the celestial powers did control human life. He may be virtually saying: 'This tyranny of spiritual forces has no basis in reality; it owes its actual power over you to your own imagination. Once realize what the Cross has done for you, and the unseen world will

H 2

CBP., ii. 741). A ninth-century legend relates how in the second century Michael saved the city of Colossae from an inundation: he cleft the rock and released the waters dammed up by a heathen crowd to overwhelm the holy fountain and the chapel built by a pagan of Laodicea who had been converted by the healing of his dumb daughter by this very fountain, itself sacred to the memory of an earlier miraculous visit of Michael. Ramsay thinks that the legend may have been founded on a historical fact, viz. an inundation that occurred in Christian times, 'or it may be an artificial legend, founded on the strange natural cleft through which the Lycus flows, and probably giving in Christian form an older pagan myth' (*CRE.*, p. 480). 'The Orthodox Church acquiesced in the continuance of the old local impersonations of the Divine power in a Christianized form' (*CRE.*, p. 466). In this way St. Michael inherited the legendary cult of the ancient god of Colossae.

2. *Later Christian angelology.*

The comparative restraint of early Christian literature and art on the subject of angels may have been partly due to the corrective influence of *Colossians* and the later angelology of St. Paul in general. But it was probably due also to the zealous anti-polytheism of apostolic and sub-apostolic Christianity at large. Christian teachers refrained deliberately or instinctively from any emphasis upon a belief which might easily be mistaken by pagan converts for a Christian counterpart of the popular belief in a multitude of gods or demi-gods. When Christian monotheism—and the doctrine of the Holy Trinity was developed and defended as a safeguard of the monotheism which Christianity had inherited from Judaism—was established beyond any danger of relapse, Christian literature and art ventured to reclaim its ancient heritage of angelology. Churches were dedicated in honour of angels and especially of archangels; Constantine built a church of St. Michael on the Bosporus. Archangels were invoked in litanies after the Holy Trinity and before the Blessed Virgin. In the fourth or fifth century a great impetus was given to Christian angelology by the treatises written in the name of Dionysius the Areopagite, in particular the treatise entitled *The Celestial Hierarchy*. These writings reflect the 'vast spiritual conglomerate' of current thought, Judaic, Hellenic, Oriental, Christian. Their angelology was mainly Jewish and Christian. The hierarchy consists of three triads derived from Jewish apocalypses and the Pauline epistles, especially Eph. i. 21 and Col. i. 16, viz. (1) Seraphim, Cherubim, Thrones—the contemplative orders; (2) Dominations,

Virtues, Powers—the regulative orders; (3) Principalities, Arch-angels, Angels—the administrative orders. Their functions are two-fold—to represent, convey, and fulfil the activities of God, and to lift mankind Godward along the threefold mystic path of purification, illumination, and perfection. The Dionysian writings are the ultimate source of most modern devotional interpretation of the scriptural descriptions of angels, e. g. the three pairs of wings of the seraphim (Isaiah vi. 2). Interesting examples of such interpretation are to be found in *A Book of Angels*, ch. iv. The idea of the twofold ministry of angels, Godward and manward, derived ultimately from Heb. i. 14 (see p. 91), is embodied in the familiar language of the Michaelmas collect, which has received careful treatment, historical and devo-tional, in Dean Goulburn's *The Collects* (ii. 338–48).

(v) *Angels in modern life and thought*

In our own day belief in angels occupies an uncertain and pre-carious position. There is deliberate denial of their existence, a denial based on the practical ground of the absence of any visible mani-festation, or on the theoretical ground of the superfluity of spiritual agents in a world of natural forces which are themselves adequate instruments of divine purpose and power. And there is the reluctant doubt of minds which feel the attraction of the idea of angelic ministry, but fear that the proofs and arguments of its reality are insufficient. On the other hand, belief in angels, even where it is held more or less, suffers from various faults. The first is indiscrimination, the uncritical acceptance of any and every evidence or impression. All biblical statements and references are regarded as equally authoritative. The ninefold order of the Dionysian angelarchy is treated as an established truth, and made the basis of a mystical interpretation which may provide satisfying or stimulating food for meditation, but is often forced into artificial and arbitrary explana-tions, e. g. to find a meaning for this or that rank in the angelic order. The second fault is indistinctness. There is serious confusion between angels and saints which finds expression for example in the idea (based perhaps originally on a misinterpretation of Mk. xii. 25 and Acts xii. 15) of 'angel faces loved long since and lost awhile' or the idea that a friend has 'gone to be an angel', or again in the metaphorical language of poets, e. g. the 'angel in the house' or 'a ministering angel thou'. The third defect is the indecision of minds which cherish dearly or contemplate wistfully the idea of angels, but never face the question whether they actually believe in the reality of angels. Lastly there is the converse fault, the indifference of minds

whose belief is theoretical but not practical—minds which are
satisfied of the possibility or probability of angelic existences, but
are untouched by any sense of angelic influence or any desire for its
realization. Liddon used to say that the weakness of modern belief
in angels was due not to any difficulty of the reason but to a lack of
imagination.

Cardinal Newman once said that if it was the sin of the dark ages
to pay unwarrantable honour to the angels, it was no less a sin, in
an age which called itself enlightened, to pay them little honour or
none. The question is not academic or immaterial. It is a question
of intellectual honesty. The Anglican liturgy asserts still that in the
Eucharist we are in devotional fellowship 'with angels and arch-
angels and with all the company of heaven'. If that is a baseless
assertion, a pious fancy, it should be excised from the public worship
of a God who is to be 'worshipped in spirit and in truth'. And it is
a question of spiritual values. The belief in angels brings into daily
life a beauty and a solemnity which are a distinct help to holiness.
If the belief is true, it should be held more firmly; if it is not true, it
should be sacrificed to the duty and necessity of building only on
reality. The dream-life of aesthetic imagination is no basis for sound
religion.

The history of the belief in angels is an instructive example of
the working of scientific research and reconsideration. Historical
criticism has discounted the authority of much scriptural evidence
by dissipating the weight of its unity. On the other hand, the sifting
of the evidence has brought into relief the strength of what remains.
When literary and historic criticism has done its utmost to examine
and to excise, what survives the test stands out all the more vividly,
if not as an integral factor, at least as a congruent feature, of the
Gospel. Christian literature and art have introduced the angels into
Gospel scenes in which they are not mentioned in the Gospel itself.
This is not a case of the tendency of the imagination to multiply
the miraculous. It is rather an inference from the Gospel itself. The
occasional revelation of the presence of the angels is so marked and
harmonious a feature of the narrative that poet and painter have
felt justified in assuming and imagining their perpetual presence
everywhere behind the veil of the visible.

The recorded experience and teaching of the Apostles, and still
more of our Lord, will be the final battle-ground of creed and
criticism on the question of the angels. Meanwhile independent
reflection in scientific minds is coming out here and there on the side
of the angels. (a) Some disciples of the evolutionary school are

prepared to allow that the principles of continuity and gradation require or permit the idea of an angelic type of being between man and God—the highest term in the series—inorganic, organic, animal, human, angelic. (*b*) St. Paul's and St. Peter's idea of the angels as spectators of human life and divine purpose has received confirmation from modern thinkers. Dr. Latham's *Service of Angels* owes its central conception and its originating impulse to a glimpse which he caught of the sun-lit beauty of a lizard on a stone bridge in a lonely landscape in Italy, which set him wondering whether this beauty would have been wasted if it had not met his eye. Sir Oliver Lodge is credited with the significant suggestion that it is more and more incredible that man should be the sole intelligent spectator of a wonderful universe which contains so many wonders lying beyond the range of his experience or his faculties. The philosophical interpretation of the universe is assuming more and more the warmth of personality. Scientific minds may yet come to see that research into the mechanical or chemical processes of nature is quite reconcilable with the belief in the personal ministry of spiritual agencies applying or accompanying the action of natural forces with the warmth of devotion to the glory of God and the good of man.

Belief in the ministry of angels is therefore more likely to be confirmed than to be confuted by the progress of scientific thought. The question still remains, what should be the attitude of Christian minds towards the angels? Interesting materials for an answer to this question are provided by a study of Christian hymnology. *Lex cantandi lex credendi.* Our hymns ought to be kept true to the soundest theology, for they are the most powerful of influences for the shaping of popular belief. A glance through a score of hymns relating to angels, whether modern compositions or modern translations of ancient or medieval hymns (e. g. J. M. Neale's versions of the hymns of Archbishop Rabanus Maurus) reveals no trace of worship paid to angels in their own right. There is contemplation of the activities of the angels and of their fellowship with humanity in the worship of God; there is prayer to God for the exercise of angelic ministry on human behalf; there is thanksgiving for the experience of that ministry. There is also direct invocation of the angels, and that in hymns from Puritan as well as Catholic pens. Beside Athelstan Riley's 'Ye watchers and ye holy ones, raise the glad strain, Alleluia' may be set Baxter's 'Ye holy angels bright, assist our song' and Lyte's 'Angels, help us to adore Him'. Such invocation, however, is rhetorical rather than doctrinal, poetical rather than practical. It is not a prayer for their ministry to the needs of humanity, but a call

for their co-operation with the Church in the adoration of God. It is
a metaphorical ornament of Christian devotion. Along with the
angels are invoked the praises of the saints living and departed, and
even of the heavenly bodies, e.g. 'ye blessed souls at rest . . . ye
saints who toil below' (Baxter)—the Blessed Virgin, patriarchs,
prophets, apostles, all saints triumphant (Riley)—'Sun and moon,
bow down before Him, dwellers all in time and space, praise with us
the God of grace' (Lyte). In the popular devotions of the Latin
Church, St. Michael is the subject of direct and real invocation for
protection and assistance in human need. Such invocation of angels
is part of the doctrinal problem of the invocation of saints, defended
by the same explanations, and open to the same objections, e.g. that
historically it is a transformation and, despite all transformation, an
adoption of lingering cults of local paganism—that doctrinally it is
a derogation of the unique supremacy and sufficiency of the Son of
God—and that practically it is a dissipation of the energy of Christian
devotion. Christian piety loses rather than gains, and the sense of
truth is subtly weakened, by any form of devotion which it is hard
to reconcile with the letter or the spirit of apostolic teaching. Yet
the danger of superstition is less imminent and less real than the
danger of unspirituality. And there is nothing in the New Testament
that condemns, and much that commends, the reverent remembrance
and vivid realization of the heavenly and earthly ministry of the
angels, so long as it is confined to that conception of angels which
is an inseparable part of the story and teaching of our Lord, and an
occasional yet integral part of the general teaching of St. Paul
rightly viewed. Doctrinal conceptions are meant not for ornament
but for use. They have a contribution to make not merely to the
wealth of mystical contemplation but also to the strength of spiritual
endeavour.

VIII

THE VALUE OF THE EPISTLE FOR MODERN THOUGHT

THERE is something arresting in the contrast between the original
purpose of the epistle and the purposes which it is serving to-day.
Here is a pastoral epistle from a Jewish-Christian apostle to a
Phrygian-Christian community of the first century which vanished
from the map of Christendom a thousand years ago. It was drawn
from him by the emergence and prevalence of a strange syncretistic
'philosophy' which at this distance almost defies the attempts of
scholarship to give it an affiliation and a name. It is still being read

in the public worship of congregations and edited for the instruction
of students belonging to peoples that have behind them now nineteen
centuries of social evolution, of scientific discovery, and of philosophical development. What value can such a document have to-day
beyond its value as material for the reconstruction of a past stage of
human experience and the illustration of an early stage of Christian
history? The question may be stated in another form which itself
points towards the answer. Why was this epistle circulated, preserved,
and canonized? Partly on the ground of its authorship; it came from
the pen of a leading apostle. Partly on the ground of its contents;
despite its sometimes obscure and ambiguous references to a religious
situation not familiar to other churches at the time or to any church
at a later time, it was felt to contain teaching of positive and permanent value on the great truths of the Christian faith and the principles of the Christian life. That teaching has been given very different applications in different ages. Its Christology was quoted in the
second century against the more distinctive and developed forms of
Gnosticism which had moved away from the early Judaistic associations and connexions of that school of thought, and also against
the Arians and the Manichaeans of the fourth century. The theological champions of the Reformation found, in its anti-ascetic
and anti-ceremonial protests, weapons and ammunition for their
attacks upon catholic tradition and discipline; and it was a true
instinct which led them to see in these protests principles of permanent validity, even though they misapplied those principles
through failure to recognize other principles of truth and value in the
very practices which they used St. Paul's teaching to condemn.

The present value of the epistle lies in various directions, corresponding more or less closely to the various phases of the miscellaneous
movement which it was intended to combat.

(i) Abstinence from foods and drinks

The epistle has a bearing upon various questions of abstinence,
occasional or permanent, in matters of food and drink.

1. The campaign against alcoholic beverages is being based more
and more upon prudential or altruistic grounds, upon the damage
done to health or thrift, or upon the social force of good or evil
example, and the Christian principle of self-sacrifice for the sake of
weaker brethren. But as far as that campaign is inspired by belief
in the inherent evil of the thing in itself, it comes within the scope of
the apostolic protest against making such prohibitions an integral
part of the Christian religion.

2. Vegetarianism is finding new advocates on spiritual grounds. Dr. Lyttelton in an article on 'Foods and Fads' in the *Nineteenth Century* (May 1929) remarks: 'Bernard Shaw bluntly but truly said that vegetarianism makes for the higher life, meaning, presumably, that it is an antidote to grossness of mind. . . . To abstain from flesh as much as possible is to give powerful aid to the subjugation of the lower desires.' St. Paul would scarcely have quarrelled with such a plea, made on behalf of 'many thousands of young men who . . . are in reality longing for this antidote'. But the tenor of his teaching in *Colossians* and elsewhere suggests that he would have warned such advocates against the danger of centring the effort after spirituality in fighting the lower nature with weapons of food rules instead of lifting the whole effort to the higher plane of that mystical communion with Christ which is to transform the entire nature of man.

3. The religious observance of fasting is a complex question which only comes at certain points within the scope of St. Paul's teaching in *Colossians*. As an *imitatio Christi*, whether in correspondence to His example or in response to His teaching, it lies outside and beyond any Pauline judgement. But as a principle of personal or ecclesiastical discipline it must be judged by the grounds on which it is urged. The substitution of fish for meat, for example, is in danger of becoming a 'tradition of men', a conventional custom, quite compatible with a self-indulgence in quality or quantity of food which is the very antithesis of the spiritual idea for which fasting stands. But it has a physiological explanation which gives it a moral significance. Its original idea was that fish is nutritive without being stimulative, and this idea brings the fish-day within the sphere of discipline of the body for the sake of the soul, and therefore within the scope of the criticism to which the vegetarian is liable. And the language of Col. ii. 16, 23 suggests that St. Paul would have condemned any teaching which advocated any particular form of self-denial on grounds which ignored the principle that the spirit of self-denial is the one thing needful, and can only find expression in personal rules which are appropriate to the circumstances of the individual case.

(ii) *Astrology and magic*

The break-down of the old pagan religion of mythology left the Graeco-Roman world to believe that life was either at the mercy of capricious or at least incalculable forces, Chance or Fortune, or under the dominion of irresistible forces, Fate or Necessity. Theoretically the two views are mutually exclusive; if everything is fixed, nothing can be fortuitous. Practically the two co-existed in the same mind; men alternated between the worship of Fate and the worship of Chance. The astrology which claimed to ascertain the fate written in the movements of the stars varied from respectable science to disreputable superstition. The use of the term 'mathematician' in Latin for 'magician' suggests that there was an easy descent from high research to low cunning. There is no clear reference in *Colossians* to astrology or to magic, though astral powers probably lie behind the term 'elements' (*stoicheia*). But both were part of the background of Anatolian syncretism. It is probable that the black arts of Ephesus (Acts xix. 19) were practised in other districts of Asia. In any case the providence of the love of God and the supremacy and sufficiency of Christ, which are the basic principles of St. Paul's answer to the Colossian heresy, are also the final answer to all astrological and magical superstitions in every age. And such superstitions die hard or revive readily. The Great War brought a recrudescence of superstition as well as a revival of faith. People who ought to know better are wavering between Christian faith and pagan fatalism, between prayer and magic. Palmistry, crystal-gazing, horoscopic predictions, find no lack of dupes and victims. Friday and the number thirteen, amulets and mascots, and the prayer-chain with its promises and warnings dependent not upon the using of the prayer but upon its copying and forwarding, these and kindred aberrations have a real hold upon minds otherwise sane and sound. Fear and doubt find expression in a blind credulity in any and every practice that promises safety or certainty. M. Allier in his *Le Non-civilisé et nous* (ch. iv. *La magie dans les sociétés supérieures* and especially ch. v. *Au seuil de la magie*, pp. 174–228) produces ample and arresting evidence of the fact that civilization is still haunted by the superstitions of savagery, not merely as survivals of a prehistoric ancestry but as a sort of spontaneous creation in modern minds. It is sometimes possible to shame or frighten the devotees of these superstitions by pointing out the fallacy or peril of all such attempts to ascertain or to evade destiny —by convincing them that these things are the very abdication of reason and the very disintegration of conscience. The idea of wresting the secrets of life and death from the supposed instruments of their supreme Lord by processes which are destitute of any intellectual or moral discipline, the idea of escaping from disaster by the aid of devices that have no relation to human personality or divine purpose—such ideas are fraught with danger to all that is noblest in man. But their final condemnation lies in the fact that they are irreconcilable with the faith of the Gospel. Superstition and magic are in stark antithesis to true reverence and faith. In a world planned by a providence of God which permits human responsibility and requires human co-operation, in a world ruled by the Christ who holds in His hands the keys of life and death, and reigns supreme over stars and storms, over men and angels, in a world whose final law is not power but love, and whose life is guided by the indwelling Spirit of God, magic and superstition are disloyalty and treason to known truth. The antidote for their prevention or their cure lies in belief in the loving purpose of God and in the supremacy of Christ in the work of the universe and His sufficiency for all needs of humanity. The purpose at the heart of the universe is a loving purpose. All who are prepared to respond to its call know that under its control the chaos and uncertainty of life are converging for their true welfare (Rom. viii. 28), and that nothing in the whole world can wrest their lives out of the hand of God which they have seen in 'Christ Jesus our Lord' (Rom. viii. 38–9). In *Colossians* these convictions are gathered up into the sweep of a great thanksgiving; the fear and doubt which dominated men's lives in a dark world vanished when they were lifted into 'the kingdom of the Son of His love' (i. 13). Life is now but a question of 'holding fast the Head' whose sympathy understands and whose power unifies everything.

(iii) *Science and Christology*

St. Paul's insistence upon the truth that the creation and coherence and continuity of the natural world are due to the personal activity and supremacy of the Son of God in the cosmic system has found a new application in relation to modern science or rather the philosophies, scientific or popular, which purport to interpret the facts of science into a theory of the universe.

1. *Angels and Laws of Nature.*

Graeco-Oriental thought attributed natural phenomena to the influence of celestial beings whose cosmic powers seemed to call for some measure of adoration or some method of propitiation. That belief has a modern counterpart in the popular, if not scientific, idea of laws of nature. Those laws are regarded sometimes as active forces which control physical processes, whereas they are in fact merely intellectual concepts which explain those processes. Extremes meet; and minds that would ridicule angel-worship are prone to attach to these laws of nature a deterministic authority to which is paid a veneration almost akin to superstition. The laws of nature thus misregarded are supposed to preclude miracle, and thus practically to limit the liberty of God in the world of His own creation. They are like the Necessity behind Zeus in the old Hellenic mythology. There is more than a superficial resemblance between the Destiny of ancient syncretistic faiths, with its hierarchy of angelic agencies, and the Determinism of modern secularistic philosophies with its system of natural laws. Neither involves necessarily the denial of the existence of God; both involve practically the denial or the derogation of His liberty of action.

Arbitrary criticism says that St. Paul 'knew nothing' of the conception of angels as the instruments of divine activity in the life of the world and humanity. It would be truer to say that he is not concerned in this epistle to establish the right doctrine of angelic ministry but only to vindicate the rightful place of Christ as the sovereign of the universe. That conception of angelic ministry is consistent with the most rigid monotheism and the most vigorous theism, and it is not incapable of combination with the idea of natural forces working in accordance with natural laws, i. e. on methodical lines which express the mind of God; 'order is heaven's first law'. Angels may be personifications of forces or personalities in charge of forces. The recognition of angels as departmental servants is as tenable a view as the veneration of angels as sub-sovereigns is untenable. St. Paul is content to refute the perilous idea of angelic sovereignty; his refutation is quite compatible with the idea of angelic service.

2. *Christ and evolution.*

The outstanding idea of the Christology of *Colossians* is the conception of Christ's sovereignty as embracing the natural as well as the spiritual order. Here St. Paul is in advance of modern thought, yet in accord with its most advanced ideas. The theory of evolution is admitted by the leaders of scientific thought to be entirely consistent with the belief in divine creation; evolution is simply a method of creation. An eminent scientist has lately insisted on the distinction between two concepts of evolution. There is evolution *within* the universe, the evolution of individual organisms struggling and surviving in the conflict with rival organisms and varying environments; and there is the evolution *of* the universe itself. 'The universe itself has no environment. It has everything within itself. It is not in time. Time and space are within it' (Dr. Brown in the *Journal of Philosophical Studies*, Jan. 1929, p. 42). It is this greater evolution that St. Paul sees and interprets in advance. The unity of the universe is for him a personal unity, the unity of relation to a divine personality. St. Paul sees in Christ the goal and the agent of evolution. He is not merely *salvator hominum* but also *consummator omnium*, the living reconciliation of the universe. In Christ stand revealed at once the purpose of God and the possibilities of man. He stands at the heart of the world as He stands at the centre of history. He is the divine revelation in advance of human research; and the history of thought since He came has been partly the recognition and partly the verification of that revelation. In the light of that revelation it is clear that evolution is not merely a process but a purpose. Nature and humanity are not merely working, they are being wrought, into conformity with that purpose. Christ is the ultimate goal of evolution. He is the direct goal of human evolution; the second Adam is the visible standard seen in advance towards which humanity is being guided and fashioned. He is also the indirect goal of natural evolution. Man is now a partner of God in that evolution, a partner with Christ; '*we* must work the works of Him that sent me' (John ix. 4, R.V.). Man's task is to bring all natural forces, as he discovers and understands them, into the service of Christ. But the whole process of cosmic evolution is not only 'unto Christ'; it is also 'through Christ'. He is the true *anima mundi*, the soul of the world of which Stoic philosophy caught a glimpse. And man's share in the process depends for its faithfulness and its efficacy upon his being 'in Christ'; 'he that believeth on me, the work that I do shall he do also, and greater works than these shall he do, because I go unto the Father' (John xiv. 12). The reconciliation of the universe depends upon the reconciliation of humanity. The Incarnation has linked together the power and purpose of God with the response and co-operation of man. 'All things are yours, and ye are Christ's, and Christ is God's' (1 Cor. iii. 23). St. Paul doubtless knew something of the scientific thought of his day; but his cosmology has its origin in reflection upon his own faith and experience. It is at once a prophecy and an interpretation of the processes that modern science has discovered and the problems that it has set for modern philosophy. St. Paul sees at the heart of the universe a purpose, and he sees that purpose unveiled in Christ. The universe is not a system of self-working forces; it is the working out of a divine purpose in which Christ is at once the creative agent, the constant guide and the culminating glory; and 'in Christ' man too finds a glory of his own in the fulfilment of that purpose and meanwhile in co-operation with its process.

3. *The reconciliation of philosophy and faith.*

The philosophy to which science has to leave the final interpretation of the universe is undergoing a remarkable transformation. The current of thought is setting steadily towards the spiritual. History is repeating itself. Graeco-Roman philosophy in the time of Christ had become or was becoming religious. It had turned from the speculative problem of the nature of the universe to the practical problem of the moral unity of life. The philosopher had become the preacher, the missionary, the spiritual director, a threefold activity vividly depicted in Dill's *Roman Society from Nero to Marcus Aurelius*, and in Glover's *Conflict of Religions in the Early Roman Empire*. Modern philosophy shows no signs of such a conversion. But it is looking already in the direction of religion. Dr. A. W. Robinson in his *Christianity of the Epistles* indicates two phases of this movement. (1) The best modern philosophy is acknowledging frankly and generously the value of religious and mystical experience as a basis for the interpretation of what is called Reality, i. e. the ultimate nature of the universe, and for the unification of all knowledge and thought. In other words, the immediate and intuitive consciousness of the human spirit as popularly distinguished from the human mind is being recognized as valid evidence for scientific study, as a factor in the cosmic problem which promises to be a solution of the problem. (2) Philosophy is teaching now 'the priority of the whole' over the parts of existence. The finite, the temporal, the material, are being recognized as subordinate to the infinite, the eternal, the spiritual. Professor Whitehead of Cambridge tells us that even in the physical world the whole is greater than the sum of its parts. Dr. W. Brown, Wylde Reader in Mental Philosophy at Oxford, in the *Journal of Philosophical Studies* (Jan. 1929, p. 42) insists that 'change, the apparent sequence of development, is not self-explanatory. We have to bring in the conception of something else, namely, a background which does not change. . . . What emerges is not merely a consequence of previous change, but it represents or manifests a characteristic of the timeless or eternal background, of the Absolute or God. So that even within the realm of biology we are faced with a contrast between the temporal and eternal, and we find that for an adequate rational appreciation of the situation we must assume the Eternal.'

The philosophical conception of this higher unity is still tentative and indefinite. Its idea of the Absolute is perilously impersonal, and the idea of human personality stands or falls ultimately with the idea of the personality of the Absolute; the soul of man depends upon the spiritual reality of God. Yet with all its uncertainty and vagueness the new philosophy is grasping the spiritual as a clue to the divine. It is erecting an altar to a yet philosophically unknown God. We are in sight of a new reconciliation between philosophy and religion, a

I

reconciliation based upon belief in the unity of truth, a reconciliation which shall fulfil the prophecy of that preface to the Fourth Gospel which links Christian experience with pre-Christian philosophy, 'the Word was made flesh'. Modern philosophy by a deliberate resignation or rather suspension of faith set itself to do for our vaster wealth of world-knowledge what ancient Greek philosophy did for its own far narrower range of knowledge, viz. to see how far it could reach towards God. Now it stands in a somewhat similar position to that of Greek philosophy just before the Christian era. The metaphysical is reaching out its hand to the spiritual. The hope of reconciliation suggests and demands a fresh advance from both sides. The time seems to have come for philosophy to reclaim and resume the faith which it resigned or waived in the interests of independent thought, and to begin again at the Christian end of things, to start afresh with the conceptions of the New Testament, particularly with the great conceptions of the Pauline epistles, accepting them and using them in the true scientific spirit as working hypotheses, and endeavouring to find a synthesis between these religious conceptions and the philosophical conclusions thus far reached. On the other hand, Christian thought should study its own position afresh. 'We ought to look upon the activities of modern philosophy as a not unfriendly challenge to a deeper and more determined investigation into the wealth which is ours in the Christian inheritance, believing that there are fresh discoveries yet to be made, as well as forgotten or neglected treasures to be brought to light again' (Robinson, p. 57).

The contribution of Christian thought to the approaching reconciliation lies in the presentation of the great conceptions which we believe are the answer to the questions which philosophy is asking, the goal towards which the explorations of philosophy ought to lead and are in fact leading. *Colossians* is a treasury of such conceptions.

(1) The first is the idea of absolute creation as against any theory of emanations. The modern theory of evolution has taken the place of the ancient theory of emanation. The root idea of both is impersonal tendency. The Christian conception of absolute creation, inherited from Hebrew faith, stands for personal action. Already biology has abandoned the mechanical interpretation of evolution; such phrases as 'purposive tendency' and 'latent directivity', at once logical self-contradictions and practical confessions, are half-way houses on the road to a franker acknowledgement of personal action. One eminent scientist, Professor J. A. Thomson, has boldly confessed that 'evolution is a series of great inventions'. Dr. Robinson

pleads urgently for a final abandonment of the refusal 'to trace the presence of a transcendent purpose working by methods which allow for liberty within the boundaries of law'.

(2) *Colossians* takes us a long step farther. The Hebrew belief in absolute creation is not only confirmed by Christ; it is concentrated in Christ. The transcendent purpose is revealed in a triumphant personality. The philosophical conception of the synthesis of causes is realized in the personal sovereignty of Christ. Not only has God liberty of action within the realm of a natural law which is the expression of His own mind. Christ is the living revelation of the character and purpose of that law. If for man 'love is the fulfilling' of the moral law, for God 'love is the fulfilling' of natural law. And the law of divine love, if we may so describe the divine purpose enpressed in the laws of nature, means liberty for the life of man; he walks erect in a world of which Christ is at once the saviour and the sovereign, the centre and the significance.

(3) *Colossians* lays implicit stress upon the dependence of spiritual progress upon the 'fullness' of Christ, i.e. upon the identity of the historic Christ with the eternal Christ. Dr. Robinson rightly doubts whether modernist Christology is justified in laying stress upon the humanitarian aspect of the person of Christ on the ground that 'we should start from and define everything in the terms of the things we know best'. He calls attention to the assurance of the philosophers 'that what we know first and most intimately is the fact of the spiritual reality'; and he quotes appropriately the remark of John Caird that 'it is of the very nature of the moral and spiritual life that its ideal is not a finite one—our aim as spiritual beings is not likeness to man but likeness to God, participation in a divine and eternal life'. This is precisely the point of St. Paul's teaching in *Colossians*. The spiritual progress of the Christian life is not represented there as consisting in the moral effort of imitation of the example of the earthly life of Jesus Christ. That *imitatio Christi* has its place in St. Paul's idea of the Christian life, e.g. Rom. xv. 3, 1 Th. i. 6, 1 Cor. xi. 1, though when he pleads the example of Christ as a motive for humility (Phil. ii. 5) or for generosity (2 Cor. viii. 9), it is not the example of His behaviour on earth but the example of His condescension in coming to live on earth—it is the example not of the human Christ but of the divine Christ. In Col. iii. 13 the duty of forgiveness is based not upon Christ's forgiveness of the penitents of the Gospel story, but upon His forgiveness of Christians, i.e. upon the atonement brought home to them when they were baptized into union with the Christ who died and rose again. Two things stand out clearly in

I 2

Colossians. (*a*) Spiritual progress is represented as resulting from a mystical experience, the experience of communion with the ascended Christ who is also immanent in the hearts of the faithful. It lies not in the following of a moral example, even of the example of the human or the divine life of Christ; it lies in the spiritual power of His presence. (*b*) The 'fullness' of Christ is not merely the wealth of instruction and inspiration that lie in the Christ of the Gospels; it is the whole power and love of God which dwell in Christ as they have dwelt in Him from all eternity. The 'historic Christ' is not ignored; but He is regarded as the historical revelation of an eternal Christ.

(4) If a humanitarian Christology is ruled out by *Colossians*, so is a merely sociological Christianity. The philosophical doctrine of the 'priority of the whole' is certainly in harmony with St. Paul's insistence upon the fellowship of the Body as the ultimate motive of personal conduct and the necessary condition of individual progress; but the ruling factor is the peace of Christ (Col. iii. 15). 'For St. Paul it was not enough to win assent to a general principle of corporate living. For him all that was vital in applied Christianity depended upon holding not only the Body but the Head' (Robinson, p. 60). This fundamental truth needs continually restating in an age of diffused Christianity, in which the leaven of Christian thought and life has lost its distinctness in the social mass which it has leavened, and society is content with a more or less Christian public opinion which has forgotten that its original source is the Christian faith. If Christian ideas and influences are to be maintained in their purity and their power, they must not only be corrected or confirmed by constant reference to their historical origin as it stands embodied in the New Testament; they must be refreshed and renewed by conscious communion with their living Source. Social reform depends upon spiritual regeneration. The kingdom of God depends upon the recognition of Christ as not merely the Law but the Lord of all life. And that is the central truth of the Epistle to the Colossians.

IX

THEOSOPHY AND CHRISTIANITY

SCIENCE is becoming more and more modest and hesitant on matters of thought as distinct from knowledge—more and more sceptical of its own adequacy as an interpretation of 'reality'—more and more conscious that its results, apart from their utilitarian value, are but materials for philosophy to weave into a world-view

(*Weltanschauung*) or world-theory (*Weltgedanke*). Modern Theosophy claims to be at once a science and a philosophy. This twofold claim lies outside the scope of this book, which is concerned with the claim, disavowed by theosophists but undeniably implied in its principles, to be the true interpretation of Christianity and all religions. Yet it is probable that its present vogue is largely due to its fascination as a philosophy of science and religion. It is coming to be recognized at last that the ordinary man, though he fights shy of the history or technique of philosophy, has none the less a philosophy of his own, in the sense of an idea of the world, as certainly as he has a theology in the sense of an idea of God. The rise and extension of strange creeds and cults are proof enough that all the time, while philosophy was regarded as a thing of indifference to the ordinary man, 'multitudes of people were thirsting for some kind of metaphysical explanation of the world, and were in danger of being carried off by theories and speculations of the weirdest description, if nothing stronger and saner could be provided for them' (A. W. Robinson, *The Christianity of the Epistles*, p. 47).

Despite their apparent novelty, these latter-day faiths are essentially ancient heresies in modern dress—conceptions of life and the world that made a bid for supremacy in late pagan and early Christian thought, and failed—theories of God and man that were tried and found wanting. Theosophy, New Thought, Christian Science, are thinly-disguised pantheism; they efface or obscure that ultimate distinction between God and man which is the very essence of religion. They mistake the undeniable affinity and correspondence between divine and human nature for an identity which is to be realized at last in some form of absorption of the human individual into the divine absolute. At the same time Theosophy illustrates the affinity between pantheism and polytheism which is so characteristic of the Indian thought-world to which modern Theosophy so clearly owes its origin or its substance. Its nebulous impersonal Absolute leaves the universe devoid of personality, and the void is filled with an array of divine *Logoi* (or emanations from the Absolute) and semi-divine hierarchs, which is virtually a new polytheism. *Colossians* provides a final answer and an effective antidote to all such fantastic errors. It presents a Christian mysticism in which the personality of God, the unique supremacy of Christ, the intimate union of the soul with God in Christ, the corrective and confirmatory influence of the corporate life of the Church, are all asserted in their rightful places and in their true relation to each other; and withal the Christian soul retains the distinct existence which is vital to any rational idea of moral responsibility and spiritual perfection. *Colossians* in fact contains all the elements of a philosophy of Christian mysticism.

It is impossible to miss or to mistake the resemblance between the Colossian heresy and the teaching of modern theosophy. Colossianism claimed to be a 'philosophy'; the term 'theosophy', had it been already current, would have been even more appropriate. The resemblance between this early theosophy and its modern counterpart is manifold. There is a resemblance in their origins. Both are invasions of eastern ideas into western minds. Colossianism was an early phase of the Gnosticism which endeavoured to capture first Greek thought and then the Christian faith and to fuse them into a world-view based on the two Oriental conceptions of the evil nature of matter and the redemption of the soul by knowledge. Theosophy is a revival, and a reclothing in modern garb, of a later phase of Gnosticism. Its fundamental idea is the underlying unity of all faiths, an idea which rests upon the constant mistaking of incidental resemblances for essential identity; but its basic conceptions are predominantly Oriental, and in particular Indian, e. g. the impersonality of the Absolute, the law of *karma* (i. e. the quasi-physical law of the consequences of moral action), and the doctrine of reincarnation.

There is a corresponding resemblance in the character of the two movements. They are not indeed exact counterparts or complete parallels. Colossianism includes a Judaistic element derived from its immediate environment. Theosophy is far more comprehensive and systematic, more deliberate in its syncretism, and more historical in its claims. But they are essentially alike in their general principles and in their spiritual outlook. Both exalt secret knowledge above simple faith. Both make the acquisition of this knowledge dependent upon a personal illumination gained by ascetic or mystic discipline. Both claim to be a superior type or a truer interpretation of the Christian religion. Both claim to give access to a spiritual hierarchy of guardians and communicators of secret truths. Both owe their attractive power to the fascination that exists 'in daring novelties of intellectual speculation, and the more so when these are combined with rules and disciplines that promise to lead to mystical illumination' (Robinson, *The Christianity of the Epistles*, p. 49). Both pride themselves on their higher spirituality, and by a strange nemesis upon self-chosen paths of salvation end in a relapse into subtle materialism. The Colossian teachers through 'their constant preoccupation with the thought of the malignity of matter' sought relief and deliverance in practices that were more physical than spiritual. Theosophical teachers through their theories of human nature as a series of subtle bodies functioning on different etheric planes come to explain sacramental grace, the working of prayer, the influence of consecrated things and places, by theories of floating thought-forms and magnetic vibrations.

The Theosophical Society represents a vigorous revival of ancient and medieval mystical and occult philosophies. The rediscovery of the teaching of Oriental religions, the realization of latent psychical powers in human nature, the revolt against exclusivism and traditionalism in some current forms of Christian theology, the recognition of the continuity of human evolution—all these factors have combined to create a demand for a more complete synthesis of all knowledge and belief. Modern Theosophy offers to supply this demand. The stated objects of the Society—(1) 'to form a nucleus of the universal brotherhood of humanity without distinction of race, creed, sex, caste or colour', (2) 'to encourage the study of comparative religion, philosophy and science', (3) 'to investigate the unexplained laws of nature and the powers latent in man'—contain nothing in itself incompatible with loyalty to the faith of Christendom and the authority of the Church. At one point only would St. Paul have demurred to the definition of brotherhood; and that is the significant addition of 'creed' to the distinctions which are to be ignored. St. Paul's idea of universal brotherhood has for its key-note 'Christ is all and in all' (Col. iii. 11). For Theosophy Christ is not the keystone of human unity. To the Christ of Theosophy we shall have occasion to return later. Here it is sufficient to note that the greatest caution is necessary in reading theosophical literature. Theosophists use the language of Christian adoration, but in senses which are not those of the Christian faith; their language sounds so Christian that their disciples fail to recognize how far they are being carried from the Christian position. St. Paul's warnings to the Colossians (i. 23, ii. 4, 8) might well be repeated to Christians fascinated by the attractions of theosophical teaching. The Theosophical Society indeed disclaims any authoritative or obligatory body of teaching or any official identification with the views propounded by its leaders. But its literature contains a large amount of common positive teaching which embodies a definite and distinctive view of the universe, and it avows that 'its mission is to spread these truths in every land', not only 'the basic truths' of 'the immanence of God and the solidarity of man' but also the 'secondary teachings' which are 'the common teachings of all religions, living or dead', including *karma* and reincarnation. We are justified therefore in describing and discussing as 'Theosophy' teaching not merely published but pushed by the Society.

We are not concerned here with Theosophy in all its aspects, but only with those features which come within the scope of the teaching of St. Paul in *Colossians*. For the examination of theosophical teaching in all its contents and bearings the reader will find guidance in the bibliography appended to this introduction.

1. The 'traditions of men' play a dominant part in the sphere of theosophical authority. It is scarcely improper to add 'the traditions of women', for the latest cleavage in the ranks of theosophists has broken out along the lines of adhesion to the teaching of Madame Blavatsky or of Mrs. Besant, both prophetesses being clothed by their respective adherents with an almost papal infallibility. But in the background of their dogmatic expositions of the secrets of life there hover mysterious figures known as Mahatmas or Masters, a shadowy apostolate of reincarnate sages of the East who have been behind the scenes, 'divine teachers, superhuman men, often called the White Brotherhood'. For them reincarnation is no longer a necessary and compulsory stage in their own evolution, but a voluntary sacrifice for the elevation of humanity. Meanwhile they constitute the Occult Hierarchy, creating and sending forth thought-forms to be absorbed and given out again by men of genius, and working in conjunction with the Angels of the Nations in the guiding of human affairs. St. Paul's answer to the Colossian adepts is a valid answer to all such appeals to occult tradition. The substance of the Christian faith rests indeed upon tradition in the first instance till experience verifies and replaces tradition; but it is not the jealously guarded tradition of the results of speculative or intuitional penetration into the secrets of the universe—it is the open tradition of apostolic witness to the facts of an historic Life lived among men and to the spiritual significance of those facts. Nowhere in *Colossians* or in any other epistles is there any suggestion or confirmation of the idea of a body of secret teaching derived from a succession of seers and sages, known only to an inner circle of initiates who by a course of mystic discipline have been enabled to quit their physical bodies and in their astral bodies to visit Tibet and there make the acquaintance and receive the approval of the Grand White Lodge.

2. Colossianism seems to have shared with the prevalent mystery-cults something of an esoteric character. Its advocates prided themselves on the possession of mystical knowledge or on the pursuance of a mystical life, superior to the ordinary level of common Christianity, and apparently drew a distinction between the plain believer content therewith or confined thereto and the perfect disciple who

shared with them these higher mysteries. Theosophy claims similarly that it has an esoteric wisdom to reveal to an esoteric circle of disciples—that it holds the key to the inner meaning of the Christian religion as of all other religions, but can only place the key in the hands of the few who submit to a course of mystical training. For that purpose branches of the Theosophical Society advertise 'Secret Teaching Study Classes'. The whole idea is in plain contradiction to St. Paul's teaching. He insists indeed on the impossibility of understanding the deeper significance of the Christian faith without some measure of spiritual desire and capacity (see note on 'perfection' on p. 277); but he gives not the faintest hint of the existence of a body of truths hidden behind the truths that he is unfolding in his epistles for all to hear and read. He lays stress upon the fact that the whole Christian faith is meant for each and all. His insistence upon this fact is so plain that Mrs. Besant is driven to sheer perversion of his language in defence of her theory. She quotes Col. i. 26 in proof of the existence of a secret mystery behind the ordinary preaching of the Gospel, and to get her proof explains the passage thus: 'the mystery . . . now made manifest to His saints—not to the world, nor even to Christians, but only to the Holy Ones'—apparently unaware that 'saints' in the New Testament means Christians in general. But it is not a question of isolated texts. *Colossians* itself is a plain refutation of theosophical esotericism. It lays the higher Christology open before the whole Colossian congregation; it points them all to the mystical life of union with Christ; and it nowhere hints at a deeper truth or a higher life reserved for a select few.

3. Theosophy, like every other gnosticism or syncretism ancient or modern, stands or falls by the place which it assigns to Christ.

(a) The Colossian heresy appears to have virtually dethroned Christ from His unique position as the Son of God and the Saviour of mankind. If it did not actually merge Him into the hierarchy of angelic beings or celestial powers, it obscured or impaired His supremacy by recognizing in them collateral agencies in cosmic and human destiny. Theosophy, despite its repudiation of any conflict with the Christian faith, strikes at the heart of that faith by its equation of Christ with 'other Masters'. Krishna stands on the same shelf with Christ in theosophical bookstores. The early Christians died rather than see Christ admitted to a gallery of more or less divine gods. St. Paul sees in Christ not a Master but the Master—not one of many emanations of divinity but the one and only personal revelation of God in the history of humanity. He is not concerned in *Colossians* to state the grounds of this belief; it is itself the established ground on which he bases his protest against any tendency to look elsewhere for communion with God.

(b) Theosophy teaches that 'the Jesus Christ of the Churches' is a fusion of three distinct elements—historical, mythical, and mystical. It denies the identity of Jesus Christ. 'The historical Christ is a glorious being belonging to the great spiritual hierarchy that guides the spiritual evolution of humanity, who used for three years the human body of the disciple Jesus.' This Jesus was a Jew born in 105 B.C., so 'the occult records' indicate, and trained in the occult lore of the East in Egyptian and Essene brotherhoods until the time came for him to lend his body for the incarnation of a Supreme Teacher. Mrs. Besant apparently adopts the strange gnostic interpretation which saw in the descent of the Spirit after the baptism of Jesus the entry of the Christ into the body of Jesus, and in the cry of desolation upon the Cross the departure of Christ from Jesus. Afterwards, while the Christ 'visited His disciples for something over fifty years in His subtle spiritual body . . . training them in a knowledge of occult truths', the man Jesus 'perfected his human evolution' and 'became the Lord and Master of the Church founded by the Christ'. At the present time Jesus, 'clothed in a body he has taken from Syria, is waiting the time for his reappearance in the open life of men'; meanwhile 'he lives mostly in the mountains of Lebanon'. Instead of the one Jesus Christ, God and man, Theosophy gives us two persons, a Christ who is divine but not God, and a Jesus promoted from humanity to quasi-divinity. This separation of Christ from Jesus is a flagrant contradiction of the plain story of the Gospels and the plain language of the Epistles. It is absolutely irreconcilable with the history of Christian experience and thought. All the controversies over the question whether Christ is divine, and in what sense He is divine, have arisen out of the very unity which Theosophy denies, the unity of the Person whose nature was in question; the very difficulty of reconciling the two elements so unmistakably and yet so inexplicably blended, the human and the divine, arose out of the undeniable identity and unity of the Person in whom they were so blended. It is destructive of the unity of Christian hope and effort; to which is that hope and effort to look, to Jesus or to the Christ? It is fatal to any coherent and consistent interpretation of those uniquely valuable evidences of the faith of the early Church, the first written documents extant of the history of Christianity, viz. the epistles of St. Paul. Is he speaking of two persons or of one, and if two, then of which of the two in this or that particular sentence? It is doubtful whether the strange gnostic interpretation of the gospel story mentioned above was current as early as A.D. 60 and might therefore have been adopted by the Colossian heresiarchs. It would surely in that case have been confronted and refuted by St. Paul. But it is obvious from *Colossians*, as from earlier epistles also, that it was a freak of gnostic fancy entirely alien to the faith which St. Paul held and taught. He refers to 'Christ' or to 'Jesus' indifferently as one and the same person; 'the Christ' has almost ceased to be a title and become a name like 'Jesus'; or he combines the two in one designation, 'our Lord Jesus Christ' or 'the Christ who is Jesus the Lord'. There is no break in unity or continuity between the Son who is the eternal image of God and the Christ in whom the fullness of the Godhead dwells 'in bodily wise', and who died 'in the body of His flesh'—whose 'afflictions' were as real an experience as the 'sufferings' of the Apostle which were their sequel and completion—whose claim upon human love and loyalty lay in the fact that He was both the Creator and the Crucified, both the conqueror of death and the communicator of a new life for soul and body.

(c) The 'historical Christ' thus wrenched away from anything more than a temporary association with the Jesus of the Gospel is however only one of three Christs in the teaching of Theosophy. There is also a 'mythical Christ' and a 'mystical Christ'. The 'mythical Christ' means that the cardinal facts embodied in Christian creeds and holy days, the Incarnation, the Crucifixion, the Resurrection, the Ascension, were not historical facts but myths attached to 'the Christ of the Church' as they had been attached to similar beings in earlier religions. 'The mystical Christ' is the truth symbolized by the myth. The Christ-myth fused with the story of Jesus represents the descent of the divine Word into matter in creation and the sacrifice and crucifixion thus involved for the spiritual by its association with the material. At the same time it represents the birth and ascent of the human Christ, the higher self of man, a self-evolution of the divine element in man, typified by the gospel allegory but independent of any actual Christ of history. This fantastic mysticism is refuted once and for all by the Christian mysticism of St. Paul. There is indeed a mystical Christ in *Colossians*, the Christ of the Church and the soul, but He is not the personification of the mind of the Church, nor the deification of the inner self of the soul, but the transcendent Christ, ascended and exalted and enthroned, whose Spirit is the life of His Body the Church, and whose Presence is the life of each and all of His members. For St. Paul the Christ-life in man is always and everywhere dependent upon the reality and objectivity both of the redemption wrought by the Incarnation and of the present activity of the ascended Christ. The 'Christ in you' who is 'the hope of glory' is not the higher self of the Colossian Christian but the union of that self with the Christ who is for ever distinct from the Christian in whom He dwells and who dwells in Him.

(d) Theosophy in denying the uniqueness of the Person of Christ also denies the universality of the Christian revelation. It teaches that beneath the exoteric form of all religions there lay and still lies the same esoteric body of essential truths—that the Christianity of the Churches is only the exoteric form of the Christian religion—and that the mission of Theosophy is to reveal and restore the lost esoteric truths of this and every religion. Theosophy therefore consistently discounts and discourages the missionary claim of Christianity, for it denies that Christianity has anything essential to give which is not already contained in the esoteric truths of other religions. In India, its true home and its recognized head-quarters, Theosophy is, as Bishop Copleston said, 'virtually an anti-Christian mission'. The Rev. Dr. Horton, who had been impressed by the Order of the Star in the East and had preached in recognition of its testimony to the Second Coming of Christ, was so convinced of its real character by what he saw in India that he published in the Indian press a repudiation of his first impressions. 'Theosophy', he wrote, 'is a subtle form of denial that Christ is the Saviour of the world. . . . There is no middle course. Christ is all or nothing.' That is the essential message of *Colossians*. Already 'the truth of the gospel' was 'bearing fruit in all the world', because it was the gospel of an actual Saviour in whom centred the sovereignty of all creation, in whom lay hidden 'all the treasures of wisdom and knowledge', in whom all races and ranks of humanity were finding all that they needed and wanted, in whom mankind would realize its true unity, a Saviour who was 'all and in all'. The anti-Christian attitude of Theosophy represents the extreme recoil of modern thought from the older view which saw little or no truth in non-Christian religions. That view is essentially foreign to the Christian faith and has long ceased to dominate Christian missionary thought. Theosophy says that the faiths of the world are 'only so many different dialects of one Catholic language'. The Christian Church stands for the belief that truth and life in religion everywhere have come and are coming still through the Word at work in the world, but that all races and peoples need the fuller truth and life which can only come from conscious knowledge of the Word made flesh, the historical Christ who was and is the Son of God.

4. Subtlest perhaps of all the dangers of Theosophy is its offer to give us an irrefutable inner knowledge of Christ in compensation for

the uncertainty resulting from destructive historical criticism of the New Testament. There is something very gnostic about this depreciation of the historic element in Christianity. It is the counterpart of the gnostic depreciation of the material world. Both are foreign to the Christian faith. There is an objective element in Christian faith and life which is essential to Christianity. St. Paul's deepest mysticism in *Colossians* is rooted in historic fact. His philosophy of life is based on the central facts of the life of Christ, on the reality of the Crucifixion and the Resurrection. Historical fact is not a transient stage in Christian faith; it is the permanent basis of faith. The facts of Christ's life were the origin of the Christian Church; the knowledge of those facts is the origin of the Christian life of the individual in every age. Historical fact again is essential to the sacramental life of the Church. The sacraments are at once the reminder of historical facts in the life of Christ and the embodiment or the instrument of the spiritual forces of His heavenly life. They are the joint consecration of the historical and the material in the spiritual sphere. Theosophy philosophizes about the sacraments, sometimes in a curiously materialistic fashion; but it tends in practice to dispense with their use, because of their apparent foundation in crude belief in bare historical facts. That is why Theosophy, like Gnosticism, can never become the religion of mankind in general. It is a religion of intellectualism. The Christian religion meets the wants of all just because in creed and sacrament alike it combines the emotional and the intellectual with the historical elements of faith. What we think and feel about God is based on what we know that He has done and is doing for us in Christ. The reason why the ancient mystery-cults from Orpheism to Mithraism failed and faded away before the presence of the Christian faith was that the Christian faith was based not on fancy but on fact. *Colossians* illustrates also one other aspect of the relation between fact, faith, and life. Its first half is concerned with the relation between the Christian faith and the fact of Christ; its second half is concerned with the working out of the life created and supported by that faith. Ideas are only permanently fruitful in action when they have their ultimate source in fact; the further they move away in mystical self-propagation, the more sterile they become in all that can stimulate moral effort and guide practical duty.

When therefore the modern Gnostic offers to come to the aid of a distressed Christianity with the assurance that even if the facts of the Gospel prove to be historically untrue our faith can rest unshaken on the basis of the mystical Christ of the higher human self, we cannot but regard with suspicion such an argument coming from the lips of those who are playing fast and loose with the language of the New Testament. The mystical Christ of the Church and the soul, the Christ of our communions and our daily life, is not a substitute for the truth but a consequence of the truth of the historical Christ. The Christ who lives within us is the presence of the one eternal Christ who came in the fullness of time to live amongst men as man, and who now reigns over men, our Lord, our Saviour, and our God.

5. The attraction of Theosophy for many thoughtful Christian minds lies largely in its presentation of Christian faith and life as a quest. Christian faith is indeed a quest for truth yet to be revealed no less than a grasp of truth already revealed. St. Paul would have sympathized with such a spirit of quest. But for him the quest is not absorbed and dissipated in an attempt to seize and unite the fragments of partial truth scattered up and down the world in all the cults and myths and faiths which have ever expressed the desires and the guesses of the human mind. For him the quest is centred in the pursuit of a life of union with a living Lord in whom there lie waiting for our realization all the treasures of wisdom and knowledge, all that sages and seers have ever longed to know and hoped to find. The Christian faith is not one more contribution to the search for truth; it is the consummation and reconciliation of all truth. Jesus Christ is not a successful seeker after God; He is himself the living answer to all seekers. All spiritual knowledge lies in union with Him. The true significance of all secular knowledge lies in that union less directly but no less definitely. The world of nature and humanity will yield its inmost secrets only to those seekers who hold the clue, and the clue is the certainty that Christ Himself, as the original source of the universe, is also the ultimate secret of its unity. The Christian faith is the revelation that guides and crowns all truly scientific research.

At the same time it must be confessed that Theosophy by the very success of its propaganda is calling attention to a want which the Church has not met. The Church has provided the simple and definite doctrinal teaching required by the common needs of all souls. But it has not provided so fully for the needs of such souls as are deeply conscious of the mystery into which all known truths shade off and of the fascinating and perplexing questions on which Bible and Creed leave speculation free. There is a lesson to be learned here from the two lines on which the great early Christian teachers met and answered the gnostic theosophy of their day. Like Tertullian and Irenaeus, we must insist on the plain meaning of Scripture and the unity and continuity of the historic faith of Christendom. But also, like Clement and Origen, we ought fearlessly to claim all life and learning as food for Christian thought, and develop what might be called a true Christian theosophy, embracing the spiritual experiences of poets, saints, and mystics, and reverently speculating beyond the borders of revelation, so long as we hold fast to the historic facts of the Creed and to the sacramental communion of the Church. *Colossians* itself is a challenge to such an effort. It soars into regions where perhaps many a Colossian Christian might well fail to keep pace with the thought of the Apostle, and where certainly many modern Christians have never tried or have failed to find their way. Except for a few texts or phrases, the doctrinal portion of the epistle is unfamiliar and even unintelligible to ordinary readers. Yet it is not merely the answer to the fantastic imaginations of modern theosophy; it is the answer to the tentative approaches of modern philosophy towards a religious interpretation of the universe. This introduction will have more than fulfilled the purpose and hope of its writing if it leads and helps some parish priests to unfold to thoughtful congregations the significance of an epistle which has a message of peculiar value in days like our own, when Eastern and Western thought, philosophy and religion, are once again in contact as they were in the first century of the Christian era, and are seeking a reconciliation which shall give unity to all life. Christianity is primarily a life based upon a faith, but it is also a philosophy, and it holds the key to the reconciliation of all truth. The first necessity is that Christians should understand their own religion better. No wiser advice could be given than was given at the close of the report of the 1920 Lambeth Conference Committee on the Christian Faith in relation to Spiritualism, Christian Science, and Theosophy. 'The Committee, while pleading for a larger place to be given in the teaching of the Church to the mystical elements of faith and life, desire earnestly to advise all thinking people to safeguard their Christian position by making the fullest study and use of the treasures of knowledge to be found in Bible, Creed and Sacrament, as they have been interpreted by sound Christian scholarship and philosophy.'

X

FRIENDS AND FELLOW-WORKERS OF ST. PAUL

1. *Timothy.*

Various friends and fellow-workers of St. Paul were intimate enough to win a word of warm commendation at the close of an epistle and to have their kindly messages sent along with his own. Timothy alone is associated with St. Paul in the opening address of

Colossians and its pendant *Philemon*. In *Romans* and *Ephesians* the Apostle's name stands alone, appropriately enough in epistles which are almost treatises rather than letters. When St. Paul wrote *1 Corinthians*, Timothy was himself at Corinth or on his way thither. In *Galatians* 'all the brethren with me' are included in the opening address. In *Thessalonians* (1 and 2) Silvanus (Silas) and Timothy, so often together on missions with or for the Apostle, are mentioned in that order, Silas coming first as the fellow-evangelist, and Timothy second as the attendant of the Apostle. In *2 Corinthians*, *Philippians*, *Colossians* and *Philemon* Timothy alone is associated with St. Paul.

Timothy appears first at Lystra, his home then, if not his birthplace. His father was a Greek. His mother Eunice (2 Tim. i. 5), 'a believing Jewess' (Acts xvi. 1–3), and her mother or her husband's mother Lois had taught the boy to love the Old Testament from his infancy (2 Tim. iii. 15) before they heard the Gospel. Timothy was already 'a disciple' on Paul's second visit; perhaps he and his mother and grandmother were among the fruits of St. Paul's earlier mission there (Acts xiv. 8–23). The Christians of Lystra and Iconium spoke well of the lad, and St. Paul, impressed by the early promise of his discipleship and perhaps attracted already to the lad himself, decided to adopt him to the companionship forfeited by John Mark. To adopt as his personal attendant a youth who (probably owing to the fact that his father was a Greek) had never been circumcised might give offence to the local Jews and perhaps create a difficulty in the way of his mission; and St. Paul circumcised him, a striking example of his principle of conciliation without compromise (1 Cor. ix. 19–23).

Timothy was soon promoted to higher service than personal attendance. He was not arrested with Paul and Silas at Philippi. Silas was a fellow-evangelist of the Apostle; Timothy was still in the background among 'them that ministered unto' the Apostle (cp. Acts xix. 22). When St. Paul was hurried away by sea from danger at Beroea by the anxiety of Christian friends, Silas and Timothy were left behind. From Acts xviii. 5 it would seem that they rejoined St. Paul at Corinth; but from 1 Th. iii. 2, 6 it is evident that the reunion took place at Athens (cp. Acts xvii. 15, 16), for Timothy was sent thence on a confidential mission to Thessalonica to see how the Thessalonian Christians were faring under persecution. On his return to Corinth he shared with St. Paul and Silas the preaching of 'the Son of God, Jesus Christ' (2 Cor. i. 19).[1] It is probable, though not certain, that he

---

[1] Silas disappears after *2 Corinthians*. He may have felt that the deepening intimacy between Timothy and the Apostle left no further need or room for his own presence; or he may have felt the call of work in other directions, perhaps

accompanied Paul from Corinth to Jerusalem and Antioch, and on his next journey westwards to Ephesus. From Ephesus he was sent with Erastus on a mission to Macedonia (Acts xix. 22), apparently to prepare the way for St. Paul's intended visit there. On this same journey or on a separate occasion Timothy was sent to Corinth (1 Cor. iv. 17) as the Apostle's 'beloved and faithful child in the Lord', to remind the Corinthians of his 'ways in the Lord', i.e. the standards of faith and life which the Apostle had upheld and applied there 'as everywhere in every church'. The letter was probably sent direct to Corinth by sea, while Timothy was working his way round through Macedonia; and the Apostle bespeaks for him a reception which will encourage him to deal fearlessly with the religious situation at Corinth. Nobody is to 'despise him' as a youngster or a subordinate, 'for he worketh the work of the Lord, as I also do'. Cp. Rom. xvi. 21, where, writing from Corinth, either to Rome or perhaps to Ephesus, Paul calls him 'my fellow-worker'. On his last journey to Jerusalem Paul was accompanied by Timothy at least 'as far as Asia' (Acts xx. 4).

Timothy next appears in attendance upon St. Paul at Rome. The Apostle was anxious for news of his people at Philippi, and hoped to send Timothy in search of this encouragement. Such an errand called for a man of unselfish sympathy and unstinted devotion. Timothy was his choice. 'I have no man like-minded who will care truly for your state.' The Greek word for *like-minded* cannot mean 'so dear unto me' (A.V. mg.) nor 'sharing my outlook', but only 'with a heart like his'. The Greek word for *truly* may also mean *naturally* (A.V.) or *genuinely* (R.V.). The corresponding adjective is used of Timothy in 1 Tim. i. 2, 'my *true* child in faith', or less accurately with A.V. 'my own son in the faith'. All three meanings are required to do justice to the word: 'with the same natural devotion, inherited from the apostle, his spiritual father' (McNeile, *St. Paul*, p. 238). In confirmation of this tribute St. Paul appeals confidently to the Philippians' own experience of Timothy. 'Ye know the proof of him, that as a child serveth a father, so he served with me in furtherance of the Gospel' (Phil. iii. 19–22).

The training of Timothy culminated in his pastorate over the Church at Ephesus. Its date and duration are vexed questions of historical criticism beyond the scope of this sketch. It may have been a temporary charge pending the expected return of St. Paul (1 Tim. i. 3, iii. 14, 15); or it may have been a sort of apostolic dele-

---

in special devotion to missionary work among his Jewish countrymen. He was associated later with St. Peter (1 Pet. v. 12).

K

gacy, a stage in the transition from apostolate to episcopate. Tradition makes Timothy the first bishop of Ephesus. It was certainly episcopal in its responsibilities; they included the direction of the order of worship (1 Tim. ii. 1 ff.), the admission of bishops (presbyters) and deacons (1 Tim. iii. 1–13), the oversight of the widows of the Church (1 Tim. v.) and the preservation of true doctrine and right discipline in general. In 1 Tim. iv. 14 St. Paul refers to some kind of ordination. (a) There was a gift of God for the work (cp. 2 Tim. i. 6, 7, 'a spirit of power and of love and of discipline'). (b) This gift was given 'by prophecy' (cp. 1 Tim. i. 18, 'the prophecies which went before on thee', R.V. mg. 'which led the way to thee'), apparently the inspired testimony of the 'prophets' of the Church in approval of his selection, or their exhortation of the minister-elect, in the latter case the prototype of the modern ordination sermon. (c) The gift was given through the laying on of the hands of the Apostle (2 Tim. i. 6) and of the presbytery, the 'elders' of the Church (1 Tim. iv. 14). Bishop Chase (*Confirmation in the Apostolic Age*, pp. 35–41) gives weighty reasons for regarding 2 Tim. i. 6, 7 as a reference to the confirmation of Timothy by St. Paul on his first visit to Lystra. In any case 1 Tim. iv. 14 is clearly his ordination. But it is uncertain whether this took place (1) on his appointment as assistant to St. Paul at Lystra, or (2) on his commissioning as St. Paul's deputy, either at Ephesus when St. Paul was leaving for Macedonia or at Rome before Timothy's departure for Ephesus. The balance of probability is in favour of the later commission. The earlier appointment at Lystra was scarcely formal or important enough to require a solemn rite. And the language of 1 Tim. i. 18, iv. 14 seems clearly to relate to his entry upon his present work at Ephesus.

Timothy had his weaknesses. He was frequently sick (1 Tim. v. 23), and naturally timid and hesitant (cp. the reference to his fear in 1 Cor. xvi. 10). No surer proof of the authenticity of the Pastoral Epistles could be found than the frankness of their references to his temptations and dangers—see 1 Tim. iv. 7, 12, 14, v. 21, 22, vi. 20, 2 Tim. i. 6–8, ii. 1–3, 16, 22—'a shrinking from opposition and hardship, a want of strength in the exercise of his authority, a need of warning against youthful lusts, and perhaps a tendency to pay to erroneous doctrines and ideas more attention than they deserved' (McNeile, *St. Paul*, p. 242). Yet to St. Paul he is not merely 'my beloved child' (2 Tim. i. 2), and 'my own son in the faith' (1 Tim. i. 2 A.V.) but 'my true child in faith' (1 Tim. i. 2 R.V.); throughout he has not only the affection but the confidence of his spiritual father and apostolic chief. When the prospect of martyrdom is in sight, the Apostle craves in that last crisis the happiness and support of the companionship of his son and servant in the Gospel (2 Tim. iv. 9). The desire was fulfilled. It seems to have brought Timothy into peril. The writer of *Hebrews* tells his readers that 'our brother Timothy has been set at liberty' (xiii. 23), or perhaps 'acquitted', and that he hopes to come with Timothy to see them. Nothing else is known of this imprisonment or trial; it may have been at Rome after the martyrdom of St. Paul or later at Ephesus; nor again of Timothy's association or acquaintance with the unknown apostolic writer of *Hebrews*. Tradition states that after a long episcopate he was martyred at Ephesus in an attempt to hold the people back from the wild orgies of a local pagan festival, and that his remains found a final resting-place at Constantinople. He is remembered in the Greek and Armenian Churches on 22 January, in the Coptic on 23 January, in the earlier Latin calendars on 27 September and in the later on 24 January. It was a strange oversight that omitted from the many welcome new names in the Calendar of the Revised Prayer Book of 1927–8 the name of the nearest and dearest of the friends and fellow-workers of St. Paul.

2. *Tychicus.*

There are three stages in the association of Tychicus with St. Paul.

(1) Towards the end of the third missionary journey the news of a Jewish plot led St. Paul to abandon the voyage from Achaia direct to Syria and to return through Macedonia. At this point we are given a list of his companions, Acts xx. 4. Three belonged to Macedonia, viz. Sopater of Beroea and Aristarchus and Secundus of Thessalonica; four to Anatolia, viz. Gaius of Derbe, Timothy of Lystra, and two 'Asians', i.e. natives or residents of the Roman province of Asia, viz. Tychicus and Trophimus. Trophimus was an Ephesian, Acts xxi. 29; it is probable that Tychicus was too. The movements of the little band of friends are hard to follow in detail. A.V. and R.V. state that they went on in advance to Troas, where they waited for Paul and Luke. A variant text says simply that they came to Troas and waited there; this would be consistent with their having sailed from Achaia to Asia and then gone north to Troas. Such a journey would not be a waste of time, if they wanted to see friends in Asia, for St. Paul may have already made the decision not to call at Ephesus himself, Acts xx. 16. But the narrative reads as though they all went through Macedonia. They all apparently 'accompanied him into Asia', A.V. or 'as far as Asia', R.V. The latter rendering reads as though some of them at least may have

K 2

remained in 'Asia' when St. Paul pursued his voyage to Jerusalem. But some manuscripts omit 'as far as Asia' or 'into Asia', implying that they all went the whole way. Trophimus certainly went to Jerusalem, Acts xxi. 29; apparently Aristarchus, Acts xxvii. 2; and perhaps Tychicus, for the narrative gives the impression that he was a twin-friend of Trophimus. Tychicus has been identified with the 'earnest' brother mentioned in 2 Cor. viii. 22; but this is mere conjecture.

(2) Tychicus next appears in attendance upon St. Paul in his imprisonment, whether that was at Caesarea or at Rome. This seems a certain inference from his being sent to Colossae and to the churches to which *Ephesians* was addressed. 'I have sent' (Col. iv. 8) can scarcely mean that St. Paul had written to Tychicus asking him to go from some other place; and the personal message of information and encouragement entrusted to Tychicus implies that he was coming straight from St. Paul's side.

(3) Tychicus was in attendance on St. Paul in the second stage of his imprisonment. He had evidently returned from his mission to Asia; we can only regret that we have no record of the report that he brought back from Colossae of the effect produced by *Colossians*. In his appeal to Timothy to come to him at Rome without delay St. Paul adds that Luke is his only companion; he has sent Tychicus to Ephesus, 2 Tim. iv. 12. This can scarcely refer to the mission to Ephesus and Colossae with the epistles. It must have been a commission to take charge of the church at Ephesus and so set Timothy free to journey to Rome. When he wrote to Titus, St. Paul was intending to send either Artemas or Tychicus to Crete to relieve Titus and set him free to join the apostle at Nicopolis in Epirus, where he had decided to spend the winter. Evidently both Artemas and Tychicus were with St. Paul at Nicopolis or wherever he was at the time. The chronological order of the Pastoral Epistles is by no means certain, nor is the history of St. Paul's movements after his release from his first imprisonment. There is therefore some uncertainty as to the order of these two missions of Tychicus to Ephesus and to Crete. It is probable that the mission to Crete came first, if it was Tychicus and not Artemas that went, and that when he was sent to Ephesus, it was to enable Timothy to give all that St. Paul's dearest son in the faith could give to an apostle now facing the certainty of martyrdom. What does emerge clearly is that Tychicus has risen in the scale of spiritual service. First a welcome and helpful companion of a travelling and toiling apostle, then a trusted messenger who can explain to the Colossian Church the situation at Rome

and grasp the situation at Colossae, and finally an apostolic delegate who can safely be placed in charge of the missionary problems of Crete and the pastoral responsibilities of the Ephesian Church, he represents the fruits of an apostolic life which had given itself throughout not merely to the building of churches but to the training of leaders. St. Paul may or may not have observed and followed the Lord's plan of preaching to the crowd and then turning to the instruction and preparation of His apostles. He may or may not have deliberately faced the need of provision for the future leadership of the Church. In any case, taught by experience and led by opportunity, he did become a true *pastor pastorum*. Timothy, Titus, and Tychicus were a rich bequest to leave to orphaned churches. We cannot but regret that the apostle's martyrdom robbed Christendom of a third pastoral epistle, an epistle to Tychicus.

All certain knowledge of Tychicus ends with the New Testament. Late traditions attach him to St. Andrew after the passing of St. Paul, make him bishop of Colophon in Ionia or of Chalcedon in Bithynia, and state that he died a martyr's death.

3. *Aristarchus.*

There is no special word of commendation or note of intimacy in the reference to Aristarchus in Col. iv. 10 or in Phm. 24, where he is associated with Mark, Demas, and Luke and perhaps Epaphras as 'my fellow-workers'. But he was a frequent, if not constant, companion of St. Paul. A Macedonian (Acts xix. 29) and a Thessalonian (Acts xx. 4), he appears first at Ephesus along with Gaius as 'Paul's companions in travel'. They were seized by the crowd and hurried into the theatre, but apparently released by the town-clerk's pacification of the riot. On St. Paul's return from Achaia through Macedonia, Aristarchus and others awaited him at Troas, Acts xx. 4, 5. From the A.V. and R.V. text they seem to have come on in advance from Macedonia; they may have been with St. Paul all the way from Ephesus to Achaia and back thence to Macedonia. R.V. mg. *came* would be consistent with their having remained at Ephesus and travelled thence to Troas to meet St. Paul there. But the reference to their Macedonian homes in xx. 4 points rather to their having come on from Macedonia. That reference is probably due to the fact that they were delegates bearing the offerings of their home churches for the relief of the distressed churches of Palestine (1 Cor. xvi. 3, 4, 2 Cor. viii. 1-4, 18, 19).

His next appearance is at Caesarea, where he and the writer of this section of Acts (almost certainly Luke) embarked with St. Paul on the voyage to Rome. They are clearly distinguished from the prisoners, Acts xxvii. 1, 2. Perhaps they were given permission to accompany St. Paul by the kindly centurion in charge; or they may have offered and been allowed to accompany him in the capacity of slaves (Ramsay). The ship was to coast along Asia apparently to Adramyttium, its port of registry; thence the party would sail to Macedonia and travel by the great Egnatian road to the Adriatic. Hence perhaps the reference (Acts xxvii. 2) to Aristarchus as belonging to Thessalonica; he may have intended to return home. When the centurion seized the opportunity of a voyage direct from Myra to Rome by an Alexandrian wheat-ship, Aristarchus may have gone on homewards on the other ship, perhaps to report to the Macedonian churches upon his mission to Jerusalem as their delegate, and then rejoined the apostle at Rome; or he may have gone on with St. Paul. Ewald thinks that as a delegate of a Gentile church he must have been a Gentile. But the Gentile churches included Jewish members (Acts xvii. 4, 11–12, xviii. 8), and might well choose one of them to go to Jerusalem. Aristarchus seems clearly to be included with Mark and Jesus Justus in the description 'who are of the circumcision' (Col. iv. 11). Perhaps he was one of the 'some of them' (Jews) who 'were persuaded and consorted with Paul and Silas' at Thessalonica, Acts xvii. 4. Late traditions (5th cent.) make him (1) one of the seventy disciples, (2) bishop of Apamea in Phrygia (Greek tradition) or of Thessalonica (Roman martyrologies under Aug. 4), (3) a martyr beheaded at Rome along with Pudens and Trophimus at the same time as St. Paul—the only credible tradition of the three.

4. *Mark*.

The identity of the Mark who appears in the N.T. in three connexions and the author of the second gospel and the founder of the Alexandrian Church seems to be established beyond all reasonable doubt by the personal links of association with three apostles, Peter, Barnabas, and Paul, and by the earliest and soundest traditions of Church history. The guesses of later tradition and the vagaries of modern criticism need not be discussed here. Conjecture has identified Mark with the young man who fled naked from the scene of our Lord's arrest (Mk. xiv. 51–2), and with the son of the house where our Lord held the Last Supper. Here it must suffice to recall the most certain facts and the most probable explanations of the successive stages of his history.

He appears first as John Mark, a Jew with a Roman surname, the son of Mary, a Jewess of some social standing, whose house was the occasional home of a Christian congregation in Jerusalem and the scene of their intercession on the night of Peter's imprisonment (Acts xii. 12). During the famine of A.D. 45–6 Barnabas and Saul came to Jerusalem with relief funds from the Christians at Antioch. Barnabas was John Mark's cousin. Mark had perhaps rendered helpful and promising service in the administration of this relief. Barnabas and Saul took him with them to Antioch to help in the work there. When they went on their first missionary journey, John is mentioned in connexion with their preaching at Salamis in Cyprus (Acts xiii. 5). It has been suggested that the Greek should be rendered 'they had with them also John the synagogue minister', a reference perhaps to a subordinate office held by John at Jerusalem which may have made him specially helpful in their preaching in the synagogues of Cyprus (Chase in Hastings, *B.D.*, iii. 245). But the more obvious rendering is 'they had John also as their attendant' (A.V. 'minister'). The word denotes 'personal service, not evangelistic', including perhaps the baptizing of converts (cp. Acts x. 48; 1 Cor. i. 14), but chiefly arrangements for travel, board and lodging, messages and interviews, &c. (Swete, *St. Mark*, p. xii).

When they crossed to the mainland and decided to push into the interior, John left them and returned to Jerusalem. It must be remembered that he had not shared with them the call of the Spirit and the commission of the Church at Antioch, even if he had been present on that solemn occasion: 'he was an extra hand, taken by Barnabas and Saul on their own responsibility' (Ramsay, *St. Paul the Traveller*, p. 71). It is not clear whether he was taken from Antioch or picked up in Cyprus, the home of his cousin Barnabas, at the place where his presence is first noted. Perhaps he felt no obligation to face a more distant and dangerous campaign than had been definitely contemplated at the outset; perhaps he regarded the new departure as an intrusion into a sphere of missionary work into which Peter was probably proposing to advance direct from Antioch (Edmundson, *The Church in Rome*, p. 76); perhaps he simply yielded to the call of home and of duty to his mother. There is no hint of any resentment on the part of St. Paul at the time (Acts xiii. 13). Mark was apparently at work again at Antioch with the two apostles until the eve of their next missionary journey (Acts xv. 37). St. Paul proposed to St. Barnabas that they should visit the churches founded on their previous journey, but declined quite naturally to accept St. Barnabas's proposal to take Mark with them. The reason assigned for this refusal was that Mark had left them when they were facing the very journey on which those churches were founded. The result was 'a sharp contention' between the two comrades. It is possible that the contention was sharpened by the recent yielding of Barnabas to the reaction of the conservative Jewish Christians with the support of Peter (Gal. ii. 13)—a crisis in which Mark may have sided with his two older friends, or may even have himself influenced Barnabas (Chase, Hastings, *B.D.*, iii. 246). The surrender of Barnabas to the Judaistic party did not however prevent Paul from inviting him to join in the new missionary journey. He may have believed that the return to the opener air of the wider mission field would bring his friend back to the truer view of the freedom of the Gospel. The separation between the two friends was probably due mainly to the dispute over Mark. Paul found a new assistant in Silas; and Barnabas, who had either regarded Mark's withdrawal as justified or pardonable, or believed that he would yet make good, took him to Cyprus (Acts xv. 38–9), perhaps to gather the fruits of their earlier mission there, or to find a compensatory probation for the disappointed young missionary in fresh work in the island which was the home of Barnabas's own family (see note on Barnabas).

Ten or twelve years later Mark (the Jewish name disappears now) was at Rome with St. Paul. The interval may have been occupied with missionary labours in Egypt which gave rise to the tradition that Mark was the evangelist of Alexandria and the first bishop of the Alexandrian Church, a charge which he is said to have resigned in A.D. 61–2. It is possible that the proposal of Mark to visit Colossae should be placed at the end of his work in Cyprus, and was abandoned for the work in Egypt (Swete, *St. Mark*, p. xv). In that case St. Paul's message of commendation (the 'commandments' mentioned in Col. iv. 10) proves that Mark's early defection was already forgiven. That reference, however, reads as if the message was more recent (see note on Barnabas). What is certain is that, for whatever reason, Mark made his way to Rome about A.D. 61, either of his own initiative or at the suggestion of St Paul. 'A complete reconciliation took place, and the "attendant" of the first missionary journey became the "fellow-worker" of the Roman imprisonment' (Swete, l.c.). Any strict or narrow Judaic sympathies that Mark may have shown at Antioch had now vanished in the wider sympathies of the catholic conception of the kingdom of God. His personal devotion and his comradeship in service were now a tonic and a cordial (Col. iv. 11) to the Apostle amid the disappointments and disheartenment of his life in Rome, especially in view of Jewish indifference or opposition. Apparently Mark paid his contemplated visit to Colossae, and the Apostle felt his absence keenly. Writing to Timothy at Ephesus, he asks him to 'pick up Mark' and bring him to Rome; 'he is useful to me for ministering', 2 Tim. iv. 11. 'The reason here given assigns to Mark his precise place in the history of the apostolic age. Not endowed with gifts of leadership, neither prophet nor teacher, he knew how to be invaluable to those who filled the first rank in the service of the Church, and proved himself a true *servus servorum Dei*' (Swete, pp. xv–xvi).

It is no slight tribute to the character of Mark that he was the friend not only of Barnabas and Paul but also of Peter, in fact a living link of fellowship between the three greatest missionary apostles. In 1 Pet. v. 13, at the close of an epistle written probably after St. Paul's martyrdom, addressed to the faithful of 'the dispersion' in Asia Minor (including churches of Pauline origin), and containing reminiscences of the epistles to the Romans and the Ephesians, there is a greeting from 'her that is in Babylon, elect together with you' (almost certainly the Church in Rome) and from 'Mark my son'. Mark and his mother may have owed their conversion to Peter. But the usual term for convert is 'child' (e.g. Timothy, 1 Cor. iv. 17; Phil. ii. 22; 1 Tim. i. 2, 18; 2 Tim. i. 2, ii. 1; Onesimus, Phm. 10; Titus, Tit. i. 4); 'my son' denotes rather a young disciple to whom the apostle was 'a second father' (Swete, p. xvi). The debt of filial piety was repaid. Mark served Peter no less faithfully than he had served Paul, but in a different and new way; and in serving Peter served unconsciously the future of all Christendom. The history of the present 'Gospel according to St. Mark' lies beyond the scope of this note. It is enough to state that in its original form it consisted of a series of lessons penned by Mark as the 'interpreter' of Peter's teaching of the gospel story, for the benefit primarily of Christian converts and catechumens at Rome.

For the end of Mark's life of service we are dependent upon traditions varying in date and value. They tell the story of a mission to the Church of Aquileia in N. Italy, a martyrdom and burial at Alexandria, and finally the removal of his remains to Venice, where his memory is perpetuated by the Cathedral of St. Mark and by the city ensign on which is blazoned the lion, the mystical emblem of the Gospel according to St. Mark.

5. *Barnabas.*

Barnabas appears first as Joseph, a Cypriote by birth but a Levite by blood, a convert to the faith apparently won by the message of the day of Pentecost, who in the wave of Christian fellowship which swept over the first Christian community sold his land like others

blest with this world's goods, and laid the price at the apostles' feet
for the needs of poorer brethren. His case is singled out in Acts (iv.
36–7) perhaps as a foil to the case of Ananias and Sapphira, but
perhaps as an indication of a life-long record of unselfishness. His
name Joseph (A.V. Joses) is lost henceforward in the surname
Barnabas, 'son of exhortation' R.V., better perhaps as in A.V. 'son
of consolation', i.e. a man whose nature made him a constant source
of refreshment and encouragement. The surname was given by the
apostles, who seem to have recognized from the first his capacity for
sympathy and inspiration. It was his influence that overcame the
reluctance of the apostles to welcome Saul, the converted persecutor,
Acts ix. 26, 27. It is possible that Barnabas and Saul had known
each other before; Cyprus and Tarsus were not far distant, and
Barnabas as a Hellenist may have visited the schools of Tarsus
(Milligan, Hastings, *B.D.*, i. 247). But this supposition weakens rather
than enhances the significance of this first example of Barnabas's
peculiar value to the Church. Recognizing unselfishly the fruits of
other men's missionary work at Antioch, when the Church at
Jerusalem sent him to visit that new Christian centre, he was content for a time to build on their foundation, and then went to Tarsus
to find Saul and bring him to share in the growing work at Antioch,
Acts xi. 20–7. Together the two friends carried to Jerusalem the
offering of the Christians at Antioch for the relief of famine-stricken
sufferers, Acts xi. 27–30. Together they went forth at the call of the
Spirit and with the blessing of their fellow 'prophets and teachers'
at Antioch to face the unknown work of a more distant mission field
(Acts xiii. 1–4)—first Cyprus, the home of Barnabas, then Antioch
in Pisidia, Iconium, Lystra, Derbe, whence they returned to their
home-base in the greater Antioch of Syria. Together before the
Church in Jerusalem they defended the cause of Christian freedom
against Judaistic limitations, and returned again to continue their
work in Antioch. But their relative positions had altered. 'Barnabas
and Saul' in the earlier stages of their joint work, they become 'Paul
and Barnabas' from Cyprus onwards. The change is vividly illustrated by the names given to them by the Lycaonians who took them
for gods. Barnabas they called Zeus, Paul they called Hermes
'because he was the chief speaker' (Acts xiv. 12); it was the difference between grave and dignified benevolence and alert and eloquent
leadership. Paul had come to the front, and the unselfish Barnabas
was content to take the lower place. The only exception to this
change in the order of their names is in the story of the council at
Jerusalem (cp. Acts xv. 2, 22, 35 with xv. 12, 25), where the name

of Barnabas stands first, perhaps as the more acceptable and influential name of the two in Jerusalem.

Shortly after their return to Antioch their comradeship was broken. Barnabas, Levite and Cypriote, the link between Judaism and Hellenism, the mediator between the narrower and the wider views of the Gospel, was 'carried away' by the plausible arguments of the Judaistic visitors from Jerusalem—'even Barnabas', writes Paul pathetically (Gal. ii. 13)—a worse disappointment even than Peter's relapse into Judaistic ways. Still the two friends seem to have gone on working together. The breach came when Paul suggested another joint mission into Asia Minor, and Barnabas proposed to take Mark again. Paul refused to trust the young assistant who had turned back from their first joint mission. The difference of personal feeling was perhaps sharpened by the memory of the recent division over the question of principle. The two apostles parted in pain, and went their separate ways with their chosen companions, Barnabas to Cyprus with Mark, Paul to Asia Minor with Silas—Paul with the blessing of the congregation at Antioch, Barnabas apparently without any such token of the Church's commendation. It is not necessary to suppose that all grateful remembrance of his work had been overshadowed by any misunderstanding of his attitude on the question of the Law and the Gospel, or by disapproval of his defence of Mark. Paul was going to the resumption of an earlier mission for which he and Barnabas had been solemnly committed to the grace of God. Barnabas was going, however reluctantly, to a task of his own choice, not obviously at the outset a missionary enterprise.

There is no record of any reunion of the two separated friends. But 'whenever Paul mentions Barnabas, his words imply sympathy and respect' (Ltft. on Gal. ii. 13). He refers to Barnabas in 1 Cor. ix. 6 as labouring like himself in a spirit of self-denial, waiving even the justest of claims upon his converts for support. In Gal. ii. 13 'even Barnabas' is a touch of affection as well as regret. And in Col. iv. 10 the reference to Barnabas by way of commendation of Mark is a proof of high esteem. It has been suggested that this reference implies that Barnabas was known at Colossae not merely by repute but by personal intercourse—that Barnabas on hearing of Paul's imprisonment resolved to visit him in Rome, travelled first to Alexandria to see Mark, urged him to leave the work already organized there and to find a new field of service in Asia Minor, wrote to Colossae to prepare the way for him (the 'commandments' of Col. iv. 10), and took him first to Rome to regain the confidence of

Paul and 'secure a few words of commendation from the Apostle as a further credential' (Edmundson, *The Church in Rome*, pp. 166–8). There is little or no evidence for this attractive reconstruction of lost history. Neither is there for the inference from Mark's rejoining St. Paul that Barnabas had died before the epistle to Colossae was written. See notes on Col. iv. 10, pp. 308, 322.

Tertullian attributes *Hebrews* to Barnabas, without much justification. The so-called *Epistle of Barnabas*, an early Alexandrian writing, is too anti-Judaic in its attitude and tone to be the work of a mediator soul like the Barnabas of the New Testament. Late and conflicting traditions state (1) that he preached the Gospel in Rome and then became the founder and first bishop of the Church of Milan— on which tradition the see of Milan based its claim to metropolitan authority over N. Italy, and (2) that he died a martyr's death and was buried at Salamis in Cyprus—on the strength of which tradition the Cyprian Church in the fifth century claimed and won its independence of the Patriarchate of Antioch.

6. *Luke*.

The name (Gr. *Loukas*, Lat. *Lucas*) is probably an abbreviation of Lucanus, cp. Silas for Silvanus. These contracted names ending in *-as* are frequent in the case of slaves. Luke may have been a freedman, like Antistitius the surgeon of Julius Caesar and Antonius Musa the physician of Augustus (Plummer, I.C.C., *St. Luke*, p. xviii). The obvious inference from Col. iv. 11 is that Luke was a Gentile. The third gospel and the Acts are dedicated to a Theophilus, a Gentile of high rank (Lk. i. 3), apparently a friend or patron, perhaps even a convert or disciple of the writer. Luke may have been a Syrian of Antioch—a supposition supported by his intimate knowledge of Antioch in the Acts—or more probably a Greek of Philippi, where he spent a long time (see the evidence of the 'we' sections of Acts). Ramsay (*St. Paul the Traveller*, p. 202) suggests that he was the Macedonian whom Paul saw in his vision at Troas, where he may perhaps have just met Luke for the first time. Recent historical criticism has vindicated the tradition that Luke was the author of the third gospel and of the Acts. From the 'we' sections of the Acts it seems evident (1) that if the addition 'when we were gathered together' in the *Codex Bezae* of Acts xi. 28 is correct, Luke was at Antioch with Barnabas and Saul about A.D. 46, (2) that he accompanied Paul from Troas to Philippi on the second missionary journey about A.D. 51 (Acts xvi. 10–17), and about six years later rejoined him at Philippi on the third missionary journey, went with him to

Jerusalem (Acts xx. 5–xxi. 18), and shared his perilous voyage to Rome (Acts xxvii. 1–xxviii. 16). An early tradition embodied in the Collect for St. Luke's Day identifies him with 'the brother whose praise in the gospel is spread through all the churches' (2 Cor. viii. 18, A.D. 56), the delegate chosen by the Macedonian churches to accompany St. Paul in charge of the relief fund for the distressed churches in Judaea. 'The gospel' here of course has no reference to the third gospel, which was written probably some twenty years later; it refers to assistance given in the preaching of the gospel in Macedonia and elsewhere.

The only direct references to Luke in the N.T. date from his association with St. Paul at Rome, (1) as a fellow-worker during his first confinement (Col. iv. 14, Phm. 24), and (2) at one stage of his later imprisonment his one and only companion (2 Tim. iv. 11). Late traditions of little value make him one of the seventy disciples, or the nameless companion of Cleophas on the walk to Emmaus. From Lk. i. 1–3 it is practically certain that he was not an original witness of our Lord's ministry. Tertullian implies that he was a convert of St. Paul's own making. If he was a native of Antioch, he may well have been a student at Tarsus; or the school of Tarsus, the rival of Alexandria and Athens, may have attracted a student even from Macedonia. Or they may have met at Antioch as *Codex Bezae* implies.

Various traditions assign to Luke different spheres of missionary activity, presumably after Paul's death—from Italy to Gaul, and from Dalmatia to Africa—and place his death, by sickness or by martyrdom, in Achaia or in Bithynia, and the final resting-place of his remains in Constantinople. A sixth-century tradition makes him a painter as well as a physician. Bishop Alexander in his *Leading Ideas of the Gospels* (pp. 83–146) brings out vividly Luke's special contribution to Christianity, in particular (1) the idea of the universality of the Gospel of grace, an idea derived from his own experience as a Gentile convert, a missionary, and a companion of St. Paul, (2) the psychological insight of a physician into the healing of body and soul, (3) the painter's sense of beauty and poetry in religion which has made the third gospel the inspiration of Christian art in every succeeding age.

7. *Demas.*

Nothing is known for certain about Demas beyond the references to his name in Col. iv. 14, where his greeting to the Colossians is coupled with Luke's; in Phm. 24, where he is included by St. Paul among 'my fellow-workers', along with Epaphras perhaps, and certainly with Mark, Aristarchus, and Luke; and in 2 Tim. iv. 10, where the apparently close association between Demas and Luke is broken, Luke remaining the Apostle's sole companion, since 'Demas forsook me, having loved this present world, and went to Thessalonica'. But both early tradition and later speculation have been busy with his name. A late scholiast on 2 Tim. iv. 10 adds: 'and there he became a priest of idols', a relapse into stark paganism. In the apocryphal *Acts of Paul and Thekla* Demas and Hermogenes appear as false friends of the Apostle treacherously endeavouring to secure his arrest at Iconium, and as false teachers denying any resurrection but the spiritual resurrection of conversion to a new life—the very heresy attributed in 2 Tim. ii. 17 to Philetus and Hymenaeus. But these passages belong to a series of interpolations intended to connect *Acta Theklae* with circumstances and persons mentioned in 2 Tim. (Ramsay, *Ch. in Rom. Emp.* pp. 377, 392, 417). Neither in the case of Demas nor of Hermogenes (2 Tim. i. 15) does the language of St. Paul suggest alienation or apostasy, or anything more than personal desertion at a critical moment. Hermogenes and other Christians from the province of Asia 'cut' St. Paul, either in Asia or at Rome; Demas 'left him in the lurch' at Rome. During the first confinement Demas apparently remained true to his friend. In Col. iv Demas is the only companion named without a word of commendation or affection. Bengel wonders whether the reason was that Demas wrote the epistle at the Apostle's dictation, and therefore omitted any note of praise for himself. But the absence of any word of commendation must not be pressed as an indication that his loyalty was already open to doubt or suspicion; in Phm. 24, written at the same time, he shares the general commendation implied in the expression 'my fellow-workers'. His defection during the second imprisonment may have been due to fear of personal danger or to impatience of hardship or to preference of self-interest. St. Paul simply says that 'he loved this present world'. It is an obvious and deliberate contrast to the description of faithful servants of Christ in the day of the Lord in the previous verse as 'them that have loved His appearing', i.e. have set their hearts upon the prospect of the coming of Christ in His glory. If Demas was a Thessalonian (like Aristarchus), he may have gone home for reasons of private interest. Chrysostom interprets: 'he chose a life of comfort at home rather than a life of hardship and danger in my company'. Jeremy Taylor (*Ductor Dubitantium*, I. ii. 5, 19) distinguishes between the love of the world (1 John ii. 15) which is 'criminal and forbidden to all Christians' and the love of the world (2 Tim. iv. 10) which 'to other Christians is not unlawful, but inconsistent with the duties of evangelists in the great necessities of the Church'. Demas, he says, was 'a good man, but weak in his spirit and too secular in his relations'. By a curious slip the learned bishop, taking *Colossians* and *Philemon* as later than *2 Timothy*, inferred that Demas returned to his earlier loyalty.

Demas is probably a shortened form of *Demetrius*. It has been suggested that he may have been identical with Demetrius the silversmith of Ephesus (Acts xix. 24) and also with the Demetrius whose character won the outspoken admiration of St. John and his Christian contemporaries (3 John 12). This double identification would give 'a very striking picture of the conversion of a staunch idolator, a period of faithful discipleship, a relapse into worldliness, and a final and triumphant recovery' (Brown, *Pastoral Epistles*, p. 84). But the identification is precarious and improbable in view of the commonness of the name Demetrius.

THE EPISTLE TO THE COLOSSIANS

CHAPTER I

I. THE CHURCH AT COLOSSAE, I. 1–14.

(i) *The Address*, I. 1–2.

Paul, an apostle of Christ Jesus by no ambition or achievement of my own but by the choice and will of God, and Timothy our brother in the faith, yours and mine, to the Christians at Colossae, called to a life of holiness and faithfulness and brotherhood in Christ: may the blessing of God our Father rest upon you in all spiritual power and peace.

I 1 PAUL, an apostle of Christ Jesus through the will of God,

1. *an apostle of Christ Jesus.* In the opening address of nine of his thirteen extant epistles St. Paul describes himself as *apostle*; in seven of these it is the only designation. The title *apostle* may have been used deliberately whenever the apostolic status of St. Paul was denied or disparaged, or some heresy or dissension called for an assertion of apostolic authority. Such was the case more or less with the churches in Galatia and at Rome, Corinth, and Colossae. On the other hand, (1) there is little or no trace of either trouble in *Ephesians*. Perhaps the title of apostle in the opening address of that encyclical letter was meant as an unobtrusive reminder of the relation of the writer to all the churches addressed. But in any case it was natural for St. Paul to begin this letter in the same way as the letter to Colossae written at the same time. (2) Both at Thessalonica and at Philippi there were disorders and errors to be corrected; and yet there is no initial assertion of apostolate in those letters to those churches. The Thessalonian epistles were the earliest, and the habit of writing as 'Paul an apostle' may have come later. Perhaps the attempt to find special reasons for the use or omission of the title *apostle* is after all as superfluous as it is precarious.

through the will of God. The same phrase follows the term 'apostle' in 1 and 2 Cor. and in Eph. In Gal. i. 1 St. Paul states definitely that he received his apostolic authority from no human source and through no human channel 'but through Jesus Christ and God the Father who raised him from the dead'. But there he is confronting a Judaistic revolt against his authority. Here there is no evidence of any challenging of his authority at Colossae. The will of God is contrasted, if contrast there be, not with any rival claim of authority but with any claim of personal merit or attainment of his own. The same phrase is used in 2 Tim. i. 1, and coupled there with the thought of

L

and Timothy [1]our brother, 2 [2]to the saints and faithful brethren

[1] Gr. *the brother.*
[2] Or, *to those that are at Colossae, holy and faithful brethren in Christ.*

the promise of life in Christ. In 1 Tim. i. 1 the same idea is expressed in more vivid language, 'according to the commandment of God our Saviour and of Christ Jesus our hope'. The will of God was both an original choice and an abiding command, cp. Tit. i. 3, where St. Paul speaks of his entrustment with the preaching of the gospel as a divine command, and 1 Cor. ix. 16–17, where he speaks of 'the necessity laid upon me'. The fuller language of these descriptions of apostolate in the three Pastoral Epistles has been contrasted with the simpler and briefer language of the other epistles and cited as an argument against the Pauline authorship of the Pastorals. But these more intimate personal confessions, with their notes of obedience, faith, promise, and hope, are just what St. Paul in his last years might have been expected to pour out to a younger colleague. See note on 'grace and peace' in verse 2.

The thought of the will of God was constantly present with St. Paul. It is expressed in Rom. i. 10 and xv. 32 in his eager and prayerful anticipations of a visit to Rome, and in Acts xxi. 14 in his refusal to avoid the danger of death at Jerusalem. It reads like an echo of the prophecy of Ananias in Acts xxii. 14, 'the God of our fathers appointed thee to know his will'.

Timothy our brother. 'The brother' in the Greek is not to be taken as a special designation of Timothy in particular. It occurs as a designation of Sosthenes in 1 Cor. i. 1 and of Apollos in 1 Cor. xvi. 12, and as part of the description of Tychicus in Col. iv. 7 and Eph. vi. 21 and of Onesimus in Col. iv. 9. Sometimes a note of closer personal intimacy is struck, e.g. 'my brother Titus' in 2 Cor. ii. 13, and of Epaphroditus in Phil. ii. 25 'my brother and fellow-worker and fellow-soldier'. Timothy himself is called 'our brother and God's minister' in 1 Th. iii. 2, where 'our' is in antithesis to 'God's'. But where there is no reason for the specification of the relationship by a personal pronoun, the definite article in Greek is itself a virtual possessive pronoun to be defined by the context—here an implied or unemphatic 'our'.

2. *to the saints and faithful brethren in Christ which are at Colossae.* The Syrian deacon Ephraem (4th cent.) took the saints to be the baptized and the faithful the catechumens. But the single definite article in the Greek indicates clearly that they are the same persons. The word *saints* is almost certainly here, as in Rom. i. 7, 1 Cor. i. 2, Phil. i. 1, not an adjective ('holy') but a substantive; it has become a customary designation of the Christian community. So too has the term *brethren.* Yet they retain something of their original adjectival meaning. Bengel remarks that 'saints' indicates their relation to

God, 'brethren' their relation to other Christians; they are brethren to each other and to St. Paul and his companions. The one ambiguous term in the description is 'faithful'. Is it 'believing', or 'trusty'? The Gr. word *pistos* is used in both senses in the N.T. But in the sense of *believing* it 'never occurs as a mere epithet of those who are known to be already believing: thus *believing brethren* would be tautology' (Lukyn Williams). 'It would add nothing which is not already contained in *saints* and *brethren*' (Ltft.). These criticisms are too drastic. 'Faithful' does here strike a distinct note. 'Saints' may be regarded as marking the objective aspect of the Christian life, the consecration of the Christian by the call of God. In that case 'faithful' may well mark the subjective aspect of that life, the response of faith. If 'trusty' or 'stedfast' be the right interpretation, it finds a parallel in the description of Onesimus in iv. 9 as 'the faithful and beloved brother' and of Silvanus in 1 Pet. v. 12 as 'our faithful brother'. Lightfoot thinks that St. Paul is hinting at the defection of some of the brethren: 'he does not directly exclude any, but he indirectly warns all'. But (1) it is surely a forced rendering to take 'faithful brethren' as a narrowing down of 'the saints' to those who are remaining true to the faith; the two terms bracketed by the one article must be co-extensive. (2) The use of 'faithful' in Eph. i. 1 rules out any such hint. There it is the counterpart of 'saints'; why not here also? It is unlikely that St. Paul would use 'faithful' in different senses in two letters written at the same time to partly identical destinations. Both addresses are identical but for the addition of 'brethren'. And but for that addition probably the meaning of 'faithful' here would have never been disputed.

The term *brethren* has given rise to the question why St. Paul did not address the epistle to the Church at Colossae. Various reasons have been suggested. (1) St. Paul writing to a Christian community with which he had no personal acquaintance as a congregation preferred to lay stress upon the fundamental bond of Christian brotherhood between himself and its members. (2) St. Paul only used the term *ecclesia* in writing to churches founded by himself, e.g. Thessalonica, Corinth, Galatia. This argument however ignores the fact that the term *ecclesia* is not used in the address to the Church at Philippi. (3) Lightfoot notes that the earliest epistles are addressed to the *ecclesia*, but the later epistles from Romans onwards are addressed to 'the saints'. He offers no explanation of this change in the mode of address. In Acts *ecclesia* is used 24 times, *the disciples* 20 times, *the saints* 4 times only. It is possible that as the years passed, St. Paul thought less of the existence of the Christian community and more of its character as a school of holiness and of its members as a new influence in the world, the *tertium genus* as they came to be called, distinct from Jew and pagan. (4) It has been suggested that the Christians at Colossae were not yet organized as a church. It is true

in Christ *which are* at Colossae: Grace to you and peace from
God our Father.

that there is no evidence of an organized ministry at Colossae such as
appears in Phil. i. 1. But the argument from silence cannot be pressed
so far. It is obvious that this epistle was addressed to the Colossians
as a Christian community, whose 'order' the apostle beholds from
afar with admiration (ii. 5).

The phrase *in Christ* may belong to 'faithful brethren', and especially to 'faithful', i.e. stedfast in their allegiance to Christ; but it
is best taken as belonging to the whole description and as simply
denoting 'Christians'.

grace and peace. The customary greeting in Greek correspondence,
as is obvious from the evidence of the papyri, was *chairein*, lit. (I bid
you) rejoice. St. Paul substitutes a word derived from the same root
but already far removed from its associations, the word *charis*,
'grace', which is found in the N.T. in the earlier Greek sense of *charm*
or *pleasure*, e.g. Lk. iv. 22, Col. iv. 6, Eph. iv. 29, all with reference
to the winning tone or content of language in conversation; but in
the overwhelming majority of cases in the N.T. the word denotes not
merely favour but in a peculiar sense the favour of God, His willingness to give and forgive, and then the giving and finally the gift. It
is in brief the love of God in its action and its effect. The customary
Hebrew greeting was 'peace', *shalom*, mod. Arab. *salaam*. The two
greetings, Greek and Hebrew, are found combined in 2 Macc. i. 1.
But in the form common to practically all the apostolic epistles, viz.
'grace and peace', it seems to have been a creation of St. Paul.
Grace is 'the source of all real blessings', peace 'their end and issue'
(Ltft.). In 1 and 2 Tim. and in 2 John and Jude a third blessing or
prayer is added, viz. 'mercy' (Gr. *eleos*). In 1 and 2 Tim. the addition
of 'mercy' sounds like an implicit confession of an aged apostle,
conscious that the imperfection of all ministerial life and labour needs
the forgiveness of divine compassion.

from God our Father. The traditional text here adds 'and from the
Lord Jesus Christ'. This phrase is undoubtedly part of the original
text in Eph. i. 2. Here the evidence of the manuscripts indicates that
it is an addition by a later hand, consciously or unconsciously assimi-
lating this passage to the usual form of the opening blessing. It has
been suggested that St. Paul omitted our Lord's name in order to lay
stress on the supremacy of the Father as the source of all spiritual
life, by way of guarding against any wrong inference from the
sovereignty of Christ which is the main theme of the epistle. But it
is improbable that the omission of our Lord's name was deliberate.
Needless perplexity is caused by the attempt to find a theological
purpose in every variation from St. Paul's customary phrases.

(ii) *Thanksgiving and intercession for their Christian life*, I. 3–14.

1. *Thanksgiving for their faith, love, and hope, for the growth and fruit of the Gospel, and for the work of Epaphras*, I. 3–8.

We thank God the Father of our Lord Jesus Christ constantly in our prayers on your behalf for all that we have heard of your faith in Christ Jesus and the love that you have for all who have answered the call to the Christian life. That faith and that love are linked both in our minds and in your experience with the thought of the great hope beyond that is yours already, secured and centred in the unseen world above,—that hope of which you first heard in those early days when the truth of God embodied in the Gospel was brought home to you. That Gospel found a home with you, as it has found a welcome in every part of the world, bearing fruit and gaining ground elsewhere as it has done and is doing amongst you, ever since the day when you heard the message and came to know the grace of God in all its simple reality, as you learned it from the teaching of Epaphras, our dear fellow-servant. He has been indeed a faithful minister of Christ in our stead and on our behalf,—your instructor and my informant, for it was he who revealed to us the strength of the Christian love which is one of the fruits of the Spirit in your life.

3 We give thanks to God the Father of our Lord Jesus Christ,

3. *We give thanks to God.* The phrase used in 2 Cor. i. 3 and Eph. i. 3 is 'Blessed be God'. The variation recalls the alternating use of 'blessed' and 'gave thanks' in our Lord's institution of the Eucharist.

With one exception all the epistles written by St. Paul to churches begin with a thanksgiving for their spiritual progress. The one exception is *Galatians*, which begins with an expression of pained surprise at their lapse from the true faith. This practice is not due merely to a desire to begin with a word of encouragement. It embodies a fundamental principle. It sets an example for all who carry the burden of pastoral care; the secret of Christian optimism is to be found not merely in the faith which leads to intercession but also in the hope which flows from thanksgiving. It indicates the rightful place of thanksgiving in all Christian devotion, private and public. A fuller study of the standards of primitive worship and a deeper insight into the laws of the spiritual life have restored thanksgiving in recent years to its proper position. The publication of *Sursum Corda* in 1899 gave it a larger place and a wider outlook. Later devotional literature has given it an earlier place in the order of Christian prayer. Thanksgiving should not follow but precede intercession. That is the order of the Lord's Prayer. The debt of gratitude should be paid before the demands of need are stated. It is also the order suggested by experience. A survey of the grounds for thanksgiving revives the spirit of hope, and provides fresh material for petition. For St. Paul's view of the place of thanksgiving in the Christian life see note on iv. 2.

praying always for you, 4 having heard of your faith in Christ
Jesus, and of the love which ye have toward all the saints,

God the Father of our Lord Jesus Christ. A.V. *God and the Father.*
R.V. is right in omitting the 'and' in accordance with the evidence
of the best MSS. here and in iii. 17. The usual form is 'the God and
Father of our Lord Jesus Christ'. It is 'confined to initial benedic-
tions and other places of special solemnity' (Hort on 1 Pet. i. 3), e.g.
Rom. xv. 6, 2 Cor. xi. 31. A.V. in Rom. xv. 6 and 2 Cor. i. 3 has 'God,
even the Father', elsewhere 'the God and Father'. Some commentators have found a difficulty in this description of God as the God of Jesus
Christ, as though it implied that the Son of God was not Himself God.
The difficulty was not felt by the apostolic writers, e.g. 'I ascend unto
my Father and your Father, and my God and your God', John xx. 17.
St. Paul states the relationship even more boldly in Eph. i. 17, 'the
God of our Lord Jesus Christ, the Father of glory'. Neither St. Paul
nor St. Peter nor St. John sees any contradiction in giving to Christ
the attributes of God and yet recognizing that God is His God as well
as His Father.

praying always for you. R.V. here seems to miss the point. St.
Paul is not insisting here on his habit of praying for the Colossians,
but on his habit of giving thanks for their faith, love, and hope.
'Always' belongs to 'give thanks', and 'praying' is an incidental
note of time, 'whenever we pray' or 'in our prayers'. The insistence
on his prayers in themselves comes when he passes from thanksgiving
to intercession in verse 9.

4. *your faith in Christ Jesus.* Our English 'in' is ambiguous. It has
to do duty for one Greek preposition which indicates faith *directed
towards* Christ, and for another which sometimes has this meaning
but usually indicates faith as part of the life lived *in union with*
Christ. The latter is the preposition used here, and in its usual sense.
Christ is not merely the object of faith but also its inspiration.

toward all the saints. The word 'all' is fatal to the suggestion that
'the saints' here are the distressed Christians of Judaea described
simply as 'the saints' in 1 Cor. xvi. 1, 2 Cor. viii. 4, ix. 1, 12. 'All the
saints' may mean all local Christians without any distinction of
social status or personal acquaintance, as is clearly the case in Rom.
i. 7, xvi. 15, 2 Cor. i. 1, xiii. 12, Phil. i. 1, iv. 21, 22, Heb. xiii. 24. The
phrase has a wider range in Eph. iii. 18, where the idea is that the
fullness of the faith requires the fellowship of all Christians for its
perfect comprehension, and in 1 Th. iii. 13, where it denotes the
presence of all the saints at the Coming of Christ, and in Rev. viii. 3,
the prayers of the whole body of the saints. In Eph. vi. 18 'supplication for all the saints, and on my behalf' seems to imply this wider
range. Here and in Phm. 5 and Eph. i. 15, parallel passages, the
reference seems to be local.

5 because of the hope which is laid up for you in the heavens,

5. *because of the hope.* The connexion of the phrase is not obvious. (1) It has been taken with 'we give thanks'. In that case (*a*) the hope itself may be the third ground of the thanksgiving of the apostle, the faith, love, and hope of the Colossians. (*b*) St. Paul may mean not that the faith and love were the actual subject of his thanksgiving, but that the report of their faith and love were the occasion which prompted the thanksgiving, in which case the hope itself is strictly speaking the subject of the thanksgiving. The second of these interpretations attaches too much importance to the grammatical analysis of the sentence. It is impossible to exclude the faith and love from the contents of the thanksgiving. Nor can that thanksgiving be limited to the occasion of any particular news from Colossae; *always* clearly indicates a constant habit. Both interpretations are doubtful. The word 'we give thanks' is too remote to be taken directly with 'because of the hope'. (2) The words 'because of the hope' have been taken in connexion with the love for the saints. This connexion has been criticized on the ground that it attributes their love to an apparently selfish motive, viz. the hope of a future reward. But the idea of the connexion between the hope and the love is rather that the hope in question, being a common hope, draws men together in brotherhood and fellowship. They love and serve each other as joint-heirs of a spiritual destiny. 'Christianity knows nothing of a hope of immortality for the individual alone, but only of a glorious hope for the individual in the Body, in the eternal society of the Church triumphant' (Mozley, *Univ. Sermons*, pp. 70–1). (3) The objection just noticed vanishes if the phrase 'because of the hope' is taken in connexion with both their love and their faith. Both flow from and rest upon the hope of eternal life which inspires both faith and love by giving a new outlook upon all life.

Whatever view be taken of the analysis of the sentence, it is impossible to avoid the impression that in substance the ground of St. Paul's thanksgiving is the familiar triad of Christian graces. It is instructive to note the different settings and aspects in which the triad occurs. In 1 Th. i. 3 (a thanksgiving as here) the three graces come in the order of practical experience: faith prompts action, love sustains labour, hope inspires perseverance. In 1 Cor. xiii. 13 they come in the order of spiritual value: 'the greatest of these is love'. Here they come in the order of temporal sequence: 'faith rests on the past; love works in the present; hope looks to the future' (Ltft.). Hope is here the dominant note, and still more in 1 Pet. i. 3–22, which is an amplification of the triad, first hope, then faith, then love. Here again, as in 1 Pet. i, the hope is not the hope they feel within themselves but the hope they see above and beyond, cp. Rom. viii. 24, Gal. v. 5. It is the 'treasure in heaven' of the Gospels (Mt. vi. 20, 21,

whereof ye heard before in the word of the truth of the gospel,
6 which is come unto you; even as it is also in all the world

Lk. xii. 34, xviii. 22). The future glory casts a new light on the
present struggle. Their faith and love have an eternal perspective.

The hope in question is not defined. (1) It may refer to the *parousia*,
the day of the Lord, the final revelation of Christ as king and judge,
or (2) to the prospect of the life beyond awaiting the individual soul
on its departure, or (3) in view of the frequent use of 'heavens' in the
sense of the unseen world or the spiritual sphere, it may refer to a
present object of hope, cp. i. 27 'Christ the hope of glory', 1 Tim. 1
'Christ Jesus our hope'. There may be a reference to the *parousia* in
i. 22, i. 28, iii. 4. But the vision of the Kingdom as an imminent
climax recedes into the background of St. Paul's thought in this
later group of epistles. They are concerned mainly with the idea of
the Church as the Kingdom in the making.

ye heard before. Not (1) before the fulfilment of the hope, or (2)
before the writing of this epistle, but (3) in the early days of their
discipleship. Lightfoot sees an implied contrast between the earlier
and truer teaching of Epaphras and the recent false teaching current
at Colossae. But there is no clear allusion to that heresy in the present
context or anywhere in this opening section; and it is improbable
that St. Paul intended to give any such subtle hint in the midst of
this whole-hearted thanksgiving.

in the word of the truth of the gospel. In Gal. ii. 5, 14 'the truth of the
gospel' is clearly the true gospel as contrasted with its false Judaistic
presentation. But here the emphasis is not on 'truth' but on 'gospel',
to which the following relative 'which' belongs. *Word* (Gr. *logos*)
may refer (1) to the message itself, i.e. 'as part of the message of
truth, namely, the gospel' or 'as part of the message of truth contained in the gospel', or (2) to the delivery of the message, i.e. 'in the
course of the preaching of the truth contained in the gospel'.

6. *which is come unto you.* The semicolon of the R.V. after these
words makes too sharp a break. There would be no point in St. Paul's
thus laying stress on the obvious fact that the Gospel had reached
Colossae. What he is laying stress upon is the fact that the arrival
of the Gospel at Colossae was part of a world-wide movement.

even as it is also in all the world. Cp. i. 23, 1 Th. i. 8. The digression
marks the catholic outlook of a missionary soul. It may be (1) a hint
of warning against the narrow interests of a self-centred compla-
cency, though their love for all the saints seems to rule out this idea,
or (2) a note of encouragement for his readers, reminding them that
the Gospel is winning all along the line, or (3) an expression of the
apostle's own thankfulness as from the centre of the Empire he surveys
the progress of the Gospel, or (4) a contrast between the catholicity
of the true Gospel and the merely local character of false gospels.

bearing fruit and increasing, as *it doth* in you also, since the day
ye heard and knew the grace of God in truth; 7 even as ye
learned of Epaphras our beloved fellow-servant, who is a faith-

The phrase *in all the world* was no rhetorical exaggeration. There
were doubtless many cities and townships still untouched by the
Gospel even in provinces already evangelized. But the Gospel had
been preached already in most provinces of the Empire, viz. Palestine,
Syria, Cilicia, Galatia, Phrygia, Asia, Pontus, Bithynia, Macedonia,
Achaia, Italy. It is probable that Egypt, Gaul, and Africa also had
been visited by apostles or evangelists. The Acts of the Apostles are
practically the Acts of St. Peter and St. Paul. We cannot infer from
the Acts that the other apostles stayed at home. In any case the
chain of Christian outposts reached from East to West. 'All the
world' is a true statement in the sense of every quarter of the Empire.
'The Church, it is true, was only established in a few centres, and
embraced at the most several thousands of adherents; but these
were representative of the human race in all its main divisions. The
experiment for which Paul himself was chiefly answerable had
succeeded. Christianity had advanced its claim to be a religion for
all mankind, and all mankind had now potentially accepted it'
(Scott, *Apologetic of the N.T.* p. 184).

bearing fruit and increasing. Lightfoot points out that *bearing
fruit* indicates the 'inherent energy' and 'inner working' of the
Gospel, while *increasing* indicates its 'external growth' and 'outward
extension'. The Christian faith was both a transforming force and a
travelling fire. It was changing the life as well as covering the face of
the Empire. The two words recall to mind the two parables of the
leaven and the mustard seed—the influence of the Christian faith and
the increase of the Christian fellowship.

7. *Epaphras our beloved fellow-servant.* The name Epaphras is an
abbreviation of Epaphroditus. Such affectionate abbreviations were
common in Greek, and this Greek habit extended to Latin as well as
Greek names, e.g. Lukas (Lucanus, in some MSS. of the Old Latin
version of St. Luke's Gospel), Silas (Silvanus in the Epistles). But it
is practically certain that Epaphras is not identical with the Epaphroditus who is mentioned in *Philippians*, apparently a native of Philippi
(Phil. ii. 25), while Epaphras was a native or at least an inhabitant
of Colossae (Col. iv. 12). Epaphras was the founder of the Church at
Colossae. The 'also' of the traditional text might suggest that Epaphras was only a later accessory in this work; but the best MS.
authority is in favour of the omission of the word. It has been inferred from Col. iv. 12–13 that it was Epaphras who had evangelized
also the neighbouring towns of Laodicea and Hierapolis. The
reference there to his labour on their behalf does not strictly convey
more than a sense of spiritual responsibility which may or may not

ful minister of Christ on [1]our behalf, 8 who also declared unto
us your love in the Spirit.

¹ Many ancient authorities read *your*.

imply that they owed to him the origin of their faith. But the
coupling of Christians of those two towns with the Colossians
justifies, even if it does not require, that inference.

Epaphras was on a visit to Rome when this epistle was written.
In Phm. 23 St. Paul calls him his 'fellow-prisoner', a title given also
to Aristarchus in Col. iv. 10. See note there on the question whether
the title refers to companionship in confinement at Rome or in the
captivity of the service of Christ. Tradition makes him the first
bishop of Colossae; but the tradition may be an inference from this
epistle, which contains all that is known of him for certain.

minister of Christ. The primary idea of the Greek word *diakonos*
is attendance upon a person, and its secondary idea attention to a
task. The Latin equivalent *minister* has the same meanings in the
same order. The word is used of the relation of Tychicus to St. Paul,
in Acts xx. 4, just as in Acts xix. 22 Timothy and Erastus and others
are described as 'ministering' to St. Paul. They were companions
and helpers in his life and work. In Eph. vi. 21 and Col. iv. 7 Tychicus
is 'the beloved brother and faithful minister' of the apostle, though
the addition of the words 'in the Lord' indicates that the service
rendered to the apostle is part of the service of Christ. But mostly in
the N.T. the word is used of Christian ministry, either the official
diaconate or the ministry in general. It is instructive to note the
different aspects marked in various contexts. (1) It denotes the officer
or servant of *a society*, (*a*) of a local church, e.g. Rom. xvi. 1 Phoebe
the *diakonos* of the Church at Cenchreae, Phil. i. 1 the bishops and
deacons at Philippi, 1 Tim. iii. 8, 12 deacons at Ephesus, (*b*) of the
Church Catholic, e.g. St. Paul himself in Col. i. 25. (2) It denotes the
servant of *a cause*, a truth, a principle. The apostles are ministers of
a new covenant, 2 Cor. iii. 6, the agents or advocates of a new relationship between God and man. Satan's 'ministers' may disguise
themselves as 'ministers of righteousness', 2 Cor. xi. 15. In Gal. ii.
17 St. Paul, repudiating the idea that the Christian doctrine of
justification by faith is in any way anti-ethical or immoral, asks
indignantly whether Christ can be 'a minister of sin'. In Rom. xv. 8
Christ is described as 'a minister of circumcision for the truth of God',
i.e. the agent of the divine fulfilment of the spiritual promise of a
covenant of which circumcision was the sign and seal. St. Paul describes himself as 'a minister of the Gospel', Col. i. 23, Eph. iii. 7.
(3) It denotes the servant of *a person*. An imperial officer is 'a
minister of God for good', Rom. xiii. 4 (cp. our Lord's words to
Pilate, John xix. 11). Satan has 'his ministers', the false apostles
who perverted or opposed the true gospel of Christ, 2 Cor. xi. 15.

The apostle and his fellow-evangelists are ministers of God, 2 Cor. vi. 4, 1 Th. iii. 2; of Christ, 2 Cor. xi. 23, Col. i. 7, 1 Tim. iv. 6. The Christian minister is an officer of a divine society, an exponent of a divine system of faith and life, a servant of a divine sovereign.

on our behalf. The traditional text has 'on your behalf'. (1) This might refer to services rendered to St. Paul by Epaphras as the representative of the Colossians, just as Epaphroditus came not merely to cheer St. Paul by his presence but to relieve the Apostle's necessities with gifts from Philippi (Phil. ii. 25, 'your messenger and minister to my need', iv. 18), and just as St. Paul wished to keep Onesimus to minister to his comfort on behalf of Philemon, Phm. 13. But this interpretation would put a false meaning upon *minister of Christ*; such services could only be remotely and indirectly regarded as the service of Christ, as being a sort of fulfilment of our Lord's words, 'Ye did it unto me', Mt. xxv. 40. (2) The reference might be to the work done by Epaphras in the spiritual interests of the Colossians. This seems to be the idea of the A.V. 'for you'. (3) But the evidence of the MSS. is decisive for the reading 'our'. Epaphras had been Paul's missionary as well as Christ's minister. In his preaching mission at Colossae, undertaken perhaps by a commission from St. Paul or at least in response to a suggestion from him, he had virtually been St. Paul's substitute and representative. This interpretation is supported by the word *also* in the following clause. Epaphras had brought the news of the Gospel from Paul to Colossae; he had also brought back to Paul from Colossae the news of the fruits of the Gospel. St. Paul is silent upon the sadder side of the news which Epaphras brought, the news of the strange perversion of the Gospel which was the occasion of the writing of this epistle. Epaphras must have been his informant; but the only possible indication of the fact is implied in the reference in iv. 12–13 to the stress of the anxiety which drove Epaphras to earnest intercession on behalf of his tempted disciples at Colossae and its neighbour cities.

8. *your love.* Commentators have insisted on narrowing this love down to one of three alternatives, (1) love for God, (2) love for all the saints, (3) love for St. Paul. If St. Paul had meant only the first or the third, he would surely have added the few words needed to make his meaning plain. The second is the more probable, if we must choose. But it is best to take this love in the widest sense, as the central grace of the Christian triad, the fruit of faith and the fount of hope. There is no need to distinguish, still less to separate, its objects. St. Paul and the saints at Colossae and elsewhere would all find a place in hearts in which the first place was given to God.

in the Spirit. The Greek text has the preposition 'in' but no definite article, but the absence of the article is not conclusive against the rendering of the R.V. In ii. 5 'the spirit' is contrasted with 'the flesh'; absent in the flesh, St. Paul is present at Colossae in spirit.

2. *Prayer for their progress in knowledge, service, strength, and thanksgiving,* I. 9–12.

Hearing his news, we share his joy. We too, ever since we learned of your conversion, have been praying for you unceasingly, and asking in particular that you may be given in the fullest measure that knowledge of the will of God which brings with it every kind and degree of spiritual insight and intelligence. We pray that this knowledge may find expression in a life which shall be at every step worthy of your Christian profession and of the approval of Christ,—a life bearing fruit in every good work, and in that very work growing in moral stature through fresh knowledge of God,—a life that is being strengthened steadily with a strength which is the result and the revelation of the power of God at work in human life,—a life of increasing perseverance and patience and indeed happiness also,—a life of constant thanksgiving to the Father.

9 For this cause we also, since the day we heard *it*, do not

Chrysostom takes the same meaning here; the Colossians had shown a deep affection in spirit for the apostle whom they had never seen in the flesh. But any idea of this contrast is foreign or forced in the present context. The reference is almost certainly to the Holy Spirit. It is the only mention of the Holy Spirit in this epistle. The Apostle's attention is concentrated by the crisis at Colossae upon the supremacy and centrality of the Son of God. But any inference therefrom that the Spirit was occupying little place in his theology or his thoughts at this time is ruled out by the frequency and variety of his references to the Spirit in the contemporary epistle to the Ephesians. Gentiles and Jews alike have access to God 'in one Spirit', Eph. ii. 18. In the four other passages the Greek phrase is identical with the phrase in the present verse. The Gentiles are being built up into a habitation of God 'in the Spirit', ii. 22. 'The secret of the Christ' was now revealed to apostles and prophets 'in the Spirit', iii. 5. Christians are to find the fullness of experience not in wine but 'in the Spirit', v. 18. They are to pray at all seasons 'in the Spirit', vi. 18. Even in this epistle there are virtual references to the working of the Spirit in the 'spiritual wisdom and understanding' of i. 9 and the 'spiritual songs' of iii. 16.

In the present passage the Holy Spirit is regarded as the inspirer of the new grace of Christian love. Cp. Gal. v. 22, where love is the first of the graces which are 'the fruit of the Spirit'; Rom. v. 5, where the love of God is 'poured into our hearts by the Holy Spirit'; Rom. xv. 30, where St. Paul pleads for the prayers of his readers 'by our Lord Jesus Christ and by the love of the Spirit', i.e. the mutual love of Christians that is born of the presence of the Spirit in their hearts; 2 Cor. vi. 6, where among the marks of a faithful ministry the phrase 'in the Holy Spirit' is followed immediately by 'in love unfeigned'.

9. *For this cause.* As in Eph. i. 15, the phrase looks back to the whole of the preceding paragraph. Thanksgiving leads on to inter-

cease to pray and make request for you, that ye may be filled
with the knowledge of his will in all spiritual wisdom and under-

cession. Spiritual progress is not a human performance but a divine
process; its proper result is not pride but prayer. Moreover, by this
time the Apostle's experience had taught him that the evangelistic
stage of Christian missionary work must pass into the pastoral, an
experience repeated in every modern mission field. 'It is much easier
to evangelize than to Christianize' (Burton, *The Call of the Pacific*,
p. 96).

we also. Not (1) 'we as well as Epaphras'; there is a vivid picture
of his prayers for the Colossians in iv. 12, but so far he has only been
mentioned as reporting their progress; but (2) 'we on our part', in
response to the news of their progress. (3) The position of 'also' in
the Greek, attached emphatically to 'we', forbids its being taken as
introducing the intercession, 'not only thank God but also pray'.

pray and make request for you. This rendering and punctuation of
the R.V. gives both words the same construction and value. The
A.V. 'to pray for you, and to desire' suggests more clearly the distinction between general prayer on their behalf and the particular
petitions which follow.

The prayers in St. Paul's epistles have a unity of their own, but it
is the unity of spiritual coherence rather than literary composition.
Thought leads on to thought, and the prayer ends far away from its
beginning. It resembles the flowing stream of petition of the Greek
liturgies rather than the clean-cut antitheses and balanced framework
of a Latin collect. It is capable of logical analysis, and the analysis
is instructive and helpful so long as it is not read back into the mind
of the apostle. Four distinct petitions can be seen in this prayer for
the spiritual progress of the Colossians,—progress in knowledge, in
service, in strength, in thanksgiving. Yet the prayer is not a mere
combination of independent petitions; they represent a sequence of
steps in progress. Knowledge is to issue in service; strength is the
reward of service: thanksgiving is the crown of the whole experience.
The three steps thus crowned correspond to the three elements of the
Christian life,—creed, conduct, character. Creed determines conduct,
and conduct develops character.

the knowledge of his will. The pronoun 'his' refers obviously to God,
whose name is implied in the very idea of prayer. Of the 45 occur-
rences of the substantive 'knowledge' in the Greek N.T. one (Eph.
iii. 4) is the word translated 'understanding' in this verse; in 28 cases
the word is the simple noun *gnosis*; in 16 it is the compound *epignosis*, and it is this word which is used here and in iii. 10. Until
recently most commentators interpreted *epignosis* as a fuller and
more perfect kind of knowledge. Lightfoot remarks on this verse that
in the LXX and the N.T. *epignosis* is 'used especially of the know-

standing, 10 to walk worthily of the Lord [1]unto all pleasing,

[1] Or, *unto all pleasing, in every good work, bearing fruit and increasing &c.*

ledge of God and of Christ, as being the perfection of knowledge'. But the exhaustive discussion of the word by Dr. Armitage Robinson (*Epistle to the Ephesians*, pp. 248-54) concludes with the judgement that '*gnosis* is the wider word and expresses "knowledge" in the fullest sense: *epignosis* is knowledge directed towards a particular object, perceiving, discerning, recognizing: but it is not knowledge in the abstract: that is *gnosis*'. This judgement is borne out by the use of the two words in this epistle. *Gnosis* is the word in ii. 3, 'in Christ are all the treasures of wisdom and knowledge hidden'. In the three cases where *epignosis* is used, i. 9, 10 and iii. 10, the reference is to the practical recognition of divine truth. The knowledge here in question is knowledge not merely of the nature but of the will of God. In Indian religious philosophy and its modern child Theosophy, the ultimate aim of thought is the mystery of divine being; in the Christian faith it is the revelation of divine purpose for human life. What St. Paul desires for the Colossians is not intellectual satisfaction but spiritual insight,—not the solution of metaphysical problems but the recognition of moral principles, and those viewed in their origin and character as the expression of a personal will.

This knowledge is then analysed. It takes the form of spiritual wisdom and spiritual understanding. Wisdom (Gr. *sophia*) is the highest form of knowledge,—insight into primary and absolute truth, cp. Eph. i. 17, where it is coupled with revelation (Gr. *apocalypsis*). In the parallel passage Eph. i. 8 wisdom is coupled with prudence (Gr. *phronesis*); here with understanding (Gr. *synesis*). Aristotle defines them both as applications of wisdom to the details of life. 'While *synesis* is critical, *phronesis* is practical; while *synesis* apprehends the bearings of things, *phronesis* suggests lines of action'—so Lightfoot paraphrases Aristotle's distinction between the two.

10. *to walk worthily of the Lord.* 'The end of all knowledge, the Apostle would say, is conduct' (Ltft.). The verb *walk*, frequently used in N.T. of a course of life, a manner of conduct, has its origin in the LXX, where it represents the Heb. *halak*, lit. *walk*, metaph. *live*. It is coupled with *worthily* also in 1 Th. ii. 12, 'worthily of God', and Eph. iv. 1, 'worthily of your calling'. In Phil. i. 27, writing to the Church in a Roman colony where he had claimed his rights as a Roman citizen, St. Paul substitutes the metaphor of citizenship,— 'behave as a citizen worthily of the gospel of Christ'. The metaphor of a walk represents the Christian life as a course of individual action; the metaphor of citizenship suggests rather the idea of social relations. The phrase in 1 Th. ii. 12 might point to *the Lord* here as referring to God; but 'the Lord' in St. Paul's epistles is almost invariably Christ. In that case we may recognize in the word *spiritual* in the preceding

bearing fruit in every good work, and increasing [1]in the knowledge of God; 11 [2]strengthened [3]with all power, according to

[1] Or, *by*.   [2] Gr. *made powerful*.   [3] Or, *in*.

clause a reference to the Holy Spirit, and see a trinitarian sequence—
the will of the Father, the guidance of the Spirit, the example of the
Son. 'The spirit of the Lord' in Isaiah xi. 2 is described as 'the spirit
of wisdom and understanding'; and the two Greek words in the LXX
there are the *sophia* and *synesis* of the present passage.

unto all pleasing. The Greek noun translated 'pleasing' occurs only
here in the N.T. It was once regarded as having a bad connotation
(i.e. obsequiousness) in later as in classical Greek, but the evidence
of the papyri and of Philo proves that it had the sense of giving honest
satisfaction or winning merited approval, and was frequently used
of seeking or meriting divine approval, even without any distinct
mention of God or the gods. The word means more than the mere
fact of giving pleasure; it means seeking to please. In most cases it
connotes also the idea of service in the interests of others, an idea
frequent in the papyri letters and in monumental inscriptions, though
there the idea is rather civic service or public spirit than personal
devotion to a friend or leader. See note on 'well-pleasing' in iii. 20.

*bearing fruit in every good work, and increasing in the knowledge of
God.* This division of the two participles in A.V. and R.V. gives a
satisfying antithesis, 'yielding fruit in service, gaining ground in
knowledge'. But in the order of the Greek there is a suggestive
parallelism between the results of being 'filled with the knowledge
of his will'. This knowledge is to result in insight, service, and
strength: (1) 'in all wisdom ... to walk worthily ... unto all
pleasing', (2) 'in every good work ... bearing fruit and increasing
... in (through) the knowledge of God', (3) 'in all strength ...
strengthened ... unto all perseverance' &c. It is doubtful therefore
whether the two participles should be separated and attached respectively to work and knowledge. The life of good works is both a harvest
and a growth; the tree yields fruit and goes on growing. The text is
uncertain. The best supported reading has no *in* before *knowledge* but
the simple instrumental dative, 'through the knowledge of God',
that knowledge being thus regarded as the divine influence by which
the fruits are produced and the growth of the life itself fostered.

11. *strengthened with all power.* In the Greek both noun and verb
are forms of the same word, 'strengthened with all strength' or 'made
powerful with all power'. The sequence of the language is more exactly
rendered 'filled with the knowledge of his will ... in all strength,
being strengthened according to the might of his glory'. Something
more is meant than strength of character as a natural endowment. It is
the strength of conviction given by the knowledge of the will of God.

according to the might of his glory. This strength is a response and

the might of his glory, unto all patience and longsuffering with joy;

3. *Thanksgiving to the Father for their admission to an inheritance of light, their transference to a realm of love, their redemption from sin,* I. 12–14.

A life of constant thanksgiving to the Father, who has enabled us to enter unto a part and place of our own in the inheritance of the saints in a new world of light,—who rescued us from the realm and rule of darkness, and lifted us into the kingdom of the Son who is the revelation of His love, and in whom we have found the redemption that we need, the forgiveness of our sins.

12 giving thanks unto the Father, who made [1]us meet to be

[1] Some ancient authorities read *you.*

a correspondence to the omnipotence of God's self-revelation. The R.V. is more careful than the A.V. to use particular English words to mark the different Greek synonyms for strength. There are four Greek words, all four found in Eph. i. 19, 20. *Ischus* has given us no English word ; *dunamis* has given us 'dynamic'. Both words indicate inherent or latent power. *Kratos,* usually translated 'might', denotes power as seen in its superiority or its vindication,—hence the compounds autocratic, democratic, aristocratic, &c. *Energeia,* our 'energy', is the actual exertion of power. The language of St. Paul in this passage is precise. The Christian life is dynamic ; it is endued with strength as the result of the omnipotent action (Gr. *kratos*) of the glory of God. 'Glory' is the character of God revealed by His action. Man's moral strength depends upon his realization of this character of God. It is his response and reaction to divine revelation, a revelation not merely of truth but of grace—not merely of doctrinal principle but of spiritual power.

unto all patience and longsuffering. The two English words both convey the idea of resignation or submission. The Greek word translated *patience* conveys the more active idea of perseverance or endurance. Trench (*N.T. Synonyms,* liii, p. 198, 12th ed. 1894) distinguishes *patience* as relating to things and *longsuffering* to persons. Lightfoot describes *patience* as 'the temper which does not easily succumb under suffering' and *longsuffering* as 'the self-restraint which does not hastily retaliate a wrong'. A better translation would be 'unto all perseverance and patience'.

with joy. To connect this phrase with *giving thanks* is to weaken its force. It is almost a truism to say that thanksgiving is prompted or accompanied by joy. The phrase comes best as the climax to perseverance and patience, 'even to the extent of finding or keeping happiness therein'. Cp. James i. 2, 3.

12. *giving thanks unto the Father.* The connexion of the participle is uncertain. (*a*) It may be a resumption and extension of the Apostle's

partakers of the inheritance of the saints in light; 13 who de-
own thanksgiving, though that would be an abrupt reversion to the
original subject of the main sentence, now rather remote. (b) It goes
more naturally with the preceding participles as part of the Apostle's
prayer for their progress in insight, service, strength, and finally in
thanksgiving. This interpretation is confirmed by the variant reading *you* in the next clause, 'made you meet'. But it is consistent with
the accepted reading *us*, which need not be limited to St. Paul and
his companions. Bengel, taking the thanksgiving as St. Paul's own,
regards verses 12–20 as a thanksgiving for the conversion of the Jews,
passing in verse 21 into a thanksgiving for the conversion of the
Gentiles. But the passage is too catholic in its language to be so
narrowed. The thanksgiving for which St. Paul prays as the last
stage in the progress of the Colossians is gathered into the sweep of
a thanksgiving, both his and theirs, which embraces all the faithful
and passes into a survey of the whole creative and redemptive work
of God in Christ.

The thanksgiving is threefold, for light, love, and liberty. They
have been admitted to a new world of light, translated into a realm
of love, redeemed to a life of liberty. The three ideas are found combined in very similar language in St. Paul's speech before Agrippa
in Acts xxvi. 18, cp. also his words to the presbyters at Miletus in
Acts xx. 32.

who made us meet. The Greek verb occurs elsewhere in the N.T.
only in 2 Cor. iii. 6, 'who *made us sufficient* as ministers of a new
covenant'. It means to equip for a task, to qualify for a position.
Some early manuscripts, versions, and patristic quotations have
another reading, 'called', which arose either through a scribe's
misreading of the very similar uncial letters of the two Greek verbs,
or through the greater familiarity of the idea of calling in such a
context. The Vatican MS. has a conflation, i.e. a combination of both
readings, viz. *called and made meet*, which recalls the sequence in
Rom. viii. 30, 'whom he called them he also justified', but has no
support in other MSS. and is obviously a scribe's attempt to solve the
textual problem.

to be partakers of the inheritance. Lit. 'for a share in the inheritance'
or better 'for a portion which consists in the inheritance'. The same
Greek phrase is found in the LXX of Ps. xv. (xvi.) 5, 'the Lord is the
portion of my inheritance'. There is no idea of division or distribu-
tion; each believer enters upon the entire inheritance of grace and
truth. Cp. St. Paul's correction of the separatism and protectionism
of religious partisanship at Corinth, 'all things are yours', 1 Cor. iii.
21–3.

the inheritance of the saints. Two Greek words for *inheritance*
alternate in LXX and N.T., viz. *kleros* (here and Acts xxvi. 18) and
kleronomia (e.g. Col. iii. 24, Acts xx. 32, Gal. iii. 18, Eph. i. 14, 18 and

M

v. 5, Heb. ix. 15, 1 Pet. i. 4). *Kleros* denotes rather the possession itself, *kleronomia* either possession itself or the position of the prospective or actual possessor. The idea of succession to an earlier possessor is not inherent in the word but only incidental in certain contexts. 'The dominant biblical sense of *inheritance* is the enjoyment by a rightful title of that which is not the fruit of personal exertion,' says Westcott (*Hebrews*, p. 170), who aptly recalls Aristotle's definition that inheritance is by birth and not by gift, and points out the spiritual fulfilment of this definition in the fact that the inheritance of the believer, the Israelite of the old and the Christian of the new dispensation, is not an unconditioned gift but a gift dependent upon a filial relation. Bengel (ii. 305) remarks *partem sorte non pretio datam*, i.e. the title of the inheritance is not human acquisition but divine adoption. The history of this idea of spiritual inheritance begins with the promise to Abraham. The original idea is the promised land as the home of the people of God, but it passes into the idea of the mutual relation between God and Israel which is Israel's destiny; God is Israel's inheritance, and Israel is God's inheritance. At a later stage this national idea becomes individual, e.g. in the Psalmist's consciousness of life as a personal relation to God. In the N.T. inheritance refers to the blessing conveyed by divine sonship, a blessing variously described as salvation (Heb. i. 14) or the kingdom of God (1 Cor. vi. 9, 10, xv. 50, Gal. v. 21, Eph. v. 5, James ii. 5). Here therefore the inheritance of the saints may be (*a*) their future glory, a parallel to the hope laid up for them in heaven (verse 5), or (*b*) their present dignity, cp. the language of the Catechism, 'inheritors of the kingdom of God'. The Colossians have been both enabled and ennobled by their enrolment in the spiritual peerage of the Christian dispensation.

in light. (1) Taken with the verb this phrase means 'enabled us by the revelation of His light', i.e. lifted us in the light of the Gospel into the fellowship of the faithful. (2) Taken with *the saints*, it would seem to mean the faithful departed, cp. the prayer of commemoration in the Revised Prayer Book of 1927, 'that encouraged by their examples and strengthened by their fellowship we also may be found meet to be partakers of the inheritance of the saints in light'; but it is doubtful whether at this early date Christian thought was much occupied with the thought of the faithful departed, except as to their place in the *parousia*, the Coming of Christ (1 Th. iv. 13–18, 1 Cor. xv. 51–2). The angels are called 'the holy ones' in the O.T. and in apocryphal writings, but it is doubtful whether they are meant by or included in 'the saints' here or in 1 Th. iii. 13. (3) The most natural attachment is to the inheritance or to the clause as a whole; the portion of the saints is in the kingdom of light.

13. *who delivered us out of the power of darkness.* In Isaiah ix. 2 the day of liberation for the oppressed Israelites is compared to the light

livered us out of the power of darkness, and translated us into

shining in the darkness. But a more probable origin of the metaphor is to be found in the prophecy of the conversion of the Gentiles in Isa. xlii. 7, 'to bring them that sit in darkness out of the prison house', which is echoed in the passage in St. Paul's speech before Agrippa in which he describes the call and commission of Christ which made him an apostle to the Gentiles (Acts xxvi. 18).

The Greek word for *delivered* denotes an exhibition of strength, the mighty hand and outstretched arm of rescue so frequent in prophet and psalmist as a symbol of the divine deliverance of the chosen people from their enemies, which became for Christian preachers the type of spiritual liberation from the bondage of sin. The same word is used in 1 Th. i. 10, where the present tense denotes that this deliverance is either a continuous process or a future certainty. There the deliverance is from the wrath of a coming judgement; here it is from the spiritual darkness of heathen life, and has already been effected by conversion.

The Greek word *exousia* here translated *power* means not strength but authority. Lightfoot remarks that the word passes from the original idea of liberty of action into two senses combined in our English word *licence*, viz. (1) authority, i.e. delegated power, and (2) tyranny, i.e. unrestrained or arbitrary power; and he interprets the word here in the latter sense. 'The transference from darkness to light is here represented as a transference from an arbitrary tyranny to a well-ordered sovereignty.' But Abbott (p. 207) insists that the idea of disorder here and in Lk. xxii. 53, 'this is your hour and the power of darkness', is supplied by the context and not implied in the word itself. Cp. Rev. xii. 10, where the word is used of 'the authority of his Christ' which is identified with 'the kingdom of God'. Nor is the idea of delegation inherent in the word itself. In Acts i. 7 and Jude 25 it is used of the authority of God. Yet that idea seems to be implied in Lk. xxii. 53, and it is assumed in Chrysostom's pathetic confession of the misery of evil in the present passage,—'it is hard to be simply under the devil, but still harder that he should have authority'. In the remarkable parallel in Acts xxvi. 18 the turning from darkness to light is described also as the turning from the power (*exousia*) of Satan to God. Augustine takes the darkness to be the devil personified; but this idea is disproved by Eph. vi. 12, 'against the world-rulers of this darkness', where Satan and his host are distinguished from the darkness, which is a description of 'the characteristic and ruling principle of the region in which they dwelt before conversion to Christ' (Abbott).

translated us into the kingdom. The very same phrase occurs in Josephus (Antiqu. ix. 11, 1) of Tiglath-Pileser who 'transferred into his kingdom' by wholesale deportation the conquered inhabitants of

M 2

Redemption in the N.T. is a complex idea. (1) In Lk. i. 68, ii. 38 it is the liberation of the Jewish city and nation, the goal of wistful expectation on the part of devout Jews; so too in Lk. xxi. 28, though there the idea perhaps includes the hope of freedom for persecuted Christians. (2) Here and in Rom. iii. 24 it is liberation from a state or sense of guilt, the freedom of the forgiven soul, a past and present experience. (3) In Rom. viii. 23 it is the redemption of the body from the limitations of this earthly life. (4) In 1 Cor. i. 30, where Christ as the divine revelation of the true wisdom is described as being to us 'righteousness, sanctification, and redemption', the order of the words points to redemption as the final destiny of the Christian, probably including soul and body.

the forgiveness of our sins. Here again *our* is an interpretation, not a translation; the Greek has simply 'the forgiveness of (the) sins'. The Greek word for *forgiveness* here is *aphesis*, the remission of a debt or a penalty, or perhaps the removal or cancelling of the offence viewed as a bad mark. It has nothing of the warmth of our word *forgiveness*, which while conveying the same idea as remission also connotes the idea of the love which gives the forgiveness, an idea conveyed in Greek by the word translated 'forgive' in iii. 13, which is a derivative of *charis*, 'grace', i.e. the love that forgives and helps. The phrase 'forgiveness (remission) of sins' occurs twice in St. Paul's speeches in Acts xiii. 38 and xxvi. 18, but never (except here and Eph. i. 7) in the epistles, where St. Paul uses instead such expressions as 'justification' and 'righteousness', cp. Acts xiii. 39, where the justification of the believer is mentioned by way of explanation of the remission of sins. Lightfoot suggests that the definition of redemption as the forgiveness of sins here and in Eph. i. 7 may 'point to some false conception of redemption put forward by the heretical teachers', and quotes in support of this idea patristic references to the later Gnostic use of *redemption* as a technical term for Gnostic formularies of initiation, e.g. 'perfect redemption consists in this very knowledge of the unspeakable Greatness' (Irenaeus, i. 13. 4), and the Marcosian formula of baptism 'into union and redemption and fellowship with the spiritual powers' or again 'into angelic redemption', which may have meant the same redemption which angels received or more probably the redemption ministered by angels. It is possible that 'the communication of similar mystical secrets, perhaps connected with their angelology, was put forward by these Colossian false teachers as an *apolutrosis*'. St. Paul in that case is insisting here that redemption is not merely an intellectual process but a moral experience.

II. CHRIST THE TRUE MYSTERY, I. 15–II. 7.

(i) *The mystery of the person of Christ*, **I. 15–23.**

1. *His relation to God and creation*, I. 15–17.

He is the visible expression of the invisible God. He stands at the head of all creation, both in priority and in supremacy. In Him was centred the creative energy which gave birth to the universe,—everything in heaven and on earth, the visible and the invisible world,—every form or degree of majesty, lordship, princedom, authority. He is the living channel and the living goal of all creation. He takes precedence of all things; in His person the whole order of things finds its unity and its continuity.

15 who is the image of the invisible God, the firstborn of all

At this point the Apostle moves on to higher ground. All that has just preceded is an enumeration of the blessings for which the *Colossians* have to give thanks to God the Father—admission to the inheritance of the saints, transference from the realm of darkness to the sovereignty of divine love, redemption from the bondage of sin. In the second of these blessings the Son appears in union with and in subordination to the Father; He is the regent of the kingdom, the establisher of the new world of love; He is the agent of redemption, the channel of divine forgiveness. Here the thought of the operation of Christ carries the Apostle away to the mystery of His person; and the pastoral injunction of thanksgiving passes into a theological exposition of the place of Christ in the world of nature and religion. The Apostle launches forth into the great theme of the epistle, the uniqueness and supremacy of Christ. It is the positive constructive answer in advance to the error analysed and refuted in a later passage (ii. 8–23). But it has a permanent value which requires a separate exposition in an additional note (p. 171).

15. *the image of the invisible God.* 'In the passage which follows St. Paul defines the Person of Christ, claiming for Him the absolute supremacy (1) in relation to the universe, the natural creation (15–17), (2) in relation to the Church, the new moral creation (18); and he then combines the two, 'that in all things he might have the pre-eminence', explaining this twofold sovereignty by the absolute indwelling of the *pleroma* in Christ, and showing how as a consequence the reconciliation and harmony of all things must be effected in Him' (19–20), Ltft. A distinction has been sometimes made between two stages of the history of the Son. The relation to the universe has been taken to refer to the pre-existent Son, and the relation to the Church to refer to the Son Incarnate. But the recurrent 'is' indicates clearly that the reference throughout is to the ascended Christ who is now

creation; 16 for in him were all things created, in the heavens

what He has always been; cp. John xvii. 5, 'glorify thou me with thine own self with the glory which I had with thee before the world was'.

the first-born of all creation. The term *first-born* (Gr. *prototokos*) has a double history. (1) It is applied in the O.T. to Israel as the first-born of God (Ex. iv. 22, Jer. xxxi. 9), 'the prerogative race' (Ltft.), and later to the Messiah (Ps. lxxxix. 27, cp. Gal. iii. 16) as 'the ideal representative of the race' (Abbott). (2) The synonym *first-begotten* (Gr. *protogonos*) and the similar expression 'eldest son' are applied by Philo, the Helleno-Hebraic philosopher of Alexandria, to the Logos, the divine Reason or Word, as denoting 'the original conception, the archetypal idea, of creation, which was afterwards realized in the material world' (Ltft.). 'As the Person of Christ was the Divine response alike to the philosophical questionings of the Alexandrian Jew and to the patriotic hopes of the Palestinian, these two currents of thought meet in the term *prototokos* as applied to our Lord, who is both the true Logos and the true Messiah' (Ltft.). (3) In the N.T. it is used (*a*) literally of the human birth of Jesus, Lk. ii. 7 'her first-born son', where the word looks backward rather than forward, indicating her precedent virginity rather than implying subsequent motherhood; (*b*) metaphorically (a) here of the relation of the preincarnate Christ to the created universe, (β) of the relation of the risen Christ to the Church, Rom. viii. 29, Col. i. 18, Rev. i. 5, (γ) absolutely in Heb. i. 6 of His entry into the world, either the Incarnation or the Resurrection or the Second Coming, (δ) of all Christians in Heb. xii. 23, 'the Church of the first-born enrolled in heaven', a description of the communion of the saints, living and departed, all alike eldest sons of God in a family where there is historical succession from generation to generation of the faithful, but no priority of spiritual status as between generations or within any generation.

16. *in him were all things created.* This statement should of itself have ruled out any idea of Christ being included among created beings. Far from being Himself a creature, even the first in order and the foremost in rank of things created, He is the source, the agent, the goal of all creation. Two questions arise here, (1) the contents of the universe, (2) the relation of the universe to Christ. On the latter question see additional note, p. 171. The world of created things is described in two ways. (*a*) It is regarded as a whole. The Greek word *all things* without an article denotes all things regarded individually; with the article, as here, it denotes all things collectively, and might be translated 'the universe' or 'the whole order of things'. (*b*) It is then classified. The universe includes heaven and earth themselves, but St. Paul is thinking primarily of powers and beings, and classifies them first by their abode and then by their character,

and upon the earth, things visible and things invisible, whether
thrones or dominions or principalities or powers; all things have

(1) things in the heavens and things on earth, the plural 'heavens'
probably referring to the idea of seven heavens (cp. St. Paul's own
reference to 'the third heaven' in 2 Cor. xii. 2) common in the Jewish
apocalyptic literature and perhaps prominent in the Colossian heresy;
(2) things visible and things invisible, a division familiar to Greek
philosophy from Plato onwards. The two classifications must not be
pressed rigidly. They overlap or cross each other. Sun and moon
and stars are visible but in the heavens. The human soul is invisible
but on earth. But human beings may be included, soul and body,
among the visible. It is clear from the following words that by the
invisible world St. Paul means the world of spiritual beings and
powers, angelic or astral or both.

thrones, dominions, principalities, powers. These have been taken
as referring to terrestrial rulers and authorities, cp. e.g. 'the rulers
of this world' in 1 Cor. ii. 6, 8. Even there the reference may be to
the hierarchy of celestial powers, cp. Eph. vi. 12. That is almost
certainly the reference here. Earthly potentates may perhaps be
included, but the primary reference of the Apostle is to the world of
spiritual beings and forces. There is no warrant here for attributing
to St. Paul any idea of a distinct and rigid gradation or an exhaustive
and precise enumeration of the celestial powers. The lists vary. In
Rom. viii. 38 among the forces that are powerless to separate Christians from the love of God are mentioned 'angels, principalities,
powers' (Gr. *dunameis*). In 1 Cor. xv. 24 among the forces to be
abolished by the sovereignty of Christ are mentioned 'all (every)
rule (principality) and all (every) authority (Gr. *exousia*) and power'
(Gr. *dunamis*). In Eph. vi. 12 the forces against which the Christian
has to wrestle are described as 'the principalities, the powers (Gr.
exousiai), the world-rulers of this darkness, the spiritual hosts of
wickedness in the heavenly places'. Most pertinent of all, in Eph. i.
21, an obvious parallel to the present passage, the forces above which
the ascended Christ is enthroned are described as 'all (every) rule
(principality) and authority (Gr. *exousia*) and power (Gr. *dunamis*)
and dominion'. *Throne* is peculiar to the present passage, *power*
(*dunamis*) to Eph. i. 21. And the order of the names is different in
the two passages. Nor is there any warrant for attributing to St.
Paul a deliberate acceptance of the belief in such an ordered hierarchy.
In Eph. i. 21 he adds 'and every name that is named not only in this
world but also in that which is to come', i.e. 'every dignity or title
(whether real or imaginary) which is reverenced' (Ltft.). 'The various
lists that he produces are probably nothing more than echoes or
repetitions of the descriptions of the world of spirits current in
the language of the day' (M. Jones, *Expositor*, May 1918). These

descriptions vary very considerably. Both the names and their sequences vary in the lists given in Jewish apocryphal writings and in Christian literature from Origen to the pseudonymous Dionysius Areopagiticus. The only agreement seems to be that on the whole *thrones* and *dominions* stand at the head of the orders, and *principalities* and *powers* come in a second class. Probably the different names used by St. Paul are selected or intended by him to denote different aspects of superhuman agency rather than different orders of superhuman agents.

thrones. This name has been interpreted as meaning (1) spirits occupying thrones around the throne of God, the seats of highest honour in the court of the heavenly King, cp. the thrones of the apostles round the throne of Christ, Mt. xix. 28, Lk. xxii. 30, and the thrones of the twenty-four elders representing the Jewish and the Christian Church in Rev. iv. 4 (cp. also xi. 16, xx. 4); (2) spirits supporting or forming the throne of God, as His chariot rests upon the cherubim in Ezek. i. 26, ix. 1 ff., xi. 22, Ps. xviii. 10, xcix. 1, 1 Chron. xxviii. 18; (3) more probably, in line with the other names, a type of rank and power, in this case viceregal or judicial, 'St. Paul perhaps preferring personifications of abstract terms to direct personal appellations, as more suitable to the vague and mysterious nature of these exalted beings' (L. Williams).

dominions, i.e. dominations, lordships; the Greek word is derived from *kurios*, lord. It has been suggested that as the word *kurios* was the Greek equivalent of the Roman imperial title *dominus*, so the word *dominion* here conveys an idea of despotism lacking in *throne* (Williams, p. 45). In 2 Pet. ii. 10 and Jude 8 it is used of legitimate authority, whether divine or human, despised and disregarded by false teachers. Here it refers like *thrones* to angelic powers, cp. *Ascension of Isaiah*, vii. 21, 'worship neither angels nor lordships nor thrones'.

principalities, powers. Cp. Eph. i. 21. The Greek words thus translated occur frequently in conjunction. They refer (1) to human authorities in Lk. xii. 11, where, coupled with synagogues, they refer to Jewish and Roman tribunals; in Lk. xx. 20 (in the singular) 'the rule and authority of the (Roman) governor'; Tit. iii. 1, all civil authorities; (2) to spiritual powers; (*a*) sometimes good spirits; Christ is 'the head of all (every) principality and power', Col. ii. 10; the Church is a living revelation of the wisdom of God 'to the principalities and powers in the heavenly places', Eph. iii. 10; (*b*) sometimes evil spirits; the invisible enemies of the Christian soul, Eph. vi. 12; the hostile powers conquered by Christ upon the Cross, Col. ii. 15; (*c*) sometimes indeterminate or neutral, e.g. Rom. viii. 38, 1 Cor. xv. 24, though the reference to enemies in the latter context suggests hostility to Christ. On the Greek word translated here *power* (*exousia*) see note on verse 13. The Greek word here for *principality* (*arche*),

been created through him, and unto him ; 17 and he is before all things, and in him all things ¹consist.

¹ That is, *hold together.*

like the Latin *princeps* and its derivatives, means (*a*) beginning or first cause, (*b*) first place in office or power. In Rev. iii. 14 it is used of Christ as 'the beginning of creation'; in Jude 6 of the position forfeited by the disobedient angels. The R.V. is not consistent in its translations of the three Greek terms *arche, exousia, dunamis.* Such consistency is hard to maintain in varying contexts. Nor is it easy to find or safe to press distinctions between the meanings of the Greek words as used in reference to spiritual powers. In fact St. Paul seems to exhaust all available synonyms for such powers in order to insist the more strongly upon the truth that all forces, powers, and beings whatever in the universe, whatever their character and capacity, are subordinate and subject to the Son of God.

17. *he is before all things.* The Vulgate has *ante omnes,* i.e. before all beings, but the recurrence of the unmistakable neuter in the context is decisive for the neuter here also, embracing not only the angelic hierarchy but the entire universe. 'All things' here has no article in the Greek ; it is distributive, 'every created thing or being'. 'Before' denotes not superiority in rank but priority in time. Bengel remarks : *ante omnia, etiam tempus, i.e. ab aeterno.* From the glimpse of the future convergence of the universe upon Christ St. Paul returns to the past and the present, or rather to the eternal and its expression in time. *He* (lit. *himself*) is emphatic, meaning either (*a*) He and no other, or (*b*) He in His own person as distinct from creation, or (*c*) He by virtue of His divine nature. The verb *is* may be (*a*) the copula with 'before all things' for predicate, in which case the clause simply asserts His priority to the created order, or (*b*) the substantive verb 'exists', in which case the present tense asserts not merely the pre-existence of Christ but His eternity, cp. John viii. 58, 'before Abraham was I am', and Exod. iii. 14, 'I AM' as the name of God.

in him all things consist. R.V. marg. *hold together.*

Additional Note.—**The Christology of St. Paul in i. 15-17.**

It is instructive to note the context and occasion of St. Paul's great theological expositions. In *Romans,* that great elaboration of the relation of Law and Gospel, Judaism and Christianity, a reference to Jews and Greeks in his explanation of his desire to visit the Church in Rome leads on to a survey of the world's religious history and then to the exposition of the Gospel as the revelation of true religion. The first epistle to Corinth is mainly a series of answers to questions raised by news or inquiries from the Corinthian Church, but each of these answers widens out into a statement of some fundamental or comprehensive truth ; e.g. the unfolding of the Gospel as the true 'wisdom of God' arises out of a reference to the partisan dissensions within the Church at Corinth. In *Philippians* the great passage on the Incarnation as the condescension of the eternal Son comes in support of an appeal for self-effacing humility in Church life. In *Ephesians* the explanation of 'the mystical union betwixt Christ and the Church' comes as the ideal and the inspiration of mutual devotion in Christian marriage. This occasional and incidental character of St. Paul's introduction and treatment of great truths is seen vividly in contrast with the systematic outline of the Epistle to the Hebrews, which despite its closing personal touches is more of a treatise than an epistle. It suggests three reflections: (1) The argument from silence which is sometimes used to support statements that St. Paul 'had no idea' of this or that aspect of truth or 'did not take' this or that view is obviously precarious and presumptuous. The great truths appear in his epistles just when and where they appear to him to contain the final answer or the full explanation needed for a particular question. They cannot be combined into a system of theology which can be taken as representing the whole of St. Paul's Christian thinking. (2) The great truth is not viewed absolutely and therefore completely. It is viewed in relation to some particular issue, and only therefore in those phases of its contents which have some bearing on that issue. The passage in which it is stated is not an abstract definition but a practical application. (3) Truth is viewed as the inspiration of action and the foundation of conduct. St. Paul would probably have repudiated pragmatism as an adequate theory of truth. But he would probably have assented to what is true in pragmatism, and that is not that efficacy is the sole and sufficient standard of doctrinal verity, but that the final verification of truth is to be found in experience. Hence his constant reference from duty back to doctrine. One of the most striking examples is in 2 Cor. viii. 9, where in the midst of his appeal to the Corinthians to give generously for the relief of the Judaean Christians he suddenly reminds them of 'the grace of our Lord Jesus Christ, that though he was rich yet for your sakes he became poor'. The self-sacrifice of the Incarnation comes into view as the motive power of Christian generosity.

The relation of Christ to the universe is twofold: it is a relation to God (image), and a relation to created things (first-born). *Image* (Gr. *eikon*) denotes (1) resemblance, (2) representation, (3) revelation. It is the term used by Philo to describe the Logos, not merely the reason, i.e. the purpose of God, but the word, i.e. the revelation of God. It is a synonym of *character*, the Greek word applied to Christ in Heb. i. 3, 'the effulgence of His glory and the *express image* of His substance'. It is used in the N.T. literally of the head on a coin (Mt. xxii. 20), and metaphorically of man as 'the image and glory of God' (1 Cor. xi. 7), and of the likeness to Christ wrought out in the Christian by his union with Christ (1 Cor. xv. 49, Rom. viii. 29, 2 Cor.

iii. 18, Col. iii. 10). The fact that it is used with reference to man rules out the idea of Hilary (*De Syn.* 73) adopted by Ellicott and other commentators, that 'image denotes perfect equality'. In the case of Christ that is true, but it is not conveyed by the word *eikon* but implied in the context, e.g. 'all the fullness' in verse 19.

Chrysostom and most early Christian writers, under the mistaken idea that 'image' meant resemblance in all respects, argued that the image of the invisible must itself be invisible. But the word 'invisible' here is obviously contrasted with 'image'. In Rom. i. 20 'the invisible things of God' (i.e. the attributes of the divine nature) are to be seen clearly by reflection upon the works of His creation. Here St. Paul goes further: the Son is the revelation of the unseen Father, cp. the language of 2 Cor. iv. 4, 'that the light of the Gospel of the glory of Christ, who is the image of God, should not dawn upon them', with iv. 6, 'to give the light of the knowledge of the glory of God in the face (i.e. person or presence) of Jesus Christ'. The same idea is expressed more plainly still in John xiv. 9, 'he that hath seen me hath seen the Father', and i. 18, 'no man hath ever seen God; the only begotten Son . . . he hath declared him'. Lightfoot remarks that 'the epithet *invisible* must not be confined to the apprehension of the bodily senses, but will include the cognisance of the inward eye also'. God is not to be known in Himself by intellectual effort but by acceptance of His living revelation in Christ. In a sense it is true to say (though it is only half the truth) that we do not believe in Christ because we believe in God; we believe in God because we believe in Christ.

It would be an error and a loss to see in the language of St. Paul only or even chiefly and primarily an answer to dangerous tendencies in philosophy and religion. The conception given here of Christ in relation to God and to the world has an inherent validity and value, a message and a majesty of its own, apart from any reference to prevalent heresies. But it is a gain to recognize that this conception does supply the answer and the antidote to the peril of two current tendencies. (1) Over against the idea of angels and other spiritual beings, often entitled 'sons of God', St. Paul's exposition claims for Christ a sonship of an absolute and unique character, a sonship which sets Him far above any sonship that may be predicated in any sense or degree of any other beings, angelic or human. His sonship is a personal and immediate revelation of God Himself. (2) Over against the tendency to fill the gap between humanity and a God hidden in remote transcendency with a series of emanations and agencies that seemed or promised to make known the unknowable and to make visible the invisible, St. Paul's exposition claims for Christ the glory of being the one adequate and complete communication not merely between God and man but actually of God to man. And this exposition is given in a language and a context which prove that, whatever it was for Philo, for St. Paul it was not a theory of philosophy but a truth of religion.

Two ideas have been seen in the expression *the first-born of all creation*, viz. priority to all creation, and sovereignty over all creation. (1) The idea of priority to all creation is obvious and indisputable. There is however some doubt as to the exact meaning of the Greek word translated 'creation'. In the N.T. it is used (*a*) of the act or process of creation, Rom. i. 20, (*b*) of the created universe, Rom. viii. 22, (*c*) of any single created thing, Rom. viii. 39. In 2 Cor. v. 17 what St. Paul says of any man in Christ may be translated 'he is a new creation', R.V., or 'there is a new creation', R.V. marg. Opinion is divided as to whether here the right translation is 'all creation' or 'every creature'. 'The first-born of all creation' might conceivably mean the first product of the process of creation. 'The first-born of every creature' suggests priority and superiority to any and every creature, i.e. something distinct from all products of creation. It suggests or confirms the idea inherent in *prototokos* 'first-born' as contrasted with *protoktistos* 'first-created', which, as patristic writers note, St. Paul refrains from using. *First-born* implies more than priority; it implies a relationship to God which cannot be predicated even of angels or men, much less of other creatures. (2) The idea of sovereignty over creation is not so certain. Lightfoot is right in observing that whereas the idea of priority is more peculiarly in line with the thought of the Logos, the idea of sovereignty is more in line with the thought of the Messiah. But the passages which he quotes in support of the idea of sovereignty as implied in *prototokos*, e.g. Ps. lxxxviii. 28, cp. Rom. viii. 29, will not bear the stress laid upon them (see Abbott, p. 211).

The history of the interpretation of this text illustrates vividly the danger of opportunist exegesis even with the best of intentions. Patristic writers of the second and third centuries interpreted the expression rightly as referring to the Eternal Word. But when the Arians early in the fourth century pointed to this text as proving that the Son was a creature, the orthodox theologians of the day, by way of evading the difficulty, insisted that the passage referred not to the pre-existent Son but to the Son Incarnate. This interpretation surrendered the whole position. They were driven to explain 'creation' as referring to the new spiritual creation. They sacrificed the Deity of the Incarnate Son in an attempt to save the eternity of the pre-incarnate Son. And the whole field of cosmogony was virtually ceded to the very heresy which St. Paul is here ruling out by his assertion of the eternal supremacy of Christ. When the Arian heresy had ceased to be a peril to the Christian faith, catholic theology returned to the only view which does justice to the whole passage, viz. the view that the Christ there set forth as the first, the full and the final revelation of God is the Christ eternal, incarnate, ascended—one unbroken unity and continuity of Divine Sonship.

The relation of creation to Christ is stated by St. Paul in three phrases, viz. *in him . . . through him . . . unto him.* (1) '*In him* were all things created'. Philo, for whom the Logos was the mind of God at work, describes the Logos as the home of the ideal world or the world in idea, which took visible shape in the actual world of creation. Origen and Athanasius and the Schoolmen of later ages adopted this view in a Christian form. 'The apostolic teaching is an enlargement of this conception (of Philo), inasmuch as the Logos is no longer a philosophical abstraction but a Divine Person' (Ltft.). 'The Son of God is the intelligible world, that is, things in their idea. In the creation they come forth from Him to an independent existence' (Olshausen). But this view is scarcely compatible with the past tense 'were created', which refers clearly not to the pre-existence of the ideas of things in the Word, but to their expression in the historical act of creation. Moreover, in view of the use of the phrase 'in Him' in the epistles to describe the relation of the Church to Christ, it seems clear that 'the Eternal Word holds the same relation to the Universe which the Incarnate Christ holds to the Church' (Ltft.). It is life and not merely thought that is thus indicated. Cp. John i. 4, 'in Him was life'. It is life and not merely action; 'through Him' denotes the action of the Word, but 'in Him' goes further back. 'He is the source of its life, the centre of all its developments, the mainspring of all its motions' (Ltft.).

(2) *Through him,* cp. Heb. ii. 10. The statement that 'in Him were all things created' is now analysed and explained. (*a*) The aorist tense there referred to creation as a historical fact; here the perfect tense denotes 'a completed and continuing fact', a permanent relation, not merely creation but preservation and development, cp. John v. 17, 'my Father worketh even until now, and I work'. (*b*) The idea of creation being centred in Christ is seen now to involve two ideas, which are the contents rather than the consequences of the original idea. One is that the creative activity of God flowed through Christ as the living agent of the Father; the other is that it flows back to Christ as the living climax of the process. The phrase 'through Him' is used in Rom. xi. 36 of God, 'of (from) Him and through Him and unto Him are all things' (creation as a whole). Liddon saw here a distinction between the three Persons of the Holy Trinity, but the Holy Spirit could scarcely be described as the goal of divine action, though Moberly in *Atonement and Personality* has brought out vividly the idea of the Holy Spirit's work as the return to God of the results of the purpose of God revealed in Christ and worked out in humanity. The reference in Rom. xi. 36 throughout is either to God the Father or more probably to the Godhead as a whole. In 1 Cor. viii. 6, where St. Paul is repudiating the idea of polytheism, God the Father is the

source of creation, 'of whom are all things', and Christ is its channel,
'through whom are all things and we through Him'. In this statement
however the first half refers to Christ's work in the natural creation,
and the second to His work in the new spiritual creation of humanity,
cp. 2 Cor. v. 17. St. Paul combines in one sentence there Christ's
work in the universe and His work in the Church, which are both
elaborated separately in the present passage. Three points are to be
noted here. (a) 'Through Him' is used of Christ and also of God the
Father or of the Godhead as a whole, but 'from Him' is never used
of Christ; God the Father is the one and only fount and source of
life, a truth safeguarded in the present passage by the very statement
that 'all things have been created through Him and unto Him', i.e.
created by God the Father—it is by the Father's will that Christ is
the channel and the goal of creation. (b) The application of the
phrases 'through Him' and 'unto Him' both to God and to Christ is
significant of St. Paul's grasp of the Deity of Christ. If the Son had
not been God to St. Paul, it is unthinkable that he would have predicated of the Son practically the same relation to the world which he
predicates of the Father. (c) The statement in 1 Cor. viii. 6 is a
sufficient answer to those critics who doubt the authenticity of
Colossians and *Ephesians* on the ground that they contain a new
Christology. Already as early as *1 Corinthians* St. Paul had grasped
the place of the eternal Christ in the creation of the universe. *Ephesians* and *Colossians* are only an elaboration of a truth seen and held
years before and taught in an epistle of unchallenged authenticity.

(3) *unto him*. Christ is the end as well as the beginning (Rev. xxii.
13), the goal of all creation. In Rom. xi. 36 'unto Him' refers to God
the Father or to the Godhead as a whole; in 1 Cor. viii. 6 definitely
to God the Father, but there a distinction is drawn between the
created world as a whole and human beings, 'of (from) whom are all
things and we unto Him', whether 'we' refers to Christians ('only
believers consciously work towards' the goal), or to all humanity, the
Jew guided by prophetic revelation, the Gentile by the revelation of
conscience and of nature, and both eventually by the revelation of
God in Christ. This double use of 'unto Him' with reference to
Christ as the immediate end and to God as the final end finds an
explanation in 1 Cor. xv. 24-8, where the mediatorial kingdom of
Christ is seen passing into the ultimate kingdom of God. Lightfoot
notes the different aspects under which the destined relation of the
world to Christ is presented in St. Paul, viz. (a) deliverance through
Christ from limitation and infirmity, sin and suffering, Rom. viii. 19 ff.
(b) subjection to the sovereignty of Christ, 1 Cor. xv. 25-7, (c) reconciliation to God, but in and through Christ, Col. i. 20, (d) consummation or recapitulation, the focussing and converging of everything
in its final development and completion upon Christ, Eph. i. 10. The
A.V. 'for him' suggests only the second of these aspects, viz. that

the world was created 'to enhance the glory of Christ' (Ellicott). But the ultimate glory belongs to God the Father, e.g. Eph. iii. 21, Phil. iv. 20, and especially Phil. ii. 11, where the confession of the Lordship of Christ is to be 'to the glory of God the Father'. The main idea of the phrase 'unto Him' is to be found under the last of the four aspects indicated above. As humanity is destined to find its unity in union with Christ, and its world-task in the service of Christ, so the whole universe, nature animate and inanimate, men below and angels above, are to find their places and fulfil their parts in a kingdom of Christ which is the realization of the Father's purpose. In the later stages of the evolution of nature, which is no antithesis to creation but only the divine method of creation, man has become an agent in the process, whether or not he realizes that he is now a partner in a divine purpose. Man is developing the resources of the created universe, while he is himself being developed by Christ. As mankind finds its true glory more and more in the service of Christ, its discovery and control of the forces of nature will bring them too into line in the service of Christ. So the whole world of men and things will become a unity of service, a synthesis of contributions to the kingdom of Christ. Man was made in the image of God. Nature is an expression of the mind of God. Christ as the living and eternal Word is the Lord of all life, and man and nature are to reflect that lordship by using in His service all the powers of life that He gave and still gives. 'All things are yours, and ye are Christ's, and Christ is God's' (1 Cor. iii. 23).

The idea of the universe owing its coherence to the mind and will of God is found in Plato and Aristotle, who use the very word used in Col. i. 17; also in Jewish thought, both Rabbinical and Hellenistic, e.g. Ecclus. xliii. 26, 'in His word all things consist', and Philo's description of the Word as 'the bond of the universe which holds all its parts together'. Lukyn Williams aptly quotes a later Rabbinical saying, 'the Holy One is the place of the world, and not the world His place', i.e. the world is in God rather than God in the world. St. Paul goes further, and sees in the eternal Christ the living bond of the world's order, the source and secret of 'that unity and solidarity which makes it a cosmos instead of a chaos' (Ltft.). Cp. Heb. i. 3, 'upholding all things by the word of his power', i.e. not merely sustaining the universe but carrying it forward to its goal. There the idea, viewed from the side of Christ, suggests active control and guidance; here, viewed from the side of the universe, it suggests rather order and unity. In the anonymous *Epistle to Diognetus* (vii. 2, early 2nd cent.) God is described as sending to men not an angel or any other minister in His service, 'but the very Artificer and Creator of the universe Himself . . . whose mysteries all the elements faithfully observe'. These 'mysteries' are what we call the laws of nature; they are mysteries as being unfathomable by human intellect, and

N

mysteries of Christ as being not impersonal tendencies but the secret counsels of the living Word. Lightfoot suggests by way of example that 'the action of gravitation, which keeps in their places things fixed and regulates the motions of things moving, is an expression of His mind'.

2. *His relation to the Church, the new creation*, 1. 18.

As in the natural world, so in the spiritual. As in the old creation, so in the new. Here however He stands in a more intimate relation. He is the Head of a Body, that Body which is called the Church. He is the source and origin of all spiritual life. He is the first-born from the dead: by His victory over death He became the pioneer and prince of the new life. Thus in every realm, natural and spiritual, He stands pre-eminent.

18 And he is the head of the body, the church: who is the beginning, the firstborn from the dead; [1]that in all things he might have the pre-eminence.

[1] Or, *that among all he might have.*

18. *and he is the head of the body.* This transition from the natural to the spiritual creation (2 Cor. v. 17), from Christ's relation to God and the world to His relation to the Church, is described by Theodoret as a transition 'from the *theologia* to the *oikonomia*', i.e. from the eternal nature and existence of the Son to His historical mission and revelation. The introduction of the idea of a new and distinct supremacy is marked by the repetition of the emphatic pronoun 'he himself' and the key-word 'first-born'.

he himself, i.e. either (1) He also in addition to His headship in the natural world, or (2) in His own person, not by any angelic deputy or representative—perhaps, in view of ii. 19 'not holding fast the Head', a glance at the heresy which was interpolating angels as intermediaries between the Head and the members of the Body.

who is the beginning. The relative gives the reason of the headship, 'inasmuch as He is'. The Greek word used here for *beginning* has two meanings, both combined here. (1) It means the first stage of a process, the first instalment of a product, e.g. LXX. Gen. xlix. 3, Dt. xxi. 17, where the first-born is called 'the beginning of his children'. Christ was the first-fruits (Gr. *aparche*) of the risen dead, 1 Cor. xv. 20, 23. But His resurrection was not merely the first of many risings to a new and undying life; it was the opening of the way of resurrection for mankind. (2) The second meaning of *arche* is therefore appropriate here, if not indispensable, viz. the originating cause, e.g. Prov. viii. 22, where Wisdom is described as the beginning of the ways of God in creation. Cp. Acts iii. 15, 'the prince of life' (Gr. *archegos*, i.e. pioneer or leader, R.V. marg. *author*), and Heb. ii. 10, 'the author of their salvation' (Gr. *archegos*, A.V. and R.V. marg. *captain*), in both of which passages the reference is to the resurrection of Christ. Cp.

John xiv. 19, 'because I live, ye shall live also'. Christ is the living cause of the new spiritual creation as well as of the old natural creation, with this difference, that while the life of the universe is due to His action and influence, the life of the Church is due to His communication of His own life to man. Christ shares the life which He gives to the Church.

the first-born from the dead. Cp. Acts xxvi. 23. In Rev. i. 5 the phrase is 'the first-born *of* the dead'. The former phrase denotes the transition from death to life; the latter the succession of all who pass through that transition. The same variation occurs with the word *resurrection*; it is 'resurrection from the dead' in Phil. iii. 11, 1 Pet. i. 3; 'the resurrection of the dead' in Rom. i. 4, 1 Cor. xv. 12, 13, 21, 42, Heb. vi. 2. Ancient commentators remark that the term *first-born* is strictly true of Christ; Lazarus and others rose again only to die again; 'Christ being raised from the dead dieth no more', Rom. vi. 9. There may be in 'first-born' here a reference to Ps. ii. 7, 'thou art my son, this day have I begotten thee', which St. Paul at Antioch interpreted of the resurrection, Acts xiii. 33.

that he might have the pre-eminence, once again the emphatic pronoun, 'He and none other', or 'He again in things spiritual as well as things natural'. The tense too is significant, lit. 'might become pre-eminent'. Christ's headship of the universe is the expression of His eternal Deity (verse 17); His headship of the Church was the result of His historical manifestation, the Incarnation and the Passion which culminated in the Resurrection. This latter connexion of ideas occurs again in Phil. ii. 9–11, where the divine exaltation of the risen and ascended Christ and the homage of the world to the name of Jesus are the sequel and reward of the condescension of the Incarnation. Cp. Rev. i. 5, where the title 'first-born of the dead' is coupled with the title 'the ruler of the kings of the earth'. 'The Resurrection carried with it a potential lordship over all humanity (Rom. xiv. 9), not only over the Church' (Swete on Rev. i. 5).

in all things. Gr. *in all* (plural), not (1) masculine, *inter omnes* (Beza), R.V. marg. *among all,* i.e. all powers, terrestrial and celestial, but (2) neuter, i.e. both in the universe and in the Church, both as the pre-existent Son and as the Incarnate Christ; or perhaps, 'in all respects'.

Dr. Burney (*Journ. Theol. Stud.* xxvii. pp. 160 ff.) propounds an ingenious theory of the origin of St. Paul's explanation of the pre-eminence of Christ in the universe, natural and spiritual. He regards Col. i. 15–18 as an elaborate exposition of the various possible meanings of the word *bereshith,* 'in the beginning', in the Hebrew text of Gen. i. 1. 'Three explanations are given of the preposition *be*; then four explanations of the substantive *reshith*: and the conclusion is that in every possible sense of the expression, Christ is its Fulfiller'. He finds the key to Gen. i. 1, 'in the beginning God created the

N 2

heavens and the earth', in Prov. viii. 22 ff., where Wisdom (i.e. Christ) is called *reshith*, the beginning of God's ways in creation. The argument is put in tabular form for the sake of clearness:

Bereshith=in *reshith*: 'in him were all things created'.
Bereshith=by *reshith*: 'all things have been created through him'.
Bereshith=into *reshith*: 'all things have been created unto him'.
Reshith   =beginning: 'he is before all things'.
Reshith   =sum-total: 'in him all things consist'.
Reshith   =head: 'he is the head of the body'.
Reshith   =first-fruits: 'who is the beginning, the first-born from the dead.

Conclusion: Christ fulfils every meaning which may be extracted from *Reshith*, 'that in all things he might have the pre-eminence'.

Space forbids a detailed examination of this theory. It must suffice here to say that while it throws a flood of light on the wealth of meaning latent in the word *bereshith* and in the profound simplicity of the opening statement of *Genesis*, it is doubtful whether St. Paul saw all this meaning in the word and its context, and still more doubtful whether he would think of making it the framework of a paragraph in an epistle which contains no quotation from the Old Testament and perhaps no reminiscence of Old Testament language. The theory may throw light upon the meaning of St. Paul's own language in this paragraph; but that is no warrant for reading these coincidences back into the mind of St. Paul.

Additional Note.—Christ the Head of the Body

The headship of Christ as taught by St. Paul relates to mankind, to the Church, and to all terrestrial and celestial powers. (1) 'The head of every man is Christ', 1 Cor. xi. 3. St. Paul is insisting that subordination is a principle which runs through all life. Woman is subordinate to man, man to Christ, Christ to God. But it is a subordination which is consistent with intimate union: cp. John xiv. 28, 'my Father is greater than I', with John x. 30, 'I and my Father are one'. (2) Christ is 'the head of all principality and power', Col. ii. 10. Here the headship denotes sovereignty over all natural or spiritual forces and beings, with special reference by implication to the angelic powers enthroned by false teachers in the seat of world-rule. (3) Christ is the Head of the Church, cp. Col. ii. 19, Eph. i. 22, iv. 15, v. 23. It is instructive to note the connexion between the headship of Christ and the headship of man. In 1 Cor. xi. 3 ff., where St. Paul is speaking of the congregational life of the Church, his reference is to the headship of man over woman in the whole order of created life, and that headship is viewed as a step in a ladder of subordination in which both man and Christ are both superordinate and subordinate, man over woman but under Christ, Christ over man but under God. Headship is in both cases balanced by subordination;

it is a link in an ascending chain of service. In Eph. v. 23 it is the headship of man within the home that is in view—not the general relation of the sexes in the Church and in society, but the intimate relation of husband and wife. Here the headship of Christ which is cited as the mystical counterpart and moral example to which the headship of the husband should conform is the headship of Christ over the Church; and its key-note is protective care, for 'He is the saviour of the Body'.

It is true that the Church is in one sense a body of Christians; but the Greek word for body, *soma*, is not used in the sense of an organization formed by the coming together of individuals or units, but only, literally or metaphorically, in the sense of an organism. To St. Paul the Church is not a body or the body of Christians, but the Body of Christ. The expression is used (1) of the natural body of Christ, as the instrument of His atoning Passion, Rom. vii. 4, cp. Heb. x. 10, 1 Pet. ii. 24, and as the revelation of the glory of His Resurrection, Phil. iii. 21; (2) of the Church as His mystical Body, which is viewed (*a*) as a body over which Christ reigns as head distinct from the body, e.g. here and in i. 24, Eph. i. 23, v. 23, (*b*) as a body including Christ as its head, or rather animated by the personality of Christ, e.g. 1 Cor. xii. 12, Rom. xii. 5. In other words Christ is regarded sometimes as the Head, sometimes as the Body, cp. John xv. 5, 'I am the vine, ye are the branches'. There is a constant interchange between these two ideas of the relation of Christ to the Body, viz. headship and identity. It is their combination which makes the difference between the two supremacies of Christ. He is supreme over creation but supreme in the Church; distinct from creation but identified with the Church. Membership of the Body is entered by baptism, 1 Cor. xii. 13. Its life is fed by 'a communion (participation) of the Body of Christ', which is not merely a personal sacrament of union with Christ but a social sacrament of the unity of the Body, 1 Cor. x. 16, 17. It is the spiritual home in which not only racial distinctions (Jew and Gentile) are merged in fellowship (Col. i. 22) but personal dissensions are lost in peace (Col. iii. 15). Its unity is created and preserved by the one indwelling Spirit, Eph. iv. 4. Its development is both a building and a growth, and depends upon the loving service of its members, Eph. iv. 12, 16, and their willingness to suffer on its behalf, Col. i. 24, and also upon the divine sustenance derived from its Head, Col. ii. 19, Eph. iv. 16.

The idea of the Body is elaborated by St. Paul for two purposes. In 1 Cor. xii. 14 ff. and Rom. xii. 4, 5 he uses it to illustrate and enforce the duty of mutual consideration and co-operation between the various members with their different gifts and functions. In *Colossians* and *Ephesians* he uses it to illustrate their relations to Christ. In the latter case the figure of the head suggests the two ideas of supremacy and sympathy. As in the human body the afferent

nerves communicate to the head the sensations of every organ, and
the efferent nerves originate and control the movements of every
organ, so in the mystical body of Christ the Head is conscious of the
experience of every member, and prompts and guides the action of
every member, unless it be paralysed or dislocated by sin.

3. *Invested with all the fullness of Divine Being, He is by His life and
death the reconciliation of the universe to God, I. 19-20.*

*That pre-eminence is His by right. It was the purpose and pleasure of
the Father that the whole content and fullness of divine being should reside
in Him. By virtue of this incarnation of the divine life in Him there is an
atoning power in His mission to the world. It was the purpose of the Father
through Him to reconcile the whole world to Himself—to make the sacrifice
of His life upon the Cross the basis and bond of a new peace, and in this
reconciliation through the life and death of the Son to include both worlds,
heaven as well as earth, the invisible world of higher beings as well as the
visible world of humanity.*

19 ¹For it was the good pleasure *of the Father* that in him
    ¹ Or, *For the whole fulness* of God *was pleased to dwell in him.*

19. *For it was the good pleasure of the Father.* The train of thought
implied in *for* depends upon the meaning of the indwelling of the
'fullness' in Christ, on which see note on p. 183. A.V. *for it pleased
the Father.* The Greek text has only the bare verb 'it pleased' or
'was pleased'. R.V. marg. takes 'the fullness' to be the subject of
the verb. Whatever the construction, the sense is the same; the full
content of deity dwelt in Christ. But the various constructions
advocated by ancient and modern commentators raise interesting
and important questions of theology, or give different turns to the
remainder of the sentence. (1) The supplying of *God the Father* as
the subject presents the simplest theology. The Father is the sole
'fount of deity'. At first sight the past tense of the verb seems to
suggest that the Son's deity was conferred at some point in time, and
to imply that there was a time when He either did not exist or was
not completely divine. But even if the reference is to the deity of
the pre-existent Christ, the aorist tense may refer not to a particular
moment in the history of the Godhead but to an eternal purpose, a
timeless act of the Father's will. But the ellipse of such a subject as
God with this verb has no parallel, though a similar ellipse does
occur with other verbs in James i. 12, iv. 6. The last preceding
mention of God as the subject of a sentence (verse 12) is too remote
to justify the supplying of the word 'God' or 'the Father' here.
(2) The supplying of *Christ* as the subject 'confuses the theology of
the passage hopelessly' (Ltft.). On this supposition, unless the
pronoun *him* is to be taken to mean something different in *unto him*
from what it means in the other three cases of its occurrence in these
verses (19, 20), it must refer to Christ, and indicate that it is to Christ

should all the fulness dwell; 20 and through him to reconcile

that all things are to be reconciled, whereas reconciliation is to God the
Father, e.g. 2 Cor. v. 19. This difficulty is removed or reduced by
some interpretations of the meaning of reconciliation, for which see
note on 'reconcile' below. But there is a graver difficulty. To make
the indwelling of the Godhead in the Son and the reconciliation of
the world to Himself or to the Father an act of the Son's own will is
to create a second distinct source of the will of the Godhead, and to
make the Son an independent author of divine purpose, in contradiction to the underlying idea of the whole passage and to the whole
tenor of our Lord's few recorded but unmistakable references to
His subordination to the will of the Father. (3) Grammatically the
simplest construction is to take *all the fullness* as the subject, as in
R.V. marg. This interpretation does not involve the giving of
independent existence to the attributes of the Godhead, as was done
by the later Gnostic theory of personified emanations such as
Wisdom. The phrase here means God or the Godhead in all the
fullness of its being. Cp. ii. 9, 'in him dwelleth all the fulness of the
Godhead' or 'of Deity', with the LXX of Ps. lxviii 17, 'God was
pleased to dwell therein'.

all the fullness—evidently the same thing that is described in
ii. 9 as 'the fulness of the Godhead', i.e. of the nature of God. The
meaning of this term, Gr. *pleroma*, is not explained here or in ii. 9,
but apparently is assumed to be known to the Colossians. It was
probably familiar to them as a technical term in the teaching of the
Colossian syncretists, though they regarded this fullness as residing
not in Christ, or in Christ alone, but in the 'elements', i.e. the
celestial powers. In the later developments of Gnosticism the term
is used to denote the sum-total of the emanations from the Godhead.
See additional note below.

dwell. There are two Greek words, both compounds of the simple
verb *dwell*, but one denoting transitory, the other permanent dwelling, e.g. LXX Gen. xxxvi. 44 (xxxvii. 1), where both occur in a
contrast between the sojournings of Isaac and the settled residence
of Jacob. The latter word is used here. Later Gnostics regarded the
plenitude of divine nature in Christ as both partial and transient,
some of them teaching that the divine nature or being descended
upon Jesus at His baptism and departed from Him on the Cross.
The false teachers at Colossae may have held some such view, and
St. Paul's use of this word here and in ii. 9 may be a deliberate
insistence upon the permanence of the divine in Christ.

Additional Note.—The Pleroma

The word *pleroma* is both (1) passive, the thing filled or fulfilled
or the fulfilment, and (2) active, the thing which fills or fulfils. The

ambiguity of the term is obvious already in the one case of its use by St. Paul in his earlier epistles, Rom. xiii. 10, 'love is the fulfilling of the law', where love may be the thing which fulfils the law or the law itself as fulfilled, i.e. either the performance or the perfection of the law. Two questions arise in these later epistles, (a) the grammatical sense of *pleroma* in various contexts with their theological implications, (b) the purely theological significance of the word with its practical bearings. (a) In Col. i. 19 and ii. 9 and Eph. iii. 19 it clearly signifies not the fulfilment or perfection of God as a stage in His history but the things which make up the idea of God, the various attributes and aspects of the divine nature. In Eph. i. 23, where the Church as the Body of Christ is described as 'the fulness of him that filleth all in all', the word may be active, i.e. the Body which is the complement of the Head, or passive, i.e. the Body which is filled with the life of Christ (see note on *bodily* in ii. 9). In Eph. iv. 13, where 'the fulness of Christ' is the goal of the growth of human life, not exactly a synonym for perfect manhood but rather the standard of this perfection, the term seems to be passive, i.e. either the maturity which consists in being filled with the grace of Christ, or the maturity which reaches the height of the perfection of Christ's character. (b) The purely theological question is, when did this *pleroma* come to dwell in Christ? Three answers have been given to this question: (1) from all eternity, in which case the *pleroma* denotes the divine nature of the Son, cp. Phil. ii. 6, 'being already in the form of God', i.e. identical in nature with the Father; (2) in the Incarnation, in which case *pleroma* lays stress on the fact that the Christ who became incarnate was not merely a being of some kind or degree of divinity but 'God of (from) God'; (3) at the Resurrection, viewed as the first step in the exaltation of Christ. The third interpretation is disputable. It is true that in Rom. i. 4 the Resurrection is the vindication or revelation of Christ as the Son of God, and in Phil. ii. 9 the Passion is viewed as the reason of this vindication, entitling Jesus to receive 'a name above every name'. But in neither case is there any justification for the idea that the Deity of Christ dated from the Resurrection. On the other hand, if *pleroma* denotes not the fullness of the divine nature but the fullness of divine grace, then the indwelling of this fullness may be regarded as coming in the Incarnation or at the Resurrection. If it was the Resurrection that led to the recognition of the Deity of Christ, and gave Him a wider range for the exercise of the powers of Deity, the Incarnation was the revelation as well as the restriction of Deity in a human life. Cp. John i. 16, 'of his fulness (*pleroma*) we all received, and grace for grace', i.e. grace in increasing measure or succession—a statement which became still truer of the risen and ascended Lord, but was true already of the ministry before the Passion.

The context of the reference to the *pleroma* in Col. i. 19 is not

decisive. It is true that it is appended to the assertion of the supremacy
of the risen Christ, but it may be intended to indicate the inevitability
of this supremacy or of the Resurrection itself; Christ could not but
be supreme, could not but rise again to glory, since He possessed by
virtue of the Incarnation the fullness of Divine Being. It is true on
the other hand that the purpose of the indwelling is stated to be the
reconciliation of the universe through the peace created by the Cross;
but this reconciliation, including, as it evidently does, angelic as well
as human life, may have been regarded by St. Paul as won in principle
by the Cross but only realized in fact by the experience of the
Resurrection.

all things ¹unto ²himself, having made peace through the
        ¹ Or, *into him.*   ² Or, *him.*

20. *through him to reconcile all things unto himself.* 'Through him'
evidently refers to Christ. As the pre-incarnate Son was the Father's
agent in the creation of the natural world, the universe (verse 16),
so the incarnate Son is the Father's agent in the creation of the new
spiritual world, the Church. The Greek word used for *reconcile* here
and in i. 22 and Eph. ii. 16 is a compound of the simple verb translated 'reconcile' in Rom. v. 10, 2 Cor. v. 18–20. The compound verb
denotes either complete reconciliation or restoration from a present
state to a previous state or to an ideal state originally intended but
not yet reached. A similar compound noun occurs in Acts iii. 21,
'the restoration of all things'. The significance of this reconciliation
is not quite clear. (1) In the light of the references to reconciliation
in *Romans* and *2 Corinthians* it would seem here also to mean the
reconciliation of alienated humanity to God. In that case the
reconciliation of the Colossians in verses 21, 22 is introduced as a
particular example of the working of that reconciliation. (2) In view
of the wide range contemplated in 'all things, whether things upon
the earth or things in the heavens', the reconciliation has been
interpreted not merely of the atonement for human sin but of the
reunion of the whole disintegrated universe in subordination to
Christ, the restoration of a disordered world to its intended unity
under the headship of Christ—'unto him' in the Greek text referring
in this case not to God but to Christ, cp. 'created unto him' in
verse 16. In that case the transition to the experience of the Colossians in verses 21, 22 might be stated thus: 'this world-wide reconciliation is not a distant dream, a pious hope, without any bearing
upon your life; as far as humanity is concerned, it is operating
already, and in that operation you have already shared.'

having made peace, i. e. *by making peace* or *making peace thereby.*
The peace and the reconciliation are not quite identical. If the
reconciliation is the restoration of a discordant universe to harmony,
the peace made by the Cross is the first step in that restoration;

liberty of the glory of the children of God' (Rom. viii. 21). The world of nature is to share in the freedom of redeemed and transformed humanity, i. e. is to be brought into closer correspondence to the purpose of God. It is not quite true that 'reconciliation implies enmity' which 'cannot be predicated of unreasoning and lifeless things' (Abbott). Its meaning depends on the context, and here it may mean the harmonizing of discord, the remedying of disorder, in the natural world. 'This restoration of universal nature may be subjective, as involved in the changed perceptions of man thus brought into harmony with God' (Ltft.), or it may be objective, i. e. man once himself restored to harmony with God might be able to bring the forces of nature into more effective subservience to the beneficent purpose of God. It is true that useful discoveries and inventions were made by 'pagan' minds in search of truth, both in ancient and in modern times. But the immense advance of recent ages in the utilization of natural forces for the welfare of humanity does seem to be in some way connected with the reverent spirit of research which is one of the fruits of the recognition of the Lordship of Christ. And in any case the Great War has taught men the horror of the misuse of natural forces for destructive purposes, and set them longing for more of the Spirit of Christ to turn the same forces to constructive and beneficial uses, in accordance with the mind of a God who is love. This would be a real reconciliation of the world of nature to God. Cp. also the prophecy of the pacification of the brute creation in Isaiah xi. esp. 9, 'they shall not hurt nor destroy in all my holy mountain'—'the knowledge of the Lord' shall bring peace between man and beast and between man and man.

Additional Note.—**Reconciliation and the Angels**

Things in the heavens would seem in the light of other references in *Colossians* and *Ephesians* to include and perhaps primarily to denote angelic beings. The difficulty of understanding in what way angels need reconciliation to God has driven some commentators, ancient and modern, to suggest other interpretations, e. g. the devil and his angels, who are yet to be reconciled by the love of God and redeemed into the service of God, or the souls of those who departed this life in the fear of God but in ignorance of the work of Christ (cp. 1 Pet. iii. 19-20), and are yet to be gathered into the retrospective sweep of His reconciling power. Both these interpretations are pure supposition without any suggestion in text or context. Others have taken a desperate refuge in the idea that 'heaven and earth' was a Hebrew way of describing this lower world. Abbott raises the fascinating question whether the things in the heavens may not mean the inhabitants of other worlds. The difficulties involved in the idea of a reconciliation of the angels in general (as distinct from fallen or evil angels) are not conclusive against that idea. It is true that in

the biblical references to angels there is no suggestion of any real
counterpart to human sin that requires atonement. It is true also
that in so far as the reconciliation depends upon the assumption of
humanity by Christ this has no counterpart in His relations with
the angelic world. On the other hand, there is a suggestion of
imperfection in angelic life, e. g. Job iv. 18, and perhaps in the
celestial sphere as a whole, Job xv. 15; and though this is not the
same thing as enmity, it does imply the need of more intimate union
with God or an advance to higher perfection through Christ. In
particular the association of angels with the promulgation of the
Law (see pp. 97–8) seems to have suggested to the Apostle the idea
of 'a certain lack of harmony with the divine plan of redemption'.
And apart from the possibility of any such angelic need of personal
reconciliation in any sense, there is something to be said for the
suggestion that the angelic order as a whole awaits closer association
with the life and purpose of God, either through the destruction of
the hostile forces within that order, the evil spirits, or through the
participation of the angels in the glory and joy of human redemption,
cp. Eph. iii. 10, Lk. xv. 7, 10. It should be noted in this connexion
that whereas in the order of creation (verse 16) heaven precedes
earth, here in the order of reconciliation earth precedes heaven; the
earthly world, the scene of the reconciling Cross, comes first, and
then the process or influence of this reconciliation on earth reacts
upon the heavenly world.

An entirely different interpretation is suggested by the possibility
that the 'things in earth and heaven' are to be taken as governed
not by 'reconcile' but by 'making peace', as Chrysostom and
Augustine read the passage. In that case the reconciliation consists
in the making of peace between earth and heaven, between men and
angels. Bengel remarks on Lk. xix. 38, 'peace in heaven', and
Lk. ii. 14, 'peace on earth', that what those in heaven call peace
on earth, those on earth call peace in heaven. Christ is in a true
sense the living bridge between heaven and earth; the angels of
God are to be seen ascending and descending upon the Son of Man,
John i. 52.

Yet, after all, the labour of the interpreters may have been misapplied or superfluous. They may have erred in 'attempting to turn
what is practically a hypothetical statement into a categorical
assertion'. 'St. Paul has in mind throughout this part of the epistle
the teaching of the false teachers at Colossae, who knew, forsooth, all
about the celestial hierarchy, with its various orders, some of which
were doubtless regarded as not entirely in harmony with the Divine
will. The apostle no more adopts their view here than he adopts their
hierarchical system. The point on which he insists is that all must
be brought into harmony, and that this is effected through Christ'
(Abbott). And if there is a subsidiary point, it is that the angels, far

from being agents or plenipotentiaries in the process of reconciliation, as the Colossian teachers held, were themselves included in the process, and as far as they needed any share in the experience of a reconciled universe, owed that blessing to Christ.

4. *The place of the Colossians in this reconciliation,* I. 21–22.

In this reconciliation you too, Phrygians, Greeks, Romans, find a place beside the people of His flesh. You had drifted away from God into alienation and antagonism: you were living a life of evil ways and works. But now Christ has brought you back into touch with God. Living a human life in a human body, He has reconciled you to God by the death which He died in that body. The purpose of that reconciliation is to present you in the sight of God here and hereafter as souls devoted to His service, free from all blemish or blame.

21 And you, being in time past alienated and enemies in your mind in your evil works, 22 yet now [1]hath he reconciled

[1] Some ancient authorities read *ye have been reconciled.*

21. *alienated and enemies in your mind.* In the absence of any further definition and in view of the context, this must refer to their relation and attitude to God. Grammatically 'in your mind' may refer to both the alienation and the hostility, and probably does. They represent two stages of the pagan mind, the drifting away from God and the turning against God. (1) The idea of alienation is explained in *Ephesians*, first (ii. 12) as alienation from the spiritual commonwealth of Israel and exclusion from the covenants of promise, with the twofold result of hopelessness and godlessness, and then again (iv. 18) as alienation from 'the life of God', i. e. the life inspired and sustained by the knowledge of God. The passive participle must not be pressed as implying any idea of the process of alienation by their own action or by evil influences; it is 'estranged' rather than 'banished', though there may be an allusion to their having fallen under an alien power, the power of darkness (verse 13). It simply denotes their condition, whatever was its cause. In Eph. iv. 18 two causes are indicated—the ignorance of the mind, the hardening or blinding of the heart. (2) The Greek word translated *hostile* is sometimes passive, 'hated'. But the active sense is required here. (*a*) It is the sense in which it is used in Rom. v. 10 and viii. 7 and elsewhere in N.T. The exception in Rom. xi. 28 is explained by the context. (*b*) It is required by the phrase 'in mind', which cannot be explained as Meyer explains it, 'hated on account of your mind'. (*c*) Reconciliation in the N.T. is always the reconciliation of men to God, not of God to men. It is the action and the proof of divine love. 'It is the mind of man, not the mind of God, which must undergo a change, that a reunion may be effected' (Ltft.).

in your evil works. Not the cause but the effect of their alienation.

in the body of his flesh through death, to present you holy and without blemish and unreproveable before him:

It found expression in a corrupt life. This sequence is brought out plainly in Eph. iv. 19. Cp. Rom. i. 21–32, where St. Paul traces the falling into unnatural vices back to the failure to grasp the truths of natural religion.

now hath he reconciled. The text is uncertain, the construction irregular. (*a*) There are three readings : (1) the traditional text, 'he reconciled'; (2) 'having been reconciled'; (3) 'ye were reconciled'. The first gives the simplest construction; but if it was the original text, it is hard to understand why it was ever extruded by a more difficult reading. The participle in the second reading, being in the nominative case, is out of connexion with the accusative 'alienated and hostile', but points to a passive verb as probably the original text. The third, though it has only slight MS. authority, is probably the true reading. (*b*) The construction in either case is broken. An English commentary can only state, without any discussion of the grammar of the Greek, the different ways in which sense can be made of the sentence as a whole. (1) 'And you too, though once alienated . . . yet God has reconciled.' In this case 'to present you' gives the result of the reconciliation. God reconciles men to Himself, and then presents them to Himself; He wins their hearts by His atoning love, and then their lives by His sanctifying grace. (2) 'You too, alienated as you once were . . . you were reconciled'—the irregular substitution of a passive verb serving to lay stress upon their experience of reconciliation rather than upon the reconciling action of God. In this case 'to present you' must be taken as meaning 'that you may present yourselves before God'. (3) 'And you, once alienated . . . but now reconciled, it is the good pleasure of the Father' (carried on from verse 19) 'to present to Himself.' (4) 'And you who were once alienated and hostile (but now you have been reconciled) it is the good pleasure of the Father to present to Himself.' In the last two cases the reconciliation is only a stage in the process of human salvation; the stress is laid on the final purpose of God, the perfecting of human character.

22. *in the body of his flesh.* Three explanations have been offered of this emphatic addition 'of his flesh'. (1) The phrase was intended to insist on the reality of our Lord's human nature as against the error known as *docetism* (from the Greek *dokein*, to seem), which arose from the idea that a divine being could not submit to the physical realities of human life; our Lord's human nature was therefore only an appearance, not a reality. It is doubtful, however, whether this heresy took definite shape before the end of the first century. (2) The phrase was intended 'to combat a false spiritualism which took offence at the doctrine of an atoning sacrifice', as Lightfoot puts it, only to remark that if this was what St. Paul meant, he would surely have brought out the point more clearly. (3) Lightfoot regards the phrase as intended to distinguish the natural body of Christ from His mystical Body the Church. It is instructive to note that Marcion, a docetist on this point, omitted the words 'of his flesh' from his edition of St. Paul, and took 'the body' to mean the Church, and that Tertullian in his reply to Marcion insisted that the words must refer to the only body in which Christ could die, viz. a physical body: 'He died not in the Church but for the Church, giving body in exchange for body, a natural body for a spiritual body,' viz. the Church. (4) The phrase has been taken as an allusive reply to the false teaching current at Colossae, in which the angels, who have no physical body, were given a share in the work of reconciliation. In that case St. Paul is insisting that the reconciliation was effected by Christ's sharing the nature and experience of man in a way in which the angels could not. Here again it is doubtful whether St. Paul would have left such an important point just touched allusively without any clearer reference. On the whole it is best to take the phrase as laying stress upon the real humanity of Christ as an integral part of the work of reconciliation, without any deliberate reference to any particular heresy which ignored or depreciated that human instrument of reconciliation.

holy and without blemish and unreproveable. The last two terms denote not status but character; probably therefore *holy* should be similarly interpreted, i. e. not merely consecrated in aim but sanctified in action. In that case *holy* is a positive and the other two words a negative description of the Christian life. There is some doubt as to whether the second Greek word means here blameless, as in classical Greek and in Phil. ii. 15, or unblemished, as in the Septuagint, where it is used of sacrifices, and in Heb. ix. 14, 1 Pet. i. 19. The last word undoubtedly means blameless or unblameable, cp. 1 Cor. i. 8. The last two words may therefore mean (1) 'without blemish and without blame', Vulg. *immaculatos et irreprehensibiles*, or less probably (2) they may refer respectively to character and reputation, 'blameless and unblamed', not merely free from any moral fault but recognized as faultless. The first two words occur together again in Eph. i. 4 and v. 27. Here the perfecting of human life is viewed in a practical light as the purpose and the result of the reconciliation effected by the Cross. In *Ephesians* it is viewed in a more eternal and mystical light. In Eph. i. 4 it is part of the eternal purpose of God, which found expression in the election of the faithful. In Eph. v. 27 the faithful are viewed as a body, the Church which is the Bride of Christ; and the perfecting of the Church is viewed as the purpose of Christ's love for the Church, a love seen in the sacrifice of His own life and in the sacramental cleansing of the life of the Church.

before him. (1) The phrase belongs not to the words immediately preceding, as though the idea were that God and not man is the judge of the holiness and innocence of the faithful, but to the word 'present', whether the idea of this presentation is final judgement or immediate acceptance. (2) Whether the true reading is 'he reconciled' or 'ye were reconciled', it is in either case uncertain whether this phrase means 'before Christ' or 'before God'. In the light of 2 Cor. iv. 14, Eph. i. 4, Jude 24–5, it would seem to mean 'before God'; in the light of Eph. v. 27 it would seem to mean 'before Christ'. Christ gave Himself for the Church in order to win the Church to Himself. But the relation of Christ to the Church, like the kingdom of Christ in 1 Cor. xv. 23–8, is both immediate and mediatorial; the ultimate relation of the Church and the Kingdom is to God the Father or perhaps rather to the Triune Godhead. The reconciliation of man is the work of Christ; but it is the purpose of God, and it is reconciliation to God. Cp. 2 Cor. v. 19, 'God was in Christ reconciling the world unto Himself'.

Additional Note.—Presentation to God

The interesting idea of presentation to God as the end and aim of the Christian life is frequent in St. Paul. Attempts have been made to give the word either a sacrificial or a judicial significance, viz. the presentation of a sacrifice for the acceptance of God or of a life for His approval. The word is too general to be limited to either idea. It is more instructive to note the threefold aspect of presentation. (1) It is sometimes regarded as *the task of the Apostle*, betrothing a Church to a divine husband with the idea of presenting it to Christ as a pure bride (2 Cor. xi. 2), or warning and teaching the individual Christian with the idea of presenting every man perfect in Christ (Col. i. 28). (2) Sometimes it is regarded as *the effort of the Christian himself*. The Roman Christians are urged to present themselves to God 'alive from the dead', Rom. vi. 13, where the idea of the whole passage is the presentation of life with all its parts and powers for obedience in the service of God, cp. vi. 16. Timothy is to present himself to God for approval as a workman not needing to be ashamed of his work (2 Tim. ii. 15). The body is to be presented as a living sacrifice in a rational service (Rom. xii. 1); cp. the echo of this language in the Prayer of Oblation in the English Prayer Book, where the sacrifice of our life is viewed as part of the eucharistic sacrifice of praise and thanksgiving. (3) Sometimes the presentation is regarded as *the work of God*. St. Paul is sustained by the knowledge that the God who raised the Lord Jesus will raise him and his fellow workers with Jesus and present them along with the Christians of Corinth (2 Cor. iv. 14), i. e. to stand before the judgement-seat of Christ or to reign with Him in glory. Christ loved the Church and gave His life for the Church to cleanse and present it to Himself as a holy and blameless bride (Eph. v. 27). In the closing doxology of Jude's

o

viz. (1) it was the faith which the Colossians themselves had heard;
(2) it was this faith, and no other, which had been preached over all
the world; (3) it was the faith by which and for which the Apostle
himself lived. (1) It is doubtful whether the simple phrase 'which ye
heard' will bear this stress, unless 'heard' is taken as implying also
acceptance and therefore the duty of faithful retention. It is more
likely that the phrase is a simple identification of the Gospel, a mere
historical reference. But the two following clauses are unmistakably
meant as arguments. (2) The Gospel was no local movement but a
world-wide message. Chrysostom remarks: 'he brings forward the
Colossians themselves as witnesses, then the whole world . . . and
thus points to the authority of the Gospel.' Lightfoot says rightly:
'the motive of the Apostle here is at once to emphasize the universality of the genuine Gospel, which has been offered without reserve to
all alike, and to appeal to its publicity as the credential and guarantee
of its truth.' But the point of the argument is rather that the Colossians are not the only trustees of the Gospel. There is a Christian
world around them near and far with which they must maintain
communion by maintaining the common faith. (3) St. Paul's reference to his own service in the cause of the Gospel is not prompted by
the desire to vindicate his apostolic authority, which was apparently
not challenged at Colossae; nor by the desire to magnify his office as
the evangelist of the Gentile world, though this idea might well have
been brought vividly to his mind by the reference to the universality
of the Gospel; but rather by the desire to impress upon the Colossians
the fact that he was himself 'a living example and witness of the
power' of the true Gospel (L. Williams).

which was preached. The aorist tense may be (1) timeless, 'which
is proclaimed', or (2) historical, 'which was proclaimed in other parts
of the world before it came to you', or (3) ideal, 'it was done when the
Saviour . . . bade it be done, Mk. xvi. 15' (Moule). This last interpretation is in harmony with the seemingly hyperbolical language
'under heaven' (cp. Acts ii. 5); but see note on 'all the world' in
verse 6 for the justification of this assertion of the world-wide extent
of the Gospel at this date. The idea of public proclamation as by a
herald (the verb is derived from the Gr. word for herald, *kerux*)
suggests a contrast to the esoteric methods not only of the Colossian
heretical teachers but of most ancient teachers of philosophy and
religion; but it is doubtful whether St. Paul intended to hint at this
contrast.

in all creation. On the double use of the Greek *ktisis*, (1) creation
as a whole, (2) a creature, see note on verse 15. The A.V. 'to every
creature' is ruled out by the preposition *in* found in the Greek text.
'Among every creature' (Coverdale, Lightfoot) is an awkward
attempt to do justice to the preposition. Ellicott's 'in the hearing of
every creature' is intelligible, but this use of *in* (cp. 1 Cor. vi. 2,

'if the world is judged by you', i.e. in your presence as a tribunal)
would require the plural. It is simpler to adopt the meaning *creation*,
i.e. (*a*) 'in all the created world' or (*b*) 'in every part of the created
world', cp. 1 Pet. ii. 13. Lightfoot would include all creation, animate
and inanimate, and compares the chorus of praise to God and the
Lamb from all created beings in Rev. v. 13. But the reference here
is to the proclamation of the Gospel as a message for human acceptance (cp. Mk. xvi. 15); any idea of its bearing on the world of nature,
however true, is here irrelevant.

I Paul. In the Greek the addition of the personal pronoun is highly
emphatic. It occurs elsewhere only in 1 Th. ii. 18, 2 Cor. x. 1,
Phm. 19, Gal. v. 2, Eph. iii. 1. In the first three cases it might be
intended to exclude for the moment the fellow-workers associated
with the Apostle in the opening address. But in the last two cases
there is no such association. In all the cases there is a special reason
for the personal emphasis. In Gal. v. 2 it is either a protest of apostolic authority or an appeal to the record of his life by way of refuting
calumny. In Phm. 19 it reads like the formal self-designation at the
beginning of a promissory note. In 2 Cor. x. 1 it adds weight to a
pathetic personal entreaty, in 1 Th. ii. 18 to an expression of personal
affection. Here in the light of Eph. iii. 1 and iii. 7, 8 it seems to recall
the wonder of his conversion and commission (cp. 1 Cor. xv. 10) as
adding weight to his witness to the Gospel.

was made a minister. On the term *minister* see note on i. 7. Far
from magnifying his own place in the life of the Church, St. Paul
describes himself here (as in 1 Cor. iii. 5, 2 Cor. iii. 6, vi. 4, Eph. iii. 7)
by the term which denotes either the character of ministration or
service which belongs to the ordinary Christian life in general or the
lowlier office of service as distinct from the higher office of oversight.
Cp. the use of *ministry* (*diakonia*) with reference to apostolate in
Acts i. 17, 25, xx. 24, xxi. 19, 2 Cor. iv. 1, v. 18, vi. 3, Rom. xi. 13,
Eph. iii. 7. Apostolate, diaconate, presbyterate, episcopate, with
their different functions and degrees of authority, are all alike types
of service. We have here an echo of the Lord's saying in Mt. xxiii. 11,
'he that is greatest among you shall be your servant' (*diakonos*), cp.
Mt. xx. 26, Mk. x. 43, 44). This reference to his commission is a link
between two sections of the epistle. Its primary purpose is to enforce
the warning against the danger of lapse or apostasy at Colossae; but
it leads the Apostle on to a fuller unfolding of the place of his mission
and ministry in relation to the central mystery of the Christian faith.
It corresponds to the reference to his mission in Eph. iii. 'In the
Ephesian epistle this declaration is made a direct introduction to
practical exhortation (cp. ch. iv, v, vi); here it leads up to the
earnest remonstrance against speculative errors in ch. ii, which
precedes a similar practical exhortation. In both cases he dwells on
the committal to him of a special dispensation; in both he rejoices

in suffering as a means of spiritual influence; in both he declares the
one object to be the presentation of each man perfect before Christ'
(Bp. Barry).

Two ancient MSS. instead of *minister* here have *preacher* (Gr. *kerux*,
herald, from which the verb *preached* in the preceding verse is derived)
and apostle, a twofold designation which St. Paul claims in 1 Tim. ii. 7
and 2 Tim. i. 11, adding in both cases a third designation, *teacher*.
The Alexandrian MS. combines all three here, *preacher and apostle
and minister*. This reading is an obvious conflation of variants; but
it suggests nevertheless an instructive analysis of the Apostle's life-
work and the life-work of every Christian minister—message, mission,
ministry—a gospel to proclaim, a church to build, a Master to serve.

(ii) *The ministry of the Apostle of Christ*, I. 24–II. 7.

1. *A ministry of suffering for the Church's sake*, I. 24.

*That service has meant suffering, but it has been worth all that it has cost.
Even here and now I find real happiness in the sufferings that I am undergoing for your sake. The sufferings of the Church are in a real sense the
sufferings of Christ, and in all that I suffer in this frail flesh of mine on
behalf of the Church which is His Body I feel that I am helping to complete
the tale of all that is yet incomplete in the afflictions of Christ.*

24 Now I rejoice in my sufferings for your sake, and fill up

24. *Now I rejoice.* A.V. *who now rejoice*, based upon a reading
which is a clear case of dittography, the scribe repeating by accident
the last two letters of *diakonos*, which are identical with the Gr.
relative pronoun. *Now* is not inferential, 'and so I rejoice'; in its
emphatic position it must be temporal, 'at this moment' or 'in these
days'. (1) Lightfoot sees a contrast to earlier moments of depression
or repining: 'now, when I contemplate the lavish wealth of God's
mercy—now, when I see all the glory of bearing a part in this
magnificent work, my sorrow is turned to joy.' This interpretation,
however true to some phases in the Apostle's chequered experience,
has no support in the context. (2) There may be a thought of the
contrast to the days before the Apostle 'became a minister' of the
Gospel—once an enemy of the Church and the faith, but now a
willing and joyful martyr. (3) Most probably the contrast lies nearer
—'the service of the Gospel, which I entered years ago, is now
impeded by a prisoner's chain; yet the imprisonment has its com-
pensations, and at this moment I am finding a new joy in the midst
of my sufferings, as I reflect upon their significance'.

for your sake. His sufferings had no direct relation to the Colossians.
But they had been incurred in the cause of the extension of the
Gospel to the Gentiles, and in the course of missionary enterprise
among the Gentiles. Colossian Christianity had been an indirect

on my part that which is lacking of the afflictions of Christ in my flesh for his body's sake, which is the church;

result of this mission to the Gentile world; the Colossians had shared at second hand through Epaphras the benefits of St. Paul's missionary labours at Ephesus. Ultimately therefore, though not immediately, his sufferings had been for their sake.

fill up on my part. The phrase represents a single Greek word, a double compound verb. The simple compound 'fill up' occurs twice with the same substantive 'deficiency' for its object which is used here, viz. 1 Cor. xvi. 17, 'that which was lacking on your part (i.e. in maintenance and support) they (the Christians of Achaia) supplied,' and Phil. ii. 30, of Epaphroditus 'hazarding his life to supply that which was lacking in your service toward me'. The preposition *anti* in the double compound has been variously interpreted, (*a*) instead of Christ, the servant suffering as the representative of his Master, (*b*) suffering in response to and in return for Christ's sufferings for him, (*c*) in correspondence to the deficiency, i.e. suffering to meet the need, to supply the deficiency. The last is the simplest interpretation.

that which is lacking, lit. *the deficiencies.* As in 1 Th. iii. 10, 'that we may perfect that which is lacking (lit. the deficiencies) in your faith,' the plural denotes weak points in the faith of the Thessalonians to be strengthened, whereas the singular would have suggested that their faith as a whole was defective, so here the plural avoids giving the impression that 'the afflictions of Christ', whatever the phrase means, were as a whole inadequate or deficient, and suggests rather the idea that there were still afflictions to be endured by the Apostle and others to complete the tale of suffering. The afflictions in question were not imperfect but incomplete—perhaps rather not incomplete but uncompleted. Note the preposition, not '*in*' the afflictions' but '*of* the afflictions'.

Additional Note.—The afflictions of Christ

The main question about *the afflictions of Christ* is whether these are afflictions endured by Christ or by the Apostle in and for Christ. Doubt of the former explanation is raised at the outset by the fact that the Greek word used here, *thlipsis*, commonly translated 'tribulations', and denoting hardship, either galling or crushing, is never used in N.T. of the sufferings of Christ, which are called *pathemata*. But there are also theological and practical objections. (1) On the assumption that the afflictions are those endured by Christ there are three interpretations. (*a*) The view of most Roman Catholic commentators has been that the benefits of the Passion are supplemented by the sufferings of the saints, which have a merit of their own and constitute a fund or treasury from which the Church can grant indulgences. But the Roman Catholic scholar Estius, while believing this doctrine to be primitive and sound, frankly admitted that it could not be proved from this passage. Any such claim on the part of the Apostle, he says, would savour of arrogance; the afflictions of Christ here must mean the same thing as the 'sufferings for your sake'. (*b*) Lightfoot and others, viewing the sufferings of Christ in two distinct aspects, viz. 'satisfactory' and 'edificatory', i.e. atoning and sustaining, rule out the former idea but insist on the latter. 'It is a simple matter of fact that the afflictions of every saint and martyr do supplement the afflictions of Christ. The Church is built up by repeated acts of self-denial in successive individuals and successive generations' (Ltft.). The Passion of our Lord as an atonement was complete and perfect; but as an inspiration it prompted and sustained sufferings on the part of the apostles and the faithful which were in a true sense not merely its consequences but also its continuation. On the other hand, such sufferings had no independent value, for they were themselves the work of the indwelling Christ, e.g. Phil. iv. 13, 'I can do all things in him that strengtheneth me'. And apart from the inconsistency of any such claim of merit with the constant humility of St. Paul, it is incredible that he would have penned such an unguarded expression in a letter to a church already under the influence of teachers who were undermining the uniqueness and all-sufficient completeness of Christ's work. Any such suggestion of a supplementary value of apostolic sufferings might easily 'foster the delusion that either saints or angels could add anything to Christ's work. If affliction could do so, why not (it might be said) self-imposed suffering, asceticism or gratuitous self-denial?' (Abbott, p. 231). (*c*) Most ancient and modern commentators find refuge from these difficulties and objections in the idea that the 'afflictions of Christ' means the sufferings of His Body, the Church, and that they are called His afflictions because 'He really felt them'. They see this idea in Acts ix. 4, 'why persecutest thou me?' But that question only indicates that the persecution of Christians is a persecution of Christ; it does not imply that Christ Himself feels that persecution as a suffering in His own person. This same explanation holds good too of Heb. vi. 6, which has been quoted in support of this interpretation. 'It is true that Christ sympathizes with the afflictions of His people; but sympathy is not affliction, nor can the fact of this sympathy justify the use of the term "afflictions of Christ", without explanation, to mean the afflictions of His Church' (Abbott, p. 231). (2) The alternative is to regard 'the afflictions of Christ' as a description of afflictions endured by the Apostle himself. (*a*) It may mean that the afflictions of Christ are typical and prophetic of the sufferings borne by His followers in the cause of His Church, cp. Mt. xx. 23, 'my cup indeed ye shall drink'. (*b*) More probably it is an illustration of the Pauline idea of the mystical union of the Christian with Christ, by which the

Christian experiences in his own life the experiences of Christ—the Passion and Crucifixion in his own dying to the world and the flesh, Gal. vi. 14; the Burial in his baptism, Rom. vi. 4, Col. ii. 12; the Resurrection in moral renewal, Rom. vi. 4, viii. 10; in spiritual freedom, Col. ii. 12, 13, 20; in the victory of strength over weakness, 2 Cor. xiii. 4, or in final glory, Phil. iii. 10, Rom. viii. 17. This mystical union is both a present experience and a future prospect, Phil. iii. 12. It has yet to be realized in closer resemblance to the character of Christ, in fuller correspondence to the experience of Christ's own life. Both 'the power of His resurrection' and 'the fellowship of His sufferings' have yet to be realized completely, and in that order—it is the risen life that learns to suffer and to win by suffering. It is in this sense of progressive assimilation that St. Paul speaks here of his filling up on his part what still remains to be experienced of the afflictions of Christ. 'Every one when he is perfected shall be as his master.' The Apostle's tale of afflictions is not yet complete, and it is pure joy to feel that his perseverance in the path of affliction is not merely a service to the Church of Christ but the crown of his own discipleship in the service of Christ.

2. A ministry of stewardship in charge of a revelation, I. 25-27.

This ministry of mine, this life of service, is the fulfilment of a stewardship in the household of God which was conferred upon me. In the fulfilment of that stewardship it is my privilege and responsibility to dispense to you the stores of divine truth and grace—to give full expression and effect to the word of God. By the word of God I mean that mystery which had been hidden from past ages of history and from past generations of humanity, and is now at last revealed to the saints of God. Such was the eternal purpose of God—to make known to His saints the wonderful wealth of the glory of that divine mystery as it is now revealed in the calling of all the nations into His kingdom. The revelation is not merely for the world at large; it is for the individual. The mystery thus revealed is nothing less than the presence of Christ in your life, a presence which is the promise and the hope of a glorious destiny.

25 whereof I was made a minister, according to the ¹dispen-

¹ Or, *stewardship*.

25. *according to the dispensation of God,* i.e. his call to the ministry was part of the divine plan of the evangelization of the world. R.V. marg. *stewardship,* i.e. his ministry was to be exercised as a stewardship of divine truth. The Greek word *oikonomia,* which has given us *economy* and *economics,* has a twofold meaning, (1) the administration of a household (Gr. *oikos*), (2) the office of an administrator (Gr. *oikonomos,* mostly translated in A.V. and R.V. *steward*). In the Bible *oikonomia* is used of the divine ordering of the world, and in particular of the life of the Hebrew nation and Church, and of the

sation of God which was given me to you-ward, to fulfil the word

Christian Church. Hence the post-biblical use of 'the old dispensation' and 'the new dispensation' to denote the Hebrew and the Christian stages of history. In Heb. iii. 2–6 the two are contrasted to bring out the superiority of Christ as the son of the house over Moses the faithful servant. The Christian Church as the household and kingdom of God has an ordered life, of which apostles and other ministers are stewards, 1 Cor. iv. 1, ix. 17, Tit. i. 7, cp. Heb. x. 21, 1 Tim. iii. 5, 15. The word *oikonomia* itself in the N.T. (except 1 Cor. ix. 17) is confined to *Colossians* and *Ephesians*. (1) Here and in Eph. iii. 2 it is used of the divine choice and appointment of the Apostle; but here it is his mission, the privilege and responsibility of preaching the Gospel to the Gentiles; there it is his conversion, the grace of God bestowed upon him in the revelation to him of the mystery of Christ. (2) In Eph. i. 10 and iii. 9 it widens into the whole purpose and plan of God for human redemption—in iii. 9 it refers to the reservation of the 'mystery' in the mind of the Creator and its final revelation in the life of the Church, in i. 10 to the historical preparation for the consummation of divine purpose in the person of Christ. By a natural development of Christian thought the term came to be used in patristic literature of the Incarnation itself as the climax and crown of divine providence.

given to me. St. Paul was consumed with the thought of his apostolic office as a divine gift of grace, a proof of divine love and trust. In 1 Cor. ix. 17 it is *a trust* (cp. Gal. ii. 7) which sustains him even when the work is against his inclination. In Eph. iii. 2, 7, 8 it is *a grace*, a communication of divine power, cp. 1 Tim. i. 12–16, where it is also *a mercy*, a proof of the forgiveness of divine love. In Eph. iv. 11 all types of Christian ministry are described as gifts to the Church from the ascended Christ.

to you-ward. Cp. Eph. iii. 2, Rom. xv. 16. See note on 'for your sake' in verse 24. The Colossians were included in the Gentiles to whom St. Paul was sent, Acts ix. 15, xxii. 21, xxvi. 18.

to fulfil the word of God—the purpose of the stewardship. Not (1) to fulfil the promise of God (Beza), or (2) to complete the teaching begun by Epaphras, but (3) to give full effect to the message of God for mankind. Cp. Rom. xv. 19, 'from Jerusalem, ... even unto Illyricum I have fully preached (R.V. marg. *have fulfilled*) the gospel of Christ'. There are two ideas in this fulfilment. (*a*) The revelation of God in Christ was not complete until it had found a home in the minds and lives of men. (*b*) That revelation was not merely 'the glory of Israel' but 'a light to lighten the Gentiles', and it was St. Paul's special task to fulfil this wider purpose of the Gospel. For the use of the phrase 'the word of God' to denote the Gospel, see 1 Th. ii. 13, 1 Cor. xiv. 36, 2 Cor. ii. 17, iv. 2, Phil. i. 14, cp. Acts iv. 31, vi. 7, viii. 4.

of God, 26 *even* the mystery which hath been hid ¹from all ages
and generations: but now hath it been manifested to his saints,

¹ Gr. *from the ages and from the generations.*

26. *The mystery which hath been hid.* For the meaning of *mystery*
see additional note below. There is no hint here of the pagan idea of
the reservation of knowledge by the gods in jealous fear of the progress of mankind, e.g. in the legend of Prometheus or the suggestion
of the serpent in the fall-story, Gen. iii. 5. The phrase 'from ages and
generations' means not 'hidden away from the knowledge of men'
but 'hidden since the beginning of history'. The emphasis is not on
the withholding of truth from mankind, but on its contemplation in
the mind of the Creator, e.g. Eph. iii. 9. Cp. Rom. xvi. 25, 'kept in
silence through times eternal'. The silence was not absolute;
glimpses of the mystery were given to psalmist and prophet, e.g. in
various phases and forms of the Messianic hope, cp. Heb. i. 1, where
these partial divine intimations are contrasted with the full revelation
given in Christ. The reservation was temporary and preparatory,
subordinate and subservient to the main purpose of divine revelation.
Human experiences and historical processes must first develop and
converge upon the point in time and space at which the revelation
would be appropriate and apprehensible, and from which it could
travel over the whole range of civilization.

from all ages and generations. These have been taken as personal,
and by some commentators identified with 'the rulers of this world'
(Gr. *aion*) in 1 Cor. ii. 8; but the reference there is not to any divine
concealment of the revelation but to the inability of men (or perhaps
angelic or other spiritual powers) to recognize the truth when it came
in Christ. It is practically certain that ages (Gr. *aiones*) and generations (Gr. *geneai*) are periods of time. Cp. Acts iii. 21, xv. 18, Rom.
xvi. 25, 2 Tim. i. 9, Tit. i. 2, Gal. i. 5, Phil. iv. 20, 1 Tim. i. 17, 2 Tim.
iv. 18. An 'age' includes many 'generations'. Combined as they are
here and in Eph. iii. 21, 'unto all generations for ever and ever,' lit. of
the age of the ages, they signify all time, with its long periods and its
short epochs.

manifested. Three Greek words are used to denote the revelation
of the mystery, (1) to reveal, lit. unveil, e.g. Eph. iii. 5, (2) to manifest,
i.e. make visible or plain, Rom. xvi. 26, (3) to make known, e.g.
verse 27, Rom. xvi. 26, Eph. iii. 3, 10. They mark three stages or
phases of revelation, (*a*) the withdrawal of the veil from the divine
purpose, (*b*) the visible exhibition of the truth, (*c*) the bringing of
the truth home to the minds of men.

to his saints. A few MSS. add *apostles*, in which case *saints* must be
an adjective, i.e. 'to His holy apostles'. This reading is due to the
influence of Eph. iii. 5, 'unto His holy apostles and prophets,' where
on the other hand some editors translate 'to the saints, viz. His

27 to whom God was pleased to make known what is the riches
of the glory of this mystery among the Gentiles, which is
Christ in you, the hope of glory:

apostles and prophets'. A comparison of parallel passages gives a
complete survey of the stages of the revelation. It came first to the
apostles and prophets, the accredited missionaries and the inspired
preachers of the Gospel. Through their labours it came to the
constantly increasing number of converts, who became thereby the
faithful, the saints, of the first age of the Church. With the opening
of the door of faith to humanity 'without the law' it came home 'to
all the nations', Rom. xvi. 26. Finally, the redemption of humanity
in and through the Church becomes an object-lesson of the manifold
wisdom of God for the contemplation of angelic powers, Eph. iii. 10,
cp. 1 Pet. i. 12.

27. *to whom.* Either (1) the simple relative, in which case the
emphasis lies upon the fact of the revelation, or (2) the limitative
relative, like the Lat. *quippe quibus*—'his saints, namely, those to
whom God willed to make known', in which case the emphasis lies
rather or also on the choice of God.

what is the riches, i.e. how great is the wealth. The idea of riches,
so frequent in St. Paul as a description of the character or action of
God, denotes not merely wealth in possession but also wealth in
communication, e.g. Rom. x. 12, 'rich unto all that call upon Him';
not merely the wonder of omnipotence but the splendour of revelation
and the generosity of providence. See Rom. ii. 4, ix. 23, Eph. i. 7, 18,
iii. 8, 16.

the glory of this mystery. The phase must not be weakened by such
translations as 'the glorious wealth of this mystery' or 'the wealth
of this glorious mystery'. Each word must be given its full weight:
e.g. 'the splendour of the character of God as seen in this revelation'.
The *mystery* is the revelation of God in Christ; the *glory* is the wonder
of divine wisdom, love, and power so revealed; the *riches* is not merely
the infinite variety and range of that triple character, but its unstinted outpouring upon humanity. In most of the contexts of the
phrase *riches of glory* the idea of the glory of God leads up and passes
into the idea of the glory of human destiny in and through Christ.
The eternal love of God which is His glory bears fruit in the glory of
eternal life for His children.

among the Gentiles. Chrysostom is right in remarking that the
glory was seen most vividly in the conversion of the pagan world.
But the glory itself is more than the most glorious results of the
Gospel among the heathen. Those results, impressive as they were
to the mind of the Apostle, could scarcely have been realized by a
local church, even though it lay on an imperial highroad. St. Paul
has to remind the Colossians that the Gospel was a world-wide

movement, i. 6, 23. Text and context here are concerned with the mystery itself rather than its consequences. The glory lies further back, in the world-wideness of the love of God in itself.

which is Christ in you. The relative may refer to the riches or to the mystery, probably the latter in view of Eph. iii. 6, where the mystery is identified with the admission of the Gentiles to life in Christ. *Christ in you* may mean (1) *Christ within you*, the mystical indwelling of Christ in the individual Christian, whether Jew or Gentile, or (2) *Christ among you*, at work in the Gentile as well as in the Jewish world.

the hope of glory. In 'the glory of this mystery' the word *glory* denotes the present revelation of the character and purpose of God; here the eternal destiny of the Christian which is the ultimate effect of that revelation. Cp. Rom. v. 2, viii. 18. Here, as in 1 Tim. i. 1, 'Christ Jesus our hope,' the meaning is not merely that the Christian's hope is centred in Christ, but that Christ Himself is the living hope, as He is 'the way, the truth, and the life' (John xiv. 6). The glory to which the Christian looks forward is the final result of the Incarnation; it is the fruit of the mystical union of the Christian with Christ, the sublimation of humanity, Gentile as well as Jewish, by the indwelling of Christ, Rom. viii. 10, or by the guiding power of the Spirit of Christ, Rom. viii. 11.

Additional Note.—**The Christian meaning of 'Mystery'**

The word *mystery* in the N.T. is not derived from the Greek mystery-religions (Gr. *musterion*) but from the Greek Bible, where it occurs in the LXX of Dan. ii. 19, 27, 29, Tob. xii. 7, Jud. ii. 2, 2 Macc. xiii. 21, Wisd. ii. 22, vi. 22, xiv. 15, 23 (both times of heathen mysteries), Ecclus. iii. 22, xxii. 22, xxvii. 16, and always in the sense of *a secret.* Dr. Armitage Robinson (*Ephesians*, p. 240) sums the history of the word thus: 'We have found then no connexion between the N.T. use of the word "mystery" and its popular religious signification as a sacred rite which the initiated are pledged to preserve inviolably secret. Not until the word has passed into common parlance as "a secret" of any kind does it find a place in biblical phraseology. The N.T. writers find the word in ordinary use in this colourless sense, and they start it upon a new career by appropriating it to the great truths of the Christian religion, which could not have become known to men except by Divine disclosure or revelation. A mystery in this sense is not a thing which *must* be kept secret. On the contrary, it is a secret which God wills to make known and has charged His apostles to declare to those who have ears to hear it.'

It is instructive to study the uses of the word in the N.T. There are echoes of its older use in the sense of a secret. In Rev. i. 20, the mystery of the seven stars in the Lord's hand, and in Rev. xvii. 5, 7, the mystery of the woman and her name, the mystery means the

who apprehend it, since it reaches away into spheres beyond their range of mental vision' (Liddon, *Romans*, p. 216). There is an element of agnosticism, reverent true agnosticism, in the surest Christian faith. But this idea of mystery as something still undiscoverable or unintelligible is foreign to the use of the word in the N.T., where the stress is not on the secrecy but on the revelation of the secret, not on the mysterious nature of truth even after its revelation but upon the fact that while it needed to be revealed it has as a matter of fact now been revealed.

3. *A ministry for the perfecting of the saints*, I. 28–9.

It is Christ Himself therefore whom we set plainly before you. We appeal to the moral sense not merely of a favoured few but of every man: we appeal to the intelligence of every man with the offer of instruction in all true wisdom—and all this with the one aim of presenting every man to God in all that perfection of his nature which can be reached, and can only be reached, through union with Christ. With this end in view I toil and wrestle with my whole being, knowing all the time that I am only responding to the power of Christ Himself which is working itself out in me and giving me strength for my own work.

28 whom we proclaim, admonishing every man and teaching every man in all wisdom, that we may present every man

28. *whom we proclaim*, i.e. either (1) simply Christ in all the aspects of His work, or (2) Christ in you, Christ in His mystical indwelling in the Christian, or (3) Christ among you, Christ in His appeal to the Gentile world. Here the Apostle returns from his brief digression upon the meaning of 'the mystery' to the purpose of his apostolic ministry (23, 25). The emphatic *we* in the Greek may point a contrast between St. Paul and his companions and on the other hand Jewish and heretical teachers. The Christian doctrine of God is centred in the Person of Christ. The Greek word for *proclaim* denotes not the enunciation of ideas but the statement of facts. The Gospel is primarily a history; Christian doctrine is the interpretation of that history.

admonishing and teaching, moral and doctrinal instruction respectively. Meyer aptly notes the correspondence of the two words to the 'repent and believe' of our Lord's own earliest message (Mk. i. 15). Cp. St. Paul's retrospect of his own teaching at Ephesus, 'repentance toward God and faith toward our Lord Jesus Christ', Acts xx. 21, and the foundation truths of 'repentance from dead works and faith toward God' in Heb. vi. 1. But the admonition must not be limited to the preaching of repentance; it would include constructive moral teaching.

every man. The emphasis seen in the triple use of this phrase may have been intended (1) to include the Colossians, whom St. Paul had

perfect in Christ; 29 whereunto I labour also, striving according
to his working, which worketh in me [1]mightily.

[1] Or, *in power*.

not yet seen but whom he has a duty and a right to address as an
apostle, (2) to include Gentiles as well as Jews, (3) to point a contrast
to the intellectual exclusiveness of heretical teachers who reserved
much of their teaching for an inner circle, (4) to mark the care of the
Apostle for each individual soul.

in all wisdom, cp. Col. i. 9, iii. 16, Eph. i. 8: either (1) the spirit of
the teacher, i.e. with all wisdom and discrimination, or (2) the substance of the teaching, i.e. in the whole range of divine truth. In
1 Cor. i. 17, ii. 1–6 St. Paul deprecates 'wisdom' in the sense of the
display of intellectuality or the elaboration of theory; but even
there (ii. 7) he insists that there is a divine philosophy of life and
history, the interpretation of a divine revelation. Cp. Col. ii. 3, of
the treasures of wisdom and knowledge to be found in Christ.

that we may present every man perfect in Christ. On the meaning of
perfect see Additional Note on p. 277.

29. *whereunto.* i.e. with this end in view, viz. the perfecting of
every Christian man by the faithful and full presentation of the
Gospel and Person of Christ. Lightfoot takes the end in view to be
the vindication of the universality of the Gospel; 'if St. Paul had
been content to preach an exclusive gospel, he might have saved
himself from more than half the troubles of his life'. It is true that
the opposition of Jew and Gnostic alike was directed against the
universality of the Gospel, the Jew insisting on racial privilege,
the Gnostic on intellectual capacity. But *whereunto* refers not to the
special feature of the universality of the Gospel, but to its preaching
and application in general; and it is doubtful whether the idea of
such opposition is prominent or even present in the labour and
conflict of which St. Paul speaks here.

I labour also. A.V. *I also labour* is ambiguous; it might mean 'I
also' as well as other apostles and teachers. R.V. is truer to the
Greek, in which there is no emphatic 'I', and 'also' clearly belongs
to the verb, indicating either (1) the price of his preaching, 'I not
merely preach, but preach to the point or at the cost of sheer toil',
or (2) the wider range of labour involved in his mission, 'I not only
preach but toil in every way'. Lightfoot traces *labour* here and in
Phil. ii. 16, 1 Tim. iv. 10, to the severity of athletic training, and
paraphrases it 'I train myself in the discipline of self-denial', in
preparation for and as a condition of the 'striving', which he paraphrases 'I commit myself to the arena of suffering and toil'. But
the labour and the striving seem to be coincident, if not identical.
Nor is this restricted sense of 'labour' supported by its use elsewhere
in N.T. The verb is used of manual labour, as St. Paul's own practice

P

*with you in spirit, and I watch with keen delight from afar the steadiness of
your fellowship and the solidity of your faith in Christ. Go on then as you
have begun. You received and accepted Christ Jesus as the Lord of your life.
Live your daily life then step by step in union with Him. The roots of that
life are already planted deep in Him; let them stay there undisturbed. That
life rests upon Him as its foundation; let it be built up stage by stage upon
that same foundation, and strengthened constantly by a faith true to the
teaching that you received at the outset. And let that faith rise like a spring
of life within your hearts and find its outlet in continual thanksgiving.*

**II 1 For I would have you know how greatly I strive for you
and for them at Laodicea, and for as many as have not seen my**

1. *how greatly I strive for you.* R.V. brings out rightly the idea of
effort as against the 'conflict' of A.V. But it misses the force of the
Greek, 'what a *strain* I have to carry in my care for you'. The noun
agon is used (1) of the Christian life, regarded (*a*) as a fight waged by a
man's faith or a fight to be true to the faith, 1 Tim. vi. 12, 2 Tim. iv. 7,
(*b*) as a race or contest, Heb. xii. 1; (2) of the conflict with opposition
or persecution, 1 Th. ii. 2, Phil. i. 30; (3) here rather of the inward
strain of 'fear or care', A.V. mg. anxiety or prayer or both, cp. Col.
iv. 12. In the story of our Lord's 'agony' in Gethsemane the Greek
word is *agonia*, which in Greek literature is often used in the sense of
or in connexion with fear (Field, *Otium Norvicense*, p. 77). The care
of St. Paul for the Colossians is seen in his prayer for their growth in
love and knowledge (verses 2, 3); his fear in the warning against the
seductions of heresy (verse 4).

for you and for them at Laodicea. The Greek preposition in the
traditional text means 'with respect to'; the revised text adopts
another reading, a preposition with a warmer touch, 'on behalf of',
'for the sake of'. In iv. 13 the Christians at Hierapolis are mentioned
as sharing the benefit of the labour and prayers of Epaphras. Some
few inferior manuscripts add here 'and for them at Hierapolis', almost
certainly an interpolation from iv. 13. Their omission here is explained by Ewald on the supposition that they were few in number
and not yet organized as a congregation, and attended the meetings
of the congregation at Laodicea, which was nearer than Colossae.
Lightfoot suggests also another reason, viz. that they were less
exposed or attracted to the heresy rife at Colossae and Laodicea.

for as many as have not seen my face in the flesh. Better, 'and indeed
for all who have not seen'. Almost certainly a general description
including the Colossians and Laodiceans. Cp. Acts iv. 6, where the
names of Annas, Caiaphas, John, and Alexander are followed by 'and
as many as were of the kindred of the high priest'. Unless the Colossians are included here, they must be excluded by the word *their* in
the next sentence. In that case the return to *you* in verse 4 would
be intolerably abrupt, and indeed the reference to Colossians and

face in the flesh; 2 that their hearts may be comforted, they
being knit together in love, and unto all riches of the ¹full

¹ Or, fulness.

Laodiceans in verse 1 would be pointless. For evidence to prove that
St. Paul had never visited the cities of the Lycus valley, see Intr. p. 39.

2. *that their hearts may be comforted*, i.e. encouraged and confirmed.
The Greek verb has two meanings in St. Paul, (1) exhort, (2) comfort,
in the sense not of consolation but of confirmation; *comfort* in N.T.
is not an anodyne but a tonic, not relief but reinforcement, cp. its
coupling with *stablish* in 1 Th. iii. 2, 2 Th. ii. 17. It is the work of
human teachers and friends, 1 Th. iii. 2, iv. 18, 2 Cor. i. 4, Col. iv. 8,
Eph. vi. 22; the work of God, 2 Th. ii. 17, 2 Cor. i. 4. In Col. iv. 8
and Eph. vi. 22 it refers to reassurance as to the welfare of St. Paul.
Ellicott remarks here: 'surely those who were exposed to the sad trial
of erroneous teaching needed consolation'. But the context suggests
not that the faithful at Colossae were troubled by the heresy of others
but that they were being tempted into heresy themselves. 'It was
not consolation that was required but confirmation in the right faith'
(Abbott). This confirmation is defined in the following words: it is
to be found in love and knowledge, in closer unity and in deeper conviction.

they being knit together in love. Vulgate, *instructi*, i.e. either taught
or equipped. The Gr. verb means *instruct* in 1 Cor. ii. 16 (from LXX.
Isa. xl. 13) and perhaps Acts xix. 33; perhaps here, too, a counterpart
to 'speaking the truth in love', Eph. iv. 15. But the reference to love
points rather to the meaning *united*, which is the original meaning of
the word, '*brought together*'. Its use in the sense of instruction is
derived from this by various stages, (1) putting things together and
so inferring, Acts xvi. 10, (2) proving, Acts ix. 22, (3) instructing.
The original sense is found also in Eph. iv. 16, where 'the whole body'
of Christ is 'fitly framed and *knit together* through that which every
joint supplieth'.

and unto all riches. The language is condensed: 'and so brought
together to and linked together in all the wealth of conviction'.
'Wealth connotes not merely the abundance' of this conviction 'but
also its essential value' (Williams). For the dependence of the advance
in Christian truth upon the unity of Christian love cp. Eph. iii. 17, 18,
'rooted and grounded in love, that ye may be strengthened to com-
prehend with all saints', &c. The idea of moral and spiritual wealth
is a constant theme with St. Paul. Of the thirty-five examples of this
use of the 'wealth' group of words in N.T. twenty-nine occur in
St. Paul's epistles, and nine in *Colossians* and *Ephesians*. Perhaps the
wide experience of long missionary labour and then the concentrated
reflection of days of confinement had given prominence to the thought
of the splendour of God and of the Christian life. Perhaps also the

and not any truth or body of truth revealed by Christ or implicit in Christ, that constitutes the one great mystery or revelation of God. See note on the Christian meaning of 'mystery' (p. 205.) 'The life of Jesus, as it stands before us in the Gospels, is the true mystery.... The one purpose of Christ's coming was to reveal Himself' (E. F. Scott, *The Apologetic of the N.T.*, pp. 182, 208). This great Pauline doctrine is also Johannine, cp. John i. 17, 'grace and truth came by Jesus Christ'. In His coming and in His character, as the Son of God and the Eternal Word, Christ is the mystery of mysteries, the source and sum of revelation.

3. *in whom*, i.e. Christ. A.V. mg. *wherein*, i.e. in which mystery. As the mystery is Christ, the two constructions mean practically the same thing. If a distinction is pressed between the mystery as the divine plan and Christ as the divine person in whom it is realized, then (1) with the rendering *in which mystery*, 'wisdom and knowledge' might denote the objective truths, the positive contents of the mystery, (2) with the rendering *in whom*, the wisdom and knowledge would denote rather His mind into which His disciples can enter (1 Cor. ii. 16), or His own wisdom and knowledge (cp. Isa. xi. 2) which He communicates to them. The second of these interpretations suggests a wider idea. All spiritual truth is in the last resort personal. It is the communion of the mind of man with the mind of God, a communion realized to the fullest degree only in Christ. And in view of the unity of the universe as an expression of the mind of God, all truth, scientific as well as spiritual, centres in Christ, cp. Col. i. 17, Eph. i. 10.

all. Lightfoot remarks that the recurrence of *all* (e.g. ii. 2, i. 28) serves 'to emphasize the character of the Gospel, which is complete in itself as it is universal in its application'. But perhaps we ought to see here rather an insistence upon the supremacy of Christ as the unique and complete revelation of truth, in opposition to the tendency of the prevalent false teaching to break up the *pleroma* (i. 19, ii. 10) and to distribute revelation among a number of spiritual and quasi-divine beings, either as virtual rivals of Christ, or as intermediaries between Christ and man.

treasures. The Greek word *thesauros* meant (1) a receptacle for the keeping of valuables, lit. the caskets of the Magi, Mt. ii. 11; metaphorically, the heart of man as a repository of good and evil thoughts, Mt. xii. 35, Lk. vi. 45; the mind of the true scribe of the kingdom, producing things new and old, Mt. xiii. 52; (2) treasures collected and stored; material wealth, Mt. vi. 19, Heb. xi. 26, or spiritual wealth, 'treasures in heaven', Mt. vi. 20, Mk. x. 21, Mt. xix. 21, Lk. xii. 33, xviii. 22; the treasure of the glory of the Gospel contrasted with the 'earthen jar' of the body or personality of an apostle, 2 Cor. iv. 7. There may be a reminiscence of the parable of the treasure hidden in a field, though there the dominant idea is the joy of discovery and

and knowledge hidden. 4 This I say, that no one may delude

the eagerness of acquisition, Mt. xiii. 44. Cp. Ecclus. i. 25 (26), and Prov. ii. 2–5.

wisdom and knowledge. Wisdom (*sophia*) corresponds to understanding (*synesis*) in verse 2, and knowledge (*gnosis*) here to knowledge (*epignosis*) there. As for their distinction, Lightfoot's note is still quoted by commentators as conclusive. While '*gnosis* is simply intuitive, *sophia* is ratiocinative also. While *gnosis* applies chiefly to the apprehension of truths, *sophia* superadds the power of reasoning about them and tracing their relations.' There is something, however, to be said still for the simpler distinction which has come to be recognized between the two English words: wisdom is wider and deeper than knowledge; knowledge is information, wisdom is inspiration; knowledge is science, wisdom is philosophy. The coupling of the two words in the Greek under one definite article indicates a close connexion with each other which is perhaps a warning against the danger of over-distinction. In Rom. xi. 33 they occur together in the description of the mind of God; in 1 Cor. xii. 8 they appear as gifts of the Spirit to different members of the Church.

hidden. The position of the word in the Greek at the end of the sentence indicates that it is not an epithet but a predicate; it is not 'all the hidden treasures' but 'there lie all the treasures, hidden'. And the fact that the Greek word is not a passive participle (as in 1 Cor. ii. 7 and Eph. iii. 9) but an adjective indicates that the treasures have not been concealed from discovery but are simply awaiting discovery, 'so that every one must ask of Him; He it is who gives wisdom and knowledge' (Chrysostom). The Greek word *apocryphos* used here is used of hidden treasures in LXX. Isa. xlv. 3 and 1 Macc. i. 23 (both times of treasures ransacked by a conqueror); of hidden things that must be manifested, e.g. the light of the Gospel or of faith in the Gospel, Mk. iv. 22, Lk. viii. 17. Lightfoot refers to its use by the Gnostics to describe their esoteric writings, carefully guarded from publication, and perhaps also their esoteric doctrines, revealed only to the select few; and concludes that the Apostle (as with the word 'perfect', *teleios*, in i. 28) here 'adopts a favourite term of the Gnostic teachers, only that he may refute a favourite doctrine'. 'All the richest treasures', so he paraphrases, 'of that secret wisdom on which you lay so much stress, are buried in Christ, and being buried there are accessible to all alike who seek Him.' It is doubtful whether this Gnostic use of the word was current at this early date. Lightfoot's paraphrase is true enough in substance, but St. Paul is addressing not Gnostic teachers but Colossian Christians in danger of listening to a sort of Gnosticism.

4. *This I say.* The same Greek phrase looks forward in 1 Cor. i. 12, Gal. iii. 17, Eph. iv. 17. So here it might mean, 'what I mean to say

Christian teaching or instruction, 1 Th. ii. 13, iv. 1, 2, 2 Th. iii. 6, 1 Cor. xv. 1, Gal. i. 9, Phil. iv. 9. In all these cases it expresses or implies receiving from a teacher; so too here perhaps, in the light of the later words 'even as ye were taught'. Yet there is something more here perhaps than the reception of teaching about Christ. Cp. Eph. iv. 21: 'Christ was the message which had been brought to them, the school in which they had been taught, the lesson which they had learned' (Arm. Robinson). That may be all that is meant in the present passage; but it seems to verge on the deeper idea of receiving Christ into their heart and life, the presence of Christ in their hearts and not merely the presentation of His person to their minds.

Christ Jesus the Lord. It is instructive to study the different combinations of these three designations in St. Paul. (1) *Our Lord Jesus Christ* occurs 47 times and *the Lord Jesus Christ* three times, 2 Th. iii. 12, Rom. xiii. 14, Phil. iii. 20, in all of which cases there is special reason in the context for the omission of the note of personal relationship *our*. (2) *Jesus Christ our Lord* occurs only four times, Rom. i. 4, v. 21, vii. 25, 1 Cor. i. 9, all in early epistles. In (1) His relation to His disciples is placed first, followed by His personal name and then His Messianic title; in (2) His personal name and His divine mission come first, followed by His relation to His disciples. In both He is the Divine Master; in both His name precedes His title. (3) *Christ Jesus our Lord* occurs eight times. In six of these cases there is no definite article with 'Christ'; 'Christ' has almost passed from a title to a name. In Eph. iii. 11 and here the presence of the article points to the thought of His office as the promised Redeemer of mankind, the anointed Servant of God of the O.T., who is then identified with the Jesus of the Gospel and recognized as the Lord of His people. The triple designation in this order denotes the Christ of prophecy, the Jesus of history, the Lord of life. Lightfoot thinks that the Colossians are here reminded that what they received was not merely the Gospel but the Christ, 'because the central point of the Colossian heresy was the subversion of the true idea of the Christ'. 'The genuine doctrine of the Christ' which 'was seriously endangered by the mystic theosophy of the false teachers' consisted in (1) 'the recognition of the historical person Jesus, and (2) the acceptance of Him as the Lord'.

so walk in Him. Mostly in St. Paul and St. John *walk* in the sense of a course or manner of life is defined by things impersonal, (*a*) a state or condition in which the life is lived; (*b*) a standard or rule by which the life is lived. But in some passages the *walk* is defined with reference to God, (*a*) God the Father, 1 Th. ii. 12, iv. 1; (*b*) Christ, here alone, 'walk in Christ', i.e. in union with Christ, a more mystical and intimate note than walking 'worthily of the Lord' (i.e. Christ) in Col. i. 10, or 'after His commandments', 2 John 6, or again than 'my ways in Christ' in 1 Cor. iv. 17; (*c*) the Spirit,

him, 7 rooted and builded up in him, and stablished [1]in your faith, even as ye were taught, abounding [2]in thanksgiving.

[1] Or, *by*.   [2] Some ancient authorities insert *in it*.

perhaps in 2 Cor. xii. 18, and certainly in Gal. v. 16, 25, where, however, it is difficult to distinguish between the Holy Spirit operating in the Christian and the spiritual life which is the result of His operation. Thus even so practical a matter as the ordinary course of the Christian life in the world is viewed by St. Paul in relation to each Person of the Holy Trinity, as implying obedience to the will of God the Father, consciousness of union with Christ the Son of God, correspondence to the guidance of the Spirit of God.

7. *rooted and builded up in Him.* In the Greek *rooted* is a perfect participle, 'rooted in the past once and for all'; *builded up* is a present participle, 'continuing to be built from day to day, stage by stage'. In Eph. iii. 17 'rooted' is coupled with 'grounded', lit. 'founded', cp. 'grounded and stedfast' in Col. i. 23. In Eph. iii. 17 love is the soil and the foundation; in Col. i. 23 the foundation is faith or the faith; here, where St. Paul is approaching the heart of his message, the centring of the Christian life in Christ, the foundation is Christ or rather in Christ. In 1 Cor. iii. 10–14 the Christian ministry is represented as building upon Christ as the foundation or perhaps upon the foundation laid by Christ. Here, where the idea is the building up of the Christian life and character course upon course (cp. Jude 20, 'building up yourselves on your most holy faith', or better 'in'), Christ is perhaps 'the binding element' rather than the foundation. Cp. Eph. ii. 20, where He is the corner-stone of the spiritual fabric of which the apostles and prophets are the foundation, 'the centre of the Church's unity' as well as 'the basis on which the Church rests' (Ltft. on 1 Cor. ii. 11). In the present passage the idea is not the building of the Church but the building of the Christian life. In both cases what the Apostle has in mind is not the fabric so much as the process, cp. 1 Pet. ii. 4, 5. The substantive itself, used nine times by St. Paul in the general sense of spiritual 'edification' of the individual or the Church, ought in the three cases where it refers to the building of the Church (1 Cor. iii. 9, 2 Cor. v. 1, Eph. ii. 20) to be recognized as referring not to the completed fabric but to the process of building. It is not the constitution of the Church that St. Paul is describing, but its growth. Much doctrinal exposition, constructive or controversial, has gone astray through being based upon the idea of the Church as a completed building rather than a process of building or at most a building in process. The idea of a completed building tends to banish or obscure the thought of the Builder.

stablished in your faith. A.V. *in the faith.* Ltft. prefers *by your faith*, seeing in faith 'as it were, the cement of the building'; but Abbott rightly deprecates this continuation of the idea of building.

Elsewhere in St. Paul this stablishing or confirming is the work of
God, Rom. xv. 8, 1 Cor. i. 6, 8, 2 Cor. i. 21.

abounding in thanksgiving. Some ancient MSS. insert *therein* after
abounding. In that case we may translate either (1) 'abounding in
your faith with thanksgiving', i.e. growing ever richer in faith, and
thanking God for that growth, or (2) 'and in that very faith abounding
in thanksgiving', i.e. not forgetting to practise more and more the
duty of thanksgiving as a necessary part of a living faith. For the
place of thanksgiving in the Christian life see note on iv. 2. But we
may note here its contexts in this epistle. In i. 11, 12 it is a remedy for
impatience under the strain of opposition or persecution; in ii. 7 a
safeguard against dissatisfaction with the fruits of faith; in iii. 15 it
is a necessary element in the unity and peace of their corporate
Christian life, and in iii. 17 in the unity and devotion to Christ of
their individual life; in iv. 2 it is an incentive to prayer or a corrective
of mere petition in prayer. On the present passage Moffatt rightly
insists upon the pertinence of this 'apparently irrelevant' phrase.
'Gratitude to God, as Paul implies, means a firmer grasp of God.'

III. THE FALSE MYSTERY AND THE TRUE, **II. 8–III. 4.**

(i) *Christ is the final answer to the false philosophy in their midst.*

1. *It is based not upon Christ but upon human tradition and upon a belief in cosmic powers,* II. 8.

But you must be on your guard. There is a philosophy in your midst which is a barren delusion, born of a tradition of human authority and based upon a theory of ruling cosmic forces and not upon the fact of Christ. So take care that nobody shall capture you and carry you off by the lure of any such philosophy.

8 [1]Take heed lest there shall be any one that maketh spoil of you through his philosophy and vain deceit, after the tradition

[1] Or, *See whether.*

8. *take heed lest there shall be any one.* R.V. mg. *see whether.* The future indicative suggests that the danger was real, and the singular pronoun (contrast the plural of a party in Gal. i. 7) that perhaps the apostle had in mind some particular teacher. Cp. the graphic description of a typical teacher in verse 18. St. Paul had probably not met any of the Colossian heresiarchs, but he may have got exact information and a vivid impression from Epaphras.

that maketh spoil of you. In some of the best manuscripts *you* stands in a position of urgent emphasis, 'you Colossians with your wonderful record of spiritual progress and promise'. *Maketh spoil,* either (1) 'spoils', A.V., i.e. robs you of your faith or your intelligence, Vulg. *decipiat,* or more probably (2) 'carries you off as his prey', perhaps as a trophy of his adroit campaigning, or perhaps as a captive drawn back into the spiritual bondage from which Christ had delivered them, cp. Gal. v. 1, 'be not entangled again in a yoke of bondage'.

through his philosophy and vain deceit. The Greek word *philosophy* occurs only here in N.T. Elsewhere St. Paul refers to current philosophy under the name 'wisdom', Gr. *sophia,* in 1 Cor. i. 17–ii. 13, and 'knowledge falsely so called' in 1 Tim. vi. 20. For the heresies of N.T. days see Intr. pp. 71–3. The word *philosophy* here may be a quotation from the claims of the Colossian heretics. St. Paul is not condemning philosophy, Greek or Oriental, in general. His speech at Athens proves that he could recognize and appreciate and utilize elements of truth in current philosophy. Here he is condemning a heresy which posed as a philosophy, i.e. something wiser than the Christian Gospel. Philo uses the word of the Mosaic law and the Jewish religion, Josephus of the three Jewish sects, both writers perhaps with the same idea of making good the claim of Judaism to a place in the world of Hellenistic thought. It is possible that 'Colossianism' was an attempt to present the Gospel as a philosophy which

of men, after the ¹rudiments of the world, and not after Christ:

¹ Or, *elements*.

could hold its own or make terms with current philosophies. Lightfoot notes that 'in this later age, owing to Roman influence, the term
was used to describe practical not less than speculative systems, so
that it would cover the ascetic life as well as the angelic theosophy
of these Colossian heretics'. In any case St. Paul's language asserts
that this vaunted philosophy was a barren delusion. *Deceit* denotes
fallacy rather than falsity, not dishonesty so much as a misconception
at once deluded and deluding. The Greek word for *vain* here means
hollow or empty. The Colossian heresy was empty and barren; it
had no core of historical reality, no reserves of spiritual faith.

after the tradition of men. Cp. verse 22 'after the precepts and
doctrines of men', with special reference to the prohibitions and explanations of the ascetic discipline of the Colossian heresy, and
Mk. vii. 3, Mt. xv. 2 'the tradition of the elders', e.g. the ritual wash-
ing of hands. There was already a Christian *tradition*, on which
St. Paul lays great stress in his earlier epistles. In 2 Th. ii. 15, iii. 6 it
refers to principles of moral duty; in 1 Cor. xi. 2 to principles of
religious worship. The corresponding verb in 1 Cor. xi. 23 refers to
the origin and significance of the Eucharist; in xv. 3 to the resurrection of Christ. In the first three cases St. Paul is the creator of the
traditions; they are his own statements of Christian duty by sermon
or epistle (2 Th. ii. 15). In the two latter he is the channel of the
tradition; its source is the Lord Himself (1 Cor. xi. 23) or the teaching
of the original apostles (1 Cor. xv. 3). In Jude 3 the tradition is the
Christian faith as a whole; in 2 Pet. ii. 21 it is the Christian standard
of life. *Tradition* (Gr. *paradosis*) denotes the transmission of truth;
in 1 Tim. vi. 20, 2 Tim. i. 14 the word used (Gr. *paratheke*) denotes
a deposit or trust to be guarded. In the present passage *tradition*
denotes the character rather than the contents of the Colossian
heresy. (1) Its basis was not the teaching of Christ but the theories
of men. Cp. Mk. vii. 8, 9, 13, Mt. xv. 6, where our Lord insists that
the vice of the tradition lay in the fact that its explanation and
application of the law had obscured and nullified the divine principle
expressed in the law. (2) It was 'essentially traditional and esoteric'
(Abbott); 'it could not appeal to sacred books which had been before
the world for centuries' (Ltft.). Like the Gnosticism of a later age
and the theosophy of modern times, it treated Christ not as the source
of divine truth but as a subject of human teaching, and that too a
teaching derived from a succession of 'masters' and communicated
only to initiated members of an exclusive school. The term 'tradition' recurs again in the name *Kabbala* given by post-Christian
Judaism to its own mystic doctrines.

after the rudiments of the world. R.V. mg. *elements.* I. The history of the term, Gr. *stoicheion*, is instructive. (1) Its original meaning is things in a row or series, e.g. the letters of the alphabet. (2) Like our phrase 'the ABC' it came to denote the rudiments of knowledge, elementary instruction, cp. Heb. v. 12, 'the rudiments of the first principles of the oracles of God', defined or illustrated in vi. 1, 2, viz. repentance, faith, baptisms and laying on of hands, resurrection and judgement. (3) Its next meaning was the elements of life and the world, e.g. mental ideas or physical materials, e.g. LXX. Wisd. vii. 17, 'the constitution of the world and the operations of the elements', and xix. 18, 'the elements changing their order with each other, continuing always the same', cp. 4 Macc. xii. 13, and in particular the astral planets, and the physical elements, viz. fire, air, water, earth, cp. 2 Pet. iii. 10 'the elements (R.V. mg. heavenly bodies) shall be dissolved with fervent heat'. (4) In Hellenistic syncretism this philosophical use became mythological; the elements and planets were regarded as the home or the instrument of spiritual beings animating and controlling their motions. The stars were identified or associated with spirits or star-gods, and the term *elements* was applied to these personal spirits, elemental or astral. In modern Greek the word is used of local spirits haunting places or things. II. In N.T. apart from Heb. v. 12 and 2 Pet. iii. 10, where the meaning is clear, the word occurs in Gal. iv. 3, 9, Col. ii. 8, 20, with reference to some feature or phase of Judaistic or Judaeo-Gnostic teaching. (1) Some ancient writers (e.g. Clement of Alexandria and Tertullian) and most modern scholars take the term to mean rudimentary instruction, an elementary form of religious belief, appropriate or tolerable in an earlier stage of religious experience, but incompatible with the Christian revelation and its new spiritual discipline. In that case 'the rudiments of the world' may mean (*a*) teaching concerned with mundane or material things, (*b*) teaching with reference to the place of humanity in the divine purpose, (*c*) teaching about the things with which the pagan world concerns itself. But this interpretation is open to various objections. (*a*) The idea in Gal. iv. 1–11 is not teaching but control. The heir in his childhood is regarded not as a scholar under instruction but a ward under authority. The Christian is regarded not as a scholar whose education has been completed, but as a servant whose redemption has lifted him into the liberty of sonship. His knowledge of God (Gal. iv. 9) is not a clearer perception but a closer relation. (*β*) The earlier stage of religious experience is described as a bondage, in a context which implies some form of moral subjection and slavery, an idea scarcely applicable to any form of religious teaching, however crude and immature. (*γ*) The bondage is not merely 'under the rudiments of the world' (Gal. iv. 3) or 'to the weak and beggarly rudiments' (iv. 9); it is 'to them which by nature are no gods' (iv. 8). This double context of the bondage points to the rudiments as being personal, not things but beings; cp. the

Q

parallel between the rudiments and the guardians and stewards of iv. 2, and the fact that in Col. ii. 8, and perhaps also in ii. 20, the rudiments of the world are contrasted with Christ. (2) Other ancient writers suggested that the rudiments here meant the astral planets themselves, whose movements were the origin of the observance of days and months and seasons and years, Gal. iv. 10. This interpretation, though nearer the mark, misses the note of personality apparently implied in the passage. (3) Recent scholarship leans strongly to the interpretation of the rudiments as referring to the spirits or angels identified or associated in pagan and in later Jewish belief not only with the planets but also with all natural phenomena, wind, cloud, cold, heat, thunder, lightning, hail, and frost. This idea is elaborated in curious ways in Jewish apocalyptic literature, e.g. the *Book of Enoch* and the *Book of Jubilees*. But it is also illustrated perhaps by Ps. civ. 4 and by the references to angels in connexion with wind, fire, water, and sun in the *Apocalypse* (vii. 1, 2, xiv. 18, xvi. 5, xix. 17). 'From the standpoint of the freedom enjoyed by the Christians as the sons of God all differences between Jewish and pagan religion vanished for the moment; the Jew with his law and its angels and the pagan with his astral and elemental spirits both belonged to an inferior cosmic sphere' (M. Jones, p. 109). The present passage may thus be paraphrased: 'teaching which centres round the angelic beings supposed to be in control of the universe, and not round the Christ who is its source and sovereign'.

2. *But Christ is the fullness of Deity and the fulfilment of humanity, the head of all spiritual powers, the sole source of salvation through the death of their old life and their resurrection to a new life,* II. 9–13.

In Christ the full content of divine being finds its permanent embodiment and expression. You too have been enriched to the fullness of human capacity with the fullness of that divine life by your union with Christ, who is the supreme head of all dominion and authority. In Him you received the true circumcision, a spiritual circumcision: it required no operation of a human hand: it was the abandonment of the whole body of natural impulse: it was circumcision by the hand of Christ. In your baptism your old life was buried as He was buried. In that same baptism you rose to a new life as He rose, through your faith in the working of God who raised Him from the dead. You were once living a life that was spiritually dead, a life of moral transgression, a life of unrestrained and unconsecrated natural impulse. God lifted you into a new life in union with Christ and forgave your past.

9 for in him dwelleth all the fulness of the Godhead bodily,

9. *for in him dwelleth.* On the permanence of this indwelling see note on i. 19. The connexion of thought seems to run thus: 'Beware of being swept away by a philosophy which centres round a theory of cosmic powers and not round the fact of Christ. They cannot give you what you need. To Christ and to Christ alone you must look, for it is in Christ and in Christ alone that the life of God in all its fullness is made available for the life of man.'

all the fulness of the Godhead. On the word *fulness*, Gr. *pleroma*, see note on p. 183. The idea of the divine nature (as distinct from the personality of God) only occurs twice in St. Paul. In Rom. i. 20 the Gr. word is *theiotes*, Lat. *divinitas*, the character or quality of being divine, Gr. *theios*. Here it is *theotes*, the essence or content of divine being (i.e. what constitutes God, Gr. *theos*), for which later Latin fathers coined the word *deitas*, to avoid the ambiguity involved in using *divinitas* to translate both Greek words. The distinction is of the highest practical importance. The word *divine* both in Latin and in English has always included all degrees of superhumanity. In some phases of theological teaching and popular belief Christ is recognized as divine but not as God. His divinity is acknowledged, but His deity is denied or doubted. It was this distinction which divided the theologians of the Nicene age. The 'quarrel over an iota' was a fight for the deity of Christ as against any mere divinity. *Homoiousios* meant a nature similar or akin to the Father's; *homoousios* the same nature as the Father's, 'being of one substance with the Father', as the Nicene Creed asserts.

bodily. Various interpretations have been suggested : (1) *essentially*, i.e. an actual presence of the divine nature, and not a mere influence such as inspired the saints and prophets; (2) *really* or *literally*, not in a figurative sense as in the phrase 'a temple made with hands'; (3) *in its entirety*, i.e. not partially or only in some respects —an answer to the false teaching which distributed the *pleroma* between Christ and the angels—'in Christ dwelt the whole undivided fulness of the Deity, not fragmentarily but as an organic whole' (Jones). All these interpretations put an unnatural strain upon the Greek word. (4) The most natural reference is to *the human body of Christ*. Chrysostom suggests that St. Paul may have deliberately avoided saying *in His body*, which might have given the idea that the Godhead could be confined or contained within His body; he used instead a word which simply says *in bodily form*. The preceding words taken alone might seem to refer to the indwelling of the divine nature in the Eternal Word, the pre-incarnate Son, cp. note on i. 19. The addition *bodily* refers that indwelling clearly to the Incarnation; the indwelling continued in all its completeness in the Son Incarnate. Ltft. notes that the preceding words correspond to St. John's opening sentence 'the Word was God', and the word *bodily* to the later statement 'the Word became flesh'. (5) The only real rival to this interpretation is the suggestion that *bodily* refers to *the Church as the Body of Christ*. 'In Christ dwells all the fulness of the Deity, expressing itself through a body: a body in which you are incorporated, so that in Him the fulness is yours' (Arm. Robinson, *Eph.*, p. 88). But this interpreta-

10 and in him ye are made full, who is the head of all principality

tion seems to involve the reversal of the idea of the Body, for it represents the Body as dwelling in Christ, whereas the essence of the Body is that it is indwelt by Christ. And it is doubtful whether St. Paul would have introduced so remote a thought so abruptly and obscurely without any further explanation.

10. *in him ye are made full.* Some scholars make two predicates of this sentence: (1) ye are in Him, (2) ye are filled thereby or already filled. The separation is not inappropriate. St. Paul may be insisting that in view of their union with Christ any leaning towards other possible sources of help means incurring the guilt of disloyalty or the risk of disaster. But the emphasis of the context is not on their union with Christ in itself but on its consequence, the endowment of their spiritual life. The repetition of *in Him* is significant; Christ is the meeting-point of God and man, the embodiment of the life of God, and the enrichment of the life of man out of the wealth of that divine life so embodied.

This process of the filling of the life of the Christian is viewed in various lights. (1) John i. 16, 'of His fullness we all received' may refer to the earthly mission of Christ viewed in retrospect, or to the entry of each individual upon the Christian life. Here the perfect passive participle seems to denote that the Christian's experience of divine grace in Christ is complete and permanent. In Eph. i. 23 the present participle seems to denote that it is a gradual process, the progressive realization of Christ in the life of the Church. In Eph. iii. 19 this filling is the end of the process, the distant goal of the Apostle's prayer for his readers. (2) The relation of the process to the divine *pleroma* is twofold. The *pleroma* is the treasury upon which the Christian draws, John i. 16, and also the standard towards which he is developing, Eph. iii. 19, iv. 13.

A word of caution is necessary. The fullness of the Christian life must be distinguished from the fullness of the life of Christ. Christ is not 'filled' in any sense which would imply a gradual process of being filled; the fullness of God dwells in Him from eternity, before and after the Incarnation. Human nature is filled gradually, not with all the fullness of God but out of that fullness, up to the limits of its capacity, up to the fulfilment of its ideal destiny. There is no suggestion here of man becoming divine, but only of his being perfected as man by the inflow of divine love. Consciousness of union with God and correspondence to the will of God are not deification, though the language of Christian mystical experience has sometimes given occasion or currency to the idea of some such identification with God.

the head of all principality and power. Of the two ideas suggested by the term *head,* viz. (1) sovereign or superior in position, (2) source and centre of life and energy, the former is here primarily, if not solely,

uncircumcision of your flesh, you, *I say*, did he quicken together
with him, having forgiven us all our trespasses ;

cp. iii. 7, 8, Eph. i. 13, ii. 1 ff., 11, 13, 17, 22, iii. 2, iv. 17, but without
any sharp antithesis to Jewish Christians, or (2) 'you too as well as
Christ',—the spiritual resurrection of the Gentiles was another proof
of the power of God manifested in the resurrection of Christ.

dead. The idea is suggested by the occurrence of the word in the
preceding sentence. But there the word refers by implication to
their symbolic or mystical death to the old life in baptism. Here it
refers to that state of moral death in which they lay before their
conversion, cp. Mt. viii. 22, 'leave the dead to bury their own dead',
and John v. 25, 'the dead shall hear the voice of the Son of God, and
they that hear shall live'.

through your trespasses and the uncircumcision of your flesh. (1)
A.V. *in your sins*, &c., following the traditional Gr. text which has
the preposition *in*, omitted in all revised texts, or (2) 'in respect of
your sins', or far more probably (3) 'through your sins'. But the
distinction between the circumstances, the extent and the cause of
their spiritual deadness is logical rather than practical. The distinction between trespasses and uncircumcision is more important.
It is virtually the distinction between actual sin and original sin,
between sinful acts and a state of tendency to sin, cp. sins and wickedness in the General Confession. But the phrase 'uncircumcision of
your flesh' serves more than one purpose. It does denote Gentile
paganism ; but it describes it in terms of spiritual as well as ritual
reference. Their physical condition was symbolical of their moral
condition.

did he quicken. The subject of the verb is almost certainly God,
cp. the parallel Eph. ii. 5. The resurrection of Christ is nearly always
in the N.T. regarded as the act of God. God is still the subject in
'having blotted out the bond' as also in 'having forgiven'. But
verse 15 seems clearly to refer to Christ, and Christ is therefore
probably the subject in 'he hath taken the bond out of the way'.

The quickening, like the raising, is part of the convert's experience
of union with the risen Christ. But whereas the raising is one side of a
mystical or sacramental process, the counterpart of the burial of the
old life in baptism, on the other hand the contrast between the
quickening and the preceding state of moral death points not merely
to a fresh beginning but to a new energy, cp. the sequence of resurrection and revival in John v. 21, 'as the Father raiseth and quickeneth'
the spiritually dead. Lightfoot deprecates the dilemma of choice in
interpretation between immortality and regeneration ; to St. Paul
'the future glorified life is only the continuation of the present moral
and spiritual life'. That is true ; but the past tense 'quickened' and
the context surely prove that what St. Paul had in mind was the

was against us, which was contrary to us: and he hath taken it
out of the way, nailing it to the cross;

precepts of Christ and the Apostles and then the doctrines of the
Christian faith. In the light of Eph. ii. 15, where Christ is said to
have 'abolished the law of commandments contained in ordinances'
(*dogmata*), it is certain that here too the reference is to the specific
orders in which the commandments, the main principles of the divine
law, found expression and application. (*b*) The bond of the law was
cancelled not by apostolic teaching nor by Christian faith but by the
action of God. (*c*) The question in ii. 20, 'Why still submit to ordinances?' suggests a parallel or resemblance between the *dogmata* of
the false teachers and the obsolete *dogmata* of the Jewish law. (2) A
possible interpretation is 'the bond which was against us by virtue
of its specific obligations of obedience to ordinances'. (3) Eph. ii. 15
is in favour of the R.V. The idea of *written* is implied in the word
bond, Gr. *cheirographon* (Lat. *chirographum*). The bond consisted in
or was expressed in specific ordinances.

against us . . . contrary to us. The former expression refers to 'the
validity of the bond', the latter 'describes its active hostility' (Ltft.).
It was not only a standing condemnation; it was a standing conflict.
The Greek word *contrary*, however, does not in itself denote hostility
but opposition or obstacle. In Eph. ii. 15 the 'enmity' which is
defined as 'the law of commandments contained in ordinances' refers
to the antagonism between Jew and Gentile. Here the law is regarded
rather as creating an external barrier, an internal discord. Cp. Rom.
vii. 7–11, 19–24, where the law is described in its working as revealing
and intensifying the conflict between obedience and disobedience,
between duty and inclination. Cp. also 2 Cor. iii. 6, where 'the letter
killeth' both hope and effort. Bengel notes that the validity of the
law as a condemnation is dealt with by its cancellation; its intervention as an obstacle is dealt with by its removal right out of the way.

and he hath taken it out of the way. The word *it* in the Greek is
emphatic, 'the very bond itself'. There is a sudden change in the construction which marks a break in the continuity of thought. (1) The
perfect tense indicates the abiding and present result; the thing
has gone, and we are free. And the change of construction may be
due to 'the feeling of relief and thanksgiving which rises up in the
Apostle's mind at this point' (Ltft.). (2) The removal of the bond is
not merely another stage of the process. The finite verb introduces a
new and distinct description, which has an explanatory note of its
own in the participle 'nailing'. (3) The change does not require a
new subject for the verb, but it does suggest that the change from
God to Christ as the subject of the sentence, a change which seems
necessary in verse 15, may be most appropriately made at this point.

Objection has been taken to the introduction of Christ as the

subject at this point on the ground that the forgiveness and cancellation are dissociated thereby from the Cross, and the work of
redemption is thus divided between the Father and the Son—the
Father forgiving sin and cancelling the bond, the Son removing and
destroying the bond. It is true that the removal and destruction of
the bond do belong more closely to the preceding stages of forgiveness and cancellation than to the following stage, the victory over
the hostile spiritual powers. But even if for this reason we continue
to regard God as the remover and destroyer of the bond, this only
postpones the difficulty. The victory upon the Cross itself in the next
verse seems to demand Christ as the victor, cp. the parallel Eph. ii.
15. It seems impossible to regard that conflict and victory as the
personal experience and achievement of God the Father; that view
approaches perilously near to the heresy known as Patripassionism.
Christ emerges unmistakably as the conqueror of evil in that last
scene. The only question that is disputable is whether or not He
comes into view as the liberator of mankind in the preceding scene.
In any case St. Paul and his commentators are alike innocent of any
idea of a discontinuity or division between the action of the Father
and the Son. The whole action is one throughout, and this unity is
not broken by any interpretation which sees a transition from the
Father to the Son at the point where the Cross itself comes into sight.

   nailing it to the cross. The metaphor has been interpreted as an
allusion (1) to a supposed custom of driving a nail through an
abrogated decree and hanging it up in public to proclaim thus its
abrogation, (2) to the custom of hanging up spoils of war in temples.
(3) Chrysostom lays stress on the actual rending of the bond thus
nailed. (4) Deissmann (*L.A.E.*, p. 337) refers to the custom of cancelling a bond by crossing it with the Greek cross-letter *X*, but admits
that this is no explanation of the nailing of the bond to the cross. It
is rather an illustration of the erasure of the bond. (5) The point of
the phrase, however, lies not in the nailing itself but in the nailing to
the cross; the bond of the law 'was rent with Christ's body and
destroyed with His death' (Ltft.). It is possible that St. Paul was
thinking of the brazen serpent fastened to a standard for the healing
of the snake-bitten Israelites whose faith was to see in the emblem of
the dead serpent a sign and proof of a plague conquered, Numb. xxi.
9. Cp. Wisdom xvi. 7, 'he was not saved by the thing that he saw,
but by thee, the Saviour of all', and John iii. 14, 'even so must the
Son of Man be lifted up'. It is possible again that he was thinking of
the 'title', the 'superscription of his accusation' (Mk. xv. 26), which
was fastened, perhaps nailed, to the Cross, the title of identification
and condemnation. St. Paul may have seen in that ironical description 'King of the Jews' the true explanation of the Cross, viz. the
acceptance and thereby the abolition of the curse of the law, cp.
Gal. iii. 13.

powers, he made a show of them openly, triumphing over them in it.

tyranny was crushed into impotence, the claims of angelic control reduced to nullity, by the victory of the Cross over sin and death. If the question is asked, how the angels were dethroned and their power broken by the Cross, the answer is partly that metaphor cannot always or completely be analysed into theology, partly that St. Paul is confronting here implicitly, as in the next two paragraphs (16–19, 20–3) he confronts expressly, an eclectic or syncretistic heresy in which a new ascetic legalism was combined with a mystic angelology, and his reply to both is that the Gospel of the Cross was not merely the abrogation of the old Law and of any idea of angelic mediation or intervention connected therewith, but also the condemnation of any idea of subjection to law as an instrument of salvation or to angels as an object of devotion. The Cross opened the new way of faith and closed the old way of works. It was the revelation of the free grace of God, and it abolished thereby not only the curse of an unfulfilled law (Gal. iii. 13), not only the cleavage of an exclusive law between Jew and Gentile (Eph. ii. 14, 16), but also the binding claim of any particular demands of legal moralism (Eph. ii. 15). Christ is 'the end of the law unto righteousness to every one that believeth', Rom. x. 4, i.e. in Christ law as a principle comes to an end, and the way to righteousness is open to faith. 'Christ is the end of law as death is the end of life' (Gifford). The two parallels meet in the death of Christ. The Cross is the termination and the destruction of the old order and the victory and triumph of the new.

made a show of them openly. Here and in some MSS. of Mt. i. 19 the verb is the simple verb which occurs in papyri and inscriptions in the sense of publication, exposure, or display, without any idea of shame. The compound verb is used in Heb. vi. 6 of renegades 'putting the Son of God to an open shame', and in Mt. i. 19 of Joseph's refusal 'to make a public example' of his betrothed. The idea here is not the shaming of the vanquished powers but their exhibition for the assurance of their victims. Cp. the uplifting of the brazen serpent in Num. xxi. 9, and the 'placarding' of Christ crucified before the eyes of the Galatians, Gal. iii. 1. Bengel in the light of Eph. iv. 8 refers this display of the vanquished to the Ascension; but St. Paul here is clearly thinking of the Cross as the scene of the triumph. *Openly*, (1) lit. 'with freedom of speech', without reserve, e.g. Mk. viii. 32, Acts ii. 29; so here perhaps (Alford) of God 'declaring and revealing by the Cross' the supremacy of Christ. But the context points rather to (2) 'boldly' or 'confidently', which is St. Paul's own constant use of the word, e.g. 2 Cor. iii. 12, vii. 4, Eph. iii. 12, vi. 19, Phil. i. 20, Phm. 8, 1 Tim. iii. 13, or more probably (3) 'openly', 'publicly', cp. John vii. 4, xi. 54. Any reference here to courage or confidence on the part of Christ would seem to strike a false note. The point of the word is the publicity of the display for all the world to see.

triumphing over them. The only other occurrence of the Greek verb in N.T. is 2 Cor. ii. 14, 'thanks be unto God which always leadeth us in triumph in Christ', R.V. The A.V. 'causeth us to triumph' gives a wrong impression. The triumph there as here is Christ's own triumph. (1) On the ground that the origin of the Greek word for triumph, *thriambos*, is to be sought in the history of Greek drama, where it denotes a hymn sung in honour of Dionysus, it has been suggested that even here it may retain or echo the note of thanksgiving, the joy of victory (M. Pope, *Exp. Times*, xxi. 1). (2) In 2 Cor. ii. 14 the word clearly denotes leading in His triumphal train, either as former enemies, now willing captives (e. g. St. Paul himself, the conquered persecutor), or as soldiers serving under the Cross, or as captives rescued from the beaten foe, or as friends sharing in the triumph. (3) In the present passage the figure of a triumphal procession is inappropriate to the Cross, however appropriate to the Ascension; but the word clearly denotes a triumph as distinct from a victory. There are three phases of the glory of the conquering Christ, (1) the victory, the disarming of the foe, (2) the evidence of the victory, the display of the vanquished, (3) the vindication of the victor, the subjugation of the vanquished.

in it. (1) The pronoun may be masculine. (*a*) Those who take 'God' to be still the subject of the sentence translate *in him*, i.e. in Christ. But there is no antecedent mention of Christ in verses 13–14 to which 'in him' could refer. (*b*) The Vulg. has *in semetipso*, R.V. mg. *in himself* (Christ), cp. Tyndale 'in his awne persone'; but this adds little or nothing to the force of the statement. (2) If the pronoun is neuter, (*a*) it may refer to the bond, the idea being that the dethronement of the spiritual powers was involved in the deletion of the bond; but the Apostle's thought has already travelled far away from the bond. (*b*) The most obvious reference is to the Cross. Origen says that the Greek MSS. before him had 'on the cross'. 'The paradox of the Crucifixion is thus placed in the strongest light— triumph in helplessness and glory in shame. 'The convict's gibbet is the victor's car' (Ltft.). Cp. the line 'regnavit a ligno Deus' in the famous hymn of Fortunatus, Bishop of Poitiers in the sixth century, known as *Vexilla Regis*, translated by J. M. Neale, 'God hath reigned and triumphed from the tree'. 'From the tree' is a Christian gloss which crept into the text of the Old Latin version of Ps. xcvi. 10. Early Christian writers interpreted the passage as a prophecy of the victory of the Crucified. 'From the Cross' may be a note of time, 'from His crucifixion onwards', or it may mean 'from the Cross itself as His throne'. The same idea is expressed in some medieval crucifixes which represent the Crucified as wearing the crown and robe of a king.

R

(ii) *The fear of spiritual powers has been conquered, faith in ritual precepts has been condemned, by the Cross.*

1. *Ritual laws of food and festival are but the shadow of a reality to be found in Christ alone,* II. 16–17.

Your life is now no longer at the mercy of their domination; it has passed into the freedom of obedience to a higher law in a nobler service. Let no man therefore claim the right to judge you on questions of personal habit or religious observance,—on questions of food or drink, or annual or monthly or weekly holydays. These things were and are still but a shadow of future realities; the reality and substance to which they point is to be found in Christ.

16 Let no man therefore judge you in meat, or in drink, or in

16. *Let no man therefore judge you.* Lit. 'let not any man', perhaps pointing to some particular person, cp. verse 8; but the point cannot be pressed. *Therefore*, a practical inference from the whole preceding paragraph. The belief in angelic authority, which is the basis of the whole system of teaching current at Colossae, has been shattered by the Cross. Therefore they can and must resist any attempt to enforce the practices based on that belief. The classic prohibition of judgement on similar matters of food and times in Rom. xiv. is based on several principles, distinct but connected. (1) The brother thus judged has been already accepted by God, (2) his observance or non-observance is the result of a judgement of his own conscience as to the will of God, (3) our own judgements and actions are all subject to the judgement of God, (4) the kingdom of God is not a ritual law but a spiritual life, (5) the vital factor in all action is the motive, viz. personal conviction. There St. Paul treats observance or non-observance as immaterial because the things in themselves are indifferent. Here, too, what he condemns is not the observance of ascetic rules but the insistence upon their observance. But there is a distinct suggestion here that the things in question are not indifferent but dangerous, in so far as they involve clinging to the type when its fulfilment has arrived in Christ, and allow the prophetic shadow to obscure the spiritual reality which it foreshadowed.

in meat or in drink. More exactly, 'in eating or in drinking'. The concrete 'meat' in reference to ritual rules occurs in Mk. vii. 19, Rom. xiv. 15, 20, 1 Cor. viii. 13, 1 Tim. iv. 3, Heb. ix. 10, xiii. 9, and the concrete 'drink' in Heb. ix. 10. The words here are the abstract, the act or habit of eating and drinking, as in Rom. xiv. 17, 'the kingdom of God is not (a question of) eating and drinking', and in 1 Cor. viii. 4. The distinction brings out clearly the question at issue; it was not the nature of various foods or drinks but the ascetic principle on which the abstinence was based. The Mosaic rules were concerned almost entirely with foods, and based on the distinction between animals clean and unclean for purposes of eating. Prohibitions of drink were special and exceptional, e.g. the case of priests on

respect of a feast day or a new moon or a sabbath day: 17 which

temple duty, Lev. x. 9, and the Nazarite vow, Num. vi. 3. Later
Jewish tradition added other precautionary rules. The Essene sect
went further, and apparently abstained entirely from animal food
and from wine. References to abstinences going beyond the Mosaic
rules are found in Rom. xiv. 2, 21, 1 Tim. iv. 2, 3, Tit. i. 15, the last
two being cases of incipient Gnosticism apparently rather than
persistent Judaism. The ascetic precepts of the Colossian teachers
seem to have points of contact or resemblance with both Judaism and
Gnosticism.

feast day or new moon or sabbath day. Not 'sabbath days' as in
A.V. The Greek plural *sabbata* in the N.T. (except in Acts xvii. 2) is
always used of the single day. Nor is the plural here to be taken as
including all three sabbaths, the sabbath day, the sabbath month, the
sabbath year; the three terms here clearly refer to holydays annual,
monthly, and weekly. They occur together as a summary of the Jewish
calendar of holydays in 1 Chron. xxiii. 31, 2 Chron. ii. 4, xxxi. 3,
Ezek. xlv. 17, Hos. ii. 11, cp. Isa. i. 13, 14. In Gal. iv. 10, 'ye observe
days and months and seasons and years', the seasons correspond to
the feast days of the present passage, and the years are the sabbatical and the jubilee years. For the new moon see Num. xxviii. 11 ff.
The feast-days were the feast of unleavened bread, of harvest, and of
ingathering, Exod. xxiii. 14–17. The passover, afterwards combined
with the week of unleavened bread, was a historical commemoration,
whereas the three feasts were all agricultural, the consecration of the
three stages of the farmer's labour and the food-supply of the people.

St. Paul in Rom. xiv is pleading the cause of Christians condemned
by their Gentile fellow-Christians for keeping rules of diet and devotion. Here he is warning Christians who are being condemned by
false teachers for not keeping such rules. But the principles which he
lays down in Rom. xiv are fundamental, and apply therefore in all
cases, viz. (1) the things are in themselves indifferent, (2) they are
questions which may and must be decided by the individual conscience. These principles would hold good with regard to Christian
observance of feast or fast, Sunday or saints' days, in so far as they
were urged or observed as in any way a necessary part of the Christian
life. But they are balanced by another principle, the right of the
Church 'to decree rites and ceremonies' on the ground of their value
as a means of religious education and discipline. That principle calls
for loyal obedience of members to the Body. The individual Christian
conscience in exercising the liberty and fulfilling the duty of private
judgement must take corporate loyalty as well as personal conviction
into account in making its decision. The fellowship of a common life
involves of necessity some measure of limitation of private freedom.
See Intr., pp. 107–8.

R 2

are a shadow of the things to come; but the body is Christ's.

17. *a shadow of the things to come.* Philo compares the letter of divine oracles to the shadow, and the power behind the letter to the substance. In the N.T. the word *shadow* is used to denote (1) the material and visible as contrasted with the spiritual and invisible, e.g. Heb. viii. 5, where the earthly temple and its worship are 'a copy and a shadow of the heavenly', (2) the prophetic type as contrasted with its future fulfilment, here and in Heb. x. 1, where the law is described as 'having a shadow of the good things to come, not the very image of the things', the shadow being there distinguished both from the reality of the future dispensation of grace and from the perfect presentation even of the idea of that dispensation in typical form. The law was a prophetic foreshadowing, but even as a prophecy it was imperfect; it was a shadow and not a picture, a dim outline and not a complete expression. Here the metaphor of a shadow 'implies both the unsubstantiality and the supersession' of the Mosaic ritual.

the things to come. The Greek participle thus translated is used in general of the future in contrast to the present in Rom. viii. 38, 1 Cor. iii. 22, Heb. xi. 20. Elsewhere it is used to describe the wrath of divine judgement, Mt. iii. 7, Lk. iii. 7, Acts xxiv. 25; the age to come, Mt. xii. 32, Eph. i. 21, Heb. vi. 5; the destined Saviour, Rom. v. 14; the Christian dispensation, its blessings, Heb. ix. 11, x. 1; its faith, Gal. iii. 23; its final glory, Rom. viii. 18, 1 Pet. v. 1; the future life, 1 Tim. iv. 8; the eternal city, Heb. xiii. 14. The Christian religion, the fulfilment of the hopes of those who looked forward in the past, is itself always looking and pointing forward to yet greater things in the future.

the body is Christ's. True as it is that 'Christianity is Christ', the reality foreshadowed by all ritual and doctrinal types and preparations, yet 'the body' is not Christ Himself but 'the things to come', the Christian life, or their embodiment in the Church. And this reality, the substance of which all law and every type was but a foreshadowing, is not merely to be found in Christ; it is His possession and His gift. The Colossians are not confronted with the alternatives of retaining the shadow or acquiring the reality. As members of Christ they are already in possession of the reality; hence the folly of returning to the shadow or rather endeavouring to combine the reality with the shadow.

Body here means the substance as opposed to the shadow which it casts before the seeker after truth and righteousness, who may or may not look ahead and see the substance. But it suggests perhaps also the idea of the whole as contrasted with anything less. Even the sum total of the benefits derived from the best-meant asceticism was nothing in comparison with the fullness of Christian experience. It could only deal with fragments of life, whereas Christ is the fulfilment of the whole of life. Some early Christian interpreters, e.g. Augustine, misreading the construction of the sentence, took the body to refer to the Church, 'corpus autem Christi nemo vos convincat', i.e. 'let no man condemn you, who are the Body of Christ'.

2. Angel-worship is pride disguised as humility, II. 18.

Refuse therefore to allow anybody to pass an arbitrary verdict of censure against you in the matter of abstinence and devotion to angels, taking his stand confidently on the ground of his admission to mystic visions. Such a critic has no warrant for his pride of judgement; it is the pride of a materialistic type of intellect.

18 Let no man rob you of your prize [1]by a voluntary humility

1 Or, *of his own mere will, by humility &c.*

18. *let no man rob you of your prize.* A.V. *beguile you of your reward,* i.e. the prize or reward of Christian perseverance, cp. 1 Cor. ix. 24 and Phil. iii. 14, where the prize is defined as 'the high calling of God in Christ Jesus', i.e. the heavenly destiny of the Christian soul. Cp. the crown, the victor's garland, promised to the faithful, 1 Cor. ix. 25, 2 Tim. iv. 8, James i. 12, Pet. v. 4, Rev. ii. 10, iii. 11. The Colossians would miss their prize if they listened to the dogmatic assertions and plausible suggestions of the false teachers and looked in the wrong direction for spiritual guidance and strength. But the Greek verb represented by the whole phrase 'rob of your prize', though derived from the word *prize* found in 1 Cor. ix. 24, Phil. iii. 14, had ceased to refer to a prize, and come to denote an unfair or unfavourable decision of a judge in any matter. See note on *rule* in iii. 15. Here, then, the meaning seems to be simply, 'let no man condemn you', A.V. marg. 'judge against you'. It is the censorious criticism of verse 16 carried to the point of an arbitrary condemnation by self-constituted authorities who laid down rules of conduct for Christians, and perhaps threatened to excommunicate the non-compliant, cp. Diotrephes in 3 John 9, 10.

by a voluntary humility. Lit. *willing in humility.* (1) It has been taken as a literary Hebraism for 'delighting in humility', i.e. finding a self-conscious satisfaction in an attitude of humility. Such a Hebraism is 'foreign to Pauline and New Testament usage' (McLellan, *Expositor,* 7th series, No. 53, p. 388). Moreover, self-conscious humility is pride in disguise, and that may be St. Paul's point here. (2) *Willing* more probably belongs to the verb *condemn,* i.e. *of his own mere will,* R.V. marg. *at will,* a note of dogmatic self-assertion which accords with the assumption of authority, 'sic volo, sic jubeo; stet pro ratione voluntas'. The difficulty of the word has tempted scholars to conjectural amendments of the Greek text which have

and worshipping of the angels, [1]dwelling in the things which he
hath [2]seen, vainly puffed up by his fleshly mind,

[1] Or, *taking his stand upon.*
[2] Many authorities, some ancient, insert *not.*

no foundation in textual evidence, e.g. 'flattering you', or 'coming
to you' with an air of humility, or 'in a tone of affected humility'.
The construction adopted above, 'let no man condemn you arbi-
trarily in the matter of humility and of angel-worship', gives an
almost exact parallel to the construction of verse 16. (*a*) The humility
may be connected with the worship of angels. The Colossian teachers
perhaps advocated the worship of angelic mediators as a humbler and
less presumptuous form of worship than the immediate worship of
God, and condemned those who refrained from such angel-worship
as lacking in humility. Chrysostom describes these teachers as
urging 'that we must be brought near by angels and not by Christ,
for that were too high a thing for us'. (*b*) On the other hand, the word
humility may correspond to the asceticism illustrated by the prohibitions of verse 16, and the angel-worship to the observance of holydays. In that case the word must perhaps be interpreted in the light
of the connexion between the humbling of the soul and fasting, e.g.
Lev. xvi. 29, 31, Ps. xxxv. 13, Isa. lviii. 3, Ecclus. xxxiv. 26, and
should be translated *mortification* or *abstinence* or *self-humiliation.*

and worshipping of the angels. (1) The simplest explanation is
probably the truest, viz. the practice of worshipping angels. On this
phase of the Colossian heresy see Intr. ch. V. pp. 59, 74. The Greek
word *threskeia* denotes usually the external form of religion, a cult
rather than a creed, acts of worship rather than an attitude of worship, cp. its use of Judaism in Acts xxvi. 5 and of the visible expression of a man's religion in James i. 26, 27. This angel-worship seems
to correspond to the observance of holydays in verse 16. The feasts,
new moons, and sabbaths were connected with the movements of the
heavenly bodies and thus with the angelic orders supposed to control
those movements. Zahn (*Intr. to N.T.* E. Tr. i. 476) insists that if the
angels are the object of this worship 'we must understand by it
simply a cult devoted to the angels, and not also a speculative
pursuit of the doctrine of angels or a superstitious veneration of
them'. (2) Zahn himself (i. 478) takes the phrase in close connexion
with 'humility' in the sense of mortification, and interprets it to
mean a self-discipline and devotion characteristic of angels. 'The
false teachers probably taught that the Christian should become as
far as possible "equal unto the angels" (Lk. xx. 36), a wrong striving
after immateriality, which induced Paul elsewhere to call such
doctrines the doctrines of devils' (1 Tim. iv. 1). (3) If the angels are
not the object but the subject, there is more to be said for the interpretation which understands the humility (i.e. abstinence) and the

worship or ceremonial religion (i.e. observance of holydays) as being sanctioned and enforced by the angels in virtue of their mediation in the promulgation of the Law (Acts vii. 53, Gal. iii. 19, Heb. ii. 2). 'The Judaizers urged the wrath of avenging angels to overawe non-conformists to the Law' (McLellan, *Exp.*, p. 391). This interpretation does not limit the reference of the passage to Jews. The Greeks attributed to the demons the same guardianship and control of human life which the Jews attributed to the angels.

dwelling in the things which he hath seen. The two points on which the interpretation of this difficult phrase turns are (1) the meaning of the Greek word translated *dwelling in,* and (2) the question whether the balance of ancient textual evidence is in favour of the insertion or the omission of the word *not* before *seen.*

(1) The Greek verb is used of setting foot upon ground, entering into the possession of property, invading a country, pursuing an investigation. (*a*) R.V. represents the false teacher as living in a world of visions, which he claims to have seen, but which St. Paul regards as not real but imaginary. But it is doubtful whether the Greek word ever means *dwelling in.* (*b*) R.V. marg. *taking his stand upon* suggests that the visions are made the basis of dogmatic teaching, an idea more in accordance with the immediately preceding context than the idea of absorption in an imaginary world, though the latter is supported by its telling contrast to the holding fast of the fact of Christ, the Head of all reality. (*c*) The translations *parading his visions* (Ltft.) and *flaunting about with things that he has seen* (von Soden) are not to be got out of the Greek word, though the idea of the pride of the visionary suits the following words. (*d*) A vivid and appropriate rendering is suggested by the use of the word in a Greek inscription of A.D. 132 in connexion with the oracle at Klaros, which states that two devotees 'after their initiation *entered upon*' the further stages of the mysteries. It is quite possible that the word was part of the vocabulary of the Colossian mysteriarch. In any case he is regarded here as 'pressing forward into or poring over the mysteries of which he has caught a glimpse'. The description may be ironical. Even so it is scarcely an offence to seek truth, however mistaken the path of research may be. (2) Even if the balance of external evidence is inclined towards the omission of *not*, the internal evidence of the context seems to require its insertion. St. Paul is laying stress upon the intellectual presumption of the Colossian teachers. There is no such presumption in investigating the contents and bearing of angelic visions, if they have been actually seen. The A.V. after all gives the sense that seems to be required, *intruding into those things which he hath not seen* (cp. Ezek. xiii. 3, 'woe unto the foolish prophets that follow their own spirit, *and have seen nothing*', R.V. marg. *and things which they have not seen*)—a reference to incursions into an unseen world in search of support for his claims to

spiritual authority. Chrysostom: 'he had never seen angels, but he behaved as though he had'. For the resemblance between this pretension to supernatural knowledge and the pretensions of modern theosophists, see Intr. p. 120. Briefly, 'if we omit the negative, the Apostle is quoting the claims' of the heretical teachers; 'if we insert it, he is denying their justice' (Barry). In the former case, he may at the same time be implicitly condemning a religion which lives by sight and not by faith, or which exalts the real or supposed knowledge of the few over the faith of the many. (3) The difficulty of finding a conclusively satisfactory interpretation of the phrase in the absence of *not* has tempted scholars to conjectural emendation of the text. One such emendation would give us *treading on empty air*, i.e. 'speculating in airy nothings' (Moffatt); another, *treading the void in suspension*, like a man balancing on a tight-rope. Lightfoot favours the latter 'as expressing at once the spiritual pride and the emptiness of these speculative mystics'. Westcott and Hort (*N.T. in Gk.* ii. 127) and Zahn (*Intr. to N.T.* i. 479) prefer the former. Zahn's explanation of it is indeed applicable to the whole passage as it stands in the actual text. 'This could mean the bold flight of an unfounded speculation quite as well as the vain effort by means of asceticism to break loose from earth and soar into higher regions.' But these feats of literary conjecture, brilliant as they are, lack adequate literary evidence; and they are not so satisfying as the simpler sense of the A.V.

vainly puffed up. *Vainly* has no connexion with vanity in the sense of conceit and pride. It means (1) recklessly, without due consideration or definite reason, e.g. Mt. v. 22, of unreasonable anger; (2) in vain, fruitlessly, e.g. Gal. iii. 4, iv. 11, of wasted sufferings and labours; 1 Cor. xv. 2, of a faith that has failed or perhaps gave too superficial an assent at first. With the preceding words it would refer to the rashness of intellectual curiosity; with 'puffed up', the more probable connexion, it denotes that the conceit was either groundless and unwarranted, or barren and fruitless, cp. 1 Cor. viii. 1, where the mere knowledge which inflates intellectual pride is contrasted with the love which intensifies spiritual experience, or builds up the faith of others. *Puffed up*, i.e. inflated or distended with conceit and pride, occurs in N.T. only in St. Paul, and all six cases are in the first epistle to Corinth. It is used of the pride of a partisan, 1 Cor. iv. 6; of the pretensions of an opponent, iv. 18, 19; of self-complacency in the midst of moral scandal, v. 2; of the intellectualism which idolizes knowledge, viii. 1. Love, on the contrary, 'vaunteth not itself, is not puffed up', xiii. 4, where the former phrase marks the ostentation of manner which is the expression of the inflation of mind.

by his fleshly mind, lit. by the mind of his flesh, 'his unspiritual thoughts' (Weymouth). The Greek preposition is emphatic, inflated not merely in his mind but by his mind. The mind, Gr. *nous*, as a

faculty or part of human nature, is in itself neutral; it may be
dominated by the flesh or by the spirit. The pagan mind, ignoring
God, sinks to a lower level, to immorality (Rom. i. 28) or to loss of all
moral purpose (Eph. iv. 17). The heretical mind, perverted in outlook and corrupted in tone, loses its grasp of truth (1 Tim. vi. 5) and
its capacity for faith (2 Tim. iii. 8), or perhaps its loyalty to the faith.
On the other hand, the mind may be on the side of the law of God,
fighting hard against the flesh which is on the side of 'the law of
sin', Rom. vii. 23. It needs progressive transformation by constant
renewal through reference to the will of God as its standard, Rom.
xii. 2. It has within itself a spiritual principle which is the starting-
point of this new life, Eph. iv. 23. Here St. Paul is meeting the claim
of the Colossian teachers to the possession of a higher intelligence and
a deeper spiritual insight. He insists that their boasted intelligence
is on a lower spiritual level; it is the intelligence of a mind dominated
by the material and the secular. The flesh here denotes not immorality but materialism, 'his unspiritual thoughts' (Weymouth), or 'his
merely human intellect' (*Twentieth-Century N.T.*). Commentators
compare Rev. ii. 24, where the mysteries which the Gnostic teachers
despise simple believers for not knowing are described as 'the deep
things of Satan', in contrast to 'the deep things of God' (1 Cor. ii. 10).

3. *This heresy stands condemned by its failure to hold fast to Christ the
Head, the source and strength of the life, the unity, the growth, of the
Body,* II. 19.

*Moreover any such teacher is guilty of a fundamental error; he has no grasp
or hold of Him who is the Head, from whom the whole Body derives its
sustenance and its unity through the various points of contact and connexion,
and thus grows with a growth which is none other than the life of God at work
in human life.*

19 and not holding fast the Head, from whom all the body,

19. *holding fast the Head,* i.e. not merely (1) steadfastly adhering
to the truth about the Headship of Christ, cp. Mk. vii. 3, 4, 8, 2 Th. ii.
15, Rev. ii. 14, 15, of holding fast traditions or doctrines, but (2)
clinging to Christ Himself, cp. Rev. ii. 13, of the Church at Pergamum,
'thou holdest fast my name', where as so often in O.T. and N.T.
'name' means character or person, and the confession of the bride
in Cant. iii. 4, 'I held him fast and did not let him go'. For the idea
of spiritual growth depending on maintaining touch with Christ,
cp. the Johannine teaching of the Vine and its branches, John xv. 4,
5. The Colossian teachers laid stress apparently on advance in
spiritual knowledge and power, but their emphasis on angelic mediation or authority was inconsistent with practical belief in the supremacy and sufficiency of Christ. St. Paul insists on this as the radical

why, as though living in the world, do ye subject yourselves
to ordinances, 21 Handle not, 22 nor taste, nor touch (all which
things are to perish with the using), after the precepts and

'elements'. The distinction between *to* and *from* in this connexion
is that the former denotes simply that the new life has no relation to
the old; there is no appeal from the past, or no response from the
present; while the latter denotes more sharply the absoluteness of
the severance, whether regarded as liberation by an act of divine
grace or renunciation by an act of human faith. It was a clean cut.

from the rudiments of the world. See note on verse 8.

as though living in the world. This cannot mean simply existing in
the world. Christians 'are in the world' and must be, John xvii. 11,
15, 16. It can only mean 'living the life of the world' or 'living your
life in the world as your home', cp. iii. 7, whereas their true life was
'hid with Christ in God'. Submission to ascetic rule looked as though
they were still clinging to their old idea of the world-order or their
old attachment to the world-spirit.

why do ye subject yourselves to ordinances? The Greek is a single
word, 'why are ye *dogmatized*?' It is used of the laying down of
principles by philosophers or the issuing of decrees by rulers. The
dogmata here may be the ordinances of the Mosaic law, as in verse 14,
or more probably the ascetic rules of the semi-Judaic and semi-
Gnostic religion of the Colossian teachers. The verb may be middle,
'Why subject yourselves?' or 'allow yourselves to be subjected',
or passive, 'why are ye subject?', A.V., i.e. as being over-ridden by
rules of life. The middle is preferable; St. Paul is not arguing with
the Colossian teachers but remonstrating with Christians inclined to
accept their teaching.

21. *Handle not, nor taste, nor touch.* Some early Latin commentators
strangely take these prohibitions as St. Paul's own. He is obviously
quoting typical prohibitions from the language of the Colossian
teachers; so Coverdale, 'as when they say, touch not this, taste not
that, handle not that'. The prohibitions apparently include the
eating of certain foods and also the contact with things regarded as
unclean. They cannot be identified more precisely. But there seems
to be in their order 'a climax of strictness' (Barry), which is expressed
better by R.V. than by A.V. *Handle* implies a deliberate act; *touch*
might include any accidental contact. 'It should be noted that all
these commands are negative, not positive. They are marked by the
ordinary ascetic preference of spiritual restraint to spiritual energy'
(Barry).

22. *all which things are to perish with the using.* An obviously paren-
thetical comment of St. Paul's own. *Which things*, i.e. the things
which are not to be handled, &c. *Are to perish*, lit. 'are for corruption', i.e. are destined for corruption by the very act of consumption,

doctrines of men? 23 Which things have indeed a show of
wisdom in will-worship, and humility, and severity to the

cp. our Lord's words in Mt. xv. 17, Mk. vii. 19, which St. Paul may
have had in mind, and St. Paul's own saying in 1 Cor. vi. 13. 'The
thought is that these things which are merely material, as is shown
by their dissolution in the ordinary course of nature, have in themselves no moral or spiritual effect' (Abbott).

after the precepts and doctrines of men. Cp. the very same phrase in
LXX. Isaiah xxix. 13, quoted thence in a slightly different form by
our Lord, Mt. xv. 9, Mk. vii. 7. *Precepts*, i.e. positive rules; *doctrines*,
i.e. general instruction and explanation. The two together form 'the
tradition of men' in verse 8. *Men* may refer to Jewish teachers or to
other teachers on whose authority the Colossian teachers based their
views.

23. *Which things*, i.e. either the ordinances themselves or the precepts and doctrines of men upon which they are based. There is a
difference between the Greek relatives in this and in the previous
which things in verse 22; that means 'which particular things', i.e.
the specific objects of the prohibitions, the things prohibited; this
means 'which sort of thing', i.e. these ordinances viewed as a line of
conduct, a principle of life.

have indeed a show of wisdom. The Greek word translated *show* is
logos, which means (1) reason, (2) theory, (3) reputation. *A show of
wisdom* may mean therefore (1) a rational basis from the point of view
of their philosophy, (2) a theory of philosophy, i.e. a philosophical
theory or conception behind them, (3) more probably, a reputation
for wisdom, i.e. a plausible appearance, an apparent justification.

in will-worship. The preposition denotes the grounds on which the
reputation for wisdom was based. *Will-worship* is an exact reproduction of a Greek compound noun, one of a group of words in which
the prefix *will* denotes either wilful or officious or self-imposed or
affectatious. The worship in question is either the observance of holy
days in itself or the worship of angels with which it was associated.
The prefix *will* may be intended to suggest that the worship was
gratuitous because it was not commanded or required. But more
probably it points to the conceit of a self-imposed cult, a sort of pride
of supererogation, or the affectation of superiority on the strength of
a self-chosen type of supposedly higher devotion. The word is found
in both a good and a bad sense; here it is ambiguous. St. Paul is
quoting what is said by themselves or admitting what may be said
by others on behalf of this system of religion, but there seems to be a
touch of irony in his language.

humility. Cp. note on the word in verse 18. Here again the word
is a quotation from the claims of the new religion. But it is not certain whether it refers to the modesty and reverence which they

CHAPTER III

(iv) *In the light of the Resurrection the path of spiritual
progress lies in looking to the Ascended Christ whose
hidden life they share now, and whose glory
they will share hereafter*, **III. 1–4.**

*But why argue against these teachers on their own ground? The true
answer to these pretensions lies in another direction. Why linger at all any
longer on the lower level on which this false asceticism rests? By your union
with the risen Christ your whole life was lifted to a higher plane. Lift your
eyes and your aims therefore to that higher world where Christ is now,
enthroned at the right hand of God. View life not from a lower but from a
higher standpoint: think in terms of heaven, not of earth. You died to the
life that you were living. That death was a mystical truth, a spiritual fact,
to be realized in conscious moral experience. The life that you are now
living lies hidden where Christ is hidden in the life of God. When the time
comes for Christ to be revealed once more in the life of the world, the Christ
who is the source and standard of your true life, then you too will be revealed
in your true glory, as a reflection of the glory of God.*

III 1 If then ye were raised together with Christ, seek the
things that are above, where Christ is, seated on the right hand

1. *If then ye were raised.* A.V. *if ye be risen* suggests the question
of a present uncertainty. R.V. rightly refers clearly to a past certainty. Baptism was a symbolic burial and resurrection, ii. 12. The
resurrection to a new life involved the beginning of a new outlook or
rather uplook upon a higher order of things. The inferential particle
then must be given its full weight. 'If you died with Christ (verse 20),
and you did, then why submit still to the false asceticism of the old
lower life ? . . . But the death of Christ was only the prelude to a
resurrection. Therefore you too must have risen again; if you did
thus rise, and you did, then live the new higher life of men who have
risen again.'
the things that are above. There are two points to be noted here.
(1) St. Paul is no longer contrasting the true asceticism with the
false. His thoughts have risen to a higher plane and a wider range.
The contrast he draws now is between the secular life engrossed in
their social and material environment and the spiritual life centred
in the ascended Christ. Cp. Phil. iii. 14, 'the prize of the high (R.V.
mg. upward) calling'; iii. 19, 20, the 'citizenship in heaven'; Mt. vi.
20, the 'treasure in heaven'. (2) This higher life is to be not only the
object of their efforts (*seek*) but the subject of their reflections (*set
your minds*). 'You must not only *seek* heaven; you must also *think*
heaven', Ltft. The phrase *set your minds upon* is a translation of a
single Greek word, *phronein*, to mind, which occurs in similar connexions in Phil. iii. 19, 'who mind earthly things'; Rom. viii. 5, of

of God. 2 Set your mind on the things that are above, not on the things that are upon the earth. 3 For ye died, and your life is hid with Christ in God. 4 When Christ, *who is* [1]our life, shall

[1] Many ancient authorities read *your*.

minding the things of the flesh and the things of the spirit; Mt. xvi. 23 (Mk. viii. 33), 'thou mindest not the things of God but the things of men'; Phil. ii. 5, 'have this mind in you which was also in Christ Jesus'. *where Christ is, seated on the right hand of God.* A.V. *where Christ sitteth* misses the point of the Greek. The things above are the region where Christ is at home and at work. 'What makes the things above impressive and real is His presence. As Dr. John Duncan once put it, the great glory of God's revelation is that it has changed our abstracts into concretes' (Moffatt, *Exp.* viii. 80, p. 136). Abbott aptly quotes Erasmus: 'par enim illuc tendere studia curasque membrorum ubi iam versatur caput',—the interests and cares of the members must tend towards the place where the Head is now. The session at the right hand of God is a distinct thought, introduced as a reminder that His ascension implies ours, cp. Eph. ii. 4–6, Rev. iii. 21.

3. *for ye died, and your life is hid with Christ in God.* St. Paul returns to the thought of the symbolic death and burial of the soul in baptism. 'You rose again . . . but only to God. The world henceforth knows nothing of your new life, and (as a consequence) your new life must know nothing of the world', Ltft. Bengel remarks: 'the world knows neither Christ nor Christians, and in fact even Christians do not know themselves'; they cannot see into the inner working of their own new life. The new life is hidden from the world; it is hidden from the Christian's own observation. Cp. John xiv. 17–19; the world cannot receive the spirit of truth because it is not looking at it and therefore does not recognize it; it is not looking at Christ, but the disciples are; 'because I live, ye shall live also'. The soul, says Augustine, is not where it lives but where it loves. Nor is this 'other-worldly' life the selfish or unfruitful thing apparently implied by this epithet. 'It is just so far as life is hidden with Christ in God that it can truly display itself without stint or weariness, in meeting all the world's needs for sympathy and service' (Dawson Walker, p. 124). 'When risen with Christ you have a Treasure, a Treasurer and a Treasury. "Your life", that is your Treasure; "is hidden with Christ", He is your Treasurer; "in God", that is your Treasury. Your life is hidden for secrecy and for security. The world knows not the sons of God; they draw their strength and inspiration from a secret source, they fix their hopes upon things unseen. Their life is hidden from the eyes of men' (Ralph Erskine, quoted in Hastings, *Great Texts*, Eph. to Col., pp. 511–12).

4. *when Christ, who is our life, shall be manifested.* Some commentators translate 'when Christ shall be manifested as our life',

s

be manifested, then shall ye also with him be manifested in glory.

i.e. shall be revealed in the character of our life, reflected in our conduct. But the Greek will scarcely bear this construction. The reference is clearly to the final revelation of Christ in all His majesty. Meanwhile the new life is not merely shared with Christ; it is Christ. Cp. John xi. 25, 1 John v. 11, 12, and also Gal. ii. 20, Phil. i. 21. There is good MS. authority for the reading *your life*, but it is probably an early correction of a supposed mistake. The transcriber missed the point of St. Paul's inclusion of himself, 'my life as well as yours'. Cp. the transition from *you* to *us* in ii. 13, 14.

then shall ye also with him be manifested in glory. Cp. 1 John iii. 2, 'we know that if he shall be manifested we shall be like him'. This prospect is compensation for suffering now for and with Christ, Rom. viii. 17, 18; it is the goal of the unconscious expectation of the suffering world of nature, 'waiting for the revelation of the sons of God'. Cp. also 1 Pet. iv. 13, v. 4. Dibelius notes that in these verses (iii. 1–4) 'we have mysticism and eschatology side by side'. The combination is an effective answer in advance to those critics who insist on the incompatibility of mystical experience and eschatological expectation, or who identify St. Paul with either the one or the other predominantly or exclusively. Dibelius might have added morality to mysticism and eschatology; for St. Paul passes at once to work out this consciousness of Christ now and this contemplation of the future Coming of Christ into a practical ideal of Christian conduct. Between present experience of Christ and expectation of the future Christ lies the exhibition of Christ in daily life.

IV. THE OLD LIFE AND THE NEW, **III. 5–IV. 6.**

(i) *The dying of the old life of passion and sin,* **III. 5–11.**

1. *There must be a resolute effort to slay evil passions and to banish sins of temper and speech,* III. 5–9.

These are not pious fancies: they are mystical truths, facts of spiritual reality. Work them out into moral realities. Kill those elements of your nature which are part of your earthly life, which cling to this world as your body clings to the earth,—immorality, impurity, passion, evil desire, and that pursuit of gain which is essentially the worship of an idol, treason against God. These things bring down the wrath of God upon the sons of disobedience, upon a humanity that denies and defies its divine origin and destiny. You too like the rest of the world went that way once upon a time, when you lived in that environment. But now you are living a new life. You too like other Christians must banish all those things,—the deep-seated feeling of anger as well as the fiery outburst of temper, the spirit of malice, reckless abuse, foul language,—banish these from your lips once and for all ; and banish all falsehood from your dealings with each other.

5 ¹Mortify therefore your members which are upon the earth ;
  ¹ Gr. *Make dead.*

5. Mortify therefore. *Mortify* has weakened in common parlance into the giving of pain or offence. The American Revisers suggested *put to death* ; but R.V. mg. *make dead,* though poorer English, is an exacter translation. St. Paul refers to three stages or phases of this death of the old life, using in each case a different word. (1) There is the act of killing, the effort of destroying, e.g. the habits of the body, Rom. viii. 13. (2) There is the state of death which results, e.g. here, 'make sure that they are dead'. (3) There is the process of dying, e.g. Gal. v. 24, 'they that are of Christ Jesus have crucified the flesh, &c.'. The past tense there may denote the definite step of their baptism, or the 'complete and decisive' character of the change of life. But crucifixion was a lingering death, and may refer here to the slow and painful dying of the old life. Cp. 2 Cor. iv. 10, where 'the dying of Jesus' which the apostles are 'always bearing about in the body' may refer to the 'perpetual martyrdom' (Plummer) of His life leading up to His death, or to the agony of the crucifixion. St. Paul is not referring to the danger of death but to the process of dying ; his life was a living death, a daily cross-bearing. The Greek word in 2 Cor. iv. 10 is the rare noun corresponding to the rare verb in the present passage, which while indicating a resolute effort to be made is quite compatible with the idea of a lingering process of extinction. Perhaps St. Paul's meaning may be: 'decide to treat them as dead, and you will find sooner or later that they are dead actually'.

the which is idolatry; 6 for which things' sake cometh the wrath

sins of the pagan world. But the Pharisees were covetous, Lk. xvi. 14 (R.V. lovers of money). They are rather the two besetting sins of all human nature in the absence of true religion. As Bengel says: 'homo extra Deum quaerit pabulum in creatura materiali vel per voluptatem vel per avaritiam', though 'pleasure' in this saying has a wider range.

It is true again that the acquisition of wealth provides ways and means for sensual self-indulgence. But this connexion is accidental; what St. Paul has in mind is some essential connexion or natural affinity between the two. Both are forms of self-gratification.

Covetousness is not quite an exact rendering of the Greek word, which denotes the taking of unfair advantage rather than the mere pursuit of gain. It describes 'the disposition which is ever ready to sacrifice one's neighbour to oneself in all things, not in money dealings merely' (Ltft. on Rom. i. 29), cp. 1 Th. ii. 5, 2 Pet. ii. 3, and the use of the corresponding verb in 2 Cor. ii. 11, vii. 2, xii. 17, 18. But it is undoubtedly used of the lust of acquisition in Lk. xii. 15 (where however 'all covetousness' seems to hint at other forms of this vice) and of the lust of possession in 2 Cor. ix. 5, where it is the spirit of the grudging as contrasted with the generous giver.

the which is idolatry. Cp. Eph. v. 5, 'covetous person which is an idolater', where the MSS. vary, viz. (1) 'which (neut.) is an idolater', (2) 'who is an idolater,' (3) 'which is idolatry', apparently an attempt to amend or explain the first reading. If (2) is the right reading, it does not mean a covetous man who is also an idolater, guilty of both sins, but that a covetous man is thereby an idolater. This is still plainer here, where the relative has a causal sense, 'seeing that it is idolatry'. It is perhaps an over-refinement of exegesis to see in this description of covetousness as idolatry the philosophical idea of idolatry, viz. the exaltation of a means into an end, in this case the exaltation of an instrument of life into the object of life. St. Paul is probably here thinking of the practical idolatry of making a religion of the pursuit of wealth. Cp. our Lord's words, 'ye cannot serve God and mammon', Mt. vi. 24, where there is no need of the mistaken supposition that mammon was the name of a Syrian god; the warning against the attempt to combine devotion to the two cults is all the more forcible if mammon simply means wealth. Cp. Job xxxi. 24, 'if I have made gold my hope, and have said to the fine gold, Thou art my confidence'. This idea of wealth as a cult is common in Jewish literature, both Rabbinical and Hellenistic. Chrysostom elaborates the idea, pointing out how wealth engrosses a man's devotion and demands the sacrifice of his soul.

6. *for which things' sake,* i.e. all these forms of impurity and indulgence. A few inferior MSS. have the singular *thing's,* i.e. covetous-

of God ¹upon the sons of disobedience; 7 ²in the which ye also

¹ Some ancient authorities omit *upon the sons of disobedience*. See Eph. v. 6.
² Or, *amongst whom*.

ness. But the best MSS. have the plural, and it is more probable in
itself; St. Paul would scarcely have confined the wrath of God to one
sin on the list.

cometh the wrath of God. cp. Rom. i. 18, 'the wrath of God is revealed from heaven against all ungodliness and unrighteousness'.
In both cases the present tense denotes not prophetic certainty but
actual experience. In Rom. i. 18 *revealed* refers not to the voice of
Scripture but to the evidence of history, past and present, pointing
to something more than the natural consequences of such conduct.

upon the sons of disobedience. These words occur in all but a few of
the ancient MSS. and versions and patristic quotations. Those few
exceptions are weighty in authority, and their omission of the phrase
seems to point to its absence in the original text. Its addition may
have been due to its undoubted presence in the original text of Eph.
v. 6. With these words, the sentence draws a lesson from the actual
experience of the pagan world. Without them, it states a general
principle, the certainty of judgement, but in a bald abrupt way which
seems to call for some such phrase to complete the sense. *Sons of
disobedience*, here and in Eph. ii. 2, v. 6, means not merely (1) disobedient sons of God, nor (2) members of a disobedient family, as
though *disobedience* here (like *dispersion* used of the Jews) were a
collective noun, but rather (3) the offspring and expression of a spirit
of disobedience, cp. Eph. ii. 2, 'the spirit that now worketh in the
sons of disobedience'. A.V. has *children*, cp. 1 Pet. i. 14, 'children of
obedience'. If a distinction may be drawn, *children* suggests the
idea of heredity, 'born and bred in obedience or disobedience', while
sons suggests the idea of growing conformity, 'living their lives in
habitual obedience or disobedience'.

7. *in the which ye also walked aforetime, when ye lived in these things.*
Ye also, you, too, like the rest of the pagan world. *Walked*, 'the character of their practice' as distinct from *lived*, 'the condition of their
life' (Ltft.), cp. Gal. v. 25 'if we live by the Spirit, by the Spirit let
us also walk'. Calvin remarks that the distinction between living
and walking is the same as that between power and action, and adds
aptly that the life comes first: 'vivere praecedit, ambulare sequitur'.

Ancient MSS. and other textual authorities are decisive for the
R.V. *in these* as against A.V. *in them*. But it is impossible to decide
whether *which* or *these* is masculine or neuter. (1) If *sons of disobedience* be omitted, *which* must be neuter, referring to the preceding
vices, but *these* may be either (*a*) masculine, 'when you lived in that
society or social environment', a rendering open to two objections,
viz. that there is no personal antecedent in the context to which

... putting off &c.', i.e. cease to lie, and instead put off the old nature and put on the new. The idea of putting off the old and putting on the new is certainly mostly in the imperative, e.g. 1 Th. v. 8, Rom. xiii. 12, 14, Eph. iv. 22, 24, vi. 11, 14. But there are serious objections to the imperative here. (a) The change from the old life to the new is too comprehensive to be identified with the putting away of the particular sins just mentioned. (b) The aorist participle indicates a resolute effort made once for all. Such an effort is neither logically nor chronologically appropriate as a sequel to the continuous present 'lie not'. (2) A.V. and R.V. are probably right in taking the participles as referring to past experience, and as giving the reason for the command to refrain from falsehood and also perhaps for the preceding command 'put ye also away all these'. *Did put off* is more exact than *have put off*; the reference is to their baptism, when they abandoned the old life and adopted the new, cp. Gal. iii. 27, 'as many as were baptized into Christ did put on Christ', and Col. ii. 11, 12. Grotius traces the origin of the metaphor to the symbolical changing of the old garment for the white baptismal garment, but this explanation is doubtful in view of the frequency of the metaphor in Greek literature.

If this second interpretation is adopted, we have a clear and instructive sequence in the successive uses of the word *put*. (1) First in verse 8 comes the command to abandon various sins of temper and speech. (2) This command is justified, and its fulfilment is possible, because (verse 9) at their baptism they divested themselves of their old pagan personality with all its practices. (3) Their baptism was not merely a renunciation; it was a renewal. They clothed themselves then with the new Christian personality, which is growing by constant renewal into a life of clearer knowledge and wider freedom, verses 10, 11. (4) Therefore they can and must clothe themselves now with all Christian virtues, 12–14. This analysis brings into clear relief the distinction between the 'man', old or new, and the vices and virtues characteristic of the old and the new man respectively, or, in other words, between the character of the personality as a whole and the practices of its conduct in particular.

the old man, i.e. the former life, the unregenerated man of their pre-Christian experience. The Greek word for *old* in itself simply means *former*, sometimes with the idea of *ancient*. But in Eph. iv. 22 the context suggests the idea of decay or corruption; 'the old man which waxeth corrupt after the lusts of deceit', i.e. is doomed, not by the certainty of the final judgement, but by the working out of misguided and misguiding desire. In Eph. iv. 22 again the old personality is regarded as dying morally; it has no future, for it has no power of recovery from its evil tendencies, inherent or acquired. In Rom. vi. 6 it is regarded as ideally dead; it was crucified with Christ, and has no power to bind or burden the new man.

10 and have put on the new man, which is being renewed unto
knowledge after the image of him that created him: 11 where

10. *have put on the new man.* In Rom. xiii. 12 the Christian life is
described as the putting on of 'the armour of light' in exchange for
the works of darkness (cp. the definition of the armour of the sons of
light in 1 Th. v. 8); in Rom. xiii. 14 and Gal. iii. 27 it is the putting on
of Christ. Here again are the two stages or phases noted above, viz.
the spiritual experience of union with Christ, and the moral effort of
obedience to Christ.

The Greek language has two words for *new*, (1) *neos*, i.e. in addition
or succession to the old, new in time, young, recent, and (2) *kainos*,
new in itself, different, fresh. Here the former is used, in Eph. iv. 24
the latter, of the 'new man'. With the lapse of time the new man
ceases to be *neos*, a new experience, but it is always *kainos*, a new
character. The new man here has been taken to mean Christ Himself,
as in Gal. iii. 27, Rom. xiii. 14, cp. 1 Cor. xv. 45, 49. But here,
whether or not Christ is implied in 'the image of him that created
him', in any case the new man is clearly the Christ-man, the Christian
personality, the new life that results from the new relation to Christ.

which is being renewed unto knowledge. The verb is a derivative of
kainos, and corresponds to that adjective as used in Eph. iv. 24. But
it goes further. The new man is not merely a fresh and different
character at the outset of the Christian life. It is being continually
renewed by fresh advances in the direction of moral insight and
spiritual experience. Meyer takes *knowledge* in close connexion with
the words that follow, viz. 'unto a knowledge that is in accordance
with the image of his Creator', i.e. in accordance with the capacity
for divine knowledge with which man's mind was endowed by its
Creator. But the more natural connexion is with the verb 'being
renewed'; in that case the character and content of the knowledge are left undefined. The stress lies on the mere fact of knowledge;
the new man is always learning to understand things. Dibelius
remarks that the old man and the new man are mystical terms which
are here given a moral turn.

after the image of him that created him. The whole sentence should
be compared carefully with Eph. iv. 23-4. There the change from the
old to the new man is described first as the gradual renewal of 'the
spirit of the mind', then as the decisive step of the assumption of a
new personality, 'which after God hath been created in righteousness
and holiness of truth', R.V., a translation more accurate than the
A.V., 'is created in righteousness and true holiness', but itself too
literal to be intelligible. A better translation would be 'which was
created according to the will of God with a righteousness and holiness
that comes from the knowledge of the truth'. Here the assumption
of the new personality comes first, and then its advance by constant

the Church is itself the completion of Christ (as the body is the completion of the head), who is only realized in all His completeness when He is realized in the life of every Christian. It will be noticed that the true meaning of the phrase is much richer and deeper than its popular use in such an expression as 'my friend was all in all to me', though even here each word may be given its full value, 'in every part of my life he was all that I needed or wanted'.

Additional Note.—The passing of human distinctions

St. Paul views all human distinctions in various lights. (1) Sometimes the different classes are viewed positively as all included in the Gospel or as all capable of entrance and advance in the kingdom of God. Greeks and barbarians, wise and foolish, alike have a claim upon his mission, Rom. i. 14, where the former antithesis refers to races, the latter to individuals or perhaps classes, educated and uneducated. Jew and Greek, in that historical order of experience, find in the Gospel the saving power of God, Rom. i. 16; cp. Acts xx. 21, of the range of St. Paul's preaching at Ephesus. There is 'no distinction between Jew and Greek' in the working of the lordship and the grace of Christ, Rom. x. 12. Greeks and Jews, slaves and freemen, all alike were baptized into one Body and drank of one Spirit, 1 Cor. xii. 13. In 1 Cor. i. 22 Greeks and Jews are contrasted as types of attitude towards the Gospel, Jews demanding signs of conquering power, Greeks seeking the subtlety of a convincing philosophy. (2) Here and in Gal. iii. 28 the distinctions are viewed negatively; their permanence or their importance is denied, on the ground that they are not essential but accidental. In Gal. iii. 28 St. Paul selects three examples of the abolition of all distinctions, viz. religious (Jew and Greek), social (slave and freeman), natural (male and female). Here the distinctions selected for mention are suggested by the special circumstances of the occasion. Hence the omission of sex; it was not a burning question at Colossae as it had been at Corinth. Hence also the amplification or the analysis of the religious distinction into race, religion, and culture. In Gal. iii. 28 the line of demarcation is religious prerogative, and is viewed from the standpoint of the Jew, who is mentioned first. Here the Greek is mentioned first, and contrasted first with the Jew and then with the barbarian. Lightfoot sees here a protest against the two distinct phases of the Colossian heresy, viz. Judaistic and Gnostic. (*a*) The religious privilege which led Jew to look down upon Greek (here and elsewhere a comprehensive term for all Gentiles, the Graeco-Roman world in general) is analysed into birth and conversion. It may be racial and hereditary (Greek and Jew) or personal and acquired, viz. circumcision and uncircumcision, where circumcision indicates or includes the proselyte to Judaism. (*b*) The Greek upon whom the Jew looks down with the pride of a superior creed looks down himself upon the uncivilized barbarian with the pride of superior culture. The Colossian heresy was Greek in this respect; it attached special virtue and value to intellectual capacity and attainment. St. Paul insists that there is no inherent merit in either distinction; men of all religions and civilizations need Christ; men of all races and ranks can receive Christ. St. Paul's language must not be pressed into a repudiation of the existence of differences within the Church. They exist, and they constitute facilities or difficulties for Christian progress, and are responsible for the variations in the value of the different contributions made to the life of the Church. His position is that these differences are cancelled by the Gospel as distinctions of spiritual rank. It is no mere coincidence that both here and in Gal. iii. 28 the insistence upon the abolition of these distinctions follows immediately upon the idea of putting on of the new life. In Gal. iii. 28 that idea comes as the climax of the transition from the special discipline of the Jew to the universal sonship of all believers, 'for as many of you as were baptized into Christ did put on Christ'. In that common relation to Christ all distinctions within humanity vanished; 'ye all are one man in Christ Jesus'. Here the idea of the new life is the climax of an appeal for the abandonment of old vices. They are living a new life which is a new correspondence to the divine nature as the ideal of humanity, and in that ideal all distinctions lose their force.

(ii) *The development of the new life of grace and holiness,* **III. 12–17.**

1. *There are new habits and tempers to be formed in response to the love of God,* III. 12–14.

Remember that you too owe everything to the fact that you yourselves are the recipients of a divine choice, called to live for God, blessed with the love of God. Clothe yourselves therefore with a character that corresponds to this call,—compassion, kindness, humility, gentleness, patience. Bear with one another: forgive each other, if any of you should have a grievance against another. Follow the example of Christ: as He forgave you, so forgive in your turn. And to crown all, clothe yourselves with a spirit of love, that love which is the one thing that binds you all together in a common approach to spiritual perfection.

12 Put on therefore, as God's elect, holy and beloved, a heart

The first list of sins consisted of sins against purity and simplicity, sins that endangered the Christian life of the individual. The second list consisted of sins against fellowship, sins contrary to the principle of fellowship in Christ, and fatal to its preservation in the Church. A similar sequence is to be noted in the reasons given for the abstention from these two kinds of sin respectively. (1) They have passed from the old life to the new, and the new life is a life of growth in the knowledge and in the likeness of God. (2) They have passed into a

13 forbearing one another, and forgiving each other, if any man

Phil. ii. 4, where it is explained in two ways, (a) each thinking more highly of the merits of others, (b) each thinking of the wants and interests of others before his own. On the significance of *humility* in itself, see note on ii. 18.

meekness, longsuffering. The word *meekness* confirms the impression that St. Paul in this description of the Christian temper has in mind the temper of Christ. Meekness receives one of the beatitudes of the Sermon on the Mount. It is part of Christ's own description of Himself, 'I am meek and lowly of heart', Mt. xi. 29. St. Paul himself appeals to the Corinthians by 'the meekness and gentleness of Christ', 2 Cor. x. 1. 'It is the attitude of mind that accepts without resistance anything that God may see fit to impose, or any injury He may permit men to inflict', while 'longsuffering is rather the attitude of self-restraint, of keeping oneself in hand to prevent any outburst of anger or reprisal, however legitimate the occasion might seem to be' (Dawson Walker). Dr. Maclaren says aptly that while long-suffering does not get angry soon meekness does not get angry at all. Despite the idea of weakness or unreality which is often associated with the word, *meekness* is a better standing translation than *gentleness*; for *gentleness* applies only to an attitude towards men, while *meekness* is sometimes used of an attitude towards God, e.g. James i. 21. In St. Paul it is used of the spirit in which the penitent should be restored, Gal. vi. 1 ; in which the contentious should be corrected or instructed, 2 Tim. ii. 25 ; in which the faith should be vindicated in answer to questioning, 1 Pet. iii. 15. *Longsuffering* here, as mostly in N.T., denotes human patience under provocation or injury from men; see note on i. 11. But in 1 Tim. i. 16 it is used of the patience of Christ in the winning of Saul the persecutor, and in 1 Pet. iii. 20 of the patience of God with mankind in the days of Noah ; and in 2 Pet. iii. 15 the delay of the Second Coming is attributed to the patience of our Lord in giving sinners a chance of repentance.

13. *forbearing one another and forgiving each other.* Bengel takes forbearing to refer to present offences, forgiving to past offences; but the distinction is unduly rigid. The Greek for *each other* here is the reflexive pronoun *yourselves*, as in Eph. iv. 32. Obviously it is not the ordinary use of the reflexive; the Colossians are not being exhorted to forgive themselves. Origen suggests that as they are members of a body what they do for each other they are in a sense doing for themselves. But the idea is rather that as a Christian community they are to forgive their own members; as individuals they are to forgive as members of a community forgiving fellow members of their own body. Forbearance is a mutual or reciprocal act between individuals. Forgiveness is a corporate act of the Body of Christ, whether given formally in the name of the Body as a

have a complaint against any; even as ¹the Lord forgave you,
so also do ye: 14 and above all these things *put on* love, which is
the bond of perfectness.

¹ Many ancient authorities read *Christ*.

ministerial absolution or informally by individual members as a
private condonation. On forgiveness as distinguished from remission,
see notes on i. 14, ii. 13.

a complaint. Only here in N.T., though the verb occurs in the sense
of finding fault in Rom. ix. 19 and Heb. viii. 8. A.V. *quarrel* here,
like the same word in the P.B.V. of Ps. xxxv. 23, represents the old
use of the word in the sense of a plaintiff's action, like the Lat.
querela.

even as the Lord forgave you. The less supported reading *Christ* may
have come from Eph. iv. 32, 'even as God in Christ forgave you'; or
it may have been substituted as an interpretation of *the Lord.* On the
other hand, *Christ* may have been the original reading, and *the Lord*
a correction made in the light of Eph. iv. 32. There is no other place
in N.T. in which Christ is described directly as Himself forgiving
except His own claim as the Son of Man in Mt. ix. , Mk. ii. 10,
Lk. v. 24. It is in Christ that we find forgiveness, C.. i. 14; but in
Col. ii. 13 it is God who forgives. Meyer suggests that the thought of
Christ's forgiveness is embodied in the phrase 'the grace of our Lord
Jesus Christ'. The word *forgive* in the Greek here is a derivative of
charis, the Greek word for *grace.*

When did Christ forgive? The forgiveness was won for man by the
atoning death of the Cross; but the reference here is to the experience
of that forgiveness when they were baptized into Christ, an abiding
experience dating from their baptism 'for the remission of sins'.

so also do ye. The example of the Head is the law for the members
of the Body. Christ's forgiveness is 'at once the pattern and the
motive for the exercise of the spirit of forgiveness. We must forgive
as Christ forgave, and we must do so *because* He has forgiven us'
(Dawson Walker).

14. *above all these things.* (1) The Greek preposition may mean
in addition, either to the virtues already enjoined, or to the things
said thus far. (2) In view of the fact that *love* is governed grammatically by the initial verb *put on* in verse 12, the preposition may
be taken (as apparently in R.V.) to mean that *over* these virtues must
come love as an outer garment, completing the garb of the Christian
life, or as 'the sash or girdle which will link them into fitting unity'
(Dawson Walker). Lightfoot is surely confusing the two figures when
he describes love as 'the outer garment which holds the others in
their places'. The outer garment is meant for dignity rather than for
security.

The bond of perfectness. Vulg. *vinculum perfectionis.* The Greek

T 2

as a stage of experience is 'perfect', and (*b*) the 'natural' man (Gr. *psychicos* as opposed to *pneumatikos*, 'spiritual'), who seems to include two classes, the pagan man of the world unable or unwilling to rise to the Christian faith (ii. 14), and the disappointing Christian unable or unwilling to rise to spiritual standards or to advance in spiritual experience, 'a babe in Christ' (iii. 1, cp. Heb. v. 13), described as 'carnal' (Gr. *sarkinos* or *sarkikos*). There is no justification here for the ancient gnostic or modern theosophical idea of grades of discipleship based on differences of nature. St. Paul's grievance against the 'babe in Christ' is simply that he will not grow up as he could and should, cp. again Heb. v. 13. Neither is there any justification for the accompanying idea of an esoteric teaching confined to a higher grade of discipleship. The advanced teaching of the Christian faith is available for all Christians, and only waiting for them to give proof of desire for its reception. (2) But while St. Paul regards some Christians in 1 Cor. ii. 6 (cp. Phil. iii. 15) as 'perfect' already, in the sense of proven desire and capacity for deeper truth, elsewhere he regards perfection as the yet future and final stage of spiritual maturity, e. g. in Col. i. 28 and iv. 12, and still more plainly in Eph. iv. 13, where he looks forward to Christians as growing up in fellowship into the perfect manhood which Christ came to reveal and to communicate.

The Gr. noun *teleiotes* in Col. iii. 14, *perfectness*, occurs also in Heb. vi. 1, 'let us press on unto perfection', where the writer is anxious to carry his readers forward from 'the first principles of Christ', the rudiments of the Christian faith and life, to a perfection which seems to combine the idea of 'the full maturity of spiritual growth with the idea of a higher knowledge of spiritual truth' (Westcott). The adjective *perfect*, Gr. *teleios*, is applied frequently to the individual Christian to indicate (*a*) a comparatively advanced stage of spiritual experience and attainment, contrasted with the immaturity of those who are still in knowledge and temper mere 'babes in Christ', 1 Cor. ii. 6, xiv. 20, Phil. iii. 15, Heb. v. 14, or (*b*) the ultimate perfection of the spiritual character, Mt. v. 48, xix. 21, 1 Cor. xiii. 10, Eph. iv. 13, James i. 4, 1 John iv. 18. In Col. iii. 14 there is no contrast between maturity and immaturity; what is here described as 'perfectness' is the ideal condition of the soul or the Church. There are five possible interpretations of this *bond of perfectness*. (1) Love is the one binding and crowning virtue, the mark of the perfect Christian life; it binds all the virtues into a harmonious unity. (2) Love is 'the power which unites and holds together all those graces and virtues which together make up perfection', Ltft. following Chrysostom. The Pythagoreans called friendship the bond of all the virtues (Epictetus, *Enchir.* 37). But it is a forced rendering to take the abstract noun *perfectness* as a collective; and love is more than a connecting link between the virtues, or 'the girdle which makes all complete' (*Twent.-Cent. N.T.*), or 'the bond that makes perfection' (Moffatt). (3) Love is 'the perfect bond of union' (Weymouth). But this rendering fails to do justice to the word *perfectness*, and leaves unanswered the question what the bond binds. (4) Love is the sum of all the virtues that make the perfect character; Bengel, 'amor complectitur virtutum universitatem'. But the use of *bond* for a totality is rare outside N.T. and never occurs in N.T. Love moreover, though greatest of all, is not the sum of all Christian virtues; it has a distinctive content and character of its own. (5) Love is the bond that binds all Christians into the perfection of a common life, a Christian community. It is the crowning characteristic of a perfect Church. This idea lies behind the reading of some western manuscripts which have *unity* instead of *perfectness*. It finds support in Eph. iv. 13, where all Christians together are represented as growing up together not into individual perfection (as in Col. i. 28) but into 'the perfect man', i.e. the perfect humanity of Christ realized at last in the life of His mystical Body. Cp. also John xvii. 23, where our Lord, thinking of that unity of the Church which alone can convince and win the world, prays for the disciples 'that they may be perfected into one', and Heb. xi. 40, where the perfecting of the Israel of God depends upon the union of the saints of the old and the new dispensations, 'that they might not be perfected without us'. Cp. Col. ii. 2, 'knit together in love', and the context there.

2. *The peace of Christ must rule in the life of members of the Body,* III. 15.

And let the peace which comes with the presence of Christ be the ruling influence, the determining factor, in your hearts,—that peace to which moreover you were called not as individuals but as members of one body; and let your whole life be marked by the note of thanksgiving.

15 And let the peace of Christ [1]rule in your hearts, to the

[1] Gr. *arbitrate.*

15. *the peace of Christ.* A.V. here *the peace of God* is the true reading in Phil. iv. 7. The same variation is found in the converse phrase *the God of peace,* Rom. xv. 33, xvi. 20, 2 Cor. xiii. 11, Phil. iv. 9, 1 Th. v. 23, Heb. xiii. 20, and *the Lord of peace,* 2 Th. iii. 16, where the Lord means Christ. *The peace of Christ* is the peace which He gives, John xiv. 27, and which He is in Himself, Eph. ii. 14. Abbott sees here also the idea of a peace 'which belongs to His kingdom by virtue of His sovereignty', cp. the legal and proverbial phrase 'the King's peace'. This peace of Christ in John xiv. 27 is the peace of His presence in the soul, part of the promise of the Comforter—the peace of freedom from fear and anxiety; so too in Phil. iv. 7, and in the collect for peace at evensong. In Eph. ii. 14 it is the peace of reconin Greek MSS., *the word of the Lord* and *the word of God*. Both phrases are frequent in Acts. In the epistles *the word of God* is the usual phrase; St. Paul only uses *the word of the Lord* (i.e. Christ) in 1 Th. i. 8 and in 2 Th. iii. 1. *The word of Christ* occurs nowhere else in N.T. The weight of textual evidence is in favour of *Christ*; the other readings may well have arisen as attempts to correct an unusual phrase. (2) For purposes of explanation the alternative *the word of the Lord* (i.e. Christ) may be included. In Lk. xxii. 61, John xviii. 32, Acts xi. 16, and the plural 'the words of the Lord Jesus' in Acts xx. 35, the reference is clearly to a particular saying of Jesus. In 1 Th. iv. 15, 'we say unto you by the word of the Lord', the reference may be to an unrecorded saying of Christ's or to a direct revelation which St. Paul had received from the Lord. In 1 Tim. vi. 3, 'the words of our Lord Jesus Christ' seem to mean His recorded or remembered teaching in general. But mostly 'the word of the Lord' is the Gospel message regarded not as a message about Christ but a message from Christ through His apostles. In the present passage Lightfoot takes 'the word of Christ' to mean 'the presence of Christ in the heart as an inward monitor'. But the passages that he quotes in support, e.g. 1 John ii. 14, 'the word of God abideth in you', will scarcely bear that interpretation. Westcott takes the word of God there to be 'the Gospel message, the crown of revelation', while recognizing that the word is a living power because it is the revelation of a living God. St. Paul is probably thinking here of the teaching of Christ in general.

dwell in you. The Gr. word for *dwell in* is used by St. Paul of sin, Rom. vii. 17; of the Spirit, Rom. viii. 9, 11, 2 Tim. i. 14; of God dwelling in man as in a temple, 2 Cor. vi. 16 (a quotation from Lev. xxvi. 11, 12); of faith, 2 Tim. i. 5. Another compound of 'dwell' is used in Eph. iii. 17 of Christ dwelling in our hearts through our faith, and in James iv. 5 of the Spirit. *In you*, i.e. (1) *in your hearts*, cp. Rom. viii. 9, 11, Eph. iii. 17, or (2) *among you*, though this scarcely suits the idea of indwelling, or (3) *in you as a body*, which suits both the preceding and the following context. 'At this point the Apostle turns to the more distinctly religious side of the Christian life in its corporate aspect, as it was manifested in assemblies for worship and in social gatherings with a religious colouring' (M. Jones, p. 98).

richly. St. Paul uses this adverb in 1 Tim. vi. 17 of the wealth of God's provision for the natural enjoyment of His creatures, and in Tit. iii. 6 of the wealth of His outpouring of the Spirit. See note on *riches* in ii. 2. Here the reference seems to be to the bringing out of the wealth of truth that is contained in the teaching of Christ, 'the application of the many-sided Gospel, with its infinite resources, to every department of human activity' (M. Jones, p. 98). Cp. ii. 3, the treasures of wisdom and knowledge hidden in Christ, waiting to be brought to light and to throw light on all life's problems, and

teaching and admonishing [1]one another with psalms *and* hymns

[1] Or, *yourselves.*

Mt. xiii. 52, the scribe of the kingdom of heaven who finds in its treasury truths new and old.

in all wisdom. This phrase might go either with the preceding or with the following words. (i) In favour of the latter connexion it has been urged (*a*) that in i. 28 it is obviously the only possible construction of the Greek, 'admonishing and teaching every man in all wisdom', (*b*) that it brings out a clear parallelism between two exhibitions of the word of Christ, viz. teaching and singing, '*in all wisdom* teaching and admonishing . . . *in grace* singing in your hearts'. But this parallel is only obtained by separating 'psalms, hymns, and spiritual songs' from 'singing in your hearts' and attaching it to 'teaching and admonishing', which surely includes other methods of expression besides sacred song. Ewald avoids this objection by making the psalms, hymns, and songs a separate expression of the indwelling word of Christ, viz. (1) teaching and admonishing in all wisdom, (2) with psalms, hymns, and spiritual songs, (3) singing in your hearts, i. e. (1) mutual instruction and admonition, (2) sacred song in religious gatherings, (3) the silent music of the heart. This trisection, however, is very doubtful, cp. Eph. v. 19, where the sacred song is obviously the method of the instruction and admonition. (ii) In favour of the connexion with the indwelling of the word of Christ it may be said (*a*) that teaching and singing both have an explanation of their own added, (*b*) that 'dwell in you richly' seems to require completion. The completing phrase *in all wisdom* may mean either (1) that the word of Christ should and will bear rich fruit in every kind of wisdom, or less probably (2) that the very wealth of this indwelling truth will call for constant discrimination in its application.

teaching and admonishing one another. (1) *Teaching* refers to the Christian faith, *admonishing* to the Christian life ; the two correspond to faith and repentance respectively, though the two kinds of instruction can scarcely be separated in practice and are distinguished not by contrast but by varying degrees of emphasis. In i. 28 *admonishing* precedes *teaching* just as repentance precedes faith, e. g. Mk. i. 15, Acts xx. 21. Perhaps there St. Paul is thinking of converts and here of confirmed Christians, in whose case moral exhortation presupposes and applies doctrinal teaching. Duty is based upon doctrine. The great truths of the Christian faith are unfolded first, and then their bearing on the Christian life. (2) *One another*, as in iii. 13, is lit. *yourselves.* They are to teach and admonish, as they are to forgive, not as mere individuals, but as members of the Body. Mutual private ministrations are the life of the Body helping and healing its own members. What St. Paul is prescribing here is mutual guidance. It would seem therefore that either the reference is to social conversation as well as to religious congregations, or that at Colossae, as at

affirming that they were divinely inspired but that they were composed by spiritual men and moved in the sphere of spiritual things' (Trench, p. 301). Trench mentions Herbert's *Temple* and Keble's *Christian Year* as belonging to this class.

The word *spiritual* in Col. iii. 16 should be compared with its context in Eph. v. 18–19. (*a*) Here all sacred song is the outcome of the indwelling of the word of Christ. There it is the result of 'being filled with the Spirit'. For the combination of the two aspects of Christian experience see John xvi. 14, 15. (*b*) The contrast in Eph. v. 18 between drink and the Spirit indicates that St. Paul is 'not primarily referring to public worship but to social gatherings in which a common meal was accompanied by sacred song' (Arm. Robinson, *Eph.* p. 122). Instead of 'primarily' it would be safer to say 'exclusively'; psalms and hymns point rather to congregational worship, even if 'spiritual songs' suggests a wider use. The *agape* or love-feast, in the first days a combination of the eucharist and a social meal, took the place of the public feasts of Greek social life; and even after the separation of the eucharist from the *agape*, the latter 'retained a semi-eucharistic character' and included sacred song; cp. the reference of Gregory above to psalms sung at Christian feasts.

'Every great spiritual revival in the Christian Church has been accompanied by a corresponding outbreak and development of Christian hymnology' (M. Jones, p. 99). Our modern hymn-books owe the largest and richest part of their contents to the Methodist revival within and without the Church of England and to the Anglo-Catholic revival known as the Oxford Movement. Both these revivals were in this respect a repetition of primitive Christian experience. 'The first age of the Christian Church was characterized by a vivid enthusiasm which found expression in ways which recall the simplicity of childhood. It was a period of wonder and delight. The floodgates of emotion were opened; a supernatural dread alternated with an unspeakable joy' (Arm. Robinson, *Eph.* p. 121). Trench remarks that many of our modern hymns are not *hymns* in the original sense of the word but rather *spiritual songs*. The word *hymn* is now established beyond challenge as the generic term for all sacred poetry used in Christian worship. But in view of the predominant influence of hymns in the shaping of personal religion, modern hymnology as a branch of pastoral theology calls for careful study. Early and medieval Christian hymns were mainly objective; they were concerned chiefly with God and the Church and the Christian faith. Modern hymns are largely subjective; they give undue prominence to personal experience and aspirations. The balance needs redressing in the direction of the older type, the hymn in the original sense of the word.

4. *Their whole life must be a life of devotion to Christ and of thanks-giving to God the Father*, III. 17.

In everything that you do, in your words and in your actions, let all be done in the name and for the sake of the Lord Jesus; and let the key-note of your whole life be thanksgiving to God the Father through Jesus the Lord.

17 And whatsoever ye do, in word or in deed, *do* all in the name of the Lord Jesus, giving thanks to God the Father through him.

in word or in deed. Words as well as works are included under 'whatever ye do'. Words are actions. Cp. our Lord's words in Mt. xii. 34–7, for the responsibility of speech as an indication of the spirit of the speaker and a vindication or an indictment in the day of judgement. *Deed* is a different Greek word from *do* in 'whatever ye do'; it is *ergon*, a work.

in the name of the Lord Jesus. The double name combines the human example and the divine power. The nearest parallel is in the revised text of 1 Cor. v. 4, 'in the name of our Lord Jesus'. The phrase *in the name* is used in various forms, 'of Jesus' in Acts iv. 18, v. 40, ix. 27, Phil. ii. 10; 'of the Lord' in Acts ix. 29, James v. 14 (? Christ or God); 'of Jesus Christ', Acts x. 48, xvi. 18; 'of Jesus Christ of Nazareth' in Acts iii. 6, iv. 10; 'of our Lord Jesus Christ' in 2 Th. iii. 6, Eph. v. 20; 'of the Lord Jesus Christ' in 1 Cor. vi. 11; 'of Christ' only in 1 Pet. iv. 14, 'if ye are reproached for the name of Christ', where it is almost equivalent to the phrase in iv. 16, 'if a man suffer as a Christian'. The phrase *in the name of Christ* in one or other of these varying forms, is used of healing, Acts iii. 6, iv. 10; of preaching the Gospel, Acts iv. 18, v. 40, ix. 27, 29; of baptism, Acts x. 48 (cp. viii. 16), 1 Cor. vi. 11; of excommunication, 1 Cor. v. 4; of exorcism, Acts xvi. 18; of apostolic injunctions, 2 Th. iii. 6; of worship, Phil. ii. 10; of anointing, James v. 14; of giving thanks, Eph. v. 20. Its meaning may be (*a*) in dependence upon His grace; Chrysostom, 'calling upon Him for help'; (*b*) in obedience to His authority; (*c*) in devotion to His service; or less probably (*d*) in the consciousness of their responsibility as representing Christ to the world, cp. Mk. ix. 37, Mt. x. 40, xviii. 5, an idea which Bengel carries too far, 'ut perinde sit ac si Christus faciat'.

to God the Father. A.V. *to God and the Father* is a mistranslation of the received text, which should be translated 'to Him who is God and Father'. It is impossible to decide whether by *the Father* St. Paul means the Father of the Lord Jesus or the Father of mankind.

through him, i.e. our Lord Jesus. The pronoun may be neuter, 'through the name'. The phrase 'through the name of Christ' is found in Acts x. 43, of the remission of sins, and in 1 Cor. i. 10, of an

e.g. differences of education or domestic duty or religion, i.e. Christian or heathen. (3) Most probably it means *fairness* as distinct from justice, the spirit of equity as distinct from the letter of obligation. This is the usual sense of *fair* in connexion with *just* in classical writers on ethics, e.g. Aristotle and Plutarch.

ye also, as well as your slaves, cp. Eph. vi. 9, 'both their Master and yours', and 1 Cor. vii. 22, where a Christian slave is 'a freed man of the Lord' and a Christian freeman 'a slave of Christ'.

3. *The Christian community*, IV. 2-6.

> (a) *In itself it should be the home of prayer and thanksgiving, with a place for the Apostle in their intercessions*, IV. 2-4.
> (b) *In relation to the outsider it should exhibit*
> > (a) *a wisdom of conduct to use every opportunity of witness or influence*, IV. 5.
> > (β) *a way of conversation attractive and appropriate to inquirers and objectors*, IV. 6.

Be regular and constant in prayer; on your guard against distraction and indolence in devotion; and cherish always a spirit of thanksgiving. Pray not for yourselves only; pray at the same time for us too, that God may open before us a door for the preaching of the Gospel, an opportunity of telling the world about the revelation of God in Christ. It is for the sake of that revelation that I have incurred my present imprisonment. Pray for me that I may do justice to the glory of that revelation, and speak fearlessly as I ought to speak.

Finally, there is the world outside the Church. Be wise in your daily intercourse with that world. Seize every opportunity of witness or influence as eagerly as a merchant closes with an offer of trade, and turn it to good account for the Gospel. Let your conversation be always attractive, flavoured with the salt of true wit that brightens and cleanses everything it touches, so that you may know just the right answer to give to each critic or inquirer.

2 Continue stedfastly in prayer, watching therein with thanks-

2. *Continue stedfastly.* A single word in the Gr., used of constant attendance upon a person, e.g. Mk. iii. 9, Acts viii. 13, x. 7, or constant attention to a duty, e.g. the adherence of the first Christians to the teaching of the apostles and the fellowship, the breaking of bread and the prayers, Acts ii. 42; the concentration of the apostles upon prayer and preaching, Acts vi. 4; the disciples at prayer in the upper room, Acts i. 14. Rom. xii. 12 has the same phrase as here, 'continuing stedfastly in prayer'.

watching therein. Chrysostom remarks that continued prayer is liable to relax into inattention, and therefore even in the act of prayer we must be on our guard against wandering thoughts. The linking of prayer and watchfulness goes back to the Lord's own warning. The contexts of that warning 'watch and pray' in the

Gospels suggest two reasons for watchfulness, (1) Mk. xiii. 33 (Mt. xxiv. 42, xxv. 13), in preparation for the unknown day of the coming of the Lord, (2) Mk. xiv. 38 (Mt. xxvi. 41), in precaution against the yielding of the spirit to the flesh. The two reasons are combined in Lk. xxi. 36. In the apostolic exhortations to watchfulness in connexion with prayer there are three Greek words translated *watch*. (1) One, *agrupnein*, originally to lie awake unable to sleep, is the watch of unsleeping vigilance, Mk. xiii. 33, Lk. xxi. 36, Eph. vi. 18, all of prayer, cp. Heb. xiii. 17, of the pastoral responsibility for the care of souls. (2) Another, *gregorein* (hence the name Gregory), originally to wake up from sleep, is the watch of the awakened soul against relapse into the slumber of indifference or insensibility, e.g. Mk. xiv. 38, Mt. xxvi. 41, and here, of prayer; and frequently in N.T. in a more general sense. (3) The third, *nephein*, originally to be sober and not drunk, denotes 'a mental state free from all perturbations and stupefactions, clear, calm, vigilant' (Hort on 1 Pet. i. 13). Milligan on 1 Th. v. 6 suggests that while *gregorein* is a mental attitude, '*nephein* points rather to a moral alertness, the senses being so exercised and disciplined that all fear of sleeping again is removed'. It is used of prayer in 1 Pet. iv. 7, and coupled with *gregorein* in 1 Th. v. 6 and 1 Pet. v. 8. In 1 Th. v. 6 and 1 Pet. iv. 7 the duty of watchfulness is urged in preparation for the coming of the Lord, in 1 Pet. v. 8 in precaution against present temptation, an echo of the two reasons given by our Lord. The three synonyms indicate three aspects or conditions of prayer. (1) The practice of prayer itself needs watchful attention without which it cannot be sustained and effective. (2) Prayer is the outcome of an awakened conscience without which it will never be attempted or renewed, cp. Acts x. 11, of St. Paul after his conversion, 'behold, he prayeth'. (3) Prayer presupposes a moral self-discipline, without which it is liable to fatal neglect.

with thanksgiving. The duty of thanksgiving 'in this epistle especially assumes a special prominence by being made a refrain', Ltft. Cp. ii. 7, iii. 15, 17, iv. 2. In ii. 7 thanksgiving is a condition of the growth of faith. Here and in Phil. iv. 6 it is 'the crown of all prayer', Ltft., the note that saves prayer from selfishness or doubt. In 1 Tim. ii. 1 thanksgivings are a necessary part of the common devotions of the Church. In Eph. v. 20 and Col. iii. 17 thanksgiving is to run through all the experiences of life. In Eph. v. 4 it is the dominant note of Christian social intercourse. It can scarcely there be the prayer of thanksgiving; there may be a play upon the double meaning of the Greek adjective *eucharistos*, viz. *thankful* and *graceful*. The antidote to the poison of impurity in the conversation of society is to be found in the cleansing charm of a conversation that is full of thankful recognition of all that is sweet and beautiful in life. Cp. Rom. i. 21, where St. Paul traces the moral degradation of pagan

to speak. 5 Walk in wisdom toward them that are without,

his readers to realize in their lives the ideal of the unity of the Spirit. He seems to be saying, 'I am a prisoner, unable to visit you, but I can pray for you, and I can pen the appeal that I cannot voice in person'. Similarly in Phm. 9 his captivity adds point to his appeal to Philemon; as the ambassador of Christ and now His prisoner he might enjoin, though he prefers as a friend to entreat. For Onesimus, the penitent runaway slave, St. Paul's imprisonment had meant the opportunity of salvation; now it might mean an opportunity of service, Phm. 10, 13. The contexts in *Philippians* refer to the attitude of others towards his imprisonment. The Philippians have won a warm place in St. Paul's heart by their spiritual fellowship both in his imprisonment and in the defence and establishment of the Gospel (at his trial or on other occasions), though it is not clear whether this fellowship means that they too had suffered and worked for the Gospel, or merely that they had given proof of practical sympathy with him in his suffering and work (Phil. i. 7). His bonds had become a visible and vivid witness to Christ among the troops of the Imperial Guard (Phil. i. 13). The majority of the Christians at Rome, seeing the hand of the Lord in the Apostle's imprisonment, found therein an encouragement to still more fearless witness to the faith in their own circles (i. 14), though some factious partisans preached Christ from mixed motives, thinking to bring a sharper note of pain into the experiences of his imprisonment (i. 17). To the Colossians St. Paul appeals to remember his bonds (iv. 18), an appeal 'not for sympathy with his sufferings but for obedience to the Gospel' (Ltft.) for which he was suffering. Finally to Timothy St. Paul appeals not to be ashamed of the Gospel of 'witness to our Lord, nor of me His prisoner', but to share with him and others the hardships of the service of the Gospel (2 Tim. i. 8), and reminds him that though he himself is suffering the hardship of imprisonment, 'the word of God is not imprisoned' (2 Tim. ii. 9); it cannot be confined, and is in fact travelling freely.

The Greek word for *bonds* is sometimes used of confinement without any implication of actual fetters. But from Acts xxviii. 16, 20, 2 Tim. i. 16, it is certain that St. Paul was actually chained, not indeed with the leg-irons and double handcuffs of a condemned prisoner in gaol, but with a light chain which attached him to the soldier in whose custody he was placed as a prisoner awaiting trial, not in gaol or even in military barracks, but in a rented lodging of his own, Acts xxviii. 16, 30. He was therefore literally 'an ambassador of Christ in chains', Eph. vi. 20.

5. *Walk in wisdom.* Not the spiritual insight into divine truth which is one of the notes of progress in the Christian life (e.g. Col. i. 9, 28, ii. 3, iii. 16, Eph. i. 8, 17), but the practical wisdom of 'consecrated

common sense'; cp. the parallel, Eph. v. 15, 'not as unwise but as wise', i.e. thoughtful and careful in your conduct; and our Lord's warning, Mt. x. 16, 'be ye therefore wise as serpents and harmless (A.V. and R.V. mg. simple) as doves'.

The progress of the Gospel depends not only upon the freedom and effectiveness of the preaching of the Apostle and his fellow-workers (verses 3, 4) but also upon the consistency of the lives of converts, both in their conduct (verse 5) and in their conversation (verse 6).

toward them that are without. These outsiders are the non-Christian world. There is no contempt in the phrase but the simple recognition of a fact. The phrase has an instructive history. (1) It was a 'rab-binical phrase for Gentiles or unorthodox Jews' (Swete on Mk. iv. 11), though in the prologue of Ecclesiasticus 'they that are without' seems to denote all possible learners, primarily Jews of the Dis-persion, but also Gentiles. (2) In Mk. iv. 11 it denotes the yet un-believing Jews to whom truth is taught in parables, while to the disciples, the inner circle of believers, it is given to know the mysteries of the kingdom of God. (3) In St. Paul's letters it denotes all who are outside the Christian community, viz. Gentiles and unbelieving Jews. They are outside the range of Church discipline. It is no function of the Apostle or the Church to judge them; they are left to the judgement of God, 1 Cor. v. 12, 13. But their judgement of the conduct of Christians is not to be ignored, either by ordinary Christians, whose lives ought to make a good impression upon their non-Christian neighbours (1 Th. iv. 12), or in the case of a candidate for the office of bishop, who ought to have a good reputation in pagan society (1 Tim. iii. 7). Chrysostom remarks that greater care is needed in intercourse with people outside; within the Christian family there are many kindly allowances made. In the present passage the context suggests that the wisdom of the Colossian Christians was to be shown not only in the maintenance of the stan-dard and example of the Christian life, but also in the seizure of opportunities for witness to the Christian faith. (4) The phrase has yet another meaning and lesson for our own day. The second sense is applicable to the conditions of a mission field, with its outer and inner circles of discipleship, the crowd, the convert, the catechumen, the communicant; the third sense to the conditions of some countries where a Christian congregation or community, whether native Chris-tians or foreign Christian residents, exists in the midst of a non-Christian population. Both are in a sense applicable also to a fourth kind of 'outsider', the nominal Christians of a Christian nation. They are inside the body of the Church by virtue of their baptism, but outside its life by their own lapse or by the failure of the Church to train and keep them—'the man in the street', the 'decent pagan' of modern society. The inner circle of church-goers and church-workers

symbolic, are blended in Mk. ix. 49, 50, 'Every one shall be salted with fire ... have salt in yourselves, and be at peace one with another'. An ancient Greek commentator remarks: 'every believer shall be salted with the fire of faith toward God or of love toward his neighbour, or at least cast out the rottenness of evil'. The salt which the disciples are to keep within their hearts is 'the seasoning power, the preserving and sacrificial fire', and peace with their brethren is 'the first condition of its presence there' (Swete). In the present passage there is no trace of the sacrificial but only of the symbolic idea. The significance of the symbol is variously interpreted. (a) The warning in Eph. iv. 29 against foul talk suggests that the idea in Col. iv. 6 is the preservation of the purity of conversation. (b) In Lk. xiv. 35 stale or dead salt is thrown away as refuse 'useless for either soil or dunghill'. In view of this use of salt as manure it has been suggested that the salt of the earth in Mt. v. 13 means a fertilizing influence, an enrichment of the world's life, and that therefore here the salt signifies the fruitfulness of Christian conversation, cp. Eph. iv. 29, 'that it may give grace to the hearers'. (c) The most obvious meaning, however, in view of Mk. ix. 50, Mt. v. 13, Lk. xiv. 34, is the giving of flavour and point to Christian conversation. Cp. Job vi. 6, LXX, 'Shall bread be eaten without salt? Is there any taste in meaningless words?' Salt in the sense of spice in speech is common in classical Greek and Latin (cp. the phrase 'Attic salt'), but usually of mere wit, often degenerating into smartness or flippancy or worse. (α) The salt that St. Paul recommends may be sober good sense, as contrasted with the 'profane and vain babblings' (art. on Salt in Ency. Bibl. iv, p. 4250) of some misleading teachers, which Parry on 2 Tim. ii. 16 explains as 'secular talk without meaning or moral or religious purpose', or perhaps as contrasted with the feeble pious talk of conventional religiosity. (β) Chrysostom remarks: 'wit must not degenerate into indifference; it is possible to be witty, yet with due propriety'. This warning refers apparently to a levity that treats truths as open questions or casual opinions. Christian wit must have a point, but it must be the spear-point of conviction. (γ) The salt may be the spice which gives a piquant touch of humour or originality to conversation on religious topics. Christians are 'not only to be interested in their religion, but to make it interesting' to other people (Moffatt, Exp. viii. 80, p. 142). Charles Simeon said he could not write and did not admire 'religious letters' except on urgent occasions. 'Religion with me is only the salt with which I season the different subjects on which I write' (quoted by Moffatt, l.c.).

V. CONVERTS AND COMRADES, IV. 7–18.

(i) *Commendation of two bearers of news from Rome, Tychicus and Onesimus*, IV. 7–9.

All that concerns me you will learn from Tychicus, the beloved brother who is my trusty helper and companion in the Lord's service. I am sending him to you for this very purpose, that you may know my present circumstances and that he may bring you the comfort and encouragement that you need. With him I am sending Onesimus, the trusty and beloved brother, who is one of yourselves, a Colossian. They will tell you everything that is going on here.

7 All my affairs shall Tychicus make known unto you, the beloved brother and faithful minister and fellow-servant in the Lord: 8 whom I have sent unto you for this very purpose, that

7. *All my affairs.* Gr. *all the things relating to me.* The same phrase occurs in the parallel Eph. vi. 21, and in Phil. i. 12, i.e. the process of his appeal and imprisonment.

faithful minister and fellow-servant in the Lord. For a fuller notice of Tychicus see Intr. p. 131. *Faithful* probably belongs to both substantives. For *minister* and *fellow-servant* see note on i. 7. *Minister* here may refer (1) to the personal service rendered by Tychicus to St. Paul, Acts xx. 4, or (2) to his ministry in the service of the various churches, or (3) to the service of Christ. *Fellow-servant* strikes a deeper and higher note; the helper is no mere subordinate but a companion in the service of a common Lord. There may be a conscious distinction between the three designations, *brother* denoting the relation of Tychicus to the Christian community everywhere, *minister* his relation to the Apostle, *fellow-servant* their common relation to Christ. But *brother*, especially with the epithet *beloved*, may refer to the affectionate intimacy of disciple and apostle as fellow-Christians. The fullness of the description may be due to the fact that Tychicus was not known in person to the Colossians, and needed some commendation by way of introduction. *In the Lord* defines both *minister* and *fellow-servant.* Grammatically it might belong also to *brother*; but *brother* was already established in the sense of fellow-Christian, and needed no specifically Christian definition; and it never has any such definition as *in the Lord* or *in Christ* attached to it in St. Paul's letters, except perhaps Phil. i. 14, on which see note on i. 2.

8. *whom I have sent.* Gr. *I sent*, almost certainly, as in Eph. vi. 22, the epistolary aorist of the time of writing (= *am sending*), an appropriate use in days when letters took a long time to reach their destination. Ewald argues in favour of the ordinary past tense here, on the assumption that Tychicus and Onesimus had already left Rome to

x

the cousin of Barnabas (touching whom ye received command-

servants all have to fight the fight of the faith; they may have to suffer capture at the hands of foes of the faith. Ewald (*Komm.* pp. 288, 438) suggests that the true reading may be a Greek word signifying 'comrade in the fight'; but the conjecture is both doubtful and superfluous. (3) Other suggestions need mentioning only to be rejected, e.g. Jerome's reference to the tradition that St. Paul's parents were deported from Gischala in Palestine to Tarsus, and that perhaps Epaphras and Aristarchus or their parents had been similarly deported.

The reference may be (1) to an earlier companionship in imprisonment not recorded in Acts or Epistles, cp. 2 Cor. xi. 23, 'in prisons more abundantly', and Clement's reference (*ad Cor.* v.) to seven imprisonments of St. Paul of which we only know three, Philippi, Jerusalem-Caesarea, and Rome; (2) to some imprisonment of Aristarchus alone, as may be the case with Andronicus and Junias, who are described as Paul's fellow-prisoners in Rom. xvi. 7, i.e. 'who has been a prisoner for Christ as I have'. (3) The most obvious reference is to the present imprisonment at Rome. Aristarchus and Epaphras were perhaps not themselves in custody, but their devoted attendance upon the imprisoned Apostle made them in a sense his fellow-prisoners. From the fact that here Aristarchus and not Epaphras is called a fellow-prisoner, while in Phm. 23 it is Epaphras and not Aristarchus who is so called, it has been conjectured that perhaps they took turns to share the quarters of the prisoner Apostle.

saluteth you, i.e. sends greetings. The addition of *in Christ* (Phil. iv. 21) or *in the Lord* (1 Cor. xvi. 19) means 'Christian greetings', i.e. greetings from one Christian to another. The Greek word translated *salute* is used of (1) greetings of travellers on the road, Lk. x. 4, Mt. v. 47, or on arrival, Lk. i. 40, Mt. x. 12, Acts xxi. 7, 19, or farewells on departure, Acts xx. 1; (2) visits of respect to a person of rank or to a church, Acts xxi. 19, xxv. 13; (3) the kiss of peace in a Christian congregation, 1 Cor. xvi. 20, 2 Cor. xiii. 12, 1 Th. v. 26, 1 Pet. v. 14; (4) messages of kind remembrance at the end of letters, as here.

the cousin of Barnabas. A.V. *sister's son to Barnabas.* But the Greek word *anepsios* means *cousin* in LXX and in contemporary Greek. *Nephew* was a later meaning.

touching whom ye received commandments. For full notices of Mark and Barnabas see Intr. ch. X. *Whom* refers to Mark, not to Barnabas, who needed no commendation. The mention of Barnabas as Mark's kinsman was intended probably not to distinguish Mark from any other person of that name but to secure him more readily a favourable reception. *Ye received* cannot be the epistolary aorist, referring to this same request, 'receive him'; St. Paul is clearly

twelve miles from Colossae. The circular epistle, our *Ephesians*, a copy of which would probably be left by Tychicus at Laodicea on his way to Colossae, contained no personal greetings. These would naturally be included in *Colossians* for transmission to the congregations and individuals concerned.

Nymphas. Evidently a resident in Laodicea, singled out for special greeting as a prominent Christian citizen whose house was a centre of Christian worship. *Nymphas* may be a contracted form of Nymphodorus, Nymphias, Nymphodotus, or less probably Nymphicus or Nymphidius (see Ltft.'s note). An alternative accentuation of the Greek word would give *Nympha*, a woman's name. In that case we have an interesting parallel to Lydia, the convert and hostess of St. Paul at Philippi, herself a native of Thyatira in Asia, Acts xvi. 14, 15, 40. The Coptic fragments of the *Acts of Paul* mention a Hermocrates and his wife Nympha among St. Paul's converts at Myra in Lycia.

the church that is in their house. The manuscripts vary in their readings here (1) *her*, (2) *his*, (3) *their*. (1) The reading *her* is due to the feminine rendering of the name as Nympha. (2) The reading *his* may be a scribe's correction of the difficult reading *their*. (3) *Their* has been taken as referring to the brethren and Nymphas together and as meaning that the brethren were a congregation, perhaps a group of non-Laodicean Christians, distinct from the church of Laodicea but affiliated thereto, and meeting in the house of Nymphas (Meyer). But the obvious reference of *their* is to the owners of the house, not therefore even to Nymphas and his friends, but to Nymphas and his family.

Additional Note.—The House-Congregation

The house-congregation at Laodicea is a counterpart of the church in the house of Philemon at Colossae (Phm. 2), of Aquila and Priscilla at Ephesus (1 Cor. xvi. 19) and later at Rome (Rom. xvi. 5). Cp. the meeting of the faithful for prayer in the house of Mary in Acts xii. 12, and the breaking of bread in the upper room at Troas, Acts xx. 7, 8. Ltft. suggests that similar gatherings may be implied in the expressions 'the brethren that are with them' and 'all the saints that are with them' in Rom. xvi. 14, 15. The first clear evidence of buildings set apart for Christian worship dates from the third century, and such dedication as a general custom dates from the cessation of persecution with the conversion of Constantine early in the fourth century. In the first two centuries the faithful may have been able in some places to hire the occasional use of rooms or buildings; but they were mostly dependent upon the hospitality of some wealthier Christian who lent a room or hall in his house for the meetings of the congregation for religious or social purposes. Pearson (*On the Creed*, Art. ix) describes this 'church in the house' as 'nothing else but the believing and baptized persons of each family, with such as they admitted and

kept along with *Colossians*, not only because it was another personal link with St. Paul, but perhaps also because it was felt to have a religious value of its own as a new light on a social problem.

(ii) *The household of Philemon*

The epistle, though addressed to an individual, is not merely personal; it has a domestic background. There is a household— father, mother, son, and slave. And behind this natural household there is a spiritual household, the Christian congregation that meets in the house of Philemon for worship and perhaps also for social intercourse. This congregation is coupled with the family in the opening salutation. It may have consisted of people intimate enough with their patron-host to be interested in the affairs of his family. It may even have been intended to hear the Apostle's message on a matter that affected and concerned their Christian fellowship. But the intensely personal character of the appeal suggests that it was intended for Philemon alone. In that case the inclusion of the con- gregation in the opening address is merely a blessing to be conveyed to the congregation from an apostle who knew of their existence and their connexion with Philemon, even though he had no personal acquaintance with them. On the other hand, it is just possible that the congregation consisted of the family and the slaves and an occasional visiting friend.

Philemon was a citizen, if not a native, of Colossae, who owed his conversion to St. Paul himself, probably in the course of visits to Ephesus during the Apostle's long missionary activity in that city. He repaid this debt in part by active Christian service either at Ephesus or (perhaps also) at Colossae. He may have done something to win friends and neighbours to the Christian faith. His house was certainly the home or at least the meeting-place of one of the groups of Christians in Colossae; and this hospitality and other proofs of sympathy and generosity had won the grateful affection of the faith- ful. Traditions of doubtful value state that he became bishop of Colossae (or of Gaza), and died the death of a martyr at Colossae in the Neronian persecution; and that his house was still standing in the fourth century.

With Philemon is coupled Apphia, almost certainly his wife, for her designation as 'sister' probably denotes that she too was a Christian. Renan (*Saint Paul*, p. 360) asserts, without any evidence, that she was a deaconess. Tradition or fiction represents her as sharing her husband's martyrdom. Her inclusion in the address of the letter may be due to the remembrance of a friendship that began at Ephesus; but it may be due rather (or also) to the thought that as the mistress of the household she too was concerned with the past misbehaviour of Onesimus, and might be willing to support or at least to approve the Apostle's plea for the welcoming of the penitent.

The Archippus mentioned next to Apphia is probably the son of the house, though Chrysostom suggests that perhaps he was an intimate friend, and Theodoret that he was their instructor in the faith. There can be no doubt that he is to be identified with the Archippus of Col. iv. 17, to whom St. Paul sends there a message of encouragement or admonition to do full justice to his 'ministry'. The question what this ministry was, and where it lay, in Colossae or in Laodicea, is discussed elsewhere (see notes on Col. iv. 17 and Phm. 1). The impression derived from Col. iv. 17 that he needed to be reminded of the obligations or opportunities of his ministry is corrected or balanced by his designation in Phm. 1 as the Apostle's 'fellow-soldier'. Whatever weakness there may have been in his work for Christ, St. Paul is either still proud to call him comrade or anxious to assure his father and mother that he believes in him. One tradition makes him bishop of Laodicea—perhaps an inference from Col. iv. 17; another says that he shared the fate of his father and his mother, dying as a martyr with them at Colossae.

The slave Onesimus is the central figure of the letter. Frequent references in literature and inscriptions indicate that the name Onesimus (Gk.=helpful, useful, cp. the modern use of 'help' to describe a domestic servant) was a common name for a slave or a freedman or a person of servile descent. Phrygians in general and Phrygian slaves in particular (and they were so common that 'Phrygian' is sometimes used as a synonym for 'slave') had a bad reputation. This particular Onesimus had justified that reputation. He had robbed his master and fled to Rome, 'the natural cesspool for these offscourings of humanity' (Ltft. p. 310). There he came into touch with St. Paul. Lightfoot gives his imagination the rein in search of an explanation of this meeting. 'Was it an accidental encounter with his fellow-townsman in the streets of Rome which led to the interview? Was it the pressure of want which induced him to seek alms from one whose large-hearted charity must have been a household word in his master's family? Or did the memory of solemn words, which he had chanced to overhear at those weekly gatherings in the upper chamber at Colossae, haunt him in his loneliness, till, yielding to the fascination, he was constrained to unburden himself to the one man who could soothe his terrors and satisfy his yearnings?' We only know that he was converted by St. Paul to the Christian faith

Apostolic Canons (Hefele, i. 490) permits the ordination of a slave 'if he should prove worthy of ordination, *as our Onesimus proved worthy*, and if his master consents and sets him free and releases him from his household'. Ignatius in his letter to the Ephesians (about A.D. 107) refers with gratitude and affection to their loving and lovable bishop Onesimus, who came to meet him on his martyr journey. The language of the succeeding paragraphs contains three or four reminiscences of *Philemon*. If the Onesimus of *Philemon* was then twenty-five, he would only be seventy at the time of Ignatius's martyrdom, not too old to be living then as a bishop. But the name of Onesimus is not uncommon, and the identity of the former slave and the later bishop cannot be pressed as a certainty. Onesimus is remembered in the Greek Calendar on 15 February as a martyr put to death at Puteoli; the Latin martyrologies mention him on 16 February as stoned to death at Rome. Both Greek Calendar and Latin martyrologies mention Philemon, Apphia, and Archippus on 22 November as tortured and stoned to death at Colossae after trial before the governor of Ephesus. The Greek Calendar adds Onesimus to this group of martyrs; the Latin lists omit his name.

II

ANCIENT PARALLELS TO THE EPISTLE

Ancient literature supplies three parallels to this plea for the forgiveness of an offending slave. In the first the offender is a friend; in the second a freedman; in the third a defaulting soldier.

1. Plutarch in his *Apophthegmata Laconica*, a collection of Spartan sayings to illustrate the terse bare brevity which has become proverbial under the name of 'laconic': has preserved a note from Agesilaus king of Sparta (398–360 B.C.) written to Idraeus the Carian on behalf of an offending friend: 'If Nicias is not guilty, forgive him; if he is guilty, forgive him for my sake; anyhow forgive him.' No reason or motive is given for this plea. It is just the blunt impatient request, almost a command, of the soldier-king of a people given to going straight to the point without wasting a word.

2. The depth and beauty of *Philemon* can be best appreciated in comparison with two letters written about forty years later on behalf of an offending freedman by a Roman gentleman and provincial governor, the younger Pliny, who was born in A.D. 61, the very year in which *Philemon* was probably written, the Pliny whose correspondence with the emperor Trajan about A.D. 110 on the subject of the Christians in the province of Bithynia throws such a vivid light

upon the life of the Church and upon the problem forced upon the Roman imperial government by 'the obstinacy of these Christians'.

(a) C. Plinius to his friend Sabinianus, greeting.

Your freedman, with whom you said you were angry, came to me, flung himself at my feet, and clung there as if they were yours. He was profuse in his tears and in his entreaties, and also left much unsaid. In brief, he led me to believe in his penitence. I believe he is a truly reformed character, because he feels that he has done wrong. You will be angry, I know, and your anger will be deserved, that also I know; but mercy is most praiseworthy when anger is most justifiable. You have loved the man, and will, I hope, love him again; meanwhile it is enough that you should allow yourself to yield to his entreaties. You will be entitled to be angry again if he should deserve it, and you will have all the more excuse for your anger because you have once yielded to his entreaties. Concede something to his youth, to his tears, and to your own inclination to mercy. Don't torture him and yourself too; it is torture to a man of your gentle temper to be angry. I am afraid that if I add my entreaties to his, I may seem to be not asking but forcing you to give way. Yet I am going to add my entreaties, all the more fully and earnestly because I have already rebuked the man himself sharply and severely, threatening strictly never to plead for him in the future. I told him so, for he needed to be frightened; but I don't tell you so, for perhaps I shall plead again, and not in vain: I only hope the occasion will be such that I can decently plead and you can decently grant my plea. Good-bye.

(b) It was good of you to take back to your home and to your heart a freedman once dear to you, in response to my letter pleading for his return. You will be glad: I am certainly glad, first because I find you so tractable that you can be induced to control yourself even in the midst of your anger, and secondly because you have honoured me so far as either to obey my authority or to yield to my entreaties. So I have a word of praise and of thanks for you; at the same time I advise you for the future to show yourself willing to forgive the faults of your servants, even though there is nobody to beg them off.

There are obvious resemblances between the letters of the Roman philosopher-lawyer and that of the Christian apostle. There is the same hesitation between authority and entreaty, the same anxiety to word a plea strongly and yet to leave to a friend the virtue and satisfaction of an unfettered discretion, the same tactful attempt to view the case from the friend's standpoint and to anticipate or interpret his feelings. Yet the contrasts are no less obvious. Something of the contrast is due to the difference in the circumstances of the two cases. But the differences go deeper. The freedman stands out more vividly in the picture than Onesimus. But Pliny's interest in the man is far removed from the intimacy of St. Paul's affection

a pseudo-Pauline imitation of Pliny's letters to a friend on behalf of
an offending freedman. Holtzmann applied to *Philemon* the theory
of interpolation which he had devised to explain the relations between
Colossians and *Ephesians*, going so far as to argue that Archippus
was invented by the writer as a personal link between *Philemon* and
Colossians. Both the Tübingen school and the German critics of the
last part of the nineteenth century regarded the letter as a romantic
or allegorical essay on the subject of slavery. It never occurred to
them that at the date to which they assigned the letter it was superfluous to plead for a Christian attitude towards slaves which was
already a recognized duty, and that a late fictionist would have made
St. Paul plead directly for the emancipation of Onesimus. Yet their
theory was a curious tribute to the latent force of a letter which refrained from even suggesting the emancipation of Onesimus, and
which has yet been a very leaven of emancipatory influence in all
subsequent ages of society.

The Epistle to Philemon has won golden opinions from critics and
scholars of every type. Sabatier says that it 'gleams like a pearl of
the most exquisite purity even amid the rich treasures of the New
Testament', while on a somewhat lower level he notes aptly enough its
perfect realization of St. Paul's own precept, 'Let your speech be
always with grace, seasoned with salt' (Col. iv. 6). It is indeed a wonderful blending of the true Christian spirit with a humour at once playful and pointed. Ewald notes another combination, the blending of
'the sensibility and warmth of a tender friendship with the loftier
feeling of a commanding spirit, a teacher and an apostle'. Renan,
always the self-conscious artist, strikes a false note in his description
of the letter as 'a true little *chef-d'œuvre* of the art of letter-writing';
on the contrary the essence of its beauty lies in the very unconscious-
ness of its simplicity. It is just a letter written out of a full heart
without a thought of artistic effect or of didactic purpose. In a recent
number of the *Revue de l'Histoire des Religions* (xcvi. 5, Sept.–Oct.
1927) M. Couchoud, paying the letter incidentally a somewhat
artificial tribute as 'a flask laden with Christian perfume' and 'a
silver bell striking a noble and mysterious note', analyses it into
stanzas of rhythmic lines in illustration of his theory that St. Paul
wrote his epistles in the antithetical parallelism of Hebrew poetry,
weaving into this framework the language of Greek rhetoric, the
rhythmic style serving as 'an appeal to the ear, a help to the memory'.
M. Couchoud holds that *Philemon* was written deliberately not for
the congregation alone which met in Philemon's house but for other
churches also near and far, and that St. Paul was consciously creating

a new sacred literature in succession to the Hebrew prophets. *Philemon* was an unfortunate choice as an illustration of this theory. Its antitheses of language indeed leap to the eye in the Greek text; but they betray no sign of literary effort; they are inherent in the apostle's thought. And the suggestion that St. Paul had any idea or intention of leading the way in the creation of a sacred literature of the new Israel of God is ruled out by the obviously incidental character and occasional purpose of most of the epistles. It is still more untenable as an explanation of a note penned on behalf of a converted and reformed slave to unlock for him the door of an injured master's home and heart. St. Paul could never have dreamed that a note so penned would come to be treasured by a world-wide Church as a twofold revelation, a revelation of the greatness of his own soul, and a revelation of the spirit of the Gospel in its bearing upon the status of slavery.

IV

CHRISTIANITY AND SLAVERY

(i) *Ancient slavery*

1. *Hebrew slavery.*

The slavery with which the apostolic epistles are mainly concerned is Graeco-Roman slavery. Jewish slavery only comes into the picture in the first epistle of St. Peter, and it is significant that there the slaves are called not slaves but household-servants (1 P. ii. 18). Slavery was tolerated under the Mosaic law. But it was slavery only in name and status. In character and conditions it was scarcely to be compared with slavery in the life of other nations. The slave class was only a fraction of the population; in Ezra ii. 65 it numbers roughly a seventh (Ltft., p. 318, n. 2). It only appears occasionally in Jewish history. As an institution it was tempered by the remembrance of the bondage of the Hebrews in Egypt; and law and prophecy both insisted steadily upon the religious and social rights of the slave, whether he were bondman for debt or captive of war. The slave was a member of the household and of the congregation. The slavery of a Hebrew was terminated by the sabbatical year.

2. *Greek and Roman slavery.*

Graeco-Roman slavery was a very different thing. Athenian democracy rested on a slave basis; the slaves of Attica numbered at least three or four times as many as the free population. Elsewhere

that common service. 'He has no word of reproach for the masters on the injustice of their position; he breathes no hint to the slaves of a social grievance needing redress' (Lightfoot, p. 323).[1]

Various general considerations have been suggested by way of explaining this apostolic toleration of slavery as a social institution. 'The New Testament is not concerned with any political or social institutions; for political and social institutions belong to particular nations and particular phases of society' (Goldwin Smith, *Does the Bible sanction American slavery?* p. 95). But slavery was not a local or temporary condition; it was practically universal. And it raised a question of fundamental principle. Again, it has been said that 'nothing marks the divine character of the Gospel more than its perfect freedom from any appeal to the spirit of political revolution' (Goldwin Smith, p. 96). This is a profound truth, illustrated vividly by our Lord's disappointment of the popular hope that He would head a revolt against foreign domination. But it is doubtful whether the apostles had thought out and deliberately adopted this principle of acquiescence in the existing order of things. And it is still more doubtful whether their acquiescence was due to any calculation of the consequences of a slave revolt, which if successful would have flung civilization back to barbarism, and if unsuccessful would have riveted the chain of slavery afresh with all the added cruelty of revenge. The silence of the apostles on the essential character of slavery was probably due to their preoccupation with issues both immediate and ultimate. Their immediate task was to make men Christians, and good Christians, whether they were slaves or freemen. This they did by laying stress on the ultimate truth of their equality in spiritual freedom and responsibility as members of the Body of Christ. In this they were following the letter and the spirit of the teaching of Christ Himself. 'Instead of attacking special abuses, the Gospel lays down universal principles which shall undermine the evil' (Ltft., p. 321). As with political oppression, so with social bondage. The Gospel asserted or implied the supreme value of the individual soul in the sight of God. In the long run this truth bore fruit both in personal emancipation and in political democracy.

---

[1] St. Peter (1 P. ii. 18) does not even refer to the obligations of masters, but only to the obedience of slaves. This omission may be due to the line of thought. He is dealing with the discipline of life, and takes three examples of social subordination—citizens to governments, slaves to masters, wives to husbands. Yet he balances the last by a reminder to husbands of the spiritual equality and fellowship of marriage.

(iv) *Apostolic teaching for slaves and masters*

It is instructive to note the various ways in which apostolic teaching brought Christian faith to bear directly upon the position of the slave. (1) The position itself is transformed into a sphere of divine service. The call of Christ came home alike to pagan husbands and wives, to circumcised and uncircumcised, to slaves and freemen. It was not a call to a change of domestic or social or racial condition, but to a change of personal character by virtue of a new personal relationship, union with Christ. The converted slave is not to worry over his social bondage; he has already a higher spiritual emancipation. The Christian slave is Christ's freedman. The Christian freeman is not to pride himself upon his social liberty; he has entered upon a spiritual bondage,—he is Christ's slave. Here St. Paul digresses for a moment. Souls purchased by Christ at such a cost must not surrender their spiritual liberty to the spiritual slavery of subservience to popularity or to partisanship. Finally he returns to his main principle; each man is to be content to remain in his present position 'with God' (1 Cor. vii. 20–4). This saving clause may mean 'in the sight of God'; outward circumstances have no power over the man whose eyes are fixed upon God; as Bengel says, *Qui Deum semper spectant, sanctam circa externa habent indifferentiam.* Or it may mean 'on the side of God', in contrast to the bondage of public or partisan opinion. 'With that proviso, all secular conditions, whether of family life or caste or service, are capable of being made the expression of a Christian character' (Plummer on 1 Cor. vii. 24).

(2) The Christian faith is to transform the spirit of service. Christian slaves are to be obedient to their masters 'as unto Christ'; their obedience is to be part and proof of their religion. And their work is to be done conscientiously 'as to the Lord and not to men'; their standard is now to be the present approval of Christ (Col. iii. 22–3, Eph. vi. 5–8). Even pagan masters are to be treated with respect; and Christian masters are not to be treated with disrespect on the ground of spiritual equality, but to be served all the better because of the spiritual fellowship between master and slave (1 Tim. vi. 1, 2). Christian slaves are to be obedient and obliging, not impertinent or dishonest (Tit. ii. 9, 10). There is to be a new spirit of diligence and devotion in the slave which is to transform the character and to improve the quality of the work done. Listlessness is to vanish in whole-hearted interest in the work itself; reluctance is to vanish in a willing and loyal response to his master's instructions (cp. Col. iii. 23

z

whether they had been redeemed by private or congregational charity
or had bought their freedom out of their own savings. The custom
was originally a legal fiction. The slave was conveyed to the god, and
thus safeguarded against any subsequent claim of human ownership.
He became 'the slave of the god' and thereby 'the freedman of the
god'; both phrases occur in inscriptions.[1] This may be the source of
the phrase 'a freedman of the Lord' by which St. Paul describes the
spiritual emancipation of a Christian slave (1 Cor. vii. 22), using a
pagan term and transforming it into an expression of Christian truth.

In various directions the influence of the Church was exerted
increasingly on behalf of the slave. It insisted upon the spiritual
equality of the slave with the freeman. It worked for the removal or
mitigation of the evils of slavery; it pointed to the emancipation of
slaves as an opportunity for Christian charity. It admitted the slave
to holy orders if his master was willing to emancipate him for that
purpose. Various canons however of ancient and medieval Church
councils indicate the complexity of the problem of slavery in Christian society, and, it must be confessed, the inconsistencies of Church
practice in the ages of conflict between Christian principle and social
tradition. The Council of Elvira in Spain (soon after A.D. 300) forbade masters to tolerate the presence of idols belonging to their
pagan slaves; 'but if they fear the violence of their slaves, at least
they must keep themselves pure from all idolatry' (Hefele, i. 154).
A fourth-century council at Gangra in Asia Minor speaks of slaves
joining a new ascetic movement, adopting proudly its distinctive
garb, and deserting and despising their masters as inferior Christians
(Hefele, ii. 326). The Jews were a large community in Spain. A
joint synod and parliament at Toledo in 681 forbade Jews to own
Christian slaves or to hold office as steward over the slaves of a
Christian household,—required the emancipation of slaves in Jewish
households who became Christians,—and condemned two offenders,
—the Jew who posed as a Christian and on that ground refused to
emancipate a Christian slave, and the Christian slave in a Jewish
household who concealed his religion (Hefele, v. 211). A similar joint
assembly at Toledo in 683 enacted that as slaves and freedmen
promoted to office by the king used their new position to persecute
their former masters, such promotions should be confined to slaves

---

[1] Bishop Hicks (*Journ. Theol. Stud.* x. 40) quotes an example from Panti-
capaeum in the Crimea, A.D. 81: 'Heraklas my house-slave is to be free once and
for all, and therefore master of his own movements, on one condition, viz.
reverent and constant attendance at the place of worship.' 'The congregation
(*synagoge*) of the Jews' is a party to the deed; and the owner states, 'I set him
free at the place of worship (*proseuche*)'.

(ii) *Thanksgiving and prayer for Philemon's love and faith,* **4–7.**

My heart is full of thankfulness to my God every time that I remember you in my prayers, for all that I hear of the love and the faith seen in your devotion to the Lord Jesus and in your dealings with all the Lord's people; and I pray that this loving fellowship which is the fruit of your faith may itself have a practical result—that it may bear fruit in its turn in a clearer recognition and a fuller realization of the meaning of everything that is good in your life as you see it in relation to Christ. I pray this prayer confidently, for I have found great happiness and encouragement in your love, and especially in the fact that the hearts of the Lord's people have found relief and refreshment through you, my brother.

4 I thank my God always, making mention of thee in my prayers, 5 hearing of ¹thy love, and of the faith which thou hast

¹ Or, *thy love and faith.*

4. *my God.* This note of personal relation to God expressed by the possessive adjective is found in similar thanksgivings in Rom. i. 8, 1 Cor. i. 4, Phil. i. 3, and in other passages of a confidential character in 2 Cor. xii. 21 and Phil. iv. 19. Cp. the fuller expression in Acts xxvii. 23, 'the God whose I am, whom also I serve'. In Phil. iii. 8, and there alone, St. Paul speaks similarly of Christ, 'the knowledge of Christ Jesus my Lord', cp. the intimate confession of Gal ii. 20.

always. A.V. takes this with 'making mention of thee in my prayers'; R.V. rightly with 'I thank my God'. In 2 Th. i. 3 and 1 Cor. i. 4 it is used of thanksgiving without any reference to prayer; in 1 Th. i. 2, Col. i. 3 and Eph. i. 16, where both thanksgiving and prayer are mentioned, the 'always' clearly belongs to the thanksgiving. So practically in Phil. i. 3, where it is connected with 'making supplication', but the emphasis is clearly on the words 'with joy', which convert the phrase into an amplification of the preceding 'I thank my God'.

making mention of thee. The Greek noun means both *remembrance* and *mention.* In 1 Th. iii. 6 and 2 Tim. i. 3 it is clearly remembrance, and probably also in Phil. i. 3. Here and in 1 Th. i. 2, Rom. i. 9, Eph. i. 16, the verb *making* requires the meaning *mention.* The connexion may be 'I thank God for you and pray for you', or more probably 'I thank God for you whenever I pray for you'. The thanksgiving and the intercession together give a vivid glimpse of the private devotions of the Apostle. Not only congregations but individuals found a constant place in his prayers. Cp. 2 Tim. i. 3.

5. *hearing,* i.e. 'hearing as I do', or 'because I hear'. St. Paul's informant was probably Epaphras (Col. i. 7, 8, iv. 12) rather than Onesimus, whose information was less recent and less intimate.

love . . . faith. In the thanksgiving in Col. i. 4, 1 Th. i. 3, 2 Th. i. 3 faith precedes love, which is the fruit of faith. Here love precedes faith; the letter is an appeal to love.

Christ Jesus: 10 I beseech thee for my child, whom I have begotten in my bonds, 11 ¹Onesimus, who was aforetime

¹ The Greek word means *Helpful*.

in His service'. There may be here a contrast between the freedom of an envoy and the confinement of a prisoner, or on the other hand the word *prisoner* may be a title of honour and authority like ambassador, both conferred by Christ. *Ambassador* need not imply that St. Paul is insisting on the fact of his authority even while he is waiving its exercise. The sense may be: 'pleading in the name of Christ, and as things are suffering in the service of Christ', a double ground of appeal. [If we compare the use of the verb πρεσβεύω in the contemporary epistle Eph. vi. 20 and the stress on reconciliation as the special work of ambassadors for Christ in 2 Cor. v. 19, 20, I have little doubt that the word ambassador should be substituted for 'the aged' here. See note on Eph. vi. 20. Gen. Editor.]

10. *my child*, not *son*, as in A.V. Cp. the use of the term to describe not only converts of an apostle but members of a church in general in relation to an apostle, 1 Cor. iv. 14, 2 Cor. vi. 13, xii. 14, 1 Th. ii. 11, 3 John 4. St. Paul uses the same term of Timothy, 1 Cor. iv. 17, Phil. ii. 22, 1 Tim. i. 2, &c., and of Titus, Tit. i. 4. Here the Greek possessive adjective is emphatic, *my own child*.

whom I have begotten. Gr. *begot*. The intimate relation between the Apostle and his converts is depicted by three metaphors: (1) the *father*, as being (*a*) the transmitter of life, e.g. 1 Cor. iv. 15, where he contrasts their many 'tutors' with himself as their one spiritual father, 'for in Christ Jesus I begat you through the Gospel', and (*b*) the trainer of character, 1 Th. ii. 11; (2) the *mother*, who gives birth at the cost of pain, Gal. iv. 19, 'my little children, of whom I am again in travail until Christ be formed in you'; (3) the *nurse*, who 'cherishes' the young child as her own, 1 Th. ii. 7. It has been suggested that the origin of this father-metaphor is to be found in the Greek mysteries, in which the initiating priest or officer is called the father of the candidate for initiation, and becomes a sort of sponsor and surety for his conduct (Dibelius). But there is no real resemblance between such a sponsorship and St. Paul's offer to make good any loss incurred through the conduct of Onesimus. And the resemblance between the ideas of fatherhood in the two cases is no evidence for any borrowing on the part of St. Paul. His use of the idea of spiritual fatherhood has its origin in his own experience of that relation towards his converts, and perhaps farther back in some aspects of the relation of God to Israel in the Old Testament.

in my bonds, i.e. during my imprisonment. 'He was doubly dear to the Apostle, as being the child of his sorrows', Ltft. Here 'for the third time Philemon is made to hear the clanking of the prisoner's chain' (Beet).

unprofitable to thee, but now is profitable to thee and to me:
12 whom I have sent back to thee in his own person, that is, my

Onesimus. See note on Col. iv. 9 and Intr. p. 325. The name is held
back to the last, when its unpleasant memories for Philemon have
been discounted in advance by the Apostle's affectionate description
of the new Onesimus.

11. *unprofitable . . . profitable.* There is an obvious play, affectionate
rather than humorous, upon the name Onesimus, which means in
Greek *helpful* or *gainful.* The old Onesimus had belied his name; the
new Onesimus will live up to his name. The Gr. word translated
unprofitable only occurs here in N.T. But a cognate adjective is used
in Mt. xxv. 30 of the servant who hid his lord's talent, and in Lk. xvii.
10 of servants who do their bare duty and no more.

to thee and to me. In Greek the first person usually precedes the
second. The reversal of this order here has been explained as due to
the fact that St. Paul's reference to himself is an afterthought. It is
more likely that he had both Philemon and himself in view at the
same time. The exceptional order is due to the fact that Philemon is
the first person to be considered, as the original loser whose loss is
now to be made good.

12. *whom I have sent back to thee,* the epistolary aorist as in Col. iv. 8,
looking back to the time of writing. The Greek verb is a compound
which may mean sending back or sending on to the proper quarter.
From the present passage and from Col. iv. 7–9 it is clear that Onesimus was sent from Rome to Colossae along with the letter.

in his own person, Gr. simply *him.* The word *him,* coming after
whom has been found a difficulty. (1) It has been explained as a
Hebraism. In Hebrew a relative sentence is introduced by a relative
particle which may be defined by a personal or demonstrative pronoun.
But this Hebraism is not found in St. Paul. (2) Some ancient manuscripts and versions have *but thou* instead of *for to thee,* and insert
receive from verse 17. Hence the A.V. 'whom I have sent again: thou
therefore receive him'. But this breaks the line of thought by introducing prematurely the actual appeal for the reception of Onesimus,
which comes only in verse 17 after a careful paving of the way.
(3) Lightfoot puts a full stop after *sent,* and takes *him* as a suspended
object, picked up finally by *receive* in verse 17 after a series of digres-
sions. (4) The simplest construction is to take *him* in the sense of
himself, an emphatic addition 'to bring Onesimus vividly before the
reader and thus prepare the way for the strong contrast in the very
next words' (L. Williams).

that is, my very heart, simple words not simple to explain. (1) It
may mean, 'and that is like tearing my own heart out', or (2) less
probably 'and that means giving up my darling'. (3) It has been
interpreted in the light of *in thy stead* in the next verse. Onesimus,

emphatic. Not only had St. Paul no idea of keeping Onesimus and
so forcing Philemon to acquiesce in an accomplished fact, but he did
not even think that Philemon would regard an actual request for the
service of Onesimus as forcing his hand. Paul wants to avoid even
the appearance of any virtual compulsion. 'Any act of kindness on
your part must not even seem as though it were forced upon you.' So
he does not even ask for Onesimus to be sent back to him. He pro-
ceeds instead to plead for a welcome to be given to Onesimus, and
pleads in language which contemplates the keeping of Onesimus
permanently in his new footing in his old home. He leaves Philemon
to read between the lines, and, if he will, to hear and grant the wistful
silent plea implied in the confession that he had wanted to keep his
new son in the faith at his own side. The letter leaves us wishing that
we knew whether Philemon did understand and grant the unspoken
request.

of free will. Perhaps *as* should be understood here also. Philemon's
action must not only have the nature but the appearance of an act of
free will. If St. Paul had asked for the return of Onesimus, and
Philemon had granted the request, his consent would doubtless have
been given willingly, whatever his secret regret. But St. Paul wanted
more than a willing response to a request. He wanted a free-will
offering. The Greek word translated *of free will* means more than
A.V. *willingly.* It is used in Heb. x. 26 of sinning wilfully, and in
1 Pet. v. 2 of the discharge of Christian ministry in a setting which
implies far more than a willing fulfilment of an obligation. The very
same phrase used by St. Paul here is used in LXX. Num. xv. 3 of
the free-will offering, and the adjective *free-will* (Heb. *nedibah*) is
used frequently of those sacrifices. St. Paul may have had this use in
mind. In any case what he desires on the part of Philemon is a sacrifice inspired by his own love and not prompted by a request or even
a suggestion. That particular 'good' would be the crowning example
of 'every good thing' (verse 6) which he has prayed that Philemon's
faith may come to learn.

(iv) *Onesimus and Philemon,* 15-20.

*Behind what has happened there may be the hand of divine providence.
Perhaps after all this was the meaning of his separation from you for a time.
You were meant to get him back for eternity. He is now no longer a mere
slave: he is much more than a slave—he is now a brother, and a dearly
beloved brother. He is very much so indeed to me, once a stranger to him.
Think how much more he will be so to you, with your human relationship
now crowned and consecrated by a Christian relationship. Here then is my
plea. If you set any store by your own personal fellowship with me, give
him the same kindly reception and welcome that you would give to me.
Whatever loss you incurred through his misconduct, whatever debt he still
owes to you, put it down to my account. Here is my promissory note in my*

*own handwriting: I will make good the loss.   I refrain from laying stress on
the fact that you yourself are already my debtor, indebted to me for your very
soul.   I simply plead with you, brother, do me in my turn a Christian
kindness; give my heart the relief and refreshment that it craves in the name
of Christ.*

15 For perhaps he was therefore parted *from thee* for a season,
that thou shouldest have him for ever; 16 no longer as a
¹servant, but more than a ¹servant, a brother beloved, specially
to me, but how much rather to thee, both in the flesh and in

¹ Gr. *bondservant.*

15. *For perhaps.*   St. Paul gives here a further reason for refraining
from keeping Onesimus, or perhaps a reason in advance for the plea
yet to come.   'For if I had kept him, I might have defeated the very
purpose of God which lay hidden behind his departure.'   His temporary absence was meant to result in a return for the rest of his life
and in a new and higher relationship.

he was parted.   (1) This literal translation of a Greek passive verb
suggests that behind the reckless action of Onesimus in running away
from his master there lay the providence of God by which he was
being separated with a view to their reunion on a higher level.   Cp.
the case of Joseph; he was torn from home and sold into Egypt by
his brothers, but 'it was God that sent me before you . . . to save your
lives', Gen. xlv. 5.   (2) The strictly passive sense is often lost in this
verb.   A.V. *departed* may therefore be right.   (3) In any case St. Paul
tactfully uses a word which avoids any reminder of the wilfulness of
Onesimus; the word 'absconded' might have reawakened his master's
legitimate resentment.

have him for ever.   The Greek word for *have* here denotes either
have him back again or *have him completely*, as in Phil. iv. 18, Lk. vi. 24,
Mt. vi. 2, 5, 16.   *For ever* suggests merely duration of time.   The Greek
has here an adjective, *everlasting* or *eternal.*   The new relationship of
Onesimus to Philemon as a brother in Christ will last all his life and
beyond this life; it is a spiritual relationship, and therefore not only
everlasting in duration but eternal in character.   'Onesimus had
obtained eternal life' by becoming a Christian, 'and eternal life
involves eternal exchange of friendship', Ltft.

16. *as a servant,* i.e. bondservant, slave.   *As* is emphatic.   Onesimus
will still actually be a slave in status, but he would not be regarded
and treated as a slave, but as a dear fellow-Christian.

specially to me, lit. *very much.*   St. Paul was his father in the faith,
and therefore in a special sense his brother and friend in Christ.

much rather to thee.   If he was 'most of all' a dear brother to St.
Paul, beyond what he was to other Christians, he was so now 'more
than most of all' to Philemon, who had both regained an old servant
and gained a new friend.

20. *Yea, brother.* (1) The same particle is used to introduce an affectionate appeal in Phil. iv. 3. It is almost '*come*, brother, do me this kindness'. (2) If its affirmative connotation *yes* or *yea* is to be pressed, it may imply 'yes, you owe me all that—so let me have, &c.', or better 'yes, I am sure I can count on your waiving all objections and claims'. *Brother* has a triple reference. 'It is the entreaty of a brother to a brother on behalf of a brother', Ltft.

let me have joy of thee in the Lord, lit. *may I have,* a hope rather perhaps than a request. The pronoun is emphatic, either 'let *me* receive a benefit from you, as *you* once received from me', or 'I am pleading not merely for Onesimus but for myself; let *me* have this happiness at your hands'. The verb *have joy* means to receive profit or benefit, R.V. mg. *help.* It is used frequently in Greek literature of the return that a father may rightly expect from a child. Cp. LXX. Ecclus. xxx. 2. Goodspeed translates, 'Let me make something out of you in a Christian sense', perhaps a playful hint at Philemon's commercial instincts. But the idea of a son in the faith making his spiritual father happy is more consonant with the tone of the passage. It is the verb from which the adjective *onesimos,* i.e. *helpful,* is formed ; but it is unlikely that St. Paul in such an earnest and pathetical appeal would play thus upon the name of Onesimus, e.g. 'show me a kindness that will make the very name of Onesimus a happy remembrance for us both'; 'prove yourself an Onesimus—a useful friend (cf. 11)—to me'.

refresh my heart in Christ. cp. verse 7 and the note there on *refreshed.* *Heart* has been taken here, as in verse 12, as a reference to Onesimus: 'cheer the lad who is my darling'. But St. Paul has clearly passed on from the thought of Onesimus to the thought of his own place in the question. 'You have brought relief to many a Christian soul; bring this relief to mine.' *In the Lord* and *in Christ* denote spiritual as distinct from natural human kindness. St. Paul is pleading for generosity not from man to man but from Christian to Christian.

(v) *Hopes and greetings,* **20–25.**

(1) *The hope of a generous response to his request and of a happy answer to their prayers,* 21–22.

I write with complete confidence in your willingness to respond to my appeal, feeling certain that you will do even more than I suggest. At the same time I ask you also to arrange hospitality for me: for I trust that through the prayers of you and yours I shall be given back to you.

21 Having confidence in thine obedience I write unto thee,

21. *thine obedience.* Cp. 1 Th. iii. 4. This hint of authority seems contrary to the waiving of authority in verses 8, 9. The apparent contradiction has led some commentators to take the Greek word in